Legislators and Legislatures of Ontario

a reference guide

Volume 1 / 1792-1866

compiled and edited by
Debra Forman

Ontario

*Legislative Library,
Research and Information Services*

Forman, Debra, 1956 -
    Legislators and legislatures of Ontario
    Includes index.
    Contents: v. 1. 1792-1866. — v. 2. 1867-1929. —
v. 3. 1930-1984.
    ISBN 0-7743-9021-2 (set). – 0-7743-9022-0 (v. 1) –
0-7743-9023-9 (v. 2). – 0-7743-9024-7 (v. 3).
    1. Ontario. Legislative Assembly — History.
    2. Ontario — Politics and government.
    3. Legislators — Ontario — History.   I. Ontario. Legislative
Library, Research and Information Services.   II. Title.

JL273.F6 1984   328.713′09   84-093008-9

V.1 /46,130

CONTENTS

Volume 1

Volume 2

Legislatures of Ontario, 1867 - 1929

Volume 3

Legislatures of Ontario, 1930 - 1984

FOREWORD

Approximately 5,000 men and women have served as Members of Parliament for the Province of Upper Canada (1792 to 1841), Canada West in the United Province of Canada (1841 to 1867), and the Province of Ontario (1867 to 1984). In the past, the identification or verification of a particular member, legislature, or electoral district has proved to be a tedious and time-consuming task for researchers in Ontario's political history because the information is widely scattered in a number of sources. It is to facilitate such research that *Legislators and Legislatures of Ontario* has been compiled. Publication of this three volume reference work constituted the Legislative Library, Research and Information Services' contribution to the Bicentennial of Ontario being celebrated during 1984.

The information collected for this reference guide is the result of months of intensive and painstaking research by Debra Forman, a librarian on the staff of the Information and Reference Services section of the Legislative Library. The Library is pleased to publish this work which will fill a long-felt need in the reference collections of politicians, political scientists, historians and others who have occasion to study the legislative history of Ontario.

R. Brian Land
Director

January 23, 1984

INTRODUCTION

Purpose

Legislators and Legislatures of Ontario is a three volume reference guide that lists Members of Parliament for Upper Canada, Canada West, and the Province of Ontario, for the period 1792 to 1984. It is intended to provide an authoritative account of the province's legislative history based on primary sources.

Scope

The main body of the text consists of a chronological listing of the legislatures of Upper Canada, Canada West, and the Province of Ontario. Each legislature is divided into two lists: an alphabetical list of members and an alphabetical list of constituencies. The list of members includes session dates and legislative notes. The constituency list, with an electoral emphasis, records by-election dates, vote recounts, Representation Acts and electoral notes. Both lists provide the date of the General Election plus the following data for each elected representative:

- Name
- Party (See Explanatory Notes)
- Constituency
- Date sworn in
- Comments (Legislative, Electoral, Personal)

Together, the two lists provide a comprehensive picture of each legislature.

The guide is supplemented with numerous appendices, tables and indices, including chronological lists of Officers of the Legislative Assembly, Premiers, and Executive Councillors. Session dates and constituency tables are also included. A special feature is the comprehensive Alphabetical Index of Members, which covers the period.

Coverage

Volume 1 covers the period from 1792 to 1866; volume 2 covers the period from 1867 to 1929; and volume 3 covers the period from 1930 to 1984.

Sources

The *Journals* and the *Statutes* of Upper Canada, Canada West, and the Province of Ontario, along with the Ontario *Debates*, provided the core material for each legislature. Frederick Armstrong's *Upper Canadian Chronology and Territorial Legislation* (London, Ont: University of Western Ontario, Lawson Memorial Library, 1967) was used as a checklist for the pre-Confederation period. The *Centennial Edition of a History of the Electoral Districts, Legislatures and Ministries of the Province of Ontario 1867-1968* (Toronto: Queen's Printer, 1969) by the Province's Chief Electoral Officer and Clerk of the House, Roderick Lewis, provided a framework for Ontario's legislative history. When necessary, these sources were supplemented with city directories, biographies, histories, lists of political appointments, newspapers and archival materials.

Acknowledgements

Thanks are extended to all my colleagues at the Legislative Library of Ontario for their support, guidance and input while this work was in preparation. Special thanks are due to Denise Debney, Word Processing Operator, who typed and retyped the manuscript, as well as to Virginia Achig and Elaine Watson of the Legislative Research Service, who provided invaluable word processing assistance.

Debra Forman
Librarian, Information and Reference Services

January 23, 1984

EDITORIAL COMMENTS

Glossary

"the House was informed of . . ."   indicates the date for locating further information in the *Journals*.

"new election had been . . ."   indicates that the Writ of Election had already been issued.

"Did not take seat"   indicates that the MPP was not sworn in to the Legislative Assembly.

"Hon."   indicates an MPP's inclusion in the Executive Council; included when listed in the *Journals*.

Explanatory Notes

Resignation of Office Holders

From Oct. 12, 1842, an MPP who accepted any office of profit was required to vacate his seat. See, "An Act to make the Law for vacating the Seats of Members of the Legislative Assembly occupying Office, uniform throughout this Province," 6 Vic. 1842 C.11, S.1.

Executive and Legislative Councils

MPPs who were appointed to either Council have been indicated. Other appointees who were not elected Members were excluded. As a result, a comprehensive list of both Councils for the years 1792 to 1866 has not been provided.

Party

Given the embryonic nature of the party system between the years 1792 and 1866 Members have not been identified by party.

Electoral Districts

Names of Electoral Districts appear as they did in both the *Journals* and the *Statutes*. Inconsistencies have not been changed.

General Election

The General Election spanned several weeks, since Counties voted on different dates and the vote within each County could take a maximum of six days.

Death Dates

Only readily available death dates are included.

Representation Acts

To preserve the integrity of the original Acts, inconsistencies have not been changed.

Alphabetical Index of Members

To identify those who were Executive or Legislative Councillors and/or Officers of the House, refer to the appropriate lists.

Parliament Buildings – 1792 – 1984

Place	Year	Site
Newark	1792-1796	Contemporary writings provide various locations. Frequently mentioned are an oak tree on the property known as the Anchorage; the upper room in a Freemanson's Hall and Governor Simcoe's official residence, Navy Hall.
York	1796-1813	Two wooden buildings bordered by the bay to the south, the forest to the north and east and oak trees to the west. The adjoining plot of land was called "Government Park."
	1814	Jordan's York Hotel – the "Ball Room."
	1815-1820	"The Lawn," a residence at the northwest corner of Wellington and York Streets.
	1820-1824	A brick structure occupying the site of the old gaol at King and Berkeley Streets. Destroyed by fire, Dec. 30, 1824.
	1825-1828	The old General Hospital, King and Hospital (Richmond) Streets, west of the original Upper Canada College.
	1829-1832	The old Court House, bordered by King, Church, Court, and Toronto Streets.
	1832-1834	Front Street Parliament Buildings.
Toronto	1834-1840	Front Street.
Kingston	1841-1843	Government House.
Montreal	1844-1849	Government House. In 1846, Front Street was used by the university and medical schools for lectures. In 1848 and 1849, the buildings were temporarily used as a lunatic asylum, as the Toronto Street gaol was overcrowded.
Toronto	1849-1851	Front Street.
Quebec (City)	1852-1855	Government House.

Toronto	1855-1859	Front Street.
Quebec (City)	1859-1866	Government House.
		From 1861-1867, Front Street was used as military barracks.
Toronto	1867-1892	Front Street.
Toronto	1892-1984	Queen's Park.

General Elections – 1792 – 1984

General Election	Legislature	General Election	Legislature
Aug. 1792	1UC	Feb. 27, 1883	5th
Aug. 1796	2UC	Dec. 28, 1886	6th
July 1800	3UC	June 5, 1890	7th
May 1804	4UC	June 26, 1894	8th
May 1808	5UC	Mar. 1, 1898	9th
June 1812	6UC	May 29, 1902	10th
Apr. 1816	7UC	Jan. 25, 1905	11th
July 1820	8UC	June 8, 1908	12th
July 1824	9UC	Dec. 11, 1911	13th
July 1828	10UC	June 29, 1914	14th
Oct. 1830	11UC	Oct. 20, 1919	15th
Oct. 1834	12UC	June 25, 1923	16th
July 1836	13UC	Dec. 1, 1926	17th
		Oct. 30, 1929	18th
Mar. 1841	1CW	June 19, 1934	19th
Oct. 1844	2CW	Oct. 6, 1937	20th
Dec. 1847	3CW	Aug. 4, 1943	21st
Nov. - Dec. 1851	4CW	June 4, 1945	22nd
July - Aug. 1854	5CW	June 7, 1948	23rd
Dec. 1857 - Jan. 1858	6CW	Nov. 22, 1951	24th
June - July 1861	7CW	June 9, 1955	25th
June - July 1863	8CW	June 11, 1959	26th
		Sept. 25, 1963	27th
		Oct. 17, 1967	28th
Aug. 27 - Sept. 21, 1867	1st	Oct. 21, 1971	29th
Mar. 21, 1871	2nd	Sept. 18, 1975	30th
Jan. 18, 1875	3rd	June 9, 1977	31st
June 5, 1879	4th	Mar. 19, 1981	32nd

1UC-13UC = Upper Canada   **1CW-8CW = Canada West**   **1st-32nd = Ontario**

Session Dates of the Legislative Assembly — 1792 – 1984

Legislature	Opening	Prorogation	Dissolution
Upper Canada			
1UC	Sept. 17, 1792	June 3, 1796	*
2UC	June 1, 1797	July 4, 1800	July 7, 1800
3UC	May 28, 1801	Mar. 9, 1804	May 14, 1804
4UC	Feb. 1, 1805	Mar. 16, 1808	*
5UC	Feb. 2, 1809	Mar. 6, 1812	*
6UC	July 27, 1812	Apr. 1, 1816	Apr. 18, 1816
7UC	Feb. 4, 1817	Mar. 7, 1820	*
8UC	Jan. 31, 1821	Jan. 19, 1824	*
9UC	Jan. 11, 1825	Mar. 25, 1828	June 24, 1828
10UC	Jan. 8, 1829	Mar. 6, 1830	Sept. 10, 1830
11UC	Jan. 7, 1831	Mar. 6, 1834	Sept. 1, 1834
12UC	Jan. 15, 1835	Apr. 20, 1836	May 28, 1836
13UC	Nov. 8, 1836	Feb. 10, 1840	†
Canada West			
1CW	June 14, 1841	Dec. 9, 1843	Sept. 23, 1844
2CW	Nov. 28, 1844	July 28, 1847	Dec. 6, 1847
3CW	Feb. 25, 1848	Aug. 30, 1851	Nov. 6, 1851
4CW	Aug. 19, 1852	June 22, 1854	June 23, 1854
5CW	Sept. 5, 1854	June 10, 1857	Nov. 28, 1857
6CW	Feb. 25, 1858	May 18, 1861	June 10, 1861
7CW	Mar. 20, 1862	May 12, 1863	May 16, 1863
8CW	Aug. 13, 1863	Aug. 15, 1866	†

* Date unknown. Journals for these years are not known to be in existence.

† Writ issued for Canada West; the Province of Ontario.

Session Dates of the Legislative Assembly – 1792 – 1984 — *Continued*

Legislature	Opening	Prorogation	Dissolution
Ontario			
1st	Dec. 27, 1867	Feb. 15, 1871	Feb. 25, 1871
2nd	Dec. 7, 1871	Dec. 21, 1874	Dec. 23, 1874
3rd	Nov. 24, 1875	Mar. 11, 1879	Apr. 25, 1879
4th	Jan. 7, 1880	Feb. 1, 1883	Feb. 1, 1883
5th	Jan. 23, 1884	Mar. 25, 1886	Nov. 15, 1886
6th	Feb. 10, 1887	Apr. 7, 1890	Apr. 26, 1890
7th	Feb. 11, 1891	May 5, 1894	May 29, 1894
8th	Feb. 21, 1895	Jan. 17, 1898	Jan. 28, 1898
9th	Aug. 3, 1898	Mar. 17, 1902	Apr. 19, 1902
10th	Mar. 10, 1903	Apr. 26, 1904	Dec. 13, 1904
11th	Mar. 22, 1905	Apr. 14, 1908	May 2, 1908
12th	Feb. 16, 1909	Mar. 24, 1911	Nov. 13, 1911
13th	Feb. 7, 1912	May 1, 1914	May 29, 1914
14th	Feb. 16, 1915	Apr. 24, 1919	Sept. 23, 1919
15th	Mar. 9, 1920	May 8, 1923	May 10, 1923
16th	Feb. 6, 1924	Apr. 8, 1926	Oct. 18, 1926
17th	Feb. 2, 1927	Mar. 28, 1929	Sept. 17, 1929
18th	Feb. 5, 1930	Apr. 3, 1934	May 16, 1934
19th	Feb. 20, 1935	Mar. 25, 1937	Aug. 25, 1937
20th	Feb. 23, 1938	Apr. 14, 1943	June 30, 1943
21st	Feb. 22, 1944	Mar. 24, 1945	Mar. 24, 1945
22nd	July 16, 1945	Apr. 16, 1948	Apr. 27, 1948
23rd	Feb. 10, 1949	Sept. 27, 1951	Oct. 6, 1951
24th	Feb. 21, 1952	Mar. 31, 1955	May 2, 1955
25th	Sept. 8, 1955	Mar. 26, 1959	May 4, 1959
26th	Jan. 26, 1960	Apr. 26, 1963	Oct. 10, 1963
27th	Oct. 29, 1963	June 15, 1967	Aug. 30, 1967
28th	Feb. 14, 1968	July 28, 1971	Sept. 13, 1971
29th	Feb. 29, 1972	July 18, 1975	Aug. 12, 1975
30th	Oct. 28, 1975	Apr. 29, 1977	Apr. 29, 1977
31st	June 27, 1977	Dec. 12, 1980	Feb. 2, 1981
32nd	Apr. 21, 1981		

Speakers of the Legislative Assembly – 1792 – 1984

Speaker	Legislature	Speaker	Legislature
Hon. John Macdonell	1UC	Hon. Charles Clarke	5th
Hon. David William Smith	2UC	Hon. Jacob Baxter	6th
Hon. Samuel Street	2UC	Hon. Thomas Ballantyne	7th
Hon. David William Smith	3UC	Hon. William Douglas Balfour	8th
Hon. Richard Beasley	3UC	Hon. Francis Eugene Evanturel	8th
Hon. Alexander McDonell	4UC	Hon. Francis Eugene Evanturel	9th
Hon. Samuel Street	5UC	Hon. William Andrew Charlton	10th
Hon. Allan McLean	6UC	Hon. Joseph Wesley St. John	11th
Hon. Allan McLean	7UC	Hon. Thomas Crawford	11th
Hon. Levius P. Sherwood	8UC	Hon. Thomas Crawford	12th
Hon. John Willson	9UC	Hon. William Henry Hoyle	13th
Hon. Marshall Spring Bidwell	10UC	Hon. David Jamieson	14th
Hon. Archibald McLean	11UC	Hon. Nelson Parliament	15th
Hon. Marshall Spring Bidwell	12UC	Hon. Joseph Elijah Thompson	16th
Hon. Allan Napier MacNab	13UC	Hon. William David Black	17th
Hon. Henry Ruttan	13UC	Hon. Thomas Ashmore Kidd	18th
Hon. Allan Napier MacNab	13UC	Hon. Norman Otto Hipel	19th
		Hon. James Howard Clark	20th
Hon. Austin Cuvillier	1CW	Hon. William James Stewart	21st
Hon. Sir Allan Napier MacNab	2CW	Hon. James deCongalton Hepburn	22nd
Hon. Augustin Norbert Morin	3CW	Hon. Myroyn "Cooke" Davies	23rd
Hon. John Sandfield Macdonald	4CW	Hon. Myroyn "Cooke" Davies	24th
Hon. Louis Victor Sicotte	5CW	Hon. Alfred Wallace Downer	25th
Hon. Henry Smith, Jr.	6CW	Hon. William Murdoch	26th
Hon. Joseph Edouard Turcotte	7CW	Hon. Donald Hugo Morrow	27th
Hon. Lewis Wallbridge	8CW	Hon. Frederick McIntosh Cass	28th
		Hon. Allan Edward Reuter	29th
Hon. John Stevenson	1st	Hon. Russell Daniel Rowe	29th
Hon. Richard William Scott	2nd	Hon. Russell Daniel Rowe	30th
Hon. James George Currie	2nd	Hon. John Edward "Jack" Stokes	31st
Hon. Rupert Mearse Wells	2nd	Hon. John Melville Turner	32nd
Hon. Rupert Mearse Wells	3rd		
Hon. Charles Clarke	4th		

1UC-13UC = Upper Canada   **1CW-8CW = Canada West**   **1st-32nd = Ontario**

Lieutenant Governors, Administrators and Governors General – 1792 – 1984

Name	Office	Year
Upper Canada		
Hon. John Graves Simcoe	Lieutenant Governor	1792-1794*
Hon. Peter Russell	Administrator	*1798-1799
Hon. Peter Hunter	Lieutenant Governor	1799-1805
Hon. Alexander Grant	President	1805-1806
Hon. Francis Gore	Lieutenant Governor	1806-1808*; 1810-1811
Hon. Isaac Brock	President	1811-1812
Hon. Sir Roger Hale Sheaffe	President	1812-1813
Hon. Francis de Rottenburg	President	1813
Hon. Gordon Drummond	President	1813-1814
Hon. Sir George Murray	Provisional Lieutenant Governor	1815
Hon. Frederick Philipse Robinson	Provisional Lieutenant Governor	1815
Hon. Francis Gore	Lieutenant Governor	1815-1817
Hon. Samuel Smith	Administrator	1817-1818
Hon. Sir Peregrine Maitland	Lieutenant Governor	1818-1828
Hon. Sir John Colborne	Lieutenant Governor	1828-1836
Hon. Sir Francis Bond Head	Lieutenant Governor	1836-1838
Hon. Sir George Arthur	Lieutenant Governor	1838-1839
Rt. Hon. Charles Poulett Thomson	Governor General	1839-1840
Canada West		
Hon. Charles, Baron Sydenham	Governor General	1841
Hon. Major General John Clitherow	Deputy Governor	1841
Hon. Sir Richard Downes Jackson	Administrator	1841-1842
Rt. Hon. Sir Charles Bagot	Governor General	1842-1843
Hon. Sir Charles Theophilus Metcalfe, Baronet	Governor General	1843-1845
Rt. Hon. Charles Murray, Earl Cathcart	Administrator	1845-1846
	Governor General	1846-1847

Hon. James, Earl of Elgin and Kincardine	Governor General	1847-1854
Hon. William Rowan	Administrator during the absence of Governor General Elgin	1853-1854
Rt. Hon. Sir Edmund Walker Head	Governor General	1854-1861
Hon. Sir William Eyre	Administrator during the absence of Governor General Head	1857
Hon. Sir William Fenwick Williams	Administrator during the absence of Governor General Head	1860-1861
Rt. Hon. Charles Stanley, Viscount Monck, Baron Monck	Governor General	1861-1866
Hon. Sir John Michel	Administrator during the absence of Governor General Monck	1865-1866

Ontario

Major General, the Hon. Henry William Stisted	Lieutenant Governor	1867-1868
Hon. William Pearce Howland	Lieutenant Governor	1868-1873
Hon. John Willoughby Crawford	Lieutenant Governor	1873-1875
Hon. Donald Alexander Macdonald	Lieutenant Governor	1875-1880
Hon. John Beverley Robinson	Lieutenant Governor	1880-1887
Hon. Sir Alexander Campbell	Lieutenant Governor	1887-1892
Hon. Sir George Airey Kirkpatrick	Lieutenant Governor	1892-1897
Hon. Sir Oliver Mowat	Lieutenant Governor	1897-1903
Hon. Sir William Mortimer Clark	Lieutenant Governor	1903-1908
Hon. Sir John Morison Gibson	Lieutenant Governor	1908-1914
Lieutenant-Colonel, the Hon. Sir John Strathearn Hendrie	Lieutenant Governor	1914-1919
Hon. Lionel Herbert Clarke	Lieutenant Governor	1919-1921
Colonel, the Hon. Henry Cockshutt	Lieutenant Governor	1921-1927
Hon. William Donald Ross	Lieutenant Governor	1927-1932
Colonel, the Hon. Herbert Alexander Bruce	Lieutenant Governor	1932-1937
Hon. Albert Matthews	Lieutenant Governor	1937-1946

*   The Journals for the years 1795, 1796, 1797, and 1809 are not known to be in existence.

Lieutenant Governors, Administrators and Governors General – 1792 – 1984 — *Continued*

Name	Office	Year
Hon. Ray Lawson	Lieutenant Governor	1946-1952
Hon. Louis Orville Breithaupt	Lieutenant Governor	1952-1957
Lieutenant Colonel, the Hon. John Keiller Mackay	Lieutenant Governor	1957-1963
Hon. William Earl Rowe	Lieutenant Governor	1963-1968
Hon. William Ross MacDonald	Lieutenant Governor	1968-1974
Hon. Pauline Emily M. McGibbon	Lieutenant Governor	1974-1980
Hon. John Black Aird	Lieutenant Governor	1980-

Presidents of the Executive Council – 1867 – 1984

President	Year	Legislature
Hon. John Sandfield Macdonald	(1867-1871)	1-2 Legislatures
Hon. Edward Blake	(1871-1872)	2 Legislature
Hon. Sir Oliver Mowat	(1872-1896)	2-8 Legislatures
Hon. Arthur Sturgis Hardy	(1896-1899)	8-9 Legislatures
Hon. George William Ross	(1899-1905)	9-11 Legislatures
Hon. Sir James Pliny Whitney	(1905-1914)	11-14 Legislatures
Hon. Sir William Howard Hearst	(1914-1919)	14-15 Legislatures
Hon. Ernest Charles Drury	(1919-1923)	15-16 Legislatures
Hon. George Howard Ferguson	(1923-1930)	16-18 Legislatures
Hon. George Stewart Henry	(1930-1934)	18-19 Legislatures
Hon. Mitchell Frederick Hepburn	(1934-1942)	19-20 Legislatures
Hon. Gordon Daniel Conant	(1942-1943)	20 Legislature
Hon. Harry Corwin Nixon	(1943)	20-21 Legislatures
Hon. George Alexander Drew	(1943-1948)	21-23 Legislatures
Hon. Thomas Laird Kennedy	(1948-1949)	23 Legislature
Hon. Leslie Miscampbell Frost	(1949-1961)	23-26 Legislatures
Hon. John Parmenter Robarts	(1961-1971)	26-28 Legislatures
Hon. William Grenville Davis	(1971-)	28- Legislatures

Clerks of the Legislative Assembly – 1792 – 1984

Clerk	Year
Angus Macdonell	Sept. 26, 1792 – July 4, 1800
Donald McLean (MacLean)	May 28, 1801 – May 1813
Grant Powell	May 1813 – May 3, 1827
James Fitzgibbon	Jan. 14, 1828 – 1840
William Burns Lindsay	1841 – died, May 15, 1862
William Burns Lindsay, Jr.	May 16, 1862 – 1866
Charles Todd Gilmor	1867 – 1892
Charles Clarke	1892 – 1907
Arthur Henry Sydere	1907 – 1926
Charles Frederick Bulmer	Feb. 23, 1926 – Dec. 7, 1926
Alexander Cameron Lewis	Dec. 7, 1926 – Dec. 31, 1954
Roderick Gilmour Lewis	Jan. 1, 1955 –

Sergeants-at-Arms – 1792 – 1984

Sergeant-at-Arms	Year
George Lawe	Sept. 26, 1792 – Feb. 1, 1810
Thomas Hamilton (Deputy)	Feb. 2, 1810*
William Stanton	Feb. 1, 1811 – Feb. 1, 1812
Stephen Jarvis (Deputy)	Feb. 4, 1812*
Allan N. MacNab	May 1813 – Oct. 17, 1828
David MacNab	1828 – 1840
William Hepburn (Deputy)	Nov. 6, 1832 – Feb. 13, 1833
Andrew Stuart (Deputy)	Dec. 5, 1839*
George K. Chisholm	1841 – 1854
John Roy (Deputy)	1841*
William C. Burrage (Deputy)	May 1, 1849*
William C. Burrage (Deputy)	Oct. 2, 1852*
Donald William McDonell	June 16, 1854 – 1866
William C. Burrage (Deputy)	Oct. 23, 1854*
William C. Burrage (Deputy)	May 23, 1856*
William C. Burrage (Deputy)	June 24, 1858*
Frederick Joseph Glackmeyer	1867 – 1924
George Hunter Ogilvie	1924 – 1934
Walter Leigh Rayfield	1934 – 1935
Charles Smith Rutherford	1935 – 1941
Harry Howie Robson	1941–1947
Benjamin Handley Geary	1947 – 1971
George Reginald Soame	1971 – 1976
Thomas Stelling	1976 –

* Temporary Replacement

Legislative Librarians – 1792 – 1984

Legislative Librarian	Year
George Mayer (Librarian and Keeper of the records)	1792 – 1823
Robert Sullivan Baldwin	1820s (First appeared in Journals on Mar. 18, 1828) – resigned, Mar. 14, 1836
Alpheus Todd	1837
Jasper Brewer	1838
William Winder	1842 – 1855
Alpheus Todd	1855 – 1866
No appointment	1867 – 1869
Donald Bethune	Mar. 22, 1869 – June 30, 1869
Alexander Gordon	Nov. 1869 – died, Sept. 1870
No appointment	1870 – 1872
Samuel James Watson	July 1, 1872 – died, 1881
Rev. William Inglis	Nov. 16, 1881 – resigned Nov. 30, 1883
William Houston	Dec. 1, 1883 – resigned, 1892
William Thomas Rochester Preston	Dec. 1, 1892 – resigned, 1896
Avern Pardoe	1896 – retired, Feb. 1, 1921
Arthur Trollope Wilgress	1921 – retired, Sept. 30, 1935
Robert A. Croskery	1935 – 1936
James John Talman (Acting Librarian)	1936 – resigned, July 30, 1939
Edith Mabel King (Acting Librarian) (Librarian)	1939 – 1944 / 1944 – died, 1947
Mildred Alys Fraser (Acting Librarian) (Librarian)	1947 – 1949 / 1949 – retired, Aug. 31, 1963
Jean Rodgers Kerfoot	Sept. 1, 1963 – retired, Apr. 30, 1973
Doris Evelyn Wagg (Acting Librarian) (Librarian)	May 1, 1973 – Aug. 31, 1974 / Sept. 1, 1974 – resigned, June 30, 1977
Eileen Patricia Hay (Senior Librarian)	July 1, 1977 – Aug. 31, 1978
Reginald Brian Land (Director)	Sept. 1, 1978 –

Alphabetical Index of Electoral Districts* – 1792 – 1984

Carleton East	28th-32nd
Carleton-Grenville	30th-32nd
Chatham-Kent	28th-32nd
Cochrane	14th-16th
Cochrane North	17th-32nd
Cochrane South	17th-32nd
Cornwall	12UC-13UC; 1CW-8CW; 1st-5th; 30th-32nd
Cornwall & Stormont	6th
Don Mills	27th-32nd
Dovercourt	17th-32nd
Downsview	27th-32nd
Dufferin	3rd-18th
Dufferin-Simcoe	19th-32nd
Dundas	1UC-13UC; 1CW-8CW; 1st-18th
Durham	8UC-13UC; 1CW-4CW; 17th-29th
Durham East	6CW-8CW; 1st-16th; 30th-32nd
Durham North	30th
Durham West	5CW-8CW; 1st-16th; 30th-32nd;
Durham-York	30th-32nd
Durham, York East & Simcoe	3UC-4UC
Durham, York & Lincoln, 1st R.	1UC-2UC
Eglinton	17th-32nd
Elgin	19th-32nd
Elgin East	5CW-8CW; 1st-18th
Elgin West	5CW-8CW; 1st-18th
Erie	30th-32nd
Essex	3UC-13UC; 1CW-8CW; 1st-2nd
Essex-Kent	28th-29th
Essex North	3rd-27th; 30th-32nd
Essex South	3th-32nd
Etobicoke	27th-32nd
Forest Hill	27th
Fort William	12th-32nd
Fort William & Lake of the Woods	10th-11th

Hastings-Peterborough	30th-32nd
Hastings South	5CW-8CW
Hastings West	1st-27th
Hastings & Ameliasburgh (Twp.)	5UC-7UC
Hastings & Northumberland	1UC-4UC
High Park	17th-29th
High Park-Swansea	30th-32nd
Humber	27th-32nd
Huron	12UC-13UC; 1CW-4CW; 19th-29th
Huron-Bruce	19th-32nd
Huron & Bruce	5CW-8CW
Huron Centre	12th-16th
Huron East	3rd-11th
Huron-Middlesex	30th-32nd
Huron North	1st-2nd; 12th-18th
Huron South	1st-18th
Huron West	3rd-11th
Kenora	12th-32nd
Kent	1UC-13UC; 1CW-8CW; 1st-2nd; 28th-29th
Kent East	3rd-27th
Kent-Elgin	30th-32nd
Kent West	3rd-27th
Kingston	2CW-8CW; 1st-27th
Kingston (Town)	8UC-13UC; 1CW
Kingston & the Islands	28th-32nd
Kitchener	28th-32nd
Kitchener-Wilmot	30th-32nd
Lake Nipigon	30th-32nd
Lakeshore	27th-32nd
Lambton	5CW-8CW; 1st-2nd; 28th-32nd
Lambton East	3rd-27th
Lambton West	3rd-27th
Lanark	9UC-13UC; 1CW-4CW; 19th-32nd
Lanark North	5CW-8CW; 1st-18th
Lanark South	5CW-8CW; 1st-18th

* Electoral Districts have been indexed according to the most common spelling. For alternate spellings, consult individual legislatures.

1UC-13UC = Upper Canada   **1CW-8CW = Canada West**   **1st-32nd = Ontario**

Alphabetical Index of Electoral Districts – 1792 – 1984 — *Continued*

Muskoka-Ontario	19th-24th
Muskoka & Parry Sound	3rd-5th
Niagara	9UC-13UC; 1CW-8CW; 1st-2nd
Niagara Falls	14th-32nd
Nickel Belt	25th-32nd
Nipissing	7th-9th; 12th-32nd
Nipissing East	10th-11th
Nipissing West	10th-11th
Norfolk	5UC-13UC; 1CW-8CW; 17th-18th
Norfolk North	1st-16th
Norfolk South	1st-16th
Northumberland	8UC-13UC; 3CW-4CW; 17th-32nd
Northumberland & Durham	5UC-7UC
Northumberland East	5CW-8CW; 1st-16th
Northumberland North	1CW-2CW
Northumberland South	1CW-2CW
Northumberland West	5CW-8CW; 1st-16th
Oakville	30th-32nd
Oakwood	30th-32nd
Ontario	19th-29th
Ontario North	5CW-8CW; 1st-18th
Ontario South	5CW-8CW; 1st-18th; 28th-29th
Ontario & Addington	1UC-2UC
Oriole	30th-32nd
Oshawa	25th-32nd
Ottawa	6CW-8CW; 1st-11th
Ottawa Centre	28th-32nd
Ottawa East	12th-32nd
Ottawa North	17th-18th
Ottawa South	17th-32nd
Ottawa West	12th-16th; 25th-32nd
Oxford	8UC-13UC; 1CW-4CW; 19th-32nd
Oxford, Middlesex & Norfolk	3UC-4UC
Oxford & Middlesex	5UC-7UC
Oxford North	5CW-8CW; 1st-18th
Oxford South	5CW-8CW; 1st-18th
Parkdale	14th-32nd

Sandwich-Riverside	28th-29th
Sarnia	28th-32nd
Sault Ste. Marie	10th-32nd
Scarborough Centre	27th-32nd
Scarborough East	27th-32nd
Scarborough-Ellesmere	30th-32nd
Scarborough North	27th-32nd
Scarborough West	27th-32nd
Sherbourne	17th
Simcoe	10UC-13UC; 1CW-4CW
Simcoe Centre	6th-32nd
Simcoe East	3rd-32nd
Simcoe North	5CW-8CW; 1st-2nd
Simcoe South	5CW-8CW; 1st-5th; 12th-16th
Simcoe Southwest	17th-18th
Simcoe West	3rd-16th
Stormont	1UC-2UC; 8UC-13UC; 1CW-8CW; 1st-5th; 7th-29th
Stormont & Russell	3UC-7UC
Stormont, Dundas & Glengarry	30th-32nd
Sturgeon Falls	12th-18th
Sudbury	12th-32nd
Sudbury East	28th-32nd
Suffolk & Essex	1UC-2UC
Temiskaming	12th-16th
Thunder Bay	28th-29th
Timiskaming	17th-32nd
Toronto	6th-7th
Toronto (City)	12UC-13UC; 1CW-6CW
Toronto East	7CW-8CW; 1st-5th; 8th-11th
Toronto East - Seat "A"	12th-13th
Toronto East - Seat "B"	12th-13th
Toronto North	8th-11th
Toronto North - Seat "A"	12th-13th
Toronto North - Seat "B"	12th-13th
Toronto Northeast - Seat "A"	14th-16th
Toronto Northeast - Seat "B"	14th-16th
Toronto Northwest - Seat "A"	14th-16th
Toronto Northwest - Seat "B"	14th-16th
Toronto South	8th-11th

1UC-13UC = Upper Canada **1CW-8CW = Canada West** **1st-32nd = Ontario**

Alphabetical Index of Electoral Districts – 1792 – 1984 — *Continued*

1UC-13UC = Upper Canada　　　　**1CW-8CW = Canada West**　　　　**1st-32nd = Ontario**

Alphabetical Index of Members – 1792 – 1984

Member	Legislature	Member	Legislature
Adam Holland Acres	16th-22nd	Richard Beasley	2UC-3UC; 5UC; 9UC
Gideon Adams	6UC	Walter Beatty	8th-10th
Alfred Emanuel Ahrens	7th	William Beatty	1st
James C. Aikens	5CW-6CW	William Rabb Beatty	8th-9th
Michael Aikman	13UC	Adam Beck	10th-14th; 16th
Absalom Shade Allan	6th-7th	Hollis Edward Beckett	24th-27th
Charles Allan	6CW	Richard B. Beckett	29th
James Noble Allan	24th-29th	William George Beech	24th
John Allan	14th	Roméo Bégin	20th-22nd
John Pearman Allan	22nd	John Beikie	6UC
Henry Allcock	3UC	Aurélien Bélanger	16th-17th; 19th-22nd
Harry Marshall Allen	22nd-26th	Joseph "Albert" Belanger	28th-31st
Richard Allen	32nd	Maurice Lucien Belanger	26th-27th
Robert Aloysius Allen	19th	James Franklin Beatty Belford	16th
William John Allen	9th	Rheal Belisle	25th-26th
William Torrance Allen	14th-15th	Robert Bell	3CW; 5CW-8CW
Arthur "Nelson" Alles	21st	Robert Bell	3rd-4th
Robert Alway	12UC-13UC	Thomas Hamilton Bell	18th
Charles N. Anderson	12th-13th	George Ben	27th-28th
Edward James Anderson	19th-20th	George Benjamin	5CW-7CW
Garfield Anderson	21st-22nd	Claude Frederick Bennett	29th-32nd
James Alexander Anderson	18th	George Bennett	21st
John George Anderson	13th	John Bennett	8th
William Anderson	1st	John Bennewies	13th-14th
William Anderson, Jr.	7CW	William Berczy	10UC-11UC
William A. Anderson	10th-11th	Leo Edward Bernier	27th-32nd
William Alfred Anderson	17th	Richard Nixon Berry	16th; 18th
Philip W. Andrewes	32nd	Donald Bethune	10UC
Iain Frances Angus	30th	George Henry Bethune	19th-20th
Nathaniel Stephen Appleby	3rd-4th	James Bethune	2nd-3rd
Charles Joseph Sylvanus "Syl" Apps	27th-29th	James Whitney Bettes	4th
William Davis Ardagh	2nd	Barnabas Bidwell	8UC
Adolphus Armstrong	16th	Marshall Spring Bidwell	9UC-12UC
James Rogers Armstrong	13UC	Nelson Gordon Bigelow	7th
Milton Taylor Armstrong	19th-20th; 22nd	Herbert Biggar	5CW-6CW
Samuel Armstrong	6th	James Lyons Biggar	7CW-8CW

Name	
Samuel Henry Armstrong	13th-14th
Richard Duke Arnott	20th-21st
George Lyle Ashe	31st-32nd
Nicholas Asmussen	15th; 19th
James Atkinson	9UC
Thomas Robert Atkinson	11th; 13th-14th
Albert Zenophile Aubin	18th
Azaire Adulphe Aubin	11th-12th
James Alexander Charles Auld	24th-31st
John Allan Auld	8th-11th
Samuel Ault	7CW-8CW
Frederick Harold Avery	19th
Nicholas Awrey	4th-8th
Bowen Ebenezer Aylsworth	9th
Francis Baby	1UC; 8UC-10UC
Jean Baptiste Baby	5UC
George Washington Badgerow	4th-5th
Reuben C. Baetz	31st-32nd
Robert Bain	30th
William Alexander Baird	17th-20th
Adam Jacob Baker	3rd-4th
Morgan Baker	19th-20th
Robert Baldwin	10UC; 1CW-3CW
William Warren Baldwin	8UC; 10UC
Dalton Arthur Bales	27th-29th
William Douglas Balfour	4th-8th
Herbert Henry Ball	17th
James Simpson Ballantyne	19th-20th
Thomas Ballantyne	3rd-7th
John Roaf Barber	9th-10th
William Barber	1st-3rd
William W. Barlow	32nd
Henry Barr	7th-8th
John Barr	3rd-4th; 7th; 9th-10th
Patrick Baskerville	4th-5th
Jacob Baxter	1st-8th
John Donald Baxter	23rd
Robert Andrew Baxter	18th
Bartholemew C. Beardsley	9UC; 11UC

Name	
John Walter Scott Biggar	6th
William Hodgins Biggar	7th-8th
Frank Campbell Biggs	15th-16th
Margaret Birch	29th-32nd
Thomas Miles Birkett	17th
Archibald Bishop	2nd-7th
William David Black	13th-20th
Ambrose Blacklock	10UC
Leslie Egerton Blackwell	21st-23rd
William Hume Blake	3CW
Thomas Aston Blakelock	18th-20th
James Blanchard	18th
Thomas Blezard	4th-9th
John Blyth	5th-6th
Charles Bockus	13UC
James Bonfield	3rd-4th
Edward Blake	1st-2nd
Paul Douglas Blundy	31st
Michael George Bolan	31st
Kenneth Charles Bolton	28th
David Bonis	18th
Joshua Booth	1UC
John Bostwick	8UC
George Morss Boswell	1CW
Don Boudria	32nd
Alfred Boultbee	2nd
George Henry Boulter	1st-4th
D'Arcy Boulton	4UC
D'Arcy Edward Boulton	2nd-3rd
George Strange Boulton	9UC; 11UC-13UC
Henry John Boulton	11UC; 1CW; 3CW
William Henry Boulton	2CW-4CW
Edwin James "Ted" Bounsall	29th-31st
Thomas Gilmore Bowerman	19th
John George Bowes	5CW
Beniah Bowman	14th-16th
Charles Martin Bowman	9th-14th
Isaac Erb Bowman	8CW
John Young Bown	7CW-8CW
Philip Henry Bowyer	11th-12th

1UC-13UC = Upper Canada   **1CW-8CW = Canada West**   **1st-32nd = Ontario**

Alphabetical Index of Members – 1792 – 1984 — *Continued*

Kenneth Bryden	26th-27th	Samuel Casey	8UC
Marion Helen Bryden	30th-32nd	Willet Casey	5UC; 7UC
Isaac Buchanan	1CW; 6CW-8CW	Frederick McIntosh Cass	25th-28th
Caleb Henry Buckland	15th	Arthur Allen Casselman	21st
William Buell, Jr.	10UC-12UC	William H. Casselman	15th
William Buell, Sr.	3UC	Michael Morris Cassidy	29th-32nd
George Bukator	26th-28th	Bryan Lewis Cathcart	22nd-26th
James Edward Bullbrook	28th-30th	John Caven	8th
George T. Burke	9UC	John Cawthra	10UC
Asa A. Burnham	4CW	William Cayley	2CW-3CW; 5CW-6CW
Zaccheus Burnham	7UC; 9UC	Louis Pierre Cecile	23rd-27th
Frederick Arthur Burr	28th-30th	George Holmes Challies	18th-24th
Henry Burritt	13UC	George Chalmers	2CW
Read Burritt	3CW	Theodore F. Chamberlain	6th
Stephen Burritt	5UC	Fitzwilliam Henry Chambers	8CW
Arthur Campbell Burt	18th	William Clark Chambers	13th-14th; 16th
Daniel Burt	8th-10th	William Henry Chambers	16th
Francis Henry Burton	5CW-6CW	Napoleon Champagne	13th
Leonidas Burwell	6CW-8CW	Gordon Chaplin	22nd
Mahlon Burwell	6UC-8UC; 11UC; 13UC	John Boyle Chapple	26th
Orlando Bush	7th-8th	Thomas William Chapple	8th
Keith Elkington Butler	27th	Jean (John) Marc Chaput	24th-25th
		Brian Albert Charlton	31st-32nd
Archibald Clement Calder	17th-18th	William Andrew Charlton	7th-10th
Campbell Carlyle Calder	23rd	Samuel Charters	12th-13th
Charles Calder	9th; 11th-12th; 14th	Aurele Chartrand	22nd-24th
John Alexander Calder	14th-15th	Solomon Youmans Chesley	1CW
Francis Caldwell	12UC-13UC	John Chesser	12UC
William Clyde Caldwell	2nd; 4th-7th; 9th-10th	Arthur John Child	24th-25th
John Fullerton Callan	16th	Alexander Chisholm	12UC-13UC
Delino Dexter Calvin	1st-4th	George K. Chisholm	5CW
Colin Stewart Cameron	13th-14th	Kenneth Chisholm	2nd-7th
Douglas Colin Cameron	10th	William Chisholm	8UC; 11UC; 13UC
Duncan Cameron	9UC	Joseph "Elie" Cholette	20th
John Cameron	7UC	David Christie	4CW-6CW
John Cameron	6CW	Robert Christie	1st-2nd
John Hillyard Cameron	2CW-3CW; 5CW; 7CW-8CW	Basil Rorison Church	5CW-6CW
Malcolm Cameron	13UC; 1CW-4CW; 6CW	James Clancy	5th-7th
Malcolm Graeme Cameron	10th-11th	Robert Edwin Clapp	11th
Matthew Crooks Cameron	7CW-8CW; 1st-3rd	Hezekiah Allen Clark	16th-18th

1UC-13UC = Upper Canada   **1CW-8CW = Canada West**   **1st-32nd = Ontario**

Alphabetical Index of Members – 1792 – 1984 — *Continued*

James Conmee	5th-10th
Thomas "Ray" Connell	24th-28th
Skeffington Connor	6CW-7CW
William "Herbert" Connor	21st
Sean Gerard Conway	30th-32nd
Ephraim Cook	5CW
Herman Henry Cook	4th
James William Cook	6CW
John Cook	11UC-13UC; 1CW
John Henry Cook	21st
Simon S. Cook	1st-2nd
David Cooke	31st-32nd
George Atwell Cooke	5th
John Robert Cooke	13th-18th
Henry Sloane Cooper	15th
James Maxwell Cooper	20th
Robert Cooper	15th
Sheila M. Copps	32nd
Henry Corby	1st-2nd
John Cornwall	2UC
Joshua Cornwall	7UC
Nathan Cornwall	12UC-13UC
Thomas Moore Costello	17th
Louis Coté	18th
James Cotter	7UC
Don Cousens	32nd
Alexander Coutts	3rd
David Cowan	4UC
James Cowan	7CW-8CW
Alfred Hozack Cowling	24th-27th
Charles Winnans Cox	19th-20th; 23rd
George Albertus Cox	3rd
John Coyne	1st-2nd
Charles W. Cragg	23rd
John Alexander Craig	18th-19th
James Craig	1st-2nd
James J. Craig	11th-12th
John Craig	8th-9th
Thomas Dixon Craig	6th
William Craig	1st-2nd
Thomas Dalton	10UC
Thomas Mayne Daly	5CW-7CW; 2nd
George Augustus Dana	8th
James Charles Dance	6th
John Robertson Dargavel	11th-14th
David Davidson	10th
Montgomery "Monty" Davidson	30th-31st
Thomas Scott Davidson	14th
Myroyn "Cooke" Davies	22nd-25th
Elihu James Davis	6th-10th
Herbert James Davis	18th
William Grenville Davis	26th-32nd
Michael Norman Davison	31st
Norman Andrew Davison	26th-30th
James Dawson	2nd
Simon James Dawson	3rd
Donald Mackay Deacon	28th-29th
Thomas Deacon	2nd-3rd
Gordon H. Dean	32nd
Ian Deans	28th-31st
Jesse Delong	4CW-5CW
Joseph Clement "Gaston" Demers	27th-28th
Dante Matthew De Monte	28th
James Shannon Dempsey	22nd-25th
William Ryerson Dempsey	9th
George Denison	5th
William Donald Dennison	21st; 23rd
Thomas Roy Dent	21st-24th
Henry Ketcheson Denyes	15th
Stewart Derbishire	1CW
Hammel Madden Deroche	2nd-4th
Arthur DesRosiers	19th
George Hill Detlor	13UC
John Henry Devitt	11th-14th
Patrick Michael Dewan	19th-20th
Herbert Hartley Dewart	14th-15th
John Dickenson	8th-10th
James Dickson	7CW-8CW
Robert Dickson	10UC
Thomas Dickson	6UC

1UC-13UC = Upper Canada   **1CW-8CW = Canada West**   **1st-32nd = Ontario**

Alphabetical Index of Members – 1792 – 1984 — *Continued*

Edward Arunah Dunlop	10th-11th; 13th-14th; 17th-18th	Thomas Roberts Ferguson	6CW-8CW; 1st-2nd
Edward Arunah Dunlop	27th-28th	Walter Renwick Ferguson	13th-14th
Robert Graham Dunlop	12UC-13UC	William Ferguson	8CW
William Dunlop	1CW-2CW	Adam Johnston Fergusson	3CW-5CW
William James Dunlop	24th-26th	Colin Campbell Ferrie	13UC
John Henry Dunn	1CW	Robert Ferrie	5CW
James Wicks Dunsford	7CW-8CW	Alexander David Ferrier	1st
James Durand	6UC-7UC; 12UC; 1CW	William Herman Ferrier	28th-30th
Stanley Harding Dye	22nd	James Marshall Ferris	3rd-5th
Matthew Bulloch Dymond	25th-29th	John P. Ferris	30th
William Dynes	8th	Corelli Collard Field	6th-8th
		John Collard Field	4th
Robert "Alan" Eagleson	27th	Hugh Finlayson	6CW; 1st-3rd
John F. Eakins	30th-32nd	William Finlayson	16th-18th; 20th
Joseph Pattulo Earngey	17th	Susan A. Fish	32nd
Joseph Lees Easton	23rd	Harold Fisher	16th
Robert Gordon Eaton	29th-32nd	John Henry Fisher	11th-12th
John Charles Ebbs	13th	Harold Ferguson Fishleigh	24th-25th
George Walter Ecclestone	14th-18th	William Fitzsimmons	1st-2nd
Joseph Edgar	14th	John Ira Flatt	8th
Hugh Alden Edighoffer	28th-32nd	John Fleming	3rd
James "Frederick" Edwards	22nd-27th	John Flesher	3rd
Raymond Clare Edwards	26th	Charles George Fletcher	17th; 20th
William Henry Edwards	16th-17th	William Robertson Flett	17th
Henry Eilber	9th-14th	Billa Flint	3CW; 5CW
Goldwin Corlett Elgie	19th-20th; 22nd	Michael Hamilton Foley	5CW-8CW
Robert Goldwin Elgie	31st-32nd	John Weir Foote	23rd-25th
Alexander Leslie Elliott	20th	John Featherson Ford	15th
Frederick Wellington Elliott	18th	T. Kenzie Foster	23rd
George Elliott	13UC	Charles Fothergill	9UC-10UC
George Adam Elliott	16th	James Francis Foulds	29th-32nd
John Campbell Elliott	12th-14th	Reginald Amherst Fowler	14th-15th
Mathew Elliott	3UC-5UC	Milton C. Fox	15th
Robert Ellsworth Elliott	22nd; 24th-25th	Samuel John Fox	9th-12th
William Elliott	11UC	James Joseph Foy	9th-14th
William Herbert Elliott	18th	Thomas Howard Fraleigh	18th
Arthur Ellis	18th-19th	Alexander Fraser	10UC-11UC
Gordon Bennett Ellis	23rd	Alexander Fraser	1st-2nd
James Albert Ellis	13th	Christopher Finlay Fraser	2nd-7th
Murray J. Elston	32nd	Donald Fraser	11UC

1UC-13UC = Upper Canada   **1CW-8CW = Canada West**   **1st-32nd = Ontario**

Alphabetical Index of Members – 1792 – 1984 — *Continued*

Melville Carlyle "Bud" Germa	29th-31st	Christopher Alexander Hagerman	8UC; 11UC-13UC
William Manley German	8th-9th	Daniel Hagerman	8UC
Robert Gibbons	1st-2nd	Henry Louis Hagey	20th
Thomas Nicholson Gibbs	8CW	James Haggerty	8th
David Gibson	12UC-13UC	Raymond Louis Haggerty	28th-32nd
John Morison Gibson	4th-10th	Archibald Judson Haines	20th
Robert Wayne Gibson	26th-27th	George Grant Halcrow	15th
Thomas Gibson	2nd-8th	Eric "Ross" Hall	30th-31st
Charles Gifford	2nd	Francis William Hall	14th
Evelyn Gigantes	30th-31st	George B. Hall	7UC
Bernt Nicole Gilbertson	28th-29th	George Barker Hall	2CW
John Gilchrist	12UC; 1CW	James Hall	3CW
John Godkin Giles	2nd	Richard Reece Hall	15th
George Alexander Gillespie	14th	Stanley Leroy Hall	21st-26th
John Gillies	5th	Zachariah Adam Hall	14th
Phil A. Gillies	32nd	George Ham	8UC
John Taylor Gilmour	6th-7th	Joseph Henry Ham	14th
Reginald Victor Gisborn	25th-29th	Charles Wesley Hambly	16th; 18th
Philip Gerald Givens	29th-30th	George Hamilton	8UC-10UC
John Judah Glass	19th-20th	George Wellesley Hamilton	2nd
James Glendinning	7th	Maurice Hamilton	25th-29th
Charles Morris Godfrey	30th	Robert Hamilton	8UC
Forbes Elliott Godfrey	11th-18th	William Hamilton	8UC
Henry Thomas Godwin	7th	William Ernest Hamilton	22nd-24th
Lincoln Goldie	16th-18th	William Henry Hammell	5th-7th
George Ellis Gomme	25th-28th	Leslie Hancock	21st
Edward R. Good	28th-30th	Sidney Bernard Handleman	29th-31st
George Horace Gooderham	12th-14th	Henry Ryan Haney	2nd-3rd
William Arthur Goodfellow	21st-26th	Wilfred Smith Haney	16th-17th
Arthur St. Clair Gordon	19th-21st	John William Hanna	21st-26th
George Thomas Gordon	23rd-27th	William John Hanna	10th-14th
James Gordon	8UC-9UC	Carl David Hanniwell	22nd
James K. Gordon	32nd	George Vernon Harcourt	16th-18th
Thomas Barnes Gough	5UC	Michael Harcourt	6CW-7CW
Isaac James Gould	5th-6th	Richard Harcourt	3rd-11th
Joseph Gould	5CW-6CW	Benjamin Hardison	2UC
Joseph M. Gould	26th-27th	Arthur Sturgis Hardy	2nd-9th
Alfred Goulet	15th	William Hargraft	3rd
John M. Govenlock	15th	William Harkin	3rd-4th
Peter Gow	1st-3rd	Eric Harrington	2nd

1UC-13UC = Upper Canada   **1CW-8CW = Canada West**   **1st-32nd = Ontario**

Alphabetical Index of Members – 1792 – 1984 — *Continued*

Member	Legislature	Member	Legislature
Michael D. Harris	32nd	James Hill Hunter	3rd-4th; 7th
Robert John "Jack" Harris	26th-27th	Roger Rollo Hunter	13UC
Charles Robert Harrison	18th	George Charles Hurdman	14th
Samuel Beasley Harrison	1CW-2CW	Earl Hutchinson	18th-19th
James Hart	5th	Harry Harland Hyndman	22nd
Joseph Hartman	4CW-6CW		
James Irwin Hartt	13th-14th	Charles Ingersol	9UC; 11UC
William Harty	7th-9th	Andrew B. Ingram	6th
George Isaac Harvey	21st-23rd	Gordon William Innes	25th-26th; 28th
William Bruce Harvey	23rd-24th	Hugh Paterson Innes	12th
W. Irwin Haskett	26th-28th	William Henry Ireland	15th-18th
Richard Hatt	7UC	Mark Howard Irish	14th
Frederick William Haultain	7CW-8CW	Donald Roy Irvine	29th-30th
Edward Michael Havrot	29th; 31st-32nd	McCausland Irvine	16th
George Douglas Hawley	4th-5th	Colin Isaacs	31st
David Davidson Hay	3rd-4th	Theodore Henry Isley	23rd
Francis Wellington Hay	14th-15th		
Joseph Longford Haycock	8th	Donald Earl Jackson	28th
William Torrance Hays	1st	George Jackson	5CW; 7CW-8CW
William Howard Hearst	12th-14th	George "Ernest" Jackson	25th
Peter Heenan	15th-16th; 19th-20th	William Jacques	14th
Wilfrid Heighington	18th-19th	Michael James	10th
Albert Hellyer	15th	Robert S. Jameson	12UC
Lorne Charles Henderson	27th-32nd	David Jamieson	9th-14th; 16th
Rufus E. Henderson	10UC	James Edgar Jamieson	16th; 18th
John Strathearn Hendrie	10th-14th	Charles Eusibius Janes	22nd-26th
Mickey Hennessy	31st-32nd	Charles William Jarvis	13th-14th
George Stewart Henry	13th-20th	George S. Jarvis	13UC
Philip James Henry	18th	William Botsford Jarvis	11UC
James deCongalton Hepburn	20th-22nd	William Jelly	4th
Mitchell Frederick Hepburn	19th-21st	James Hugh Jessiman	28th-29th
Alexander "Robert" Herbert	24th-26th	Elisha Jessop	9th-14th
John George Hess	5th-6th	Edward Jessup	11UC
Andrew Hicks	15th	Edward Jessup, Jr.	2UC
Thomas Higginson	8CW	Hamilton Dibble Jessup	2CW
Hamnett Pinhey Hill	15th	John McLellan "Jack" Johnson	30th-32nd

James Ferguson Hill	16th-19th	John Wesley Johnson	12th-14th
Solomon Hill	4UC	Thomas Hall Johnson	3CW-4CW
William James Hill	9th	Alexander Johnston	5th
Daniel Hilliard	6th	Allister Johnston	23rd-28th
Irwin Foster Hilliard	14th	George Graham Johnston	21st-26th
George Hillmer	16th-17th	James Johnston	1CW-2CW
Francis Hincks	1CW; 3CW-5CW	John Benjamin Johnston	15th
Norman Otto Hipel	18th-20th	Richard Frank Johnston	31st-32nd
James Hiscott	7th-8th	Robert Mercer Johnston	28th-30th
Archibald Hislop	9th-11th	Thomas Dalton Johnston	16th
Thomas Saunders Hobbs	8th	William "Erskine" Johnston	25th-28th
Thomas D. Hodgens	9th	William J. Johnston	15th
Charles Constantine Hodgins	11th	John Philemon Johnstone	22nd; 24th
Thomas Hodgins	2nd-3rd	Arthur C. Jolley	24th-25th
Louis M. Hodgson	27th	Edward Bigelow Jolliffe	21st; 23rd
Ronald "Glen" Hodgson	27th-29th	Charles Jones	8UC-9UC
William Marshall Chamberlain Hodgson	28th-32nd	David Jones	9UC; 12UC
Philip Hoffman	26th	David Ford Jones	8CW
John Sheridan Hogan	6CW	Ephraim Jones	1UC
Donald McDonald Hogarth	13th-15th; 17th-18th	Francis Jones	7CW-8CW
John Holmes	6CW	Henry Jones	11UC
Joseph William Holmes	9th-10th	Jonas Jones	7UC-9UC; 13UC
Karl Kenneth Homuth	15th-18th	Solomon Jones	2UC
Albert Edwin Honeywell	17th-18th	Terry David Jones	30th-32nd
Thomas Hook	14th	John Joynt	15th-16th
Augustus F. Hooper	7CW	Robert L. Joynt	9th-10th
Edmund John Hooper	1st	Thomas William Jutten	17th-18th
Caleb Hopkins	10UC; 12UC; 1CW; 3CW		
Thomas Hornor	8UC-11UC	John Kean	3rd
Richard Phillips Hotham	13UC	John Kearns	13UC
William Limburg Houck	19th-20th; 23rd-24th	Francis Henry Keefer	16th
Matthew Munsel Howard	11UC-12UC	John Joseph Kehoe	21st
Peter Howard	4UC-5UC; 7UC	William Keith	16th
John Ranson Howitt	12th	Russell Temple Kelley	22nd-23rd
Oliver Aiken Howland	8th	Morley C. Kells	32nd
William Pearce Howland	6CW-8CW	James Francis "Frank" Kelly	19th-21st
William Henry Hoyle	9th-14th	Philip Timothy Kelly	24th-25th
William Parker Hudson	5th-7th	Robert Henry Kemp	16th-17th
Stanley Joseph Hunt	21st-25th	Angus John Kennedy	16th-18th
Frederick Fraser Hunter	19th-20th	Hugh W. Kennedy	11th

1UC-13UC = Upper Canada　　　　**1CW-8CW = Canada West**　　　　**1st-32nd = Ontario**

Alphabetical Index of Members – 1792 – 1984 — *Continued*

Member	Legislature	Member	Legislature
Robert "Douglas" Kennedy	28th-32nd	James Livingston	4th
Thomas Laird Kennedy	15th-18th; 20th-25th	George Edward Lockhart	21st
Alfred Franklin Kenning	17th-18th	William Thomas Lockhart	7th
William Kerns	5th-8th	Joseph N. Lockwood	10UC
David "McMaster" Kerr	24th-25th	Thomas Long	3rd-4th
George Kerr	11th	George Longley	10UC
George Albert Kerr	27th-32nd	John Loughrin	7th-9th
Joseph Kerr	4th-5th	Samuel Lount	12UC
William J. Kerr	8UC	William Lount	1st
Vincent George Kerrio	30th-32nd	John W. Loux	6CW
Jesse Ketchum	10UC-11UC	William James Lowe	14th
George Nelson Kidd	8th-11th	Isaac Benson Lucas	9th-14th
Thomas Ashmore Kidd	17th-20th	Margarette "Rae" Morrison Luckock	21st
John Kilborn	10UC	Alexander Lumsden	9th
Hamilton Hartley Killaly	1CW	John MacVeigh Lumsden	5CW
Robert Kincaid	4th	Antonio "Tony" Lupusella	30th-32nd
James Harold King	19th-20th	Daniel Luton	1st
Harold James Kirby	19th-20th	George Lyon	11UC; 2CW
James Kirkwood	7th	George Byron Lyon	3CW-5CW
Ronald Henry Knight	28th	*See also* George Byron Lyon Fellowes	
Vernon Charles Knowles	22nd	Robert Lyon	1st
John "Ralph" Knox	27th	Robert Adam Lyon	3rd-6th
Jacob Kohler	11th-13th	William Durie Lyon	3rd
Al Kolyn	32nd	Clayton "Harry" Lyons	24th-26th
William Abram Kribs	9th-10th	James Lyons	9UC-11UC
		James Lyons	16th-18th
Joseph Louis Labrosse	11th		
Henry George Lackner	9th-13th	Duncan MacArthur	13th
Louis Hypolite Lafontaine	1CW	Leopold Macaulay	17th-20th
James Laidlaw	4th-5th	Robert William Macaulay	24th-27th
Charles Lamarche	11th	George Macbeth	5CW-7CW
Allan Austin Lamport	20th	John Palmer MacBeth	29th-31st
Thomas Percival Lancaster	18th-19th	Morrison Mann MacBride	15th-16th; 19th-20th
John Lane	3rd	Finlay George MacDiarmid	9th-14th; 16th-17th
John Gordon Lane	29th-32nd	Donald Alexander Macdonald	6CW-7CW
Malcolm Lang	14th-16th	Donald Cameron MacDonald	25th-32nd

George Edward Langford	8th	Herbert Stone Macdonald	2nd
John Langton	4CW-5CW	John Alexander Macdonald	2CW-8CW
Edmund Antoine Lapierre	19th	John Sandfield Macdonald	1CW-8CW; 1st-2nd
Edwin Larwill	5CW	Rolland Macdonald	2CW
Francis Robert Latchford	9th-10th	Angus Macdonell (Glengary)	3UC
Abram William Lauder	1st-5th	Angus Macdonell (York)	3UC-4UC
Floyd Laughren	29th-32nd	Donald Macdonell	12UC-13UC
Frederick Vanwyck Laughton	18th	Donald Aeneas MacDonell	12UC-13UC; 2CW
Robert Laurier	20th-21st	George Macdonell	2CW
Gordon Lavergne	24th-26th	Hugh Macdonell	1UC
Patrick Daniel Lawlor	28th-31st	John Macdonell	1UC-2UC
Lawrence Lawrason	2CW	John Macdonell	6UC
Albert Benjamin Rutter "Bert" Lawrence	27th-29th	Hon. William MacDougall	3rd
Allan Frederick Lawrence	25th-29th	Robert Macfarlane	8CW
Samuel Lawrence	19th	Charles Maitland Macfie	19th-20th
Bertram Elijah Leavens	21st; 23rd	Edmund Aberdeen MacGillivray	20th-22nd
Stanley Francis Leavine	24th	Harold Arthur Clement Machin	12th-14th
Marie Charles Denis "Paul" Leduc	19th-20th	William Mack	4th; 6th-7th
John Lee	9th-10th	Alexander Grant MacKay	10th-13th
William Lees	4th-6th	Andrew Mackay	12th
George Mansfield Leeson	15th	John Pearson MacKay	20th
John Johnson Lefferty	9UC-10UC; 12UC	William John Mackay	18th
Theodore Legault	17th; 19th	A. Alexander MacKenzie	22nd-27th
Marcel Leger	23rd	Alexander MacKenzie	7CW-8CW; 2nd
Nicholas George Leluk	29th-32nd	Charles Mackenzie	6th-7th
Thomas Herbert Lennox	11th-15th	Harold Arthur MacKenzie	28th
John A. Leslie	22nd	Hope Fleming Mackenzie	6CW; 8CW
John Giles Lethbridge	15th-17th	Robert Warren Mackenzie	30th-32nd
Lloyd A. Letherby	24th-27th	William Lyon Mackenzie	10UC-12UC; 3CW-6CW
Alexander Cameron Lewis	15th-16th	Alexander Albert MacLeod	21st-23rd
Frederick William Lewis	11th	John MacLeod	6CW
John Bower Lewis	11UC-13UC	Donald Macmaster	4th
Levi Lewis	5UC	Allan Napier MacNab	11UC-13UC; 1CW-5CW
Stephen Henry Lewis	27th-31st	Charles Steel MacNaughton	25th-29th
Thomas Henry Lewis	22nd	Donald Macnish	8th-9th
W. Beverley Lewis	25th-27th	Charles "Gordon" MacOdrum	24th
Francis Baxter Leys	9th	William Macomb	1UC
John Leys	6th	Jean Baptiste Maçon	11UC
Archibald M. Little	10th	Agnes Campbell MacPhail	21st; 23rd
Edward Alfred Little	8th-11th	Robert W. MacQuarrie	32nd

1UC-13UC = Upper Canada   **1CW-8CW = Canada West**   **1st-32nd = Ontario**

Alphabetical Index of Members – 1792 – 1984 — *Continued*

Member	Legislature	Member	Legislature
Malcolm MacVicar	15th	Daniel McCraney	3rd-5th
Frank Madill	4th	Thomas McCrae	3UC
Lorne Howard Maeck	29th-31st	William McCrae	12UC-13UC
Zotique Mageau	13th-16th	Charles McCrea	13th-18th
Charles Magill	8CW	Hiram McCreary	15th
Thomas Magladery	14th-15th	James Simeon McCuaig	2nd
Thomas Magwood	7th-8th	John Arthur McCue	25th
Arthur Arnold Mahaffy	10th-13th	Angus Peter McDonald	6CW
Thomas Joseph Mahoney	16th-18th	Archibald McDonald	11UC
Mitro "Mac" Makarchuk	28th; 30th-31st	Donald McDonald	10UC-11UC; 1CW
Andrew Malcolm	9th	Donald Alexander McDonald	8CW
Finlay Malcolm	10UC	Donald Robert McDonald	9th; 12th
James Anthony Maloney	25th-26th	Ernest Nicholls McDonald	15th
Edward Malloch	12UC-13UC; 3CW-4CW	John McDonald	8CW
Benajah Mallory	4UC-5UC	John Lawrence McDonald	21st; 23rd
Anthony Manahan	13UC; 1CW	John Stevenson McDonald	8th
Remo J. Mancini	30th-32nd	Roderick McDonald	4CW-5CW
Peter Thomas Manley	24th-26th	William McDonald	13th-14th
Clare Edgar Mapledoram	24th-25th	Alexander McDonell	3UC-6UC; 8UC-9UC
Joseph "Henri" Marceau	15th; 19th	Alexander McDonell (Northumberland)	12UC-13UC
James Raglan Mark	16th	Alexander McDonell (Prescott)	12UC
Abraham Markle	6UC	Donald McDonell	9UC
Henry Markle	5UC	John McDonell	7UC
John Marks	13UC	Donald Joseph McDougal	11th-12th
Abraham Marsh	5UC	John McDougall	3rd
Duncan McLean Marshall	19th	John Lorn McDougall	6CW; 1st
Thomas A. Marshall	13th-15th	William McDougall	6CW-8CW
Elie Walter Martel	28th-32nd	Robert Herbert McElroy	11th-14th
George Frederick Marter	6th-9th	J. Earl McEwen	30th-32nd
Charles Hammond Martin	21st-23rd	James McEwing	12th
D'Arcy "Argue" Consell Martin	18th	Ross Atkinson McEwing	20th-23rd
John Strickler Martin	16th-18th	John McFarlan	13th-14th
Victor J. Martin	22nd	Duncan McFarland	3CW
William George Martin	17th-18th	Thomas William McGarry	11th-14th
John Burton Martyn	14th	Robert McGhee	5th
Robert Mercer Mason	12th-14th	William McGill	1st

James Massie	3rd	Angus McGillis	17th
Isaac Master	3rd-6th	William McGiverin	8CW
Thomas Matchett	1st	John McGowan	2nd-3rd
John Mathews	9UC-10UC	John McGregor	4UC-6UC
James Mathewson	13UC	James Fitzgerald McGuigan	31st-32nd
Arthur James Matheson	8th-13th	Charles Elmer McIlveen	29th
Donald Matheson	5CW	John McIntosh	12UC-13UC
James Arthur Mathieu	13th-15th; 17th	Alexander Fraser McIntyre	3rd
William D. Mattice	4CW-6CW	Daniel McIntyre	21st
George S. May	11th	Duncan John McIntyre	5th
Thomas Richard Mayberry	12th-13th	Robert McIntyre	8CW
William Balmer McAllister	4th	Angus McKay	6th-9th
Donald McAlpine	15th	George Prevost McKay	5th
John Alfred McAndrew	6th	John McKay	7th-8th
Duncan McArthur	20th	Thomas McKay	12UC-13UC
Frederick John McArthur	18th	Gilbert McKechnie	7th
Robert Neil McArthur	15th	Thomas McKee	2UC-3UC
Edward McBride	9UC	William J. McKee	8th-9th
Frederick George McBrien	16th-18th; 20th	Archibald McKellar	6CW-8CW; 1st-3rd
Bruce Robert McCaffrey	31st-32nd	Donald McKenzie	5th
George R. McCague	30th-32nd	Hugh McKenzie	7th
Duncan McCall	9UC-11UC	William "Darcy" McKeough	28th-31st
Simpson McCall	1st-2nd	Charles Robert McKeown	11th-14th; 16th
Lachlan McCallum	2nd	Daniel McKerlie	5CW
Malcolm Alexander McCallum	16th-17th	Robert Carson McKessock	30th-32nd
Peter Duncan McCallum	7th-8th	Robert McKim	1st-2nd; 4th-5th
Henry Wellesley McCann	5CW-7CW	Michael McKnight	16th
Milo McCargar	13UC	Daniel McLachlin	4CW; 7CW
William John McCart	10th; 12th	Alexander McLaren	8th
James Arthur McCausland	16th	James Wellington McLaughlin	4th-6th
William McCleary	7th	John McLaughlin	9th
Ross A. McClellan	30th-32nd	David McLaws	3rd
Archibald Blake McCoig	11th	Alexander McLean	13UC; 1CW; 3CW
Dugold McColl	7th	Alexander Daniel McLean	17th
Nicol McColl	1st	Allan McLean	4UC-8UC
Neil McColman	5th	Allan K. McLean	32nd
Robert John McCormick	12th-13th	Alvin Coulter McLean	18th
William McCormick	6UC-8UC	Archibald McLean	8UC-13UC
Thomas David McConkey	8CW	Murdo Young McLean	8th
Alexander McCowan	11th-13th	Nathaniel McLenaghan	7th

1UC-13UC = Upper Canada   **1CW-8CW = Canada West**   **1st-32nd = Ontario**

Alphabetical Index of Members – 1792 – 1984 — *Continued*

Member	Legislature	Member	Legislature
James William McLeod	15th	James Percy Moore	17th-18th
John McLeod	1st-3rd	John Douglas Moore	7th-8th
William Duncan McLeod	10th	Henri Morel	12th-14th; 16th-18th
James McMahon	3rd-7th	Ira Morgan	4th
George McManus	2nd	William Morgan	4th-6th
Alexander McMartin	6UC-8UC; 11UC	James E. Morin	5th-6th
Richard M. McMeekin	20th	Jules Morin	25th-26th; 28th
Gilbert McMicken	6CW	Ellis Price Morningstar	24th-29th
Gilbert McMicking	12UC-13UC	Hon. Alexander Morris	7CW-8CW; 3rd-5th
Edward B. McMillan	23rd	James Morris	13UC; 1CW
John Angus McMillan	11th	William Morris	8UC-12UC
Andrew Robinson McMillen	18th	Angus Morrison	5CW-8CW
James McMonies	8CW	Marshall Bidwell Morrison	9th-11th
Hon. John McMurrich	1st	Joseph Curran Morrison	3CW-5CW
Roland "Roy" McMurtry	30th-32nd	Thomas David Morrison	12UC-13UC
James McNabb	5UC; 7UC	William Morrison	17th-18th
Joseph McNamara	15th	Donald Hugo Morrow	23rd-30th
William Kirkpatrick McNaught	11th-13th	James Morton	7CW
Daniel McNaughton	7th-8th	William Caven Moscrip	9th
Duncan Alexander McNaughton	17th-18th	William Mostyn	3rd
John McNeil	8th	Roswell Mount	11UC
Ronald Keith McNeil	25th-32nd	Oliver Mowat	6CW-8CW; 2nd-8th
Colin McNeilledge	11UC	Robert Mulholland	5th
David McNichol	8th	Duncan "Paul" Munro	18th-19th
John Duncan "Jack" McNie	29th	Henry Munro	5CW-8CW
John Duncan McPhee	21st-24th	Hugh Munro	13th-14th
David Murdoch McPherson	8th	James S. Munro	10th-11th
William David McPherson	12th-14th	John W. Munro	9th-10th
James McQueen	13th	Malcolm G. Munroe	3rd
Thomas Baker McQuesten	19th-20th	Gilbert Hugh Murdoch	15th
George Alexander McQuibban	17th-19th	William Murdoch	21st-26th
Duncan McRae	2nd-3rd	Edmund Murney	13UC; 1CW-2CW; 4CW-5CW
Milton Duncan McVicar	19th-20th	Denis Murphy	10th
Walter William Meacham	6th-8th	Edward Joseph Murphy	18th
Thomas Mears	5UC-6UC	Thomas Alexander Murphy	17th-22nd
William George Medd	17th-18th	Thomas Murray	1st; 4th-6th

Arthur Kenneth Meen	28th-30th
Joseph Ignatino Meinzinger	22nd
Cecil George Mercer	20th
William Ralph Meredith	2nd-8th
Henry Merrick	2nd-5th
William Hamilton Merritt	11UC-13UC; 1CW-6CW
James Henry Metcalfe	4th-7th
Alexander Patterson Mewhinney	15th-17th
Joseph Michaud	10th
Daniel "Roland" Michener	22nd
James Taylor Middleton	8th
Charles Hibbert Millard	21st; 23rd
Gordon James Millen	22nd
Edward Blake Miller	17th
Frank Stuart Miller	29th-32nd
Gordon Irvin Miller	30th-32nd
John Classon Miller	3rd-4th
John Stewart Miller	6th
Robert Francis Miller	17th
Wilfred Lynn Miller	19th-21st
John Colborne Milligan	13th; 16th
Charles Henry Mills	13th-14th
Henry Mills	15th
Edward Ming	17th
Andrew Miscampbell	7th-10th
George Herbert Mitchell	21st
John Henry Mitchell	17th
Robert C. Mitchell	31st-32nd
Douglas Peter Moffatt	30th
Foster Graham Moffatt	17th
Gerald Joseph Monaghan	25th
George William Monk	2nd-7th
George Monro	2CW
Andrew Monteith	1st-2nd
John C. Monteith	10th
Joseph Dunsmore Monteith	16th-18th
Samuel "Nelson" Monteith	9th; 11th
Hugh Montgomery	11th
Wesley Montgomery	15th
Elias Moore	12UC-13UC
Thomas Patrick Murray	18th-21st
William Alexander Murray	22nd
Armstrong H. Musgrove	12th-14th
George Johnston Musgrove	14th
John Mutrie	8th-9th
Adam Henry Myers	2CW-3CW
Raymond Munro Myers	24th-26th
Thomas MacIntyre Nairn	4th; 6th
Joseph "Daniel" Nault	23rd-24th
Daniel Near	4th
Sylvester Neelon	3rd-5th
George Wesley Neely	11th-13th
Robert Nelles	3UC-4UC; 6UC-7UC
Arthur Russell Nesbitt	16th-19th
Samuel Greerson Murray Nesbitt	12th-14th
William Beattie Nesbitt	10th-11th
John Newlands	20th
Bernard Newman	26th-32nd
James Melvin Newman	22nd-23rd
William Newman	17th-19th
William G. Newman	28th-31st
Robert Nichol	6UC-8UC
William Folger Nickle	12th; 15th-16th
William McAdam Nickle	24th-26th
William Niles	5CW
Alfred Westland Nixon	11th-14th
George Adam Nixon	29th
Harry Corwin Nixon	15th-26th
Robert Fletcher Nixon	26th-32nd
William Glennie Nixon	19th-20th
William George Noden	24th-27th
Robert Addison Norman	12th-13th
Hiram Norton	11UC-13UC
Keith Calder Norton	30th-32nd
William Notman	3CW; 6CW-8CW
Wilmer John Nuttall	29th
George Oakley, Jr.	16th-18th
Hamilton Parke O'Connor	4th-7th

1UC-13UC = Upper Canada   **1CW-8CW = Canada West**   **1st-32nd = Ontario**

Alphabetical Index of Members – 1792 – 1984 — *Continued*

Member	Legislature	Member	Legislature
John O'Connor, Jr.	7CW	Charles Berkeley Powell	9th-10th
Daniel John O'Donoghue	2nd-3rd	Israel Wood Powell	1CW-2CW
Leslie Warner Oke	15th-17th	John A.H. Powell	13UC
George O'Keefe	8th	Walker Powell	6CW
Neil Leverne Olde	27th-28th	William Frederick Powell	5CW-8CW
Adam Oliver	1st-3rd	Arthur Clarence Pratt	11th-14th
Farquhar Robert Oliver	17th-27th	Josiah Johnston Preston	10th-14th
Thomas Oliver	8CW	Richard Franklin Preston	8th; 11th-14th
Hugh Patrick O'Neil	30th-32nd	Robert Henry Preston	3rd; 5th-7th
John O'Neill	15th	Thomas Hiram Preston	9th-11th
Gilbert Wellington Ostrom	6th	William Alfred Preston	11th-12th
John O'Sullivan	3rd	Henry Isaac Price	18th
Cyril Arthur Goodwin Overall	21st	Henry James Price	25th-28th
Edward William James Owens	13th-14th; 16th	James Hervey Price	1CW-3CW
		Lloyd H. Price	25th
Gaspard Pacaud	6th	William Herbert Price	14th-19th
Frederick Forsyth Pardee	9th	Albert Prince	2nd
Timothy Blair Pardee	1st-6th	John Prince	13UC; 1CW-4CW
Thomas Letson Pardo	8th-10th	John Abbot Pringle	21st-24th
Alexander A. Parent	22nd	Ada Mary Pritchard	27th-28th
George "Eamon" Park	23rd	William Proudfoot	12th-14th
Thomas Parke	12UC-13UC; 1CW	Edmund Proulx	16th-17th
Thomas Sutherland Parker	8CW	Thomas Pryde	22nd-25th
William James Parkhill	3rd-4th	Jesse Thomas Purdy	6CW
Nelson Parliament	14th-15th	Robert Allan Pyne	9th-14th
Frederick Raymond Parnell	14th		
Harry Craig Parrott	29th-31st	Leonard Joseph Quilty	26th
George W. Parry	22nd-26th		
Donald Alexander Paterson	27th-29th	Damase Racine	11th-15th
Robert Paton	7th-8th	Horace S. Racine	27th
Thomas L. Patrick	21st-25th	Thomas Radenhurst	10UC
William Patrick	4CW-7CW	Robert Keith Rae	32nd
James Colebrooke Patterson	3rd	John Carman Ramsden	15th
Peter Patterson	2nd-4th	Russell Harold Ramsay	31st-32nd
Robert John Patterson	16th	Robert Randal	8UC-11UC
Roland Patterson	19th-21st	Stanley John Randall	27th-28th

Name		Name	
David Pattie	8UC	William "Edgar" Raney	15th-17th
George Pattinson	11th-13th	Anthony McGuin Rankin	13th-16th
Richard Pattinson	6UC	Arthur Rankin	5CW; 7CW-8CW
Andrew Pattullo	8th-10th	David John Rankin	25th
William James Paul	11th-12th	Edward Walter Rathbun	11th
Benjamin Pawling	1UC	Charles Edmund Raven	18th
Thomas Paxton	1st-4th	James Rayside	4th-7th
Hugh Peacock	28th	Charles Edward Rea	23rd
Josiah Williams Pearce	10th-12th	George Read	1st-2nd
Peter William Pearson	17th	Arthur John Reaume	24th-27th
Edward Armour Peck	13th	Joseph Octave Réaume	10th-13th
George Henry Peck	27th	Daniel Reed	11th-12th
Samuel Stanley Peck	4th	Julian Alexander Arnott Reed	30th-32nd
Edward John Barker Pense	9th-11th	James Thomas Hammill Regan	13th-14th
George Perry	1st-2nd	James Reid	7th-10th
Peter Perry	9UC-12UC; 3CW	John Frederick Reid	17th-18th
David Robertson Peterson	30th-32nd	Norman Reid	12th
Paul Peterson	8UC-10UC	Thomas "Patrick" Reid	28th-32nd
Archibald Petrie	2CW	Timothy Escott Reid	28th
Nathaniel Pettit	1UC	William Henry Reid	8th-9th
Henry John Pettypiece	9th-10th	Leonard McKenzie Reilly	26th-29th
George Hector Pharand	12th	Frank Rennie	15th
Orson James Phelps	5th-6th	James Alexander Renwick	27th-32nd
Edward Thomas Philip	30th-32nd	Margaret Ellen Renwick	28th
Mackinnon Phillips	22nd-26th	Allan Edward Reuter	27th-29th
René L. Piché	32nd	Hugh Alexander Reynolds	23rd
Clifford George Pilkey	28th	Walter Bain Reynolds	20th-23rd
Joseph Albert Pinard	14th-17th	John Reginald Rhodes	29th-31st
Hamnett Pinhey	11UC	Albert Norton Richards	8CW
Walter George Pitman	28th	Stephen Richards	1st-2nd
Gordon William Pittock	27th	William Buell Richards	3CW-4CW
Andrew William Playfair	6CW	Amos Augustus Richardson	12th
Eli Playter	9UC	Charles Richardson	12UC-13UC
Paul Poisson	17th-18th	Charles Edward Richardson	18th
James Pollock	32nd	John Richardson	8th-10th
Alan William Pope	31st-32nd	Richard Richardson	3rd
Dana Harris Porter	21st-25th	Udney Richardson	13th-14th
David Porter	7th	William Richardson	4th
Maurice Berkeley Portman	7CW	William Rickard	10th
Richard Thomas Potter	28th-29th	John Keith "Jack" Riddell	29th-32nd

1UC-13UC = Upper Canada **1CW-8CW = Canada West** **1st-32nd = Ontario**

Alphabetical Index of Members – 1792 – 1984 — *Continued*

Clarke Tivy Rollins	26th-31st
Walter Ritchie Rollo	15th
George Rolph	10UC
John Rolph	9UC-10UC; 13UC; 4CW-5CW
John Henry Haines Root	24th-29th
Joseph Rorke	6th-7th
Baltis Rose	4th
Jesse Wright Rose	4CW
John Rosevear	3rd-4th
Alexander McLagan Ross	3rd-6th
Alexander Peter Ross	5th
Arthur Edward Ross	13th-15th
David Munro Ross	15th-18th
Duncan Alexander Ross	15th
Duncan Campbell Ross	11th-12th
George William Ross	5th-11th
James Ross	5CW-6CW
James Alway Ross	12th
John Sylvester Ross	7CW-8CW
Walter Ross	8CW
David Rotenberg	31st-32nd
George Albert Routledge	10th
Russel Daniel Rowe	27th-31st
William Earl Rowe	16th
Newton Wesley Rowell	13th-14th
John Rowlandson	19th
Henry "Leslie" Rowntree	25th-28th
Albert J. Roy	29th-32nd
Robert W. Runciman	32nd
Tony Ruprecht	32nd
Joseph Russell	14th
Samuel Russell	9th-10th
Richard Fletcher Ruston	28th-32nd
Henry Ruttan	8UC; 13UC
George Sterling Ryerson	7th-8th
William Ryerson	7CW
Arthur Frederick Rykert	14th
George Rykert	12UC-13UC
John Charles Rykert	6CW-7CW; 1st-3rd
Jacob Rymal	12UC

William Sexton	1st-3rd
Benjamin Seymour	2CW-4CW
Absalom Shade	11UC; 13UC
Walter Shanly	8CW
Donald Sharpe	14th
James Sharpe	7th
Alexander Laurence Shaver	17th-18th
Peter Shaver	8UC; 10UC-13UC
James Shaw	4CW-5CW
John Shaw	12th
William McNairn Shaw	1st
Robert Austin Shearer	14th
Howard N. Sheppard	32nd
George Sherwood	1CW-3CW; 6CW-7CW
Henry Sherwood	13UC; 1CW-4CW
Levius P. Sherwood	6UC; 8UC
Samuel Sherwood	3UC-4UC
Jacob Shibley	12UC
George Sylvester Shields	17th-18th
Robert Taylor Shillington	12th-13th
Marvin Leonard Shore	30th
William Shore	8th
Thomas Short	6CW
Morton Shulman	28th-29th
Yuri Shymko	32nd
Ephraim George Sills	5th
John Richard "Jack" Simonett	26th-28th
John Simpson	6CW-8CW
Leonard Jennett Simpson	18th-20th
Donald Sinclair	1st-4th
John William Sinclair	19th-20th
Victor Albert Sinclair	14th
William Edmund Newton Sinclair	13th; 15th-19th
Ephraim Frederick Singer	18th
Vernon Milton Singer	26th-30th
Frederick James Skinner	17th-18th
Thomas Kerr Slack	15th; 17th-18th
James Edward Small	12UC-13UC; 1CW-2CW
Thomas Stewart Traille Smellie	11th-12th
Alexander Mortimer Smith	8CW

1UC-13UC = Upper Canada   **1CW-8CW = Canada West**   **1st-32nd = Ontario**

Alphabetical Index of Members – 1792 – 1984 — *Continued*

George Southwick	5CW	Parshal Terry	1UC
Philip Sovereign	5UC	William Terry	10UC
Franklin Harford Spence	16th-18th; 20th	Benjamin Tett	6CW-7CW; 1st
John Purvis "Jack" Spence	25th-30th	Alexander Thom	12UC
Robert Spence	5CW	Fletcher Stewart Thomas	22nd-25th
Hazelton Spencer	1UC	Thomas David Thomas	23rd-26th
Michael A. Spensieri	32nd	Alfred Burke Thompson	9th; 11th-14th
Joseph "Wilfrid" Spooner	25th-27th	Andrew Joseph Ernest Thompson	26th-27th
John Allison Sprague	6th-7th	David Thompson	1CW-3CW; 8CW
Moses Springer	1st-4th	Hugh Christopher Thompson	9UC-11UC
Samuel Sanford Staples	15th	James Thompson	12th-14th
Wellesley Wilson Staples	18th	Joseph Elijah Thompson	15th-17th
Egerton Reuben Stedman	16th-18th	Robert Adam Thompson	10th-11th
Harry Steel	21st	Thomas Alfred Thompson	16th-17th
Elmes Steele	1CW	Timothy Thompson	2UC-3UC; 6UC
Bette M. Stephenson	30th-32nd	Wesley Gardiner Thompson	21st-22nd
Norman William Sterling	31st-32nd	William Thompson	9UC
David Barker Stevenson	3CW-5CW	Edward William Thomson	13UC
Hugh Allan Stevenson	15th	David Thorburn	12UC-13UC; 1CW
John Stevenson	1st	Robert Desmond Thornberry	21st; 23rd
K. Ross Stevenson	32nd	Robert Thorpe	4UC
Falkner Cornwall Stewart	6th	Ivan William Thrasher	27th
Harry Allan Stewart	21st-23rd	Dennis Roy Timbrell	29th-32nd
Neil Stewart	2CW	Alphonse George Tisdelle	15th
William Stewart	1CW-2CW	James Craig Tolmie	14th-15th
William Atcheson Stewart	25th-29th	Richard Tooley	2nd-4th; 6th-7th
William James Stewart	20th-22nd; 24th-25th	Thomas Tooms	15th
John Stinson	5UC-6UC	James Torrance	11th-14th
Thomas Henry Stinson	7th	Richard L. Treleaven	32nd
David Stirton	6CW-8CW	Nelson William Trewartha	16th
Thomas Stock	3rd	James Beecham Trotter	26th-28th
Valentine Stock	10th; 12th	Adelard Charles Trottier	19th-20th
John Edward "Jack" Stokes	28th-32nd	James Trow	1st
Alfred Joseph Stong	30th-31st	Martin "Leo" Troy	26th-27th
Kenneth Spenser Stover	15th	Reuben Eldridge Truax	8th-10th; 12th
Ian Thompson Strachan	19th-20th	George Tucker	8th
James McGill Strachan	1CW	James Tucker	8th-11th
Charles Alfred Strange	21st	James Brockett Tudhope	10th-12th
John Strange	12UC	John Melville Turner	29th; 31st-32nd
Maxwell W. Strange	1st	Sydney Charles Tweed	18th

Alphabetical Index of Members – 1792 – 1984 — *Continued*

Name	Designation
John Waters	4th-7th
Andrew Naismith Watson	31st-32nd
Edgar Watson	15th
John Watterworth	2nd-4th
Jacob Weager	3UC
Everett Lane Weaver	24th
William Wilson Webb	2nd
James Webster	2CW-3CW
Jonah Moorehouse Webster	15th
William Gourlay Webster	21st-22nd
William Weekes	4UC
William George Weichel	16th-17th
Robert Stanley Welch	27th-32nd
James Pearson Wells	8CW
Rupert Mearse Wells	2nd-4th
Thomas Leonard Wells	27th-32nd
William B. Wells	12UC-13UC
George "Arthur" Welsh	22nd-24th
Harold Edward Welsh	19th-20th
Asa Werden	11UC
John Wesley Westbrook	13th
John Wetenhall	3CW
Ross Mackenzie Whicher	25th-27th
Andrew Thomas White	9th
James George White	23rd
John White	1UC
John White	4CW; 6CW-8CW
John Howard White	26th-29th
Reuben White	8UC-9UC; 11UC
Solomon White	3rd-5th; 7th
Thomas Richard Whitesides	12th-13th
James Pliny Whitney	6th-14th

Name	Designation
William Wilson	11UC
Eric Alfred Winkler	28th-29th
John Joseph Wintermeyer	25th-26th
Douglas Jack Wiseman	29th-32nd
Arthur Allison Wishart	27th-28th
Leslie Emery Wismer	21st; 23rd
Alpheus Field Wood	5th-7th
Edmund Burke Wood	8CW; 1st-2nd
Samuel Casey Wood	2nd-4th
William Bruce Wood	6th-8th
Richard Woodruff	13UC
William Woodruff	10UC
Joseph Woods	1CW-2CW
Dennis Woolverton	12UC
Harry A. Worton	25th-32nd
Albert Wren	24th-26th
Amos Wright	4CW-8CW
Charles Ernest Wright	16th-17th
George Wright	4CW
Samuel Thomas Wright	17th-18th
William M. Wrye	32nd
Thomas Wylie	6th-7th
Henry W. Yager	12UC
Paul Joseph Yakabuski	27th-32nd
John Yaremko	24th-29th
Agar Yielding	5CW
Fred Matthews Young	27th-31st
James Young	6UC
James Young	4th-5th
Edward J. Ziemba	30th-31st

1UC-13UC = Upper Canada   **1CW-8CW = Canada West**   **1st-32nd = Ontario**

EXECUTIVE COUNCILS OF ONTARIO

The Ministry of the Hon. John Sandfield Macdonald: July 16, 1867 – Dec. 20, 1871
Coalition

Portfolio	Name	Constituency	Dates in Portfolio
Premier and President of the Council	Hon. John Sandfield Macdonald	Cornwall	Portfolio enacted by the B.N.A. Act, 1876, 30 & 31 Vic., C.3.
			July 16, 1867 – Dec. 20, 1871
Provincial Secretary and Registrar	Hon. Matthew Crooks Cameron	Toronto East	Portfolio enacted by the B.N.A. Act, 1876, 30 & 31 Vic., C.3.
			July 20, 1867 – July 25, 1871
	Hon. Stephen Richards	Niagara	July 25, 1871 – Dec. 20, 1871
Treasurer of Ontario	Hon. Edmund Burke Wood	Brant South	Portfolio enacted by the B.N.A. Act, 1876, 30 & 31 Vic., C.3.
			July 20, 1867 – Dec. 20, 1871
Commissioner of Agriculture and Public Works	Hon. John Carling	London	Portfolio enacted by the B.N.A. Act, 1876, 30 & 31 Vic., C.3.
			July 16, 1867 – Dec. 20, 1871
Attorney General	Hon. John Sandfield Macdonald	Cornwall	Portfolio enacted by the B.N.A. Act, 1876, 30 & 31 Vic., C.3.
			July 16, 1867 – Dec. 20, 1871
Commissioner of Crown Lands	Hon. Stephen Richards	Niagara	Portfolio enacted by the B.N.A. Act, 1876, 30 & 31 Vic., C.3.
			July 16, 1871 – July 25, 1871
	Hon. Matthew Crooks Cameron	Toronto East	July 25, 1871 – Dec. 21, 1871

The Ministry of the Hon. Edward Blake: Dec. 20, 1871 – Oct. 25, 1872
Liberal

Portfolio	Name	Constituency	Dates in Portfolio
Premier and President of the Council	Hon. Edward Blake	Bruce South	Dec. 20, 1871 – Oct. 25, 1872
Provincial Secretary and Registrar	Hon. Alexander Mackenzie	Middlesex West	Dec. 20, 1871 – Dec. 21, 1871
	Hon. Peter Gow	Wellington South	Dec. 21, 1871 – Oct. 25, 1872
Treasurer of Ontario	Hon. Alexander Mackenzie	Middlesex West	Dec. 20, 1871 – Oct. 25, 1872
Commissioner of Agriculture and Public Works	Hon. Archibald McKellar	Bothwell	Dec. 20, 1871 – Oct. 25, 1872
Attorney General	Hon. Adam Crooks	Toronto West	Dec. 20, 1871 – Oct. 25, 1872
Commissioner of Crown Lands	Hon. Richard William Scott	Ottawa	Dec. 21, 1871 – Oct. 25, 1872

The Ministry of the Hon. Oliver Mowat: Oct. 25, 1872 – July 21, 1896
Liberal

Portfolio	Name	Constituency	Dates in Portfolio
Premier and President of the Council	Hon. Oliver Mowat	Oxford North	Oct. 25, 1872 – July 21, 1896
Provincial Secretary and Registrar	Hon. Timothy Blair Pardee	Lambton	Oct. 25, 1872 – Nov. 25, 1873
	Hon. Christopher Finlay Fraser	Grenville South	Nov. 25, 1873 – Apr. 4, 1874
	Hon. Archibald McKellar	Bothwell	Apr. 4, 1874 – July 23, 1875
	Hon. Samuel Casey Wood	Victoria South	July 23, 1875 – Mar. 19, 1877
	Hon. Arthur Sturgis Hardy	Brant South	Mar. 19, 1877 – Jan. 18, 1889
	Hon. John Morison Gibson	Hamilton Hamilton West (1895-)	Jan. 18, 1889 – July 21, 1896
Treasurer of Ontario	Hon. Adam Crooks	Toronto West Oxford South (1875-)	Oct. 25, 1872 – Mar. 19, 1877
	Hon. Samuel Casey Wood	Victoria South	Mar. 19, 1877 – June 2, 1883
	Hon. James Young	Brant North	June 2, 1883 – Nov. 1, 1883
	Hon. Alexander McLagan Ross	Huron West	Nov. 2, 1883 – Sept. 16, 1890
	Hon. Richard Harcourt	Monck	Sept. 16, 1890 – July 21, 1896
Commissioner of Agriculture	Hon. Archibald McKellar	Bothwell	Oct. 25, 1872 – July 23, 1875
	Hon. Samuel Casey Wood	Victoria South	July 23, 1875 – June 2, 1883
	Hon. James Young	Brant North	June 2, 1883 – Nov. 1, 1883
	Hon. Alexander McLagan Ross	Huron West	Nov. 2, 1883 – May 1, 1888
	Hon. Charles Alfred Drury	Simcoe East	May 1, 1888 – Sept. 29, 1890
	Hon. John Dryden	Ontario South	Sept. 30, 1890 – Apr. 16, 1895
			On Apr. 16, 1895, Portfolio changed to Minister of Agriculture.
Minister of Agriculture	Hon. John Dryden	Ontario South	Portfolio enacted Apr. 16, 1895, 58 Vic., C.10.
			Apr. 16, 1895 – July 21, 1896
Attorney General	Hon. Oliver Mowat	Oxford North	Oct. 25, 1872 – July 21, 1896

Commissioner of Crown Lands	Hon. Richard William Scott	Ottawa	Oct. 25, 1872 – Dec. 4, 1873
	Hon. Timothy Blair Pardee	Lambton Lambton West (1885-)	Dec. 4, 1873 – Jan. 18, 1889
	Hon. Arthur Sturgis Hardy	Brant South	Jan. 18, 1889 – July 21, 1896
Minister of Education	Hon. Adam Crooks	Toronto West	Portfolio enacted Feb. 10, 1876, 39 Vic., C.16.
			Feb. 19, 1876 – Nov. 23, 1883
	Hon. George William Ross	Middlesex West	Nov. 23, 1883 – July 21, 1896
Commissioner of Public Works	Hon. Archibald McKellar	Bothwell	Oct. 25, 1872 – Apr. 4, 1874
	Hon. Christopher Finlay Fraser	Grenville South Brockville (1880-)	Apr. 4, 1874 – May 30, 1894
	Hon. William Harty	Kingston	May 30, 1894 – July 21, 1896
Minister Without Portfolio	Hon. Erskine Henry Bronson	Ottawa	Portfolio enacted Mar. 19, 1910, 10 Edw. VII, C.4.
			Sept. 16, 1890 – July 21, 1896

The Ministry of the Hon. Arthur Sturgis Hardy: July 21, 1896 – Oct. 21, 1899
Liberal

Portfolio	Name	Constituency	Dates in Portfolio
Premier and President of the Council	Hon. Arthur Sturgis Hardy	Brant South	July 21, 1896 – Oct. 21, 1899
Provincial Secretary and Registrar	Hon. William Douglas Balfour	Essex South	July 21, 1896 – until his death, Aug. 19, 1896
	Hon. Elihu James Davis	York North	Aug. 28, 1896 – Oct. 21, 1899
Treasurer of Ontario	Hon. Richard Harcourt	Monck	July 21, 1896 – Oct. 21, 1899
Minister of Agriculture	Hon. John Dryden	Ontario South	July 21, 1896 – Oct. 21, 1899
Attorney General	Hon. Arthur Sturgis Hardy	Brant South	July 21, 1896 – Oct. 21, 1899
Commissioner of Crown Lands	Hon. John Morison Gibson	Hamilton West Wellington East (1899-)	July 21, 1896 – Oct. 21, 1899
Minister of Education	Hon. George William Ross	Middlesex West	July 21, 1896 – Oct. 21, 1899
Commissioner of Public Works	Hon. William Harty	Kingston	July 21, 1896 – Oct. 21, 1899
Minister Without Portfolio	Hon. Erskine Henry Bronson	Ottawa	July 21, 1896 – Dec. 16, 1898
	Hon. James Thompson Garrow	Huron West	Dec. 16, 1898 – Oct. 21, 1899

The Ministry of the Hon. George William Ross: Oct. 21, 1899 – Feb. 8, 1905
Liberal

Portfolio	Name	Constituency	Dates in Portfolio
Premier and President of the Council	Hon. George William Ross	Middlesex West	Oct. 21, 1899 – Feb. 8, 1905
Provincial Secretary and Registrar	Hon. James Robert Stratton	Peterborough West	Oct. 21, 1899 – Nov. 22, 1904
	Hon. George Perry Graham	Brockville	Nov. 22, 1904 – Feb. 8, 1905
Treasurer of Ontario	Hon. George William Ross	Middlesex West	Oct. 21, 1899 – Feb. 8, 1905
Minister of Agriculture	Hon. John Dryden	Ontario South	Oct. 21, 1899 – Feb. 8, 1905
Attorney General	Hon. John Morison Gibson	Wellington East	Oct. 21, 1899 – Nov. 22, 1904
	Hon. Francis Robert Latchford	Renfrew South	Nov. 22, 1904 – Feb. 8, 1905
Commissioner of Crown Lands	Hon. Elihu James Davis	York North	Oct. 21, 1899 – resigned, Nov. 22, 1904 (Resigned from Executive Council, Nov. 22, 1904)
	Hon. Alexander Grant MacKay	Grey North	Nov. 22, 1904 – Feb. 8, 1905
Minister of Education	Hon. Richard Harcourt	Monck	Oct. 21, 1899 – Feb. 8, 1905
Commissioner of Public Works	Hon. Francis Robert Latchford	Renfrew South	Oct. 21, 1899 – Nov. 22, 1904
	Hon. William Andrew Charlton	Norfolk South	Nov. 22, 1904 – Feb. 8, 1905
Minister Without Portfolio	Hon. Francis Eugene Alfred Evanturel	Prescott	Nov. 22, 1904 – Feb. 8, 1905
	Hon. John Morison Gibson	Wellington East	Nov. 22, 1904 – Feb. 8, 1905

The Ministry of the Hon. James Pliny Whitney: Feb. 8, 1905 – Oct. 2, 1914
Conservative

Portfolio	Name	Constituency	Dates in Portfolio
Premier and President of the Council	Hon. James Pliny Whitney	Dundas	Feb. 8, 1905 – until his death, Sept. 25, 1914
Provincial Secretary and Registrar	Hon. William John Hanna	Lambton West	Feb. 8, 1905 – Oct. 2, 1914
Treasurer of Ontario	Hon. Arthur James Matheson	Lanark South	Feb. 8, 1905 – until his death, Jan. 25, 1913
	Hon. Isaac Benson Lucas	Grey Centre	May 13, 1913 – Oct. 2, 1914
Minister of Agriculture	Hon. Samuel "Nelson" Monteith	Perth South	Feb. 8, 1905 – Oct. 6, 1908
	Hon. James Stoddart Duff	Simcoe West	Oct. 6, 1908 – Oct. 2, 1914
Attorney General	Hon. James Pliny Whitney	Dundas	Feb. 8, 1905 – May 30, 1905
	Hon. James Joseph Foy	Toronto South Toronto South – Seat "A" (1909-1912) Toronto North – Seat "B" (1912-)	May 30, 1905 – Oct. 2, 1914
Commissioner of Crown Lands	Hon. James Joseph Foy	Toronto South	Feb. 8, 1905 – May 30, 1905 On May 25, 1905, Portfolio changed to Minister of Lands and Mines.
Minister of Education	Hon. Robert Allan Pyne	Toronto East Toronto East – Seat "A" (1909-)	Feb. 8, 1905 – Oct. 2, 1914
Minister of Lands and Mines	Hon. Francis "Frank" Cochrane	Nipissing East Sudbury (1909-)	Portfolio enacted May 25, 1905, 5 Edw. VII, C.5. May 30, 1905 – Apr. 27, 1906 On Apr. 27, 1906, Portfolio changed to Minister of Lands, Forests and Mines.

Minister of Lands, Forests, and Mines	Hon. Francis "Frank" Cochrane	Nipissing East	Portfolio enacted Apr. 27, 1906, 6 Edw. VII, C.10.
			Apr. 27, 1906 – Oct. 12, 1911
	Hon. William Howard Hearst	Sault Ste. Marie	Oct. 12, 1911 – Oct. 2, 1914
Commissioner of Public Works	Hon. Joseph Octave Réaume	Essex North	Feb. 8, 1905 – May 25, 1905
			On May 25, 1905, Portfolio changed to Minister of Public Works.
Minister of Public Works	Hon. Joseph Octave Réaume	Essex North	Portfolio enacted May 25, 1905, 5 Edw. VII, C.5.
			May 25, 1905 – Oct. 2, 1914
Minister Without Portfolio	Hon. Adam Beck	London	Feb. 8, 1905 – Oct. 2, 1914
	Hon. John Strathearn Hendrie	Hamilton West	Feb. 8, 1905 – Oct. 2, 1914
	Hon. William Armson Willoughby	Northumberland East	Feb. 8, 1905 – until his death, Apr. 28, 1908
	Hon. Isaac Benson Lucas	Grey Centre	June 3, 1909 – May 13, 1913
	Hon. Richard Franklin Preston	Lanark North	Feb. 18, 1914 – Oct. 2, 1914

The Ministry of the Hon. William Howard Hearst: Oct. 2, 1914 – Nov. 14, 1919
Conservative

Portfolio	Name	Constituency	Dates in Portfolio
Premier and President of the Council	Hon. William Howard Hearst	Sault Ste. Marie	Oct. 2, 1914 – Nov. 14, 1919
Provincial Secretary and Registrar	Hon. William John Hanna	Lambton West	Oct. 2, 1914 – Dec. 19, 1916
	Hon. William David McPherson	Toronto Northwest – Seat "B"	Dec. 19, 1916 – Nov. 14, 1919
Treasurer of Ontario	Hon. Isaac Benson Lucas	Grey Centre	Oct. 2, 1914 – Dec. 22, 1914
	Hon. Thomas William McGarry	Renfrew South	Dec. 22, 1914 – Nov. 14, 1919
Minister of Agriculture	Hon. James Stoddart Duff	Simcoe West	Oct. 2, 1914 – until his death, Nov. 17, 1916
	Hon. William Howard Hearst	Sault Ste. Marie	Dec. 19, 1916 – May 23, 1918
	Hon. George Stewart Henry	York East	May 23, 1918 – Nov. 14, 1919
Attorney General	Hon. James Joseph Foy	Toronto Southwest – Seat "A"	Oct. 2, 1914 – Dec. 22, 1914
	Hon. Isaac Benson Lucas	Grey Centre	Dec. 22, 1914 – Nov. 14, 1919
Minister of Education	Hon. Robert Allan Pyne	Toronto Northeast – Seat "A"	Oct. 2, 1914 – May 23, 1918
	Hon. Henry John Cody	Toronto Northeast – Seat "A"	May 23, 1918 – Nov. 14, 1919
Minister of Lands, Forests and Mines	Hon. William Howard Hearst	Sault Ste. Marie	Oct. 2, 1914 – Dec. 22, 1914
	Hon. George Howard Ferguson	Grenville	Dec. 22, 1914 – Nov. 14, 1919
Minister of Public Works	Hon. Finlay George MacDiarmid	Elgin West	Oct. 2, 1914 – Apr. 8, 1915
			On Apr. 8, 1915, Portfolio changed to Minister of Public Works and Highways.

Minister of Public Works & Highways	Hon. Finlay George MacDiarmid	Elgin West	Portfolio enacted Apr. 8, 1915, 5 Geo. V., C.17. Apr. 8, 1915 – Nov. 14, 1919
Minister Without Portfolio	Hon. Richard Franklin Preston	Lanark North	Oct. 2, 1914 – Nov. 14, 1919
	Hon. Arthur Edward Ross	Kingston	Sept. 24, 1919 – Nov. 14, 1919

The Ministry of the Hon. Ernest Charles Drury: Nov. 14, 1919 – July 16, 1923
United Farmers of Ontario

Portfolio	Name	Constituency	Dates in Portfolio
Premier and President of the Council	Hon. Ernest Charles Drury	Halton	Nov. 14, 1919 – July 16, 1923
Provincial Secretary and Registrar	Hon. Harry Corwin Nixon	Brant North	Nov. 14, 1919 – July 16, 1923
Treasurer of Ontario	Hon. Peter Smith	Perth South	Nov. 14, 1919 – July 16, 1923
Minister of Agriculture	Hon. Manning William Doherty	Kent East	Nov. 14, 1919 – July 16, 1923
Attorney General	Hon. William "Edgar" Raney	Wellington East	Nov. 14, 1919 – July 16, 1923
Minister of Education	Hon. Robert Henry Grant	Carleton	Nov. 14, 1919 – July 16, 1923
Minister of Labour	Hon. Walter Ritchie Rollo	Hamilton West	Portfolio enacted Apr. 24, 1919, 9 Geo. V., C.22.
			Nov. 14, 1919 – July 16, 1923
Minister of Lands and Forests	Hon. Beniah Bowman	Manitoulin	Portfolio enacted June 4, 1920, 10-11 Geo. V., C.12.
			June 26, 1920 – July 16, 1923
Minister of Lands, Forests and Mines	Hon. Beniah Bowman	Manitoulin	Nov. 14, 1919 – June 26, 1920
			On June 4, 1920, Portfolio changed to Minister of Lands and Forests.
Minister of Mines	Hon. Henry Mills	Fort William	June 26, 1920 – July 16, 1923
Minister of Public Works and Highways	Hon. Frank Campbell Biggs	Wentworth North	Nov. 14, 1919 – July 16, 1923
Minister Without Portfolio	Hon. Dougall Carmichael	Grey Centre	Nov. 14, 1919 – July 16, 1923
	Hon. Henry Mills	Fort William	Nov. 14, 1919 – June 26, 1920

The Ministry of the Hon. George Howard Ferguson: July 16, 1923 – Dec. 15, 1930
Conservative

Portfolio	Name	Constituency	Dates in Portfolio
Premier and President of the Council	Hon. George Howard Ferguson	Grenville	July 16, 1923 – Dec. 15, 1930
Provincial Secretary and Registrar	Hon. Lincoln Goldie	Wellington South	July 16, 1923 – Sept. 12, 1930
	Hon. Leopold Macaulay	York South	Sept. 12, 1930 – Dec. 15, 1930
Treasurer of Ontario	Hon. William Herbert Price	Parkdale	July 16, 1923 – Oct. 18, 1926
	Hon. Joseph Dunsmore Monteith	Perth North	Oct. 18, 1926 – Sept. 12, 1930
	Hon. Edward Arunah Dunlop	Renfrew North	Sept. 12, 1930 – Dec. 15, 1930
Minister of Agriculture	Hon. John Strickler Martin	Norfolk South Norfolk (1925-)	July 16, 1923 – Sept. 12, 1930
	Hon. Thomas Laird Kennedy	Peel	Sept. 12, 1930 – Dec. 15, 1930
Attorney General	Hon. William Folger Nickle	Kingston	July 16, 1923 – resigned, Oct. 18, 1926 (Resigned from Executive Council, Oct. 18, 1926)
	Hon. William Herbert Price	Parkdale	Oct. 18, 1926 – Dec. 15, 1930
Minister of Education	Hon. George Howard Ferguson	Grenville	July 16, 1923 – Dec. 15, 1930
Minister of Health	Hon. Forbes Elliott Godfrey	York West	Portfolio enacted Apr. 17, 1924, 14 Geo. V., C.69.
			Apr. 17, 1924 – Sept. 12, 1930
	Hon. John Morrow Robb	Algoma	Sept. 12, 1930 – Dec. 15, 1930
Minister of Labour	Hon. Forbes Elliott Godfrey	York West	July 16, 1923 – Sept. 12, 1930
	Hon. Joseph Dunsmore Monteith	Perth North	Sept. 12, 1930 – Dec. 15, 1930
Minister of Lands and Forests	Hon. James Lyons	Sault Ste. Marie	July 16, 1923 – resigned, Mar. 1, 1926 (Resigned from Executive Council, Mar. 1, 1926)
	Hon. George Howard Ferguson	Grenville	Mar. 2, 1926 – Oct. 18, 1926
	Hon. William Finlayson	Simcoe East	Oct. 18, 1926 – Dec. 15, 1930
Minister of Mines	Hon. Charles McCrea	Sudbury	July 16, 1923 – Dec. 15, 1930

The Ministry of the Hon. George Howard Ferguson: July 16, 1923 – Dec. 15, 1930 — *Continued*

Portfolio	Name	Constituency	Dates in Portfolio
Minister of Public Welfare	Hon. William George Martin	Brantford	Portfolio enacted Apr. 2, 1931, 21 Geo. V., C.5.
			Sept. 12, 1930 – Dec. 15, 1930
Minister of Public Works and Highways	Hon. George Stewart Henry	York East	July 16, 1923 – Sept. 12, 1930
	Hon. Joseph Dunsmore Monteith	Perth North	Sept. 12, 1930 – Dec. 15, 1930
Minister Without Portfolio	Hon. Sir Adam Beck	London	July 16, 1923 – until his death, Aug. 15, 1925
	Hon. Leeming Carr	Hamilton East	July 16, 1923 – resigned, May 15, 1928 (Resigned from Executive Council, May 15, 1928)
	Hon. John Robert Cooke	Hastings North	July 16, 1923 – Dec. 15, 1930
	Hon. Thomas Crawford	Toronto Northwest - Seat "A"	July 16, 1923 – resigned, May 15, 1924 (Resigned from Executive Council, May 15, 1924)
	Hon. David Jamieson	Grey South	Oct. 18, 1926 – Nov. 26, 1926
	Hon. Edward Arunah Dunlop	Renfrew North	Jan. 29, 1929 – Sept. 12, 1930
	Hon. Frederick Thomas Smye	Hamilton West	Mar. 21, 1929 – until his death, Nov. 15, 1930

The Ministry of the Hon. George Stewart Henry: Dec. 15, 1930 – July 10, 1934
Conservative

Portfolio	Name	Constituency	Dates in Portfolio
Premier and President of the Council	Hon. George Stewart Henry	York East	Dec. 15, 1930 – July 10, 1934
Provincial Secretary and Registrar	Hon. Leopold Macaulay	York South	Dec. 15, 1930 – July 31, 1931
	Hon. George Holmes Challies	Dundas	July 31, 1931 – July 10, 1934
Treasurer of Ontario	Hon. Edward Arunah Dunlop	Renfrew North	Dec. 15, 1930 – until his death, Dec. 31, 1933
	Hon. George Stewart Henry	York East	Jan. 12, 1934 – July 10, 1934
Minister of Agriculture	Hon. Thomas Laird Kennedy	Peel	Dec. 15, 1930 – July 10, 1934
Attorney General	Hon. William Herbert Price	Parkdale	Dec. 15, 1930 – July 10, 1934
Minister of Education	Hon. George Stewart Henry	York East	Dec. 15, 1930 – July 10, 1934
Minister of Health	Hon. John Morrow Robb	Algoma	Dec. 15, 1930 – July 10, 1934
Minister of Health and Labour	Hon. John Morrow Robb	Algoma	Jan. 12, 1934 – July 10, 1934
Minister of Highways	Hon. George Stewart Henry	York East	Dec. 15, 1930 – July 31, 1931
	Hon. Leopold Macaulay	York South	July 31, 1931 – July 10, 1934
Minister of Labour	Hon. Joseph Dunsmore Monteith	Perth North	Dec. 15, 1930 – until his death, Jan. 8,1934
	Hon. John Morrow Robb	Algoma	Jan. 12, 1934 – July 10, 1934 (Hon. John Morrow Robb to be called the Minister of Health and Labour.)
Minister of Lands and Forests	Hon. William Finlayson	Simcoe East	Dec. 15, 1930 – July 10, 1934
Minister of Mines	Hon. Charles McCrea	Sudbury	Dec. 15, 1930 – July 10, 1934
Minister of Public Welfare	Hon. William George Martin	Brantford	Dec. 15, 1930 – July 10, 1934
Minister of Public Works	Hon. Joseph Dunsmore Monteith	Perth North	Dec. 15, 1930 – until his death, Jan. 8,1934
Minister of Public Works and Highways	Hon. Leopold Macaulay	York South	Jan. 12, 1934 – July 10, 1934
Minister Without Portfolio	Hon. John Robert Cooke	Hastings North	Dec. 15, 1930 – July 10, 1934
	Hon. Paul Poisson	Essex North	Dec. 23, 1930 – July 10, 1934
	Hon. Henry Chadwick Scholfield	St. George	Dec. 23, 1930 – July 10, 1934
	Hon. James Percy Moore	London North	May 22, 1934 – July 10, 1934

The Ministry of the Hon. Mitchell Frederick Hepburn: July 10, 1934 – Oct. 21, 1942
Liberal

Portfolio	Name	Constituency	Dates in Portfolio
Premier and President of the Council	Hon. Mitchell Frederick Hepburn	Elgin	July 10, 1934 – Oct. 21, 1942
Provincial Secretary and Registrar	Hon. Harry Corwin Nixon	Brant	July 10, 1934 – resigned, Mar. 11, 1940 (Resigned from Executive Council, Mar. 11, 1940)
			Mar. 13, 1940 – Oct. 21, 1942
Treasurer of Ontario	Hon. Mitchell Frederick Hepburn	Elgin	July 10, 1934 – Oct. 21, 1942
Minister of Agriculture	Hon. Duncan McLean Marshall	Peel	July 10, 1934 – Oct. 12, 1937
	Hon. Patrick Michael Dewan	Oxford	Oct. 12, 1937 – Oct. 12, 1942
Attorney General	Hon. Arthur Wentworth Roebuck	Bellwoods	July 10, 1934 – resigned, Apr. 14, 1937 (Resigned from Executive Council, Apr. 14, 1937)
	Hon. Marie Charles Denis "Paul" Leduc	Ottawa East	Apr. 15, 1937 – Oct. 12, 1937
	Hon. Gordon Daniel Conant	Ontario	Oct. 12, 1937 – Oct. 21, 1942
Minister of Education	Hon. Leonard Jennett Simpson	Simcoe Centre	July 10, 1934 – until his death, Aug. 18, 1940
	Hon. Duncan McArthur	Simcoe Centre	Aug. 22, 1940 – Oct. 12, 1942
Minister of Health	Hon. James Albert Faulkner	Hastings West	July 10, 1934 – Oct. 12, 1937
	Hon. Harold James Kirby	Eglinton	Oct. 12, 1937 – Oct. 21, 1942
Minister of Highways	Hon. Thomas Baker McQuesten	Hamilton – Wentworth	July 10, 1934 – Oct. 21, 1942
Minister of Labour	Hon. Arthur Wentworth Roebuck	Bellwoods	July 10, 1934 – May 21, 1935
	Hon. David Arnold Croll	Windsor – Walkerville	May 21, 1935 – resigned, Apr. 14, 1937 (Resigned from Executive Council, Apr. 14, 1937)
	Hon. Mitchell Frederick Hepburn	Elgin	Apr. 15, 1937 – Oct. 12, 1937
	Hon. Morrison Mann MacBride	Brantford	Oct. 12, 1937 – until his death, June 5, 1938

	Hon. Peter Heenan	Kenora	June 14, 1938 – Sept. 2, 1938
	Hon. Norman Otto Hipel	Waterloo South	Sept. 2, 1938 – May 27, 1941
	Hon. Peter Heenan	Kenora	May 27, 1941 – Oct. 21, 1942
Minister of Lands and Forests	Hon. Peter Heenan	Kenora	July 10, 1934 – May 27, 1941
	Hon. Norman Otto Hipel	Waterloo South	May 27, 1941 – Oct. 21, 1942
Minister of Mines	Hon. Marie Charles Denis "Paul" Leduc	Ottawa East	July 10, 1934 – Sept. 30, 1940
	Hon. Thomas Baker McQuesten	Hamilton – Wentworth	Sept. 30, 1940 – Oct. 7, 1940
	Hon. Robert Laurier	Ottawa East	Oct. 7, 1940 – Oct. 21, 1942
Minister of Municipal Affairs	Hon. David Arnold Croll	Windsor – Walkerville	Portfolio enacted Apr. 18, 1935, 25 Geo. V., C.16.
			Aug. 8, 1934 – resigned, Apr. 14, 1937 (Resigned from Executive Council, Apr. 14, 1937)
	Hon. Mitchell Frederick Hepburn	Elgin	Apr. 15, 1937 – Oct. 12, 1942
	Hon. Eric William Blake Cross	Haldimand – Norfolk	Oct. 12, 1937 – Nov. 22, 1940
	Hon. Thomas Baker McQuesten	Hamilton – Wentworth	Nov. 22, 1940 – Oct. 21, 1942
Minister of Public Welfare	Hon. David Arnold Croll	Windsor – Walkerville	July 10, 1934 – resigned, Apr. 14, 1937 (Resigned from Executive Council, Apr. 14, 1937)
	Hon. Mitchell Frederick Hepburn	Elgin	Apr. 15, 1937 – Oct. 12, 1937
	Hon. Eric William Balke Cross	Haldimand – Norfolk	Oct. 12, 1937 – Nov. 22, 1940
	Hon. Norman Otto Hipel	Waterloo South	Nov. 22, 1940 – May 27, 1941
	Hon. Farquhar Robert Oliver	Grey South	May 27, 1941 – Oct. 21, 1942
Minister of Public Works	Hon. Thomas Baker McQuesten	Hamilton – Wentworth	July 10, 1934 – Oct. 12, 1937
	Hon. Colin Alexander Campbell	Sault Ste. Marie	Oct. 12, 1937 – Jan. 23, 1941
	Hon. Farquhar Robert Oliver	Grey South	Jan. 23, 1941 – Oct. 21, 1942

The Ministry of the Hon. Mitchell Frederick Hepburn: July 10, 1934 – Oct. 21, 1942 — *Continued*

Portfolio	Name	Constituency	Dates in Portfolio
Minister Without Portfolio	Hon. Charles Winnans Cox	Port Arthur	Dec. 18, 1936 – Oct. 12, 1937
	Hon. William Limburg Houck	Niagara Falls	Oct. 12, 1937 – Oct. 21, 1942
	Hon. Arthur St. Clair Gordon	Kent West	Oct. 12, 1937 – Oct. 21, 1942

The Ministry of the Hon. Gordon Daniel Conant: Oct. 21, 1942 – May 18, 1943
Liberal

Portfolio	Name	Constituency	Dates in Portfolio
Premier and President of the Council	Hon. Gordan Daniel Conant	Ontario	Oct. 21, 1942 – May 18, 1943
Provincial Secretary and Registrar	Hon. Harry Corwin Nixon	Brant	Oct. 21, 1942 – resigned Oct. 22, 1942 (Resigned from Executive Council, Oct. 22, 1942)
	Hon. Norman Otto Hipel	Waterloo South	Oct. 27, 1942 – May 18, 1943
Treasurer of Ontario	Hon. Mitchell Frederick Hepburn	Elgin	Oct. 21, 1942 – Mar. 3, 1943
	Hon. Arthur St. Clair Gordon	Kent West	Mar. 3, 1943 – May 18, 1943
Minister of Agriculture	Hon. Patrick Michael Dewan	Oxford	Oct. 21, 1942 – May 18, 1943
Attorney General	Hon. Gordon Daniel Conant	Ontario	Oct. 21, 1942 – May 18, 1943
Minister of Education	Hon. Duncan McArthur	Simcoe Centre	Oct. 21, 1942 – May 18, 1943
Minister of Health	Hon. Harold James Kirby	Eglinton	Oct. 21, 1942 – May 18, 1943
Minister of Highways	Hon. Thomas Baker McQuesten	Hamilton – Wentworth	Oct. 21, 1942 – May 18, 1943
Minister of Labour	Hon. Peter Heenan	Kenora	Oct. 21, 1942 – May 18, 1943
Minister of Lands and Forests	Hon. Norman Otto Hipel	Waterloo South	Oct. 21, 1942 – May 18, 1943
Minister of Mines	Hon. Robert Laurier	Ottawa East	Oct. 21, 1942 – May 18, 1943
Minister of Municipal Affairs	Hon. Thomas Baker McQuesten	Hamilton – Wentworth	Oct. 21, 1942 – May 18, 1943
Minister of Public Welfare	Hon. Farquar Robert Oliver	Grey South	Oct. 21, 1942 – resigned, Oct. 27, 1942 (Resigned from Executive Council, Oct. 27, 1942)
	Hon. Harold James Kirby	Eglinton	Oct. 27, 1942 – May 18, 1943
Minister of Public Works	Hon. Farquar Robert Oliver	Grey South	Oct. 21, 1942 – resigned, Oct. 27, 1942 (Resigned from Executive Council, Oct. 27, 1942)
	Hon. Thomas Baker McQuesten	Hamilton – Wentworth	Oct. 27, 1942 – May 18, 1943
Minister Without Portfolio	Hon. Arthur St. Clair Gordon	Kent West	Oct. 21, 1942 – Mar. 3, 1943
	Hon. William Limburg Houck	Niagara Falls	Oct. 21, 1942 – May 18, 1943

The Ministry of the Hon. Harry Corwin Nixon: May 18, 1943 – Aug. 17, 1943
Liberal

Portfolio	Name	Constituency	Dates in Portfolio
Premier and President of the Council	Hon. Harry Corwin Nixon	Brant	May 18, 1943 – Aug. 17, 1943
Provincial Secretary and Registrar	Hon. Harry Corwin Nixon	Brant	May 18, 1943 – Aug. 17, 1943
Treasurer of Ontario	Hon. Arthur St. Clair Gordon	Kent West	May 18, 1943 – Aug. 17, 1943
Minister of Agriculture	Hon. Patrick Michael Dewan	Oxford	May 18, 1943 – Aug. 17, 1943
Attorney General	Hon. Eric William Blake Cross	Haldimand – Norfolk	May 18, 1943 – Aug. 17, 1943
Minister of Education	Hon. Duncan McArthur	Simcoe Centre	May 18, 1943 – until his death, July 20, 1943
Minister of Health	Hon. Harold James Kirby	Eglinton	May 18, 1943 – Aug. 17, 1943
Minister of Highways	Hon. Thomas Baker McQuesten	Hamilton – Wentworth	May 18, 1943 – Aug. 17, 1943
Minister of Labour	Hon. Peter Heenan	Kenora	May 18, 1943 – Aug. 17, 1943
Minister of Lands and Forests	Hon. Norman Otto Hipel	Waterloo South	May 18, 1943 – Aug. 17, 1943
Minister of Mines	Hon. Robert Laurier	Ottawa East	May 18, 1943 – Aug. 17, 1943
Minister of Municipal Affairs	Hon. Eric William Blake Cross	Haldimand – Norfolk	May 18, 1943 – Aug. 17, 1943
Minister of Public Welfare	Hon. Farquhar Robert Oliver	Grey South	May 18, 1943 – Aug. 17, 1943
Minister of Public Works	Hon. Farquhar Robert Oliver	Grey South	May 18, 1943 – Aug. 17, 1943
Minister Without Portfolio	Hon. William Limburg Houck	Niagara Falls	May 18, 1943 – Aug. 17, 1943

The Ministry of the Hon. George Alexander Drew: Aug. 17, 1943 – Oct. 19, 1948
Progressive Conservative

Portfolio	Name	Constituency	Dates in Portfolio
Premier and President of the Council	Hon. George Alexander Drew	High Park	Aug. 17, 1943 – Oct. 19, 1948
Provincial Secretary and Registrar	Hon. George Harrison Dunbar	Ottawa South	Aug. 17, 1943 – Apr. 15, 1946
	Hon. Daniel "Roland" Michener	St. David	Apr. 15, 1946 – Oct. 19, 1948
Treasurer of Ontario	Hon. Leslie Miscampbell Frost	Victoria	Aug. 17, 1943 – Oct. 19, 1948
Minister of Agriculture	Hon. Thomas Laird Kennedy	Peel	Aug. 17, 1943 – Oct. 19, 1948
Attorney General	Hon. Leslie Egerton Blackwell	Eglinton	Aug. 17, 1943 – Oct. 19, 1948
Minister of Education	Hon. George Alexander Drew	High Park	Aug. 17, 1943 – Oct. 19, 1948
Minister of Health	Reginald Percival Vivian	Durham	Aug. 17, 1943 – Jan. 7, 1946
	Hon. Russell Temple Kelley	Hamilton – Wentworth	Jan. 7, 1946 – Oct. 19, 1948
Minister of Labour	Hon. Charles Daley	Lincoln	Aug. 17, 1943 – Oct. 19, 1948
Minister of Lands and Forests	Hon. Wesley Gardiner Thompson	Kent East	Aug. 17, 1943 – Nov. 28, 1946
	Hon. Harold Robinson Scott	Peterborough	Nov. 28, 1946 – Oct. 19, 1948
Minister of Mines	Hon. Leslie Miscampbell Frost	Victoria	Aug. 17, 1943 – Oct. 19, 1948
Minister of Municipal Affairs	Hon. George Harrison Dunbar	Ottawa South	Aug. 17, 1943 – Oct. 19, 1948
Minister of Planning and Development	Hon. Dana Harris Porter	St. George	Portfolio enacted Mar. 14, 1944, 8 Geo. VI, C.16.
			May 8, 1944 – Oct. 19, 1948
Minister of Public Welfare	Hon. Reginald Percival Vivian	Durham	Aug. 17, 1943 – Jan. 7, 1946
	Hon. William Arthur Goodfellow	Northumberland	Jan. 7, 1946 – Oct. 19, 1948
Minister of Public Works and Highways	Hon. George Henry Doucett	Lanark	Aug. 17, 1943 – Oct. 19, 1948
Minister of Reform Institutions	Hon. George Harrison Dunbar	Ottawa South	Portfolio enacted Mar. 27, 1946, 10 Geo. VI, C.22.
			Apr. 15, 1946 – Oct. 19, 1948

The Ministry of the Hon. George Alexander Drew: Aug. 17, 1943 – Oct. 19, 1948 — *Continued*

Portfolio	Name	Constituency	Dates in Portfolio
Minister of Travel and Publicity	Hon. George "Arthur" Welsh	Muskoka – Ontario	Portfolio enacted Mar. 27, 1946, 10 Geo. VI, C.23.
			Mar. 25, 1946 – Oct. 19, 1948
Minister Without Portfolio	Hon. George Holmes Challies	Grenville – Dundas	Aug. 17, 1943 – Oct. 19, 1948
	Hon. William Gourlay Webster	London	Dec. 13, 1944 – Oct. 19, 1948
	Hon. William Griesinger	Windsor – Sandwich	Apr. 15, 1946 – Oct. 19, 1948
	Hon. Louis Pierre Cecile	Prescott	Sept. 17, 1948 – Oct. 19, 1948

The Ministry of the Hon. Thomas Laird Kennedy: Oct. 19, 1948 – May 4, 1949
Progressive Conservative

Portfolio	Name	Constituency	Dates in Portfolio
Premier and President of the Council	Hon. Thomas Laird Kennedy	Peel	Oct. 19, 1948 – May 4, 1949
Provincial Secretary and Registrar	Hon. Dana Harris Porter	St. George	Oct. 19, 1948 – May 4, 1949
Treasurer of Ontario	Hon. Leslie Miscampbell Frost	Victoria	Oct. 19, 1948 – May 4, 1949
Minister of Agriculture	Hon. Thomas Laird Kennedy	Peel	Oct. 19, 1948 – May 4, 1949
Attorney General	Hon. Leslie Egerton Blackwell	Eglinton	Oct. 19, 1948 – May 4, 1949
Minister of Education	Hon. Dana Harris Porter	St. George	Oct. 19, 1948 – May 4, 1949
Minister of Health	Hon. Russell Temple Kelley	Hamilton – Wentworth	Oct. 19, 1948 – May 4, 1949
Minister of Labour	Hon. Charles Daley	Lincoln	Oct. 19, 1948 – May 4, 1949
Minister of Lands and Forests	Hon. Harold Robinson Scott	Peterborough	Oct. 19, 1948 – May 4, 1949
Minister of Mines	Hon. Leslie Miscampbell Frost	Victoria	Oct. 19, 1948 – May 4, 1949
Minister of Municipal Affairs	Hon. George Harrison Dunbar	Ottawa South	Oct. 19, 1948 – May 4, 1949
Minister of Planning and Development	Hon. George "Arthur" Welsh	Muskoka – Ontario	Oct. 19, 1948 – May 4, 1949
Minister of Public Welfare	Hon. William Arthur Goodfellow	Northumberland	Oct. 19, 1948 – May 4, 1949
Minister of Public Works and Highways	Hon. George Henry Doucett	Lanark	Oct. 19, 1948 – May 4, 1949
Minister of Reform Institutions	Hon. George Harrison Dunbar	Ottawa South	Oct. 19, 1948 – May 4, 1949
Minister of Travel and Publicity	Hon. Louis Pierre Cecile	Prescott	Oct. 19, 1948 – May 4, 1949
Minister Without Portfolio	Hon. George Holmes Challies	Grenville – Dundas	Oct. 19, 1948 – May 4, 1949
	Hon. William Griesinger	Windsor – Sandwich	Oct. 19, 1948 – May 4, 1949

The Ministry of the Hon. Leslie Miscampbell Frost: May 4, 1949 – Nov. 8, 1961
Progressive Conservative

Portfolio	Name	Constituency	Dates in Portfolio
Premier and President of the Council	Hon. Leslie Miscampbell Frost	Victoria	May 4, 1949 – Nov. 8, 1961
Provincial Secretary and Minister of Citizenship	Hon. John Yaremko	Bellwoods	Portfolio enacted Jan. 27, 1961, 9-10 Eliz. II, C.20.
			Jan. 27, 1961 – Nov. 8, 1961
Provincial Secretary and Registrar	Hon. George "Arthur" Welsh	Muskoka – Ontario	May 4, 1949 – resigned, Jan. 20, 1955 (Resigned from Executive Council, Jan. 20, 1955)
	Hon. William McAdam Nickle	Kingston	Jan. 20, 1955 – Aug. 17, 1955
	Hon. George Harrison Dunbar	Ottawa South	Aug. 17, 1955 – resigned, Dec. 22, 1958 (Resigned from Executive Council, Dec. 22, 1958)
	Hon. Mackinnon Phillips	Grey North	Dec. 22, 1958 – resigned, May 15, 1960 (Resigned from Executive Council, May 15, 1960)
	Hon. John Yaremko	Bellwoods	May 26, 1960 – Jan. 27, 1961
			On Jan. 27, 1961, Portfolio changed to Provincial Secretary and Minister of Citizenship.
Treasurer of Ontario	Hon. Leslie Miscampbell Frost	Victoria	May 4, 1949 – Aug. 17, 1955
	Hon. Dana Harris Porter	St. George	Aug. 17, 1955 – Mar. 28, 1956
			On Mar. 28, 1956, Portfolio changed to Treasurer and Minister in charge of the Department of Economics.
Treasurer and Minister in Charge of the Department of Economics	Hon. Dana Harris Porter	St. George	Portfolio enacted Mar. 28, 1956, 4-5 Eliz. II, C.16.
			Mar. 28, 1956 – resigned, Jan. 30, 1958 (Resigned from Executive Council, Jan. 30, 1958)
Chairman, Treasury Board	Hon. Leslie Miscampbell Frost	Victoria	Feb. 3, 1958 – Apr. 28, 1958
			As of Mar. 27, 1958, the Treasurer was

			also to be the Chairman, Treasury Board. Portfolio enacted Mar. 27, 1958, 6-7 Eliz. II, C.29.
	Hon. James Noble Allan	Haldimand – Norfolk	Apr. 28, 1958 – Nov. 8, 1961
Minister of Agriculture	Hon. Thomas Laird Kennedy	Peel	May 4, 1949 – resigned, Jan. 20, 1953 (Resigned from Executive Council, Jan. 20, 1953)
	Hon. Fletcher Stewart Thomas	Elgin	Jan. 20, 1953 – resigned, Aug. 1, 1956 (Resigned from Executive Council, Aug. 1, 1956)
	Hon. William Arthur Goodfellow	Northumberland	Aug. 1, 1956 – Nov. 8, 1961
Attorney General	Hon. Dana Harris Porter	St. George	May 4, 1949 – Aug. 17, 1955
	Hon. Archibald "Kelso" Roberts	St. Patrick	Aug. 17, 1955 – Nov. 8, 1961
Minister of Commerce and Development	Hon. William McAdam Nickle	Kingston	Portfolio enacted Jan. 27, 1961, 9-10 Eliz. II, C.18.
			Nov. 21, 1960 – Nov. 8, 1961
Minister of Education	Hon. Dana Harris Porter	St. George	May 4, 1949 – Oct. 2, 1951
	Hon. William James Dunlop	Eglinton	Oct. 2, 1951 – resigned, Dec. 17, 1959 (Resigned from Executive Council, Dec. 17, 1959)
	Hon. John Parmenter Robarts	London North	Dec. 17, 1959 – Nov. 8, 1961
Minister of Energy Resources	Hon. Robert William Macaulay	Riverdale	Portfolio enacted Mar. 26, 1959, 7-8 Eliz. II, C.26.
			May 5, 1959 – Nov. 8, 1961
Minister of Health	Hon. Russell Temple Kelley	Hamilton – Wentworth	May 4, 1949 – Aug. 8, 1950
	Hon. Mackinnon Phillips	Grey North	Aug. 8, 1950 – resigned, Dec. 22, 1958 (Resigned from Executive Council, Dec. 22, 1958)
	Hon. Matthew Bulloch Dymond	Ontario	Dec. 22, 1958 – Nov. 8, 1961
Minister of Highways	Hon. George Henry Doucett	Lanark	May 4, 1949 – resigned, Jan. 5, 1955 (Resigned from Executive Council, Jan. 5, 1955)

The Ministry of the Hon. Leslie Miscampbell Frost: May 4, 1949 – Nov. 8, 1961 — *Continued*

Portfolio	Name	Constituency	Dates in Portfolio
Minister of Highways — *Continued*	Hon. James Noble Allan	Haldimand – Norfolk	Jan. 5, 1955 – Apr. 28, 1958
	Hon. Frederick McIntosh Cass	Grenville – Dundas	Apr. 28, 1958 – Nov. 8, 1961
Minister of Labour	Hon. Charles Daley	Lincoln	May 4, 1949 – Nov. 8, 1961
Minister of Lands and Forests	Hon. Harold Robinson Scott	Peterborough	May 4, 1949 – resigned, June 3, 1952 (Resigned from Executive Council, June 3, 1952)
	Hon. Welland Stewart Gemmell	Sudbury	June 3, 1952 – until his death, June 18, 1954
	Hon. Clare Edgar Mapledoram	Fort William	July 7, 1954 – resigned, July 4, 1958 (Resigned from Executive Council, July 4, 1958)
	Hon. Joseph "Wilfred" Spooner	Cochrane South	July 23, 1958 – Nov. 8, 1961
Minister of Mines	Hon. Welland Stewart Gemmell	Sudbury	May 4, 1949 – June 3, 1952
	Hon. Philip Timothy Kelly	Cochrane North	June 3, 1952 – resigned, July 18, 1957 (Resigned from Executive Council, July 18, 1957)
	Hon. Joseph "Wilfrid" Spooner	Cochrane South	July 18, 1957 – Dec. 22, 1958
	Hon. James Anthony Maloney	Renfrew South	Dec. 22, 1958 – Nov. 8, 1961
Minister of Municipal Affairs	Hon. George Harrison Dunbar	Ottawa South	May 4, 1949 – Aug. 17, 1955
	Hon. William Arthur Goodfellow	Northumberland	Aug. 17, 1955 – Nov. 1, 1956
	Hon. William Kenneth Warrender	Hamilton Centre	Nov. 1, 1956 – Nov. 8, 1961
Minister of Planning and Development	Hon. William Griesinger	Windsor – Sandwich	May 4, 1949 – Jan. 20, 1953
	Hon. William Kenneth Warrender	Hamilton Centre	Jan. 20, 1953 – Aug. 17, 1955
	Hon. William McAdam Nickle	Kingston	Aug. 17, 1955 – Nov. 8, 1961
Minister of Public Welfare	Hon. William Arthur Goodfellow	Northumberland	May 4, 1949 – Aug. 17, 1955
	Hon. Louis Pierre Cecile	Prescott	Aug. 17, 1955 – Nov. 8, 1961
Minister of Public Works	Hon. George Henry Doucett	Lanark	May 4, 1949 – Oct. 2, 1951

	Hon. Fletcher Stewart Thomas	Elgin	Oct. 2, 1951 – Jan. 20, 1953
	Hon. William Griesinger	Windsor – Sandwich	Jan. 20, 1953 – resigned, May 6, 1958 (Resigned from Executive Council, May 6, 1958)
	Hon. James Noble Allan	Haldimand – Norfolk	May 14, 1958 – Dec. 22, 1958
	Hon. Thomas "Ray" Connell	Hamilton – Wentworth	Dec. 22, 1958 – Nov. 8, 1961
Minister of Reform Institutions	Hon. George Harrison Dunbar	Ottawa South	May 4, 1949 – July 15, 1949
	Hon. William Ernest Hamilton	Wellington South	July 15, 1949 – Nov. 16, 1950
	Hon. John Weir Foote	Durham	Nov. 16, 1950 – resigned, July 18, 1957 (Resigned from Executive Council, July 18, 1957)
	Hon. Matthew Bulloch Dymond	Ontario	July 18, 1957 – Apr. 28, 1958
	Hon. Thomas "Ray" Connell	Hamilton – Wentworth	Apr. 28, 1958 – Dec. 22, 1958
	Hon. George Calvin Wardrope	Port Arthur	Dec. 22, 1958 – Nov. 8, 1961
Minister of Transport	Hon. James Noble Allan	Haldimand – Norfolk	Portfolio enacted Apr. 3, 1957, 5-6 Eliz. II, C.26.
			June 26, 1957 – Apr. 28, 1958
	Hon. Matthew Bulloch Dymond	Ontario	Apr. 28, 1958 – Dec. 22, 1958
	Hon. John Yaremko	Bellwoods	Dec. 22, 1958 – Nov. 21, 1960
	Hon. Henry "Leslie" Rowntree	York West	Nov. 21, 1960 – Nov. 8, 1961
Minister of Travel and Publicity	Hon. Louis Pierre Cecile	Prescott	May 4, 1949 – Aug. 17, 1955
	Hon. Bryan Lewis Cathcart	Lambton West	Aug. 17, 1955 – Nov. 8, 1961
Minister Without Portfolio	Hon. George Holmes Challies	Grenville – Dundas	May 4, 1949 – Aug. 17, 1955
	Hon. Russell Temple Kelley	Hamilton – Wentworth	Aug. 8, 1950 – resigned, Jan. 18, 1952 (Resigned from Executive Council, Jan. 18, 1952)
	Hon. William Ernest Hamilton	Wellington South	Nov. 16, 1950 – resigned, Aug. 17, 1955 (Resigned from Executive Council, Aug. 17, 1955)

The Ministry of the Hon. Leslie Miscampbell Frost: May 4, 1949 – Nov. 8, 1961 — *Continued*

Portfolio	Name	Constituency	Dates in Portfolio
Minister Without Portfolio — *Continued*	Hon. Harold Robinson Scott	Peterborough	June 3, 1952 – resigned, Apr. 28, 1958 (Resigned from Executive Council, Apr. 28, 1958)
	Hon. William Kenneth Warrender	Hamilton Centre	Aug. 17, 1955 – Nov. 1, 1956
	Hon. Thomas "Ray" Connell	Hamilton – Wentworth	Nov. 1, 1956 – Apr. 28, 1958
	Hon. John Yaremko	Bellwoods	Apr. 28, 1958 – Dec. 22, 1958
	Hon. Robert William Macaulay	Riverdale	May 26, 1958 – May 5, 1959
	Hon. John Parmenter Robarts	London North	Dec. 22, 1958 – Dec. 17, 1959
	Hon. John Henry Haines Root	Wellington – Dufferin	Dec. 22, 1958 – Nov. 8, 1961
	Hon. William James Dunlop	Eglinton	Dec. 17, 1959 – resigned, Nov. 21, 1960 (Resigned from Executive Council, Nov. 21, 1960)
	Hon. Allan Grossman	St. Andrew	Nov. 21, 1960 – Nov. 8, 1961
	Hon. William Atcheson Stewart	Middlesex North	Nov. 21, 1960 – Nov. 8, 1961

The Ministry of the Hon. John Parmenter Robarts: Nov. 8, 1961 – Mar. 1, 1971
Progressive Conservative

Portfolio	Name	Constituency	Dates in Portfolio
Premier and President of the Council	Hon. John Parmenter Robarts	London North	Nov. 8, 1961 – Mar. 1, 1971
Provincial Secretary and Minister of Citizenship	Hon. John Yaremko	Bellwoods	Nov. 8, 1961 – Nov. 24, 1966
	Hon. Robert Stanley Welch	Lincoln	Nov. 24, 1966 – Mar. 1, 1971
Treasurer of Ontario Chairman, Treasury Board	Hon. James Noble Allan	Haldimand-Norfolk	Dec. 15, 1961 – Nov. 24, 1966
	Hon. Charles Steel MacNaughton	Huron	Nov. 24, 1966 – July 23, 1968
			On July 23, 1968, Portfolio changed to Treasurer of Ontario and Minister of Economics.
Treasurer of Ontario and Minister in charge of the Department of Economics Chairman, Treasury Board	Hon. James Noble Allan	Haldimand-Norfolk	Nov. 8, 1961 – Dec. 15, 1961
			On Dec. 15, 1961, Portfolio divided into Treasurer of Ontario and Minister of Economics and Development.
Treasurer of Ontario and Minister of Economics Chairman, Treasury Board	Hon. Charles Steel MacNaughton	Huron	Portfolio enacted July 23, 1968, 17 Eliz. II, C.37.
			July 23, 1968 – Mar. 1, 1971
Minister of Agriculture	Hon. William Atcheson Stewart	Middlesex North	Nov. 8, 1961 – May 18, 1966
			On May 18, 1966, (Sections 7 & 8, July 8, 1966), Portfolio changed to Minister of Agriculture and Food.
Minister of Agriculture and Food	Hon. William Atcheson Stewart	Middlesex North	Portfolio enacted May 18, 1966 (Sections 7 & 8, July 8, 1966), 14-15 Eliz. II, C.39.
			May 18, 1966 – Mar. 1, 1971
Attorney General	Hon. Archibald "Kelso" Roberts	St. Patrick	Nov. 8, 1961 – Oct. 25, 1962
	Hon. Frederick McIntosh Cass	Grenville – Dundas	Oct. 25, 1962 – resigned, Mar. 23, 1964 (Resigned from Executive Council, Mar. 23, 1964)

The Ministry of the Hon. John Parmenter Robarts: Nov. 8, 1961 – Mar. 1, 1971 — *Continued*

Portfolio	Name	Constituency	Dates in Portfolio
Attorney General —*Continued*	Hon. Arthur Allison Wishart	Sault Ste. Marie	Mar. 26, 1964 – May 18, 1966
			On May 18, 1966, Portfolio changed to Minister of Justice and Attorney General.
Minister of Commerce and Development	Hon. Robert William Macaulay	Riverdale	Nov. 8, 1961 – Dec. 15, 1961
			On Dec. 15, 1961, Portfolio changed to Minister of Economics and Development.
Minister of Correctional Services	Hon. Allan Grossman	St. Andrew – St. Patrick	Portfolio enacted July 1, 1968, 17 Eliz. II, C.27.
			July 1, 1968 – Mar. 1, 1971
Minister of Economics and Development	Hon. Robert William Macaulay	Riverdale	Portfolio enacted Dec. 15, 1961, 10-11 Eliz. II, C.30.
			Dec. 15, 1961 – resigned, Oct. 16, 1963 (Resigned from Executive Council, Oct. 16, 1963)
	Hon. James Noble Allan	Haldimand-Norfolk	Oct. 16, 1963 – Nov. 8, 1963
	Hon. Stanley John Randall	Don Mills	Nov. 8, 1963 – Apr. 11, 1968
			On Apr. 11, 1968, Portfolio changed to Minister of Trade and Development.
Minister of Education	Hon. John Parmenter Robarts	London North	Nov. 8, 1961 – Oct. 25, 1962
	Hon. William Grenville Davis	Peel	Oct. 25, 1962 – Mar. 1, 1971
		Peel North (1966-)	
Minister of Energy and Resources Management	Hon. John Richard "Jack" Simonett	Frontenac-Addington	Portfolio enacted May 18, 1966, 14-15 Eliz. II, C.41.
			Mar. 26, 1964 – resigned, June 5, 1969 (Resigned from Executive Council, June 5, 1969)
	Hon. George Albert Kerr	Halton West	June 5, 1969 – Mar. 1, 1971

Minister of Energy Resources	Hon. Robert William Macaulay	Riverdale	Nov. 8, 1961 – resigned, Oct. 16, 1963 (Resigned from Executive Council, Oct. 16, 1963)
	Hon. John Richard "Jack" Simonett	Frontenac – Addington	Oct. 16, 1963 – Mar. 25, 1964 On Mar. 25, 1964, Portfolio changed to Minister of Energy and Resources Management.
Minister of Financial and Commercial Affairs	Hon. Henry "Leslie" Rowntree	York West	Portfolio enacted May 18, 1966, 14-15 Eliz. II, C.41. Nov. 24, 1966 – resigned, Feb. 5, 1970 (Resigned from Executive Council, Feb. 5, 1970)
	Hon. Albert Benjamin Rutter "Bert" Lawrence	Carleton East	Feb. 5, 1970 – Mar. 1, 1971
Minister of Health	Hon. Matthew Bulloch Dymond	Ontario	Nov. 8, 1961 – resigned, Aug. 13, 1969 (Resigned from Executive Council, Aug. 13, 1969)
	Hon. Thomas Leonard Wells	Scarborough North	Aug. 13, 1969 – Mar. 1, 1971
Minister of Highways	Hon. William Arthur Goodfellow	Northumberland	Nov. 8, 1961 – Oct. 25, 1962
	Hon. Charles Steel MacNaughton	Huron	Oct. 25, 1962 – Nov. 24, 1966
	Hon. George Ellis Gomme	Lanark	Nov. 24, 1966 – Mar. 1, 1971
Minister of Justice and Attorney General	Hon. Arthur Allison Wishart	Sault Ste. Marie	Portfolio enacted May 18, 1966, 14-15 Eliz. II, C.52 (Executive Council Act) and Mar. 26, 1969, 17-18 Eliz. II, C.27. May 18, 1966 – Mar. 1, 1971
Minister of Labour	Hon. William Kenneth Warrender	Hamilton Centre	Nov. 8, 1961 – Oct. 25, 1962
	Hon. Henry "Leslie" Rowntree	York West	Oct. 25, 1962 – Nov. 24, 1966
	Hon. Dalton Arthur Bales	York Mills	Nov. 24, 1966 – Mar. 1, 1971
Minister of Lands and Forests	Hon. Joseph "Wilfrid" Spooner	Cochrane South	Nov. 8, 1961 – Oct. 25, 1962
	Hon. Archibald "Kelso" Roberts	St. Patrick	Oct. 25, 1962 – Nov. 24, 1966
	Hon. René Joseph Napoléon Brunelle	Cochrane North	Nov. 24, 1966 – Mar. 1, 1971

The Ministry of the Hon. John Parmenter Robarts: Nov. 8, 1961 – Mar. 1, 1971 — *Continued*

Portfolio	Name	Constituency	Dates in Portfolio
Minister of Mines	Hon. George Calvin Wardrope	Port Arthur	Nov. 8, 1961 – Nov. 23, 1967
	Hon. René Joseph Napoléon Brunelle	Cochrane North	Nov. 23, 1967 – Feb. 13, 1968
	Hon. Allan Frederick Lawrence	St. George	Feb. 13, 1968 – June 26, 1970
			On June 26, 1970, Portfolio changed to Minister of Mines and Northern Affairs.
Minister of Mines and Northern Affairs	Hon. Allan Frederick Lawrence	St. George	Portfolio enacted June 26, 1970, 19 Eliz. II, C.26.
			June 26, 1970 – Mar. 1, 1971
Minister of Municipal Affairs	Hon. Frederick McIntosh Cass	Grenville – Dundas	Nov. 8, 1961 – Oct. 25, 1962
	Hon. Joseph "Wilfred" Spooner	Cochrane South	Oct. 25, 1962 – Nov. 23, 1967
	Hon. William "Darcy" McKeough	Chatham – Kent	Nov. 23, 1967 – Mar. 1, 1971
Minister of Public Welfare	Hon. Louis Pierre Cecile	Prescott	Nov. 8, 1961 – Nov. 24, 1966
	Hon. John Yaremko	Bellwoods	Nov. 24, 1966 – Mar. 22, 1967
			On Mar. 22, 1967, Portfolio changed to Minister of Social and Family Services.
Minister of Public Works	Hon. Thomas "Ray" Connell	Hamilton – Wentworth	Nov. 8, 1961 – resigned, June 5, 1969 (Resigned from Executive Council, June 5, 1969)
	Hon. John Richard "Jack" Simonett	Frontenac – Addington	June 5, 1969 – Mar. 1, 1971
Minister of Reform Institutions	Hon. W. Irwin Haskett	Ottawa South	Nov. 8, 1961 – Aug. 14, 1963
	Hon. Allan Grossman	St. Andrew – St. Patrick	Aug. 14, 1963 – July 1, 1968
			On July 1, 1968, Portfolio changed to Minister of Correctional Services.
Minister of Revenue	Hon. Charles Steel McNaughton	Huron	Portfolio enacted June 13, 1968, 17 Eliz. II, C.29.
			July 23, 1968 – Oct. 10, 1968
	Hon. John Howard White	London South	Oct. 10, 1968 – Mar. 1, 1971

Minister of Social and Family Services	Hon. John Yaremko	Bellwoods	Portfolio enacted Mar. 22, 1967, 15-16 Eliz. II, C.23.
			Mar. 22, 1967 – Mar. 1, 1971
Minister of Tourism and Information	Hon. James Alexander Charles Auld	Leeds	Portfolio enacted Mar. 25, 1964, 12-13 Eliz. II, C.23.
			Mar. 25, 1964 – Mar. 1, 1971
Minister of Trade and Development	Hon. Stanley John Randall	Don Mills	Portfolio enacted Apr. 11, 1968, 17 Eliz. II, C.30.
			Apr. 11, 1968 – Mar. 1, 1971
Minister of Transport	Hon. Henry "Leslie" Rowntree	York West	Nov. 8, 1961 – Oct. 25, 1962
	Hon. James Alexander Charles Auld	Leeds	Oct. 25, 1962 – Aug. 14, 1963
	Hon. W. Irwin Haskett	Ottawa South	Aug. 14, 1963 – Mar. 1, 1971
Minister of Travel and Publicity	Hon. Bryan Lewis Cathcart	Lambton West	Nov. 8, 1961 – Aug. 14, 1963
	Hon. James Alexander Charles Auld	Leeds	Aug. 14, 1963 – Mar. 25, 1964
			On Mar. 25, 1964, Portfolio changed to Minister of Tourism and Information.
Minister of University Affairs	Hon. William Grenville Davis	Peel	Portfolio enacted May 8, 1964, 12-13 Eliz. II, C. 24.
		Peel North (1966-)	May 14, 1964 – Mar. 1, 1971
Minister Without Portfolio	Hon. Charles Daley	Lincoln	Nov. 8, 1961 – Oct. 25, 1962
	Hon. Allan Grossman	St. Andrew	Nov. 8, 1961 – Aug. 14, 1963
	Hon. Charles Steel MacNaughton	Huron	Nov. 8, 1961 – Oct. 25, 1962
	Hon. William McAdam Nickle	Kingston	Nov. 8, 1961 – resigned, Oct. 25, 1962 (Resigned from Executive Council, Oct. 25, 1962)
	Hon. William Arthur Goodfellow	Northumberland	Oct. 25, 1962 – resigned, Apr. 30, 1963 (Resigned from Executive Council, Apr. 30, 1963)
	Hon. John Richard "Jack" Simonett	Frontenac – Addington	Oct. 25, 1962 – Oct. 16, 1963
	Hon. George Ellis Gomme	Lanark	Jan. 12, 1965 – Nov. 24, 1966

The Ministry of the Hon. John Parmenter Robarts: Nov. 8, 1961 – Mar. 1, 1971 — *Continued*

Portfolio	Name	Constituency	Dates in Portfolio
Minister Without Portfolio — *Continued*	Hon. James Noble Allan	Haldimand – Norfolk	Nov. 24, 1966 – resigned, Jan. 31, 1968 (Resigned from Executive Council, Jan. 31, 1968)
	Hon. William "Darcy" McKeough	Kent West	Nov. 24, 1966 – Nov. 23, 1967
	Hon. Thomas Leonard Wells	Scarborough North	Nov. 24, 1966 – Aug. 13, 1969
	Hon. Fernand Guindon	Stormont	Nov. 23, 1967 – Mar. 1, 1971
	Hon. Albert Benjamin Rutter "Bert" Lawrence	Carleton East	Aug. 13, 1969 – Feb. 5, 1970

The Ministry of the Hon. William Grenville Davis: Mar. 1, 1971 –
Progressive Conservative

Portfolio	Name	Constituency	Dates in Portfolio
Premier and President of the Council	Hon. William Grenville Davis	Brampton	Mar. 1, 1971 –
Deputy Premier	Hon. Robert Stanley Welch	Brock	Sept. 21, 1977 –
Provincial Secretary and Minister of Citizenship	Hon. John Yaremko	Bellwoods	Mar. 1, 1971 – Apr. 1, 1972. On Apr. 1, 1972, the Department of Provincial Secretary and Citizenship ceased to exist. Its responsibilities were transferred to other ministries.
Provincial Secretary for Justice	Hon. Allan Frederick Lawrence	St. George	Portfolio enacted Apr. 7, 1972, 21 Eliz. II, C.1, S.3. Jan. 5, 1972 – Sept. 28, 1972
	Hon. George Albert Kerr	Halton West	Sept. 28, 1972 – resigned, Feb. 26, 1974
	Hon. Robert Stanley Welch	Lincoln	Feb. 26, 1974 – June 18, 1975
	Hon. John Twining Clement	Niagara Falls	June 18, 1975 – Oct. 7, 1975
	Hon. John Palmer MacBeth	Humber	Oct. 7, 1975 – Jan. 21, 1978
	Hon. George Albert Kerr	Burlington South	Jan. 21, 1978 – Aug. 18, 1978
	Hon. Robert Stanley Welch	Brock	Aug. 18, 1978 – Aug. 30, 1979
	Hon. Gordon Wayne Walker	London South	Aug. 30, 1979 – Feb. 13, 1982
	Hon. Norman William Sterling	Carleton – Grenville	Feb. 13, 1982 – July 6, 1983
	Hon. Gordon Wayne Walker	London South	July 6, 1983 –
Provincial Secretary for Resources Development	Hon. Albert Benjamin Rutter "Bert" Lawrence	Carleton East	Portfolio enacted Apr. 7, 1972, 21 Eliz. II, C.1, S.3. Jan. 5, 1972 – Feb. 26, 1974
	Hon. Allan Grossman	St. Andrew – St. Patrick	Feb. 26, 1974 – Oct. 7, 1975
	Hon. Donald Roy Irvine	Carleton – Grenville	Oct. 7, 1975 – Feb. 3, 1977

The Ministry of the Hon. William Grenville Davis: Mar. 1, 1971 –   — *Continued*

Portfolio	Name	Constituency	Dates in Portfolio
Provincial Secretary for Resources Development — *Continued*	Hon. René Joseph Napoléon Brunelle	Cochrane North	Feb. 3, 1977 – Apr. 10, 1981
	Hon. Russell Harold Ramsay	Sault Ste. Marie	Apr. 10, 1981 – Feb. 13, 1982
	Hon. Lorne Charles Henderson	Lambton	Feb. 13, 1982 – July 6, 1983
	Hon. Norman William Sterling	Carleton – Grenville	July 6, 1983 –
Provincial Secretary for Social Development	Hon. Robert Stanley Welch	Lincoln	Portfolio enacted Apr. 7, 1972, 21 Eliz. II, C.1, S.3.
			Jan. 5, 1972 – Feb. 26, 1974
	Hon. Margaret Birch	Scarborough East	Feb. 26, 1974 – July 6, 1983
	Hon. Bruce Robert McCaffrey	Armourdale	July 6, 1983 – Dec. 23, 1983
	Hon. Gordon H. Dean	Wentworth	Dec. 23, 1983 –
Treasurer of Ontario and Minister of Economics and Chairman, Treasury Board	Hon. William "Darcy" McKeough	Chatham – Kent	Mar. 1, 1971 – Apr. 7, 1972
			On Feb. 2, 1972, the Chairman, Treasury Board was abolished and the Chairman, Management Board of Cabinet established.
			On Apr. 7, 1972, Portfolio changed to Treasurer of Ontario and Minister of Economics and Intergovernmental Affairs.
	Hon. Frank Stuart Miller	Muskoka	Aug. 18, 1978 – July 6, 1983
	Hon. Lawrence Sheldon "Larry" Grossman	St. Andrew – St. Patrick	July 6, 1983 –
Treasurer of Ontario and Minister of Economics and Intergovernmental Affairs	Hon. William "Darcy" McKeough	Chatham – Kent	Portfolio enacted Apr. 7, 1972, 21 Eliz. II, C.3.
			Apr. 10, 1972 – Sept. 7, 1972
	Hon. Charles Steel MacNaughton	Huron	Sept. 7, 1972 – Jan. 15, 1973
	Hon. John Howard White	London South	Jan. 15, 1973 – June 18, 1975

	Hon. William "Darcy" McKeough	Chatham – Kent	June 18, 1975 – Aug. 16, 1978
	Hon. Frank Stuart Miller	Muskoka	Aug. 16, 1978 – Aug. 18, 1978
			On Aug. 18, 1978, Intergovernmental Affairs component changed to Minister of Intergovernmental Affairs.
Chairman, Management Board of Cabinet	Hon. Charles Steel MacNaughton	Huron	Portfolio enacted Dec. 17, 1971, 20 Eliz. II, C.12.
			Feb. 2, 1972 – Sept. 28, 1972
	Hon. Eric Alfred Winkler	Grey South	Sept. 28, 1972 – Oct. 7, 1975
	Hon. James Alexander Charles Auld	Leeds	Oct. 7, 1975 – Aug. 18, 1978
	Hon. George R. McCague	Dufferin – Simcoe	Aug. 18, 1978 –
Chairman of Cabinet	Hon. René Joseph Napoléon Brunelle	Cochrane North	Oct. 7, 1975 – Feb. 3, 1977
	Hon. Lorne Charles Henderson	Lambton	Feb. 3, 1977 – Aug. 30, 1979
	Hon. George R. McCague	Dufferin – Simcoe	Aug. 30, 1979 –
Minister of Agriculture and Food	Hon. William Atcheson Stewart	Middlesex North	Mar. 1, 1971 – Oct. 7, 1975
	Hon. William G. Newman	Durham North Durham-York (1976-)	Oct. 7, 1975 – Aug. 30, 1979
	Hon. Lorne Charles Henderson	Lambton	Aug. 30, 1979 – Feb. 13, 1982
	Hon. Dennis Roy Timbrell	Don Mills	Feb. 13, 1982 –
Attorney General	Hon. Dalton Arthur Bales	York Mills	Portfolio enacted Apr. 7, 1972, 21 Eliz. II, C.1.
			Apr. 10, 1972 – Feb. 26, 1974
	Hon. Robert Stanley Welch	Lincoln	Feb. 26, 1974 – June 18, 1975
	Hon. John Twining Clement	Niagara Falls	June 18, 1975 – Oct. 7, 1975
	Hon. Roland "Roy" McMurtry	Eglington	Oct. 7, 1975 –
Minister of Citizenship and Culture	Hon. Bruce Robert McCaffrey	Armourdale	Portfolio enacted June 7, 1982, S.O. 1982, C.6.
			Feb. 13, 1982 – July 6, 1983
	Hon. Susan A. Fish	St. George	July 6, 1983 –

The Ministry of the Hon. William Grenville Davis: Mar. 1, 1971 – *— Continued*

Portfolio	Name	Constituency	Dates in Portfolio
Minister of Colleges and Universities	Hon. John Howard White	London South	Portfolio enacted July 23, 1971, 20 Eliz. II, C.66.
			Oct. 28, 1971 – Feb. 2, 1972
	Hon. George Albert Kerr	Halton West	Feb. 2, 1972 – Sept. 28, 1972
	Hon. John Duncan "Jack" McNie	Hamilton West	Sept. 28, 1972 – Feb. 26, 1974
	Hon. James Alexander Charles Auld	Leeds	Feb. 26, 1974 – Oct. 7, 1975
	Hon. Harry Craig Parrott	Oxford	Oct. 7, 1975 – Aug. 18, 1978
	Hon. Bette M. Stephenson	York Mills	Aug. 18, 1978 –
Minister of Community and Social Services	Hon. René Joseph Napoléon Brunelle	Cochrane North	Portfolio enacted Apr. 7, 1972, 21 Eliz. II, C.1.
			Apr. 10, 1972 – Oct. 7, 1975
	Hon. James A. Taylor	Prince Edward-Lennox	Oct. 7, 1975 – Feb. 3, 1977
	Hon. Keith Calder Norton	Kingston and the Islands	Feb. 3, 1977 – Apr. 10, 1981
	Hon. James Francis "Frank" Drea	Scarborough Centre	Apr. 10, 1981 –
(Acting)	Hon. Bruce Robert McCaffrey	Armourdale	Sept. 29, 1983 – Nov. 21, 1983 (Appointed by Order-in-Council, during the illness of the Hon. Frank Drea.)
Minister of Consumer and Commercial Relations	Hon. Eric Alfred Winkler	Grey South	Portfolio enacted Apr. 7, 1972, 21 Eliz. II, C.1, S.23.
			Apr. 10, 1972 – Sept. 28, 1972
	Hon. John Twining Clement	Niagara Falls	Sept. 28, 1972 – June 18, 1975
	Hon. Sidney Bernard Handleman	Carleton	June 18, 1975 – Sept. 21, 1977
	Hon. Lawrence Sheldon "Larry" Grossman	St. Andrew – St. Patrick	Sept. 21, 1977 – Oct. 18, 1978
	Hon. James Francis "Frank" Drea	Scarborough Centre	Oct. 18, 1978 – Apr. 10, 1981

	Hon. Gordon W. Walker	London South	Apr. 10, 1981 – Feb. 13, 1982
	Hon. Robert Goldwin Elgie	York East	Feb. 13, 1982 –
Minister of Correctional Services	Hon. Charles Joseph Sylvanus "Syl" Apps	Kingston and the Islands	Mar. 1, 1971 – Feb. 26, 1974
	Hon. Richard Thomas Potter	Quinte	Feb. 26, 1974 – Oct. 7, 1975
	Hon. John Roxborough Smith	Hamilton-Mountain	Oct. 7, 1975 – Feb. 3, 1977
	Hon. Arthur Kenneth Meen	York East	Feb. 3, 1977 – June 23, 1977
(Acting)	Hon. John Palmer MacBeth	Humber	June 23, 1977 – Sept. 21, 1977
	Hon. James Francis "Frank" Drea	Scarborough Centre	Sept. 21, 1977 – Oct. 18, 1978
	Hon. Gordon W. Walker	London South	Oct. 18, 1978 – Apr. 10, 1981
	Hon. Nicholas George Leluk	York West	Apr. 10, 1981 –
Minister of Culture and Recreation	Hon. Robert Stanley Welch	Lincoln	Portfolio enacted Dec. 20, 1974, 23-24 Eliz. II, C.120.
		Brock	June 18, 1975 – Aug. 18, 1978
	Hon. Reuben C. Baetz	Ottawa West	Aug. 18, 1978 – Feb. 13, 1982
			On June 7, 1982, Portfolio changed to Minister of Citizenship and Culture and Minister of Tourism and Recreation.
Minister of Education	Hon. Robert Stanley Welch	Lincoln	Mar. 1, 1971 – Feb. 2, 1972
	Hon. Thomas Leonard Wells	Scarborough North	Feb. 2, 1972 – Aug. 18, 1978
	Hon. Bette M. Stephenson	York Mills	Aug. 18, 1978 –
Minister of Energy	Hon. William "Darcy" McKeough	Chatham – Kent	Portfolio enacted June 22, 1973, 22-23 Eliz. II, C.56.
			July 4, 1973 – June 18, 1975
	Hon. Dennis Roy Timbrell	Don Mills	June 18, 1975 – Feb. 3, 1977
	Hon. James A. Taylor	Prince Edward-Lennox	Feb. 3, 1977 – Jan. 21, 1978
	Hon. Reuben C. Baetz	Ottawa West	Jan. 21, 1978 – Aug. 18, 1978
	Hon. James Alexander Charles Auld	Leeds	Aug. 18, 1978 – Aug. 30, 1979

The Ministry of the Hon. William Grenville Davis: Mar. 1, 1971 – — *Continued*

Portfolio	Name	Constituency	Dates in Portfolio
Minister of Energy — *Continued*	Hon. Robert Stanley Welch	Brock	Aug. 30, 1979 – July 6, 1983
	Hon. Philip W. Andrewes	Lincoln	July 6, 1983 –
Minister of Energy and Resources Management	Hon. George Albert Kerr	Halton West	Mar. 1, 1971 – July 23, 1971
			On July 23, 1971, Portfolio changed to Minister of Environment.
Minister of the Environment	Hon. George Albert Kerr	Halton West	Portfolio enacted July 23, 1971, 20 Eliz. II, C.63.
			July 23, 1971 – Feb. 2, 1972
	Hon. James Alexander Charles Auld	Leeds	Feb. 2, 1972 – Feb. 26, 1974
	Hon. William G. Newman	Ontario South	Feb. 26, 1974 – Oct. 7, 1975
	Hon. George Albert Kerr	Burlington South	Oct. 7, 1975 – Jan. 21, 1978
	Hon. George R. McCague	Dufferin-Simcoe	Jan. 21, 1978 – Aug. 18, 1978
	Hon. Harry Craig Parrott	Oxford	Aug. 18, 1978 – Apr. 10, 1981
	Hon. Keith Calder Norton	Kingston and the Islands	Apr. 10, 1981 – July 6, 1983
	Hon. Andrew S. Brandt	Sarnia	July 6, 1983 –
Minister of Financial and Commercial Affairs	Hon. Arthur Allison Wishart	Sault Ste. Marie	Mar. 1, 1971 – Dec. 8, 1971
			Although Hon. Arthur Allison Wishart, MPP, Sault Ste. Marie, did not seek re-election in the Oct. 21, 1971 General Election, he retained his portfolio. He was listed in the Cabinet positions, released Oct. 28, 1971.
	Hon. Gordon Robert Carton	Armourdale	Dec. 8, 1971 – Feb. 2, 1972
	Hon. Eric Alfred Winkler	Grey South	Feb. 2, 1972 – Apr. 10, 1972
			On Apr. 10, 1972, Portfolio changed to Minister of Consumer and Commercial Affairs.

Minister of Government Services	Hon. James Wilfred Snow	Halton East	Portfolio enacted Apr. 7, 1972, 21 Eliz. II, C.1, S.74.
			Apr. 10, 1972 – Oct. 7, 1975
	Hon. Margaret Scrivener	St. David	Oct. 7, 1975 – Feb. 3, 1977
	Hon. John Roxborough Smith	Hamilton Mountain	Feb. 3, 1977 – June 23, 1977
(Acting)	Hon. James Alexander Charles Auld	Leeds	June 23, 1977 – Sept. 21, 1977
	Hon. George R. McCague	Dufferin – Simcoe	Sept. 21, 1977 – Jan. 21, 1978
	Hon. Lorne Charles Henderson	Lambton	Jan. 21, 1978 – Aug. 30, 1979
	Hon. Douglas Jack Wiseman	Lanark	Aug. 30, 1979 – July 6, 1983
	Hon. George Lyle Ashe	Durham West	July 6, 1983 –
Minister of Health	Hon. Albert Benjamin Rutter "Bert" Lawrence	Carleton East	Mar. 1, 1971 – Feb. 2, 1972
	Hon. Richard Thomas Potter	Quinte	Feb. 2, 1972 – Feb. 26, 1974
	Hon. Frank Stuart Miller	Muskoka	Feb. 26, 1974 – Feb. 3, 1977
	Hon. Dennis Roy Timbrell	Don Mills	Feb. 3, 1977 – Feb. 13, 1982
	Hon. Lawrence Sheldon "Larry" Grossman	St. Andrew – St. Patrick	Feb. 13, 1982- July 6, 1983
	Hon. Keith Calder Norton	Kingston & the Islands	July 6, 1983 –
(Acting)	Hon. Thomas Leonard Wells	Scarborough North	Oct. 11, 1983 – Dec. 5, 1983 (Appointment by Order-in-Council, during the illness of the Hon. Keith Norton.)
Minister of Highways and Minister of Transport	Hon. Charles Steel MacNaughton	Huron	Mar. 1, 1971 – May 28, 1971
			On May 28, 1971, the two Portfolios were amalgamated into Minister of Transportation and Communications.
Minister of Housing	Hon. Robert Stanley Welch	Lincoln	Portfolio enacted Oct. 30, 1973, 22-23 Eliz. II, C.100.
			Nov. 7, 1973 – Feb. 26, 1974
	Hon. Sidney Bernard Handleman	Carleton	Feb. 26, 1974 – Oct. 7, 1974

The Ministry of the Hon. William Grenville Davis: Mar. 1, 1971 – — *Continued*

Portfolio	Name	Constituency	Dates in Portfolio
Minister of Housing — *Continued*	Hon. Donald Roy Irvine	Grenville – Dundas	Oct. 7, 1974 – Oct. 7, 1975
	Hon. John Reginald Rhodes	Sault Ste. Marie	Oct. 7, 1975 – Jan. 21, 1978
	Hon. Claude Frederick Bennett	Ottawa South	Jan. 21, 1978 – July 3, 1981
			On July 3, 1981, Portfolio changed to Minister of Municipal Affairs and Housing.
Minister of Industry and Tourism	Hon. John Howard White	London South	Portfolio enacted Apr. 7, 1972, 21 Eliz. II, C.5.
			Apr. 10, 1972 – Jan. 15, 1973
	Hon. Claude Frederick Bennett	Ottawa South	Jan. 15, 1973 – Jan. 21, 1978
	Hon. John Reginald Rhodes	Sault Ste. Marie	Jan. 21, 1978 – until his death, Sept. 25, 1978
	Hon. Lawrence Sheldon "Larry" Grossman	St. Andrew – St. George	Oct. 18, 1978 – Feb. 13, 1982
			On Feb. 13, 1982, Portfolio changed to Minister of Industry and Trade Development and Minister of Tourism and Recreation.
Minister of Industry and Trade Development	Hon. Gordon Wayne Walker	London South	Portfolio enacted June 7, 1982, S.O. 1982, C.31.
			Feb. 13, 1982 – July 6, 1983
	Hon. Frank Stuart Miller	Muskoka	July 6, 1983 –
Minister of Intergovernmental Affairs	Hon. Thomas Leonard Wells	Scarborough North	Portfolio enacted Nov. 24, 1978, S.O. 1978, C.64.
			Aug. 16, 1978 –
Minister of Justice and Attorney General	Hon. Allan Frederick Lawrence	St. George	Mar. 1, 1971 – Feb. 2, 1972
	Hon. Dalton Arthur Bales	York Mills	Feb. 2, 1972 – Apr. 10, 1972
			On Apr. 7, 1972, Portfolio changed to Attorney General.

Minister of Labour	Hon. Gordon Robert Carton	Armourdale	Mar. 1, 1971 – Feb. 2, 1972
	Hon. Fernand Guindon	Stormont	Feb. 2, 1972 – May 31, 1974
	Hon. John Palmer MacBeth	York West	May 31, 1974 – Oct. 7, 1975
	Hon. Bette M. Stephenson	York Mills	Oct. 7, 1975 – Aug. 18, 1978
	Hon. Robert Goldwin Elgie	York East	Aug. 18, 1978 – Feb. 13, 1982
	Hon. Russell Harold Ramsay	Sault Ste. Marie	Feb. 13, 1982 –
Minister of Lands and Forests	Hon. René Joseph Napoléon Brunelle	Cochrane North	Mar. 1, 1971 – Feb. 2, 1972
	Hon. Leo Edward Berrier	Kenora	Feb. 2, 1972 – Apr. 10, 1972
			On Apr. 7, 1972, Portfolio changed to Minister of Natural Resources.
Minister of Mines and Northern Affairs	Hon. Leo Edward Berrier	Kenora	Mar. 1, 1971 – Apr. 7, 1972
			On Apr. 7, 1972, Portfolio changed to Minister of Natural Resources.
Minister of Municipal Affairs	Hon. Dalton Arthur Bales	York Mills	Mar. 1, 1971 – Feb. 2, 1972
	Hon. William "Darcy" McKeough	Chatham – Kent	Feb. 2, 1972 – Apr. 7, 1972
			On Apr. 7, 1972, Portfolio changed to Treasurer of Ontario and Minister of Economics and Intergovernmental Affairs.
Minister of Municipal Affairs and Housing	Hon. Claude Frederick Bennett	Ottawa South	Portfolio enacted July 3, 1981, S.O. 1981, C.19.
			July 3, 1981 –
Minister of Natural Resources	Hon. Leo Edward Bernier	Kenora	Portfolio enacted Apr. 7, 1972, 21 Eliz. II, C.4.
			Apr. 7, 1972 – Feb. 3, 1977
	Hon. Frank Stuart Miller	Muskoka	Feb. 3, 1977 – Aug. 18, 1978
	Hon. James Alexander Charles Auld	Leeds	Aug. 18, 1978 – Apr. 10, 1981
	Hon. Allan William Pope	Cochrane South	Apr. 10, 1981 –

The Ministry of the Hon. William Grenville Davis: Mar. 1, 1971 –   *— Continued*

Portfolio	Name	Constituency	Dates in Portfolio
Minister of Northern Affairs	Hon. Leo Edward Bernier	Kenora	Portfolio enacted July 12, 1977, S.O. 1977, C.21.
			Feb. 3, 1977 –
Minister of Public Works	Hon. James Alexander Charles Auld	Leeds	Mar. 1, 1971 – Feb. 2, 1972
	Hon. James Wilfred Snow	Halton East	Feb. 2, 1972 – Apr. 10, 1972
			On Apr. 7, 1972, Portfolio changed to Minister of Government Services.
Minister of Revenue	Hon. Eric Alfred Winkler	Grey South	Mar. 1, 1971 – Feb. 2, 1972
	Hon. Allan Grossman	St. Andrew – St. Patrick	Feb. 2, 1972 – Feb. 26, 1974
	Hon. Arthur Kenneth Meen	York East	Feb. 26, 1974 – Feb. 3, 1977
	Hon. Margaret Scrivener	St. David	Feb. 3, 1977 – Jan. 21, 1978
	Hon. Lorne Howard Maeck	Parry Sound	Jan. 21, 1978 – Apr. 10, 1981
	Hon. George Lyle Ashe	Durham West	Apr. 10, 1981 – July 6, 1983
	Hon. Milton Edward Charles "Bud" Gregory	Mississauga East	July 6, 1983 –
Minister of Social and Family Services	Hon. Thomas Leonard Wells	Scarborough North	Mar. 1, 1971 – Feb. 2, 1972
	Hon. René Joseph Napoléon Brunelle	Cochrane North	Feb. 2, 1972 – Apr. 10, 1972
			On Apr. 7, 1972, Portfolio changed to Minister of Community and Social Services.
Solicitor General	Hon. John Yaremko	Bellwoods	Portfolio enacted Apr. 7, 1972, 21 Eliz. II, C.2.
			Apr. 7, 1972 – Feb. 26, 1974
	Hon. George Albert Kerr	Halton West	Feb. 26, 1974 – June 18, 1975
(Acting)	Hon. John Twining Clement	Niagara Falls	June 18, 1975 – Oct. 7, 1975
	Hon. John Palmer MacBeth	Humber	Oct. 7, 1975 – Jan. 21, 1978

	Hon. George Albert Kerr	Burlington South	Jan. 21, 1978 – Sept. 11, 1978
	Hon. Roland "Roy" McMurtry	Eglinton	Sept. 11, 1978 – Feb. 13, 1982
	Hon. George William Taylor	Simcoe Centre	Feb. 13, 1982 –
Minister of Tourism and Information	Hon. Fernand Guindon	Stormont	Mar. 1, 1971 – Feb. 2, 1972
	Hon. John Howard White	London South	Feb. 2, 1972 – Apr. 7, 1972
			On Apr. 7, 1972, Portfolio changed to Minister of Industry and Tourism.
Minister of Tourism and Recreation	Hon. Reuben C. Baetz	Ottawa West	Portfolio enacted June 7, 1982, S.O. 1982, C.7.
			Feb. 13, 1982 –
Minister of Trade and Development	Hon. Allan Grossman	St. Andrew – St. Patrick	Mar. 1, 1971 – Feb. 2, 1972
	Hon. John Howard White	London South	Feb. 2, 1972 – Apr. 7, 1972
			On Apr. 7, 1972, Portfolio changed to Minister of Industry and Tourism.
Minister of Transportation and Communications	Hon. Charles Steel MacNaughton	Huron	Portfolio enacted May 28, 1971, 20 Eliz. II, C.13.
			May 28, 1971 – Feb. 2, 1972
	Hon. Gordon Robert Carton	Armourdale	Feb. 2, 1972 – Feb. 26, 1974
	Hon. John Reginald Rhodes	Sault Ste. Marie	Feb. 26, 1974 – Oct. 7, 1975
	Hon. James Wilfred Snow	Oakville	Oct. 7, 1975 –
Minister of University Affairs	Hon. John Howard White	London South	Mar. 1, 1971 – Oct. 28, 1971
			On Oct. 28, 1971, Portfolio changed to Minister of Colleges and Universities.
Minister Responsible for Women's Issues	Hon. Robert Stanley Welch	Brock	Directorate established May 17, 1983.
			May 17, 1983 –
Minister Without Portfolio	Hon. Edward Arunah Dunlop	York – Forest Hill	Mar. 1, 1971 – Oct. 28, 1971
	Hon. Richard Thomas Potter	Quinte	Mar. 1, 1971 – Feb. 2, 1972
	Hon. James Wilfred Snow	Halton East	Mar. 1, 1971 – Feb. 2, 1972
	Hon. Claude Frederick Bennett	Ottawa South	Sept. 28, 1972 – Jan. 15, 1973
	Hon. Margaret Birch	Scarborough East	Sept. 28, 1972 – Feb. 26, 1974

The Ministry of the Hon. William Grenville Davis: Mar. 1, 1971 – *— Continued*

Portfolio	Name	Constituency	Dates in Portfolio
Minister Without Portfolio — *Continued*	Hon. Donald Roy Irvine	Grenville – Dundas	Feb. 26, 1974 – Oct. 7, 1974
	Hon. John Duncan "Jack" McNie	Hamilton West	Feb. 26, 1974 – Oct. 7, 1975
	Hon. Dennis Roy Timbrell	Don Mills	Feb. 26, 1974 – June 18, 1975
	Hon. Sidney Bernard Handleman	Carleton	Oct. 7, 1974 – June 18, 1975
	Hon. Richard B. Beckett	Brantford	June 18, 1975 – Oct. 7, 1975
	Hon. John Howard White	London South	June 18, 1975 – Oct. 7, 1975
	Hon. René Joseph Napoléon Brunelle	Cochrane North	Oct. 7, 1975 – Feb. 3, 1977
	Hon. Lorne Charles Henderson	Lambton	Oct. 7, 1975 – Jan. 21, 1978
	Hon. Douglas Jack Wiseman	Lanark	Jan. 21, 1978 – Aug. 30, 1979
	Hon. Alan William Pope	Cochrane South	Aug. 30, 1979 – Apr. 10, 1981
	Hon. Bruce Robert McCaffrey	Armourdale	Apr. 10, 1981 – Feb. 13, 1982
	Hon. Norman William Sterling	Carleton – Grenville	Apr. 10, 1981 – Feb. 13, 1982
	Hon. Robert Gordon Eaton	Middlesex	Feb. 13, 1982 – July 6, 1983
	Hon. Gordon H. Dean	Wentworth	July 6, 1983 – Dec. 23, 1983
Minister Without Portfolio and Chief Government Whip	Hon. Milton Edward Charles "Bud" Gregory	Mississauga East	Aug. 30, 1979 – July 6, 1983
	Hon. Robert Gordon Eaton	Middlesex	July 6, 1983 –

LEGISLATURES OF UPPER CANADA
1st Legislature

General Election   Aug. 1792

Sessions of the First Legislature of Upper Canada: Sept. 17, 1792 – June 3, 1796†

First:	Sept. 17, 1792 – Oct. 15, 1792.
Second:	May 31, 1793 – July 9, 1793.
Third:	June 2, 1794 – July 9, 1794.
Fourth:	July 6, 1795 – Aug. 10, 1795.
Fifth:	May 16, 1796 – June 3, 1796.

Alphabetical List of Members

Member	Constituency	Sworn In	Comments
Francis Baby	Kent	Sept. 17, 1792	
Joshua Booth	Ontario & Addington	Sept. 17, 1792	Died, Oct. 13, 1813.
Alexander Campbell	Dundas	Sept. 17, 1792	
Philip Dorland	Prince Edward & Adolphus (Twp.)	Did not take seat	On Sept. 19, 1792, the House was informed that Philip Dorland, MPP, Prince Edward & Adolphus (Twp.), was unseated, as he had not subscribed to the Oath set forth in the Act of Parliament, as he was a Quaker. Dorland was willing to affirm, but affirmation was not considered as being legal. A new election was called.
Jeremiah French	Stormont	Sept. 17, 1792	Died, in 1805.
Ephraim Jones	Grenvill	Sept. 17, 1792	
Hugh Macdonell	Glengary, 1st R.	Sept. 17, 1792	Also listed as McDonell.
Hon. John Macdonell	Glengary, 2nd R.	Sept. 17, 1792	Also listed as McDonell. On Sept. 17, 1792, the House unanimously elected John Macdonell, MPP, Glengary, 2nd R., as Speaker. Sept. 17, 1792 – Date took chair.

William Macomb	Kent	Sept. 17, 1792	Died, 1796. (Will dated Apr. 11, 1796). No By-election was called.
Benjamin Pawling	Lincoln, 2nd R.	Sept. 17, 1792	Buried, Dec. 16, 1818, in Niagara.
Nathaniel Pettit	Durham, York & Lincoln, 1st R.	Sept. 17, 1792	
David William Smith	Suffolk & Essex	Sept. 17, 1792	Appointed to Executive Council, Mar. 2, 1796.
Hazelton Spencer	Lenox, Hastings & Northumberland	Sept. 17, 1792	Died, Feb. 1813.
Isaac Swayze	Lincoln, 3rd R.	Sept. 17, 1792	Also listed as Swayzie or Swayzé.
Parshal Terry	Lincoln, 4th R. & Norfolk	Sept. 17, 1792	Drowned, 1808, in the Don River.
Peter Vanalstine	Prince Edward & Adolphus (Twp).	June 1, 1793*	Writ of Election – Sept. 19, 1792. Return of Writ – May 31, 1793. On June 1, 1793, the House was informed of the election of Peter Vanalstine, MPP, Prince Edward & Adolphus (Twp.), in room of Philip Dorland, whose election was declared void. Died in 1811, at Adolphustown.
John White	Leeds & Frontenac	Sept. 17, 1792	Attorney General. Killed in a duel with John Small, Clerk of the Executive Council, in 1801.

†   The Journals for the years 1795 and 1796 are not known to be in existence

*   By-election

Proclamation: July 16, 1792

J. Graves Simcoe.

George the Third by the grace of God, of Great Britain, France, and Ireland, King, Defender of the Faith, and so forth, & c. & c. To all our loving subjects, whom these presents may concern:

Whereas in pursuance of an act of parliament, lately made and provided, passed in the thirty-first year of our reign, and of authority by us given for that purpose, our late province of Quebec is become divided into two provinces of Upper Canada and Lower Canada, and our lieutenant governor of the said province of Upper Canada, by power from us derived, is authorized in the absence of our right trusty and well beloved Guy, lord Dorchester, captain general and governor in chief of our said province of Upper Canada, to divide the said province of Upper Canada into districts, counties, circles or towns and townships for the purpose of effectuating the intent of the said act of parliament, and to declare and appoint the number of representatives to be chosen by each, to serve in the assembly of the said province: Know ye, therefore, that our trusty and well beloved John Graves Simcoe, esquire, our lieutenant governor of our said province of Upper Canada, in the absence of the said governor in chief, hath and by this our proclamation doth divide the said province of Upper Canada into counties, and hath and doth appoint and declare the number of representatives of them and each of them to be as hereinafter limited, named, declared, and appointed.

Constituency	Member	Sworn In	Comments
Dundas	Alexander Campbell	Sept. 17, 1792	That the third of the said Counties be hereafter called by the name of the County of Dundas; which County is to be bounded on the east by the westernmost boundary line of the County of Stormont, on the south by the river St. Lawrence, and on the west by the easternmost boundary line of the late township·of Edwardsburgh, running north twenty-four degrees west until it intersects the Ottawa or Grand River, thence descending the said river until it meets the northwesternmost boundary of the County of Stormont. The said County of Dundas is to comprehend all the islands in the said river St. Lawrence nearest to the said County, in the whole or greater part fronting

the same . . . and that the said County of Dundas, bounded as hereinbefore is described, shall and may be represented in the said house of assembly by one member.

General Election Aug. 1792.

Durham, York & Lincoln, 1st R.   Nathaniel Pettit   Sept. 17, 1792

That the thirteenth of the said Counties be hereafter called by the name of the County of Durham; which County is to be bounded on the east by the westernmost line of the County of Northumberland, on the south by lake Ontario until it meets the westernmost point of Long Beach, thence by a line running north sixteen degrees west until it intersects the southern boundary of a tract of land belonging to the Mississague Indians, thence along the said tract parallel to lake Ontario until it meets the northwesternmost boundary of the County of Northumberland.

That the fourteenth of the said Counties be hereafter called by the name of the County of York; which County is to consist of two ridings, the east and west riding; the east riding is to be bounded on the east by the westernmost line of the County of Durham, on the south by lake Ontario until it meets the easternmost boundary of a tract of land belonging to the Mississague Indians, on the west by the easternmost boundary line of said tract, running north sixteen degrees west the distance of twenty-eight miles, north seventy-four degrees east fourteen miles, thence south sixteen degrees east sixteen miles to the southern boundary of the lands belonging to the said Indians, thence along the said tract parallel to lake Ontario until it meets the northwesternmost boundary of the County of Durham.

† The Journals for the years 1795 and 1796 are not known to be in existence.

Constituency	Member	Sworn In	Comments
Durham, York & Lincoln, 1st R. — *Continued*			That the west riding of the said County be hereafter called by the name of the west riding of the County of York; which riding is to be bounded on the east by the westernmost line of a tract of land belonging to the Mississague Indians, running north forty-five degrees west to the river La Tranche, to be called the Thames, on the south by Lake Geneva, to be called Burlington bay, and a carrying place leading through the Mohawk village to where it intersects the river La Tranche or Thames, thence up the said river to the northwesternmost boundary of a tract of land belonging to the Mississague Indians. That the fifteenth of the said Counties be hereafter called by the name of Lincoln; which County is to be divided into four ridings. The first riding is to be bounded on the west by the easternmost line of the County of York, on the south by the Grand River, to be called the Ouse, thence descending the said river until it meets an Indian road leading to the forks of the Chippawa Creek, which creek is to be called the Welland, thence descending the said creek until it meets the continuation of the easternmost boundary of the late township No. 5, thence north along the said boundary until it intersects lake Ontario, thence along the south shore of lake Ontario until it meets the southeast boundary of the County of York . . . and that the Counties of Durham and York, and the said first riding of the County of Lincoln, severally bounded as hereinbefore is described, shall together send one representative, that is, the said Counties of Durham and York, and first riding of the County

of Lincoln, shall and may be represented together in the said house of assembly by one member.

General Election Aug. 1792.

Glengary, 1st R.	Hugh Macdonell	Sept. 17, 1792	Also listed as McDonell.

That the first of the said Counties be hereafter called by the name of the County of Glengary; which County is to be bounded on the east by the lines that divide Upper from Lower Canada, on the south by the river St. Lawrence, and westerly by the easternmost boundary of the late township of Cornwall, running north twenty-four degrees west until it intersects the Ottawa or Grand river, thence descending the said river until it meets the divisional lines aforesaid. The said County is to comprehend all the islands in the said river St. Lawrence nearest to the said County, and in the whole or greater part fronting the same . . . the County of Glengary, bounded as aforesaid, shall be divided into two ridings, the first riding to include the late township of Charlottenburgh . . . and that each of the said ridings shall send one representative; that is, the said first riding shall and may be represented in the said house of assembly by one member.

General Election Aug. 1792.

Glengary, 2nd R.	Hon. John Macdonell	Sept. 17, 1792	Also listed as McDonell.

That the first of the said Counties be hereafter called by the name of the County of Glengary; which County is to be bounded on the east by the lines that divide Upper from Lower Canada, on the south by the river St. Lawrence, and westerly by the easternmost boundary of the late township of Cornwall, running north twenty-four degrees west until it intersects the Ottawa or Grand river, thence descending the said river until it meets the divisional lines

Constituency	Member	Sworn In	Comments
Glengary, 2nd R. — *Continued*			aforesaid. The said County is to comprehend all the islands in the said river St. Lawrence nearest to the said County, and in the whole or greater part fronting the same . . . the County of Glengary, bounded as aforesaid, shall be divided into two ridings, . . . the second riding to comprehend such part of the said County of Glengary as is not contained in the first riding, and that each of the said ridings shall send one representative; . . . and the said second riding shall and may be represented in the said house of assembly by one member.
			General Election Aug. 1792.
			On Sept. 17, 1792, the House unanimously elected John Macdonell, MPP, Glengary, 2nd R., as Speaker. Sept. 17, 1792 – Date took chair.
Grenvill	Ephraim Jones	Sept. 17, 1792	That the fourth of the said Counties be hereafter called by the name of the County of Grenvill; which County is to be bounded on the east by the westernmost line of the County of Dundas, on the south by the river St. Lawrence, and on the west by the easternmost boundary line of the late township of Elizabethtown, running north twenty-four degrees west until it intersects the Ottawa or Grand river, thence descending the said river until it meets the northwesternmost boundary of the County of Dundas. The said County of Grenvill is to comprehend all the islands in the said river St. Lawrence nearest to the said County, in the whole or greater part fronting the same . . . and that the said County of Grenvill, bounded as hereinbefore is described,

			shall and may be represented in the said house of assembly by one member.
			General Election Aug. 1792.
Kent	Francis Baby	Sept. 17, 1792	That the nineteenth of the said Counties be hereafter called by the name of the County of Kent; which County is to comprehend all the County not being territories of the Indians, not already included in the several Counties hereinbefore described, extending northward to the boundary line of Hudson's Bay, including all the territory to the westward and southward of the said line, to the utmost extent of the Country commonly called or known by the name of Canada . . . and that the said County of Kent, as hereinbefore is described, shall and may be represented in the said house of assembly by two members.
			General Election Aug. 1792.
Kent	William Macomb	Sept. 17, 1792	That the nineteenth of the said Counties be hereafter called by the name of the County of Kent; which County is to comprehend all the County not being territories of the Indians, not already included in the several Counties hereinbefore described, extending northward to the boundary line of Hudson's Bay, including all the territory to the westward and southward of the said line, to the utmost extent of the Country commonly called or known by the name of Canada . . . and that the said County of Kent, as hereinbefore is described, shall and may be represented in the said house of assembly by two members.
			General Election Aug. 1792.
			Died, 1796. (Will dated Apr. 11, 1796). No By-election was called.
Leeds & Frontenac	John White	Sept. 17, 1792	Attorney General.
			That the fifth of the Counties be hereafter called by the name of the County of Leeds;

Constituency	Member	Sworn In	Comments
Leeds & Frontenac — *Continued*			which County is to be bounded on the east by the westernmost line of the County of Grenvill, on the south by the river St. Lawrence, and on the west by the easternmost boundary line of the late township of Pittsburgh, running north until it intersects the Ottawa or Grand River, thence descending the said river until it meets the northwesternmost boundary of the County of Grenvill. The said County of Leeds is to comprehend all the islands in the said river of St. Lawrence nearest the said County, in the whole or greater part fronting the same.
			That the sixth of the said Counties be hereafter called by the name of the County of Frontenac; which County is to be bounded on the east by the westernmost line of the County of Leeds on the south by lake Ontario, on the west by the easternmost boundary line of the late township of Ernestown, running north twenty-four degrees west until it intersects the Ottawa or Grand river, thence descending the said river until it meets the northwesternmost boundary of the County of Leeds . . . and that the said County of Leeds and County of Frontenac, severally bounded as hereinbefore is described, shall together send one representative, that is the said Counties of Leeds and Frontenac shall and may be represented together in the said house of assembly by one member.
			General Election Aug. 1792.
			Killed in a duel with John Small, Clerk of the Executive Council, in 1801.
Lenox, Hastings & Northumberland	Hazelton Spencer	Sept. 17, 1792	That the ninth of the said Counties be hereafter called by the name of the County of Lenox;

which County is to be bounded on the east by the westernmost line of the County of Addington, on the south and west by the bay of Quinte, to the easternmost boundary of the Mohawk village, thence by a line along the westernmost boundary of the late township of Richmond, running north sixteen degrees west to the depth of twelve miles, thence running north seventy-four degrees east until it meets the northwesternmost boundary of the County of Addington; and comprehending all the islands in the bays and nearest to the shores thereof.

That the eleventh of the said Counties be hereafter called by the name of the County of Hastings; which County is to be bounded on the east by the westernmost line of the County of Lenox, on the south by the bay of Quinte, until it meets a boundary on the easternmost line of the river Trent, thence along the said river until it intersects the rear of the ninth concession, thence by a line running north sixteen degrees west until it intersects the river Ottawa or Grand river, thence descending the said river until it meets the northwesternmost boundary of the County of Addington; and the said County of Hastings to comprehend all the islands in the said bay of Quinte and river Trent nearest to the said County, in the whole or greater part fronting the same.

That the twelfth of the said Counties be hereafter called by the name of the County of Northumberland; which County is to be bounded on the east by the westernmost line of the County of Hastings and carrying-place of the Presque isle d'Quinte, on the south by lake Ontario until it meets the westernmost point of the Little bay, thence by a line running north sixteen degrees west until it meets the

Constituency	Member	Sworn In	Comments
Lenox, Hastings & Northumberland — *Continued*			southern boundary of a tract of land belonging to the Mississague Indians, thence along the said tract parallel to lake Ontario until it meets the northwesternmost boundary of the County of Hastings. The said County of Northumberland is to comprehend all the islands in the said lake Ontario and bay of Quinte nearest to the said County, in the whole or greater part fronting the same . . . and that the County of Lenox (the said district, late the township of Adolphus, excepted,) with the Counties of Hastings and Northumberland, severally bounded as hereinbefore is described, shall together send one representative, that is, the said County of Lenox, except as before excepted, and the said Counties of Hastings and Northumberland shall and may be represented together in the said house of assembly by one member.
			General Election Aug. 1792.
			Died, Feb. 1813.
Lincoln, 1st R. – See Durham, York & Lincoln, 1st R.			
Lincoln, 2nd R.	Benjamin Pawling	Sept. 17, 1792	That the fifteenth of the said Counties be hereafter called by the name of the County of Lincoln; which County is to be divided into four ridings. The second riding is to be bounded on the west by the easternmost line of the first riding, on the north by lake Ontario, on the east by the river Niagara, and on the south by the northern boundary of the late townships No. 2, No. 9, and No. 10 . . . and that the said second riding of the said County of Lincoln, bounded as hereinbefore is described, shall and may be

represented in the said house of assembly by one member.

General Election Aug. 1792.

Buried, Dec. 16, 1818, in Niagara.

Lincoln, 3rd R.	Isaac Swayze	Sept. 17, 1792	Also listed as Swayzie or Swayzé.

That the fifteenth of the said Counties be hereafter called by the name of the County of Lincoln; which County is to be divided into four ridings. The third riding is to be bounded on the east by the river Niagara, on the south by the Chippawa or Welland, on the west by the easternmost boundary of the first riding, and on the north by the southern boundary of the second riding . . . and that the said third riding of the said County of Lincoln, bounded as hereinbefore is described, shall and may be represented in the said house of assembly by one member.

General Election Aug. 1792.

Lincoln, 4th R. & Norfolk	Parshal Terry	Sept. 17, 1792	

That the fifteenth of the said Counties be hereafter called by the name of the County of Lincoln; which County is to be divided into four ridings. The fourth riding is to be bounded on the east by the river Niagara, on the south by lake Erie, to the north of the Grand river or Ouse, thence up the said river to the road leading from the said Grand river or Ouse to the forks of the Chippawa or Welland, and on the north by the said road until it strikes the forks of the Welland, thence down the said Welland to the river Niagara; the said fourth riding to include the islands comprised within the easternmost boundaries of the river Niagara.

That the sixteenth of the said Counties be hereafter called by the name of the County of Norfolk; which County is to be bounded on the

Constituency	Member	Sworn In	Comments
Lincoln, 4th R. & Norfolk — *Continued*			north and east by the County of Lincoln and the river La Tranche, now called the Thames, on the south side by the lake Erie until it meets the Barlue, to be called the Orwell river, thence by a line running north sixteen degrees until it intersects the river La Tranche or Thames, thence up the said river until it meets the northwest boundary of the County of York . . . and that the said fourth riding of the said County of Lincoln, and the County of Norfolk, severally bounded as hereinbefore is described, shall together send one representative, that is, the said fourth riding of the said County of Lincoln, and the County of Norfolk, shall and may be represented together in the said house of assembly by one member.
			General Election Aug. 1792.
			Drowned, 1808, in the Don River.
Ontario & Addington	Joshua Booth	Sept. 17, 1792	That the seventh of the said Counties be hereafter called by the name of the County of Ontario; which County is to consist of the following islands: an island at present known by the name of isle Tonti, to be called Amherst island; an island known by the name of isle au Foret, to be called Gage island; an island known by the name of Grand island, to be called Wolfe island; an island known by the name of isle Cauchois, to be called Howe island; and to comprehend all the islands between the mouth of the Gananoque to the easternmost extremity of the late township of Marysburgh, called point Pleasant.
			That the eighth of the said Counties be hereafter called by the name of the County of

Addington; which County is to be bounded on the east by the westernmost line of the County of Frontenac, on the south by lake Ontario, to the westernmost boundary of the late township of Ernestown, and on the west by the easternmost boundary line of the township of Fredericksburgh, running north thirty-one degrees west until it meets the northwesternmost boundary of the County of Frontenac; comprehending within the said County all the islands nearest to it, in the whole or greater part fronting the same. . . . and that the County of Ontario and the County of Addington, severally bounded as hereinbefore described, shall together send one representative, that is, the said Counties of Ontario and Addington shall and may be represented together in the said house of assembly by one member.

General Election Aug. 1792.

Died, Oct. 13, 1813.

Prince Edward & Adolphus (Twp.)	Philip Dorland	Did not take seat

That the tenth of the said Counties be hereafter called by the name of the County of Prince Edward; which County is to be bounded on the south by lake Ontario, on the west by the carrying-place on the isthmus of the Presque isle d'Quinte, on the north by the bay of Quinte and on the east, from Point Pleasant to point Traverse, by its several shores and bays, including the late township of Ameliasburg, Sophiasburg, and Marysburg. The said County of Prince Edward is to comprehend all the islands in the said lake Ontario and bay of Quinte nearest to the said County; in the whole or greater part fronting the same . . . and that the County of Prince Edward, bounded as hereinbefore is described, together with the district of the late township of Adolphus in the County of Lenox, shall

Constituency	Member	Sworn In	Comments
Prince Edward & Aldolphus (Twp.) — *Continued*			together send one representative, that is, the said County of Prince Edward, together with the said district, late the township of Adolphus, shall and may be represented together in the said house of assembly by one member.
			General Election Aug. 1792.
			On Sept. 19, 1792, the House was informed that Philip Dorland, MPP, Prince Edward & Adolphus (Twp.), was unseated, as he had not subscribed to the Oath set forth in the Act of Parliament, as he was a Quaker. Dorland was willing to affirm, but affirmation was not considered as being legal. A new election was called.
Prince Edward & Adolphus (Twp.)	Peter Vanalstine	June 1, 1793*	By-election Date unknown.
			Writ of Election – Sept. 19, 1792. Return of Writ – May 31, 1793. On June 1, 1793, the House was informed of the election of Peter Vanalstine, MPP, Prince Edward & Adolphus (Twp.), in room of Philip Dorland, whose election was declared void.
			Died, 1811, in Adolphustown.
Stormont	Jeremiah French	Sept. 17, 1792	That the second of the said Counties be hereafter called by the name of the County of Stormont; which County is to be bounded on the east by the westernmost line of the County of Glengary, on the south by the river St. Lawrence, to the westernmost boundary of the late township of Osnaburg, and on the west by the easternmost boundary line of the late township of Williamsburgh, running north twenty-four degrees west until it intersects the Ottawa or Grand river, then descending the said river until it meets the northwesternmost

boundary of the County of Glengary. The said County of Stormont is to comprehend all the islands in the said river St. Lawrence nearest to the said County, in the whole or greater part fronting the same . . . and that the said County of Stormont, bounded as hereinbefore is described, shall and may be represented in the said house of assembly by one member.

General Election Aug. 1792.

Died in 1805.

Suffolk & Essex	David William Smith	Sept. 17, 1792

That the seventeenth of the said Counties be hereafter called by the name of the County of Suffolk; which County is to be bounded on the east by the County of Norfolk, on the south by lake Erie, until it meets the carrying-place from point au Pins unto the Thames, on the west by the said carrying-place, thence up the said river Thames until it meets the northwesternmost boundary of the County of Norfolk.

That the eighteenth of the said Counties be hereafter called by the name of the County of Essex; which County is to be bounded on the east by the County of Suffolk, on the south by lake Erie, on the west by the river Detroit to Maisonville's mill, from thence by a line running parallel to the river Detroit and lake St. Clair, at the distance of four miles, until it meets the river La Tranche or Thames, thence up the said river to the northwest boundary of the County of Suffolk . . . and that the County of Suffolk and County of Essex, severally bounded as hereinbefore is described, shall together send one representative, that is, the said Counties of Suffolk and Essex shall and may be represented together in the said house of assembly by one member.

General Election Aug. 1792.

Appointed to Executive Council, Mar. 2, 1796.

* By-election

LEGISLATURES OF UPPER CANADA
2nd Legislature

General Election   Aug. 1796

Sessions of the Second Legislature of Upper Canada: June 1, 1797 – July 4, 1800

First:	June 1, 1797 – July 3, 1797.
Second:	July 5, 1798 – July 5, 1798.
Third:	June 12, 1799 – June 29, 1799.
Fourth:	June 2, 1800 – July 4, 1800.

Alphabetical List of Members

Member	Constituency	Sworn In†	Comments
Richard Beasley	Durham, York & Lincoln, 1st R.	June 1, 1797	
John Cornwall	Suffolk & Essex	June 1, 1797	
William Fairfield	Ontario & Addington	June 12, 1799*	Writ of Election – Nov. 20, 1798. On June 12, 1799, the House was informed of the election of William Fairfield, MPP, Ontario & Addington, in room of Christopher Robinson, deceased.
Thomas Fraser	Dundas	June 1, 1797	
Robert Isaac Dey Gray	Stormont	June 1, 1797	Mr. Solicitor General.
Benjamin Hardison	Lincoln, 4th R. & Norfolk	June 1, 1797	
Edward Jessup, Jr.	Grenvill	June 1, 1797	Died, as a result of a duel with James Clark, Clerk of the Legislative Council, Jan. 4, 1800. No By-election was called.
Solomon Jones	Leeds & Frontenac	June 1, 1797	
John Macdonell	Glengary, 2nd R.	June 9, 1798	Absent from first Session.
Thomas McKee	Kent	June 5, 1800	On June 17, 1799, the House was informed of a letter from Thomas McKee, MPP, Kent,

apologizing for not attending to his service in Parliament. Duties arising from his being the Superintendant of Indian Affairs and from the death of his father had prevented him from attending.

Christopher Robinson	Ontario & Addington	June 1, 1797	Died, Nov. 2, 1798. A new election was called.
David McGregor Rogers	Prince Edward & Adolphus (Twp.)	June 1, 1797	
Hon. David William Smith	Lincoln, 2nd R.	June 1, 1797	Acting Surveyor General.

The Journals for the years 1796 and 1797 are not known to be in existence. As the practice has been to swear in the new Speaker on the first day of the first Session, the date June 1, 1797 has been given as the date the Hon. David William Smith, MPP, Lincoln, 2nd R., took the chair.

On June 1, 1797, David William Smith, MPP, Lincoln, 2nd R., was proposed as Speaker. Seconded and resolved. June 1, 1797 – Date took chair.

On June 5, 1800, the House was informed of the absence from the Country of the Speaker, the Hon. David William Smith, MPP, Lincoln, 2nd R. A new Speaker was to be chosen.

| Thomas Smith | Kent | June 1, 1797 | |
| Hon. Samuel Street | Lincoln, 3rd R. | June 1, 1797 | On June 5, 1800, Thomas Smith, MPP, Kent, proposed Samuel Street, MPP, Lincoln, 3rd R., as Speaker, in room of the Hon. David William Smith, MPP, Lincoln, 2nd R., in absentia. Seconded and resolved. June 5, 1800 – Date took chair. |

† The Journals for the years 1796 and 1797 are not known to be in existence. As the practice has been to swear in new Members on the first day of the first Session, the date June 1, 1797 has been given as the date the Members took their seats in the 2nd Parliament.

* By-election

Member	Constituency	Sworn In	Comments
Timothy Thompson	Lenox, Hastings & Northumberland	June 1, 1797	
Richard Norton Wilkinson	Glengary, 1st R.	June 1, 1797	

Constituency	Member	Sworn In†	Comments
Dundas	Thomas Fraser	June 1, 1797	General Election Aug. 1796.
			Dundas. 1800. 40 Geo. III, C.3. An Act for the more equal Representation of the Commons of this Province in Parliament, and for the better defining the Qualification of Electors. . . . That from and after the end of the present Parliament, the representation of the Commons of this Province in the House of Assembly, shall be in manner and form following, that is to say: the Counties of Dundas, Grenville, Leeds, Frontenac, and Prince Edward, be each represented by one Member.
Durham, York & Lincoln, 1st R.	Richard Beasley	June 1, 1797	General Election Aug. 1796.
Glengary, 1st R.	Richard Norton Wilkinson	June 1, 1797	General Election Aug. 1796.
Glengary, 2nd R.	John Macdonell	June 9, 1798	General Election Aug. 1796. Absent from first Session.
Grenvill	Edward Jessup, Jr.	June 1, 1797	General Election Aug. 1796.
			Died, as a result of a duel with James Clark, Clerk of the Legislative Council, Jan. 4, 1800. No By-election was called.
			Grenvill. 1800. 40 Geo. III, C.3. An Act for the more equal Representation of the Commons of this Province in Parliament, and for the better defining the Qualification of Electors. . . . That from and after the end of the present Parliament, the representation of the Commons of this Province in the House of Assembly, shall be in manner and form following, that is to say: the Counties of Dundas, Grenville, Leeds, Frontenac, and Prince Edward, be each represented by one Member.
Kent	Thomas McKee	June 5, 1800	General Election Aug. 1796.

On June 17, 1799, the House was informed of a letter from Thomas McKee, MPP, Kent, apologizing for not attending to his service in Parliament. Duties arising from his being the Superintendant of Indian Affairs and from the death of his father had prevented him from attending.

Kent. 1800. 40 Geo. III, C.3. An Act for the more equal Representation of the Commons of this Province in Parliament, and for the better defining the Qualification of Electors. . . . That from and after the end of the present Parliament, the representation of the Commons of this Province in the House of Assembly, shall be in manner and form following, that is to say: the County of Kent, shall be represented by one Member.

Kent	Thomas Smith	June 1, 1797	General Election Aug. 1796.

Kent. 1800. 40 Geo. III, C.3. An Act for the more equal Representation of the Commons of this Province in Parliament, and for the better defining the Qualification of Electors. . . . That from and after the end of the present Parliament, the representation of the Commons of this Province in the House of Assembly, shall be in manner and form following, that is to say: the County of Kent, shall be represented by one Member.

Leeds & Frontenac	Solomon Jones	June 1, 1797	General Election Aug. 1796.
Lenox, Hastings & Northumberland	Timothy Thompson	June 1, 1797	General Election Aug. 1796.
Lincoln, 1st R. – See Durham, York & Lincoln, 1st R.			
Lincoln, 2nd R.	Hon. David William Smith	June 1, 1797	Acting Surveyor General. General Election Aug. 1796.

† The Journals for the years 1796 and 1797 are not known to be in existence. As the practice has been to swear in new Members on the first day of the first session, the date June 1, 1797 has been given as the date the Members took their seats in the 2nd Parliament.

Constituency	Member	Sworn In	Comments
Lincoln, 2nd R. — *Continued*			The Journals for the years 1796 and 1797 are not known to be in existence. As the practice has been to swear in the new Speaker on the first day of the first Session, the date June 1, 1797 has been given as the date the Hon. David William Smith, MPP, Lincoln, 2nd R., took the chair.
			On June 1, 1797, David William Smith, MPP, Lincoln, 2nd R., was proposed as Speaker. Seconded and resolved. June 1, 1797 – Date took chair.
			On June 5, 1800, the House was informed of the absence from the Country of the Speaker, the Hon. David William Smith, MPP, Lincoln, 2nd R. A new Speaker was to be chosen.
Lincoln, 3rd R.	Hon. Samuel Street	June 1, 1797	General Election Aug. 1796.
			On June 5, 1800, Thomas Smith, MPP, Kent, proposed Samuel Street, MPP, Lincoln, 3rd R., as Speaker, in room of the Hon. David William Smith, MPP, Lincoln, 2nd R., in absentia. Seconded and resolved. June 5, 1800 – Date took chair.
Lincoln, 4th R. & Norfolk	Benjamin Hardison	June 1, 1797	General Election Aug. 1796.
Ontario & Addington	Christopher Robinson	June 1, 1797	General Election Aug. 1796.
			Died, Nov. 2, 1798. A new election was called.
Ontario & Addington	William Fairfield	June 12, 1799*	By-election Date unknown.
			Writ of Election – Nov. 20, 1798. On June 12, 1799, the House was informed of the election of William Fairfield, MPP, Ontario & Addington, in room of Christopher Robinson, deceased.

Prince Edward & Adolphus
  (Twp.)

David McGregor Rogers

June 1, 1797

General Election Aug. 1796.

Prince Edward & Adolphus (Twp.). 1797. 37 Geo. III, C. 17, S.1. An Act for the better Division of the County of Prince Edward into Townships. Whereas the inhabitants of the townships of Marysburg and Sophiasburg, in the county of Prince Edward, experience many difficulties from the uncommon length of the said townships; be it enacted . . . That a township shall be struck off from the southernmost parts of the townships of Marysburg and Sophiasburg, in form following: To commence in Marysburg in the limit between the lots numbers eleven and twelve, south side of the bay of Quinty, to the eastward of a small bay which leads to the Carrying-Place, to the East lake; then along the said limit south ten degrees west, the depth of three concessions, more or less, until it intersects the limit between lots numbers twelve and thirteen in the second concession, north of Black river; and then along the limit between the said lots numbers twelve and thirteen, south thirty-two degrees east, to the rear of the first concession from Black river; then south fifty-eight degrees west along the line between the first and second concessions, passing lot number thirty-two, to a small creek which empties itself into the East Lake; then south thirty-two degrees east to Lake Ontario; then westerly along the shore of the said lake to the mouth of the West lake; thence by the nearest line to the limit between lot number one in Ameliasburg, and lot number one in Sophiasburg; then north twenty degrees west, the depth of two concessions; then north seventy degrees east to the northeast angle of lot number sixteen in the second concession, nearly; then north fifty-eight and one half

Constituency	Member	Sworn In	Comments
Prince Edward & Aldolphus (Twp.) — *Continued*			degrees east to the northeast angle of a lot, numbered thirty-nine, in the third concession; then south thirty-one and one half degrees east to the rear of the second concession; then a small distance by the most direct line to the northernmost angle of lot number ten in the second concession; then along the limit between the lots numbers ten and eleven south sixty-one degrees east to the small bay first mentioned; then following the shores of the said bay and the bay of Quinty, according to its different windings and courses, to the place of beginning, which townships shall be under the same regulations and entitled to the same privileges as any other township in this province.
Stormont	Robert Isaac Dey Gray	June 1, 1797	Mr. Solicitor General. General Election Aug. 1796.
Suffolk & Essex	John Cornwall	June 1, 1797	General Election Aug. 1796.

LEGISLATURES OF UPPER CANADA
3rd Legislature

General Election   July 1800

Sessions of the Third Legislature of Upper Canada: May 28, 1801 – Mar. 9, 1804

First:	May 28, 1801 – July 9, 1801.
Second:	May 25, 1802 – July 7, 1802.
Third:	Jan. 24, 1803 – Mar. 5, 1803.
Fourth:	Feb. 1, 1804 – Mar. 9, 1804.

Alphabetical List of Members

Member	Constituency	Sworn In	Comments
Henry Allcock	Durham, York East & Simcoe	May 28, 1801	Mr. Justice. On June 11, 1801, the election of Henry Allcock, MPP, Durham, York East & Simcoe, was declared void. A new election was called.
Hon. Richard Beasley	York West, Lincoln, 1st R., & Haldimand	May 28, 1801	On Jan. 27, 1803, John Ferguson, MPP, Frontenac, proposed Richard Beasley, MPP, York West, Lincoln, 1st R. & Haldimand, as Speaker, in room of the Hon. David William Smith, MPP, Oxford, Middlesex & Norfolk, in absentia. Seconded and resolved. Jan. 27, 1803 – Date took chair.
William Buell, Sr.	Leeds	May 28, 1801	
Ralph Clench	Lincoln, 2nd, 3rd, & 4th R.	May 28, 1801	Also listed as Ralfe or Ralf.
Mathew Elliott	Essex	May 28, 1801	
John Ferguson	Frontenac	May 28, 1801	
Robert Isaac Dey Gray	Stormont & Russell	May 28, 1801	Mr. Solicitor General.
Angus Macdonell (Glengary)	Glengary & Prescott	May 28, 1801	

Angus Macdonell (York)	Durham, York East & Simcoe	July 4, 1801*	On June 29, 1801, Angus Macdonell, Clerk of the House, was thanked for his years of service, 1792-1801. On July 4, 1801, the House was informed of the election of Angus Macdonell, MPP, Durham, York East & Simcoe, in room of Henry Allcock, unseated.
Thomas McCrae	Kent	May 28, 1801	
Alexander McDonell	Glengary & Prescott	May 28, 1801	Sheriff of the Home District.
Thomas McKee	Essex	June 9, 1801	
Robert Nelles	York West, Lincoln, 1st R. & Haldimand	May 28, 1801	Also listed as Nellis.
David McGregor Rogers	Hastings & Northumberland	May 28, 1801	
Samuel Sherwood	Grenville	May 28, 1801	
Hon. David William Smith	Oxford, Middlesex & Norfolk	May 28, 1801	On May 28, 1801, David McGregor Rogers, MPP, Northumberland & Hastings, proposed David William Smith, MPP, Oxford, Middlesex & Norfolk, as Speaker. Seconded and resolved. May 28, 1801 – Date took chair. On Jan. 27, 1803, the House was informed of the absence from the Country of the Speaker, the Hon. David William Smith, MPP, Oxford, Middlesex & Norfolk. A new Speaker was to be chosen.
Isaac Swayze	Lincoln, 2nd, 3rd, & 4th R.	May 28, 1801	
Timothy Thompson	Lenox & Addington	May 28, 1801	
Ebenezer Washburn	Prince Edward	May 28, 1801	
Jacob Weager	Dundas	May 28, 1801	

* By-election

Constituency	Member	Sworn In	Comments†
Dundas	Jacob Weager	May 28, 1801	Dundas. 1798. 38 Geo. V., C.5, Ss.3, 6. An Act for the better Division of this Province. And be it further enacted by the authority aforesaid, That the Townships of Williamsburg, Matilda, Mountain and Winchester, with such of the Islands in the River St. Lawrence as are wholly, or in greater part opposite thereto, do together, constitute and form the County of Dundas. . . . And be it further enacted by the authority aforesaid, That the Counties of Glengary, Stormont, Dundas, Prescott, and Russell, do constitute and form the Eastern District.
			Dundas. 1800. 40 Geo. III, C.3. An Act for the more equal Representation of the Commons of this Province in Parliament, and for the better defining the Qualification of Electors. . . . That from and after the end of the present Parliament, the representation of the Commons of this Province in the House of Assembly, shall be in manner and form following, that is to say: the Counties of Dundas, Grenville, Leeds, Frontenac, and Prince Edward, be each represented by one Member.
			General Election July 1800.
Durham, York East & Simcoe	Henry Allcock	May 28, 1801	Mr. Justice.
			Durham, York East & Simcoe. 1798. 38 Geo. III, C.5, Ss.20, 21, 23, 25. An Act for the better Division of this Province. And be it further enacted by the authority aforesaid, That the Townships of Hope, Clarke, and Darlington, with all the tract of land hereafter to be laid out into Townships, which lies to the southward of

the small Lakes above the Rice Lake, and the communication between them and between the eastern boundary of the Township of Hope, and the western boundary of the Township of Darlington, produced north sixteen degrees west, until they intersect either of the said Lakes, or the communication between them, shall constitute and form the County of Durham. . . . Provided always, and it is hereby further enacted, That when and so soon as the said Counties of Northumberland and Durham shall make it satisfactorily appear to the governor, lieutenant governor, or person administering the government of this province, that there are one thousand souls within the said Counties, and that six of the Townships therein do hold town meetings according to law, [1802. 42 Geo. III, C.2], then the said Counties, with all the land in their rear, confined between their extreme boundaries, produced north sixteen degrees, west, until they intersect the northern limits of the province, shall, and are hereby declared to be, a separate District to be called the District of Newcastle. . . . And be it further enacted by the authority aforesaid, That the Counties of Northumberland, Durham, York, and Simcoe, do constitute and form the Home District. . . . And be it further enacted by the authority aforesaid, That Matchedash, Gloucester, or Penetangueshine, together with Prince William Henry's Island, and all the land lying between the Midland District and a line produced due north from a certain fixed boundary (at the distance of about fifty miles north-west from the outlet of Burlington Bay) till it intersects the northern limits of the Province, do constitute

† The Royal Assent to this Act was promulgated by Proclamation, bearing date January first, in the year of Our Lord, One thousand eight hundred, and fortieth of His Majesty's reign.

Constituency	Member	Sworn In	Comments
Durham, York East & Simcoe — *Continued*			and form the County of Simcoe. . . .And be it further enacted by the authority aforesaid, That the Townships of Whitby, Pickering, Scarborough, York, including its peninsula, Etobicoke, Markham, Vaughan, King, Whitchurch, Uxbridge, Gwillimbury, and the tract of land hereafter to be laid out into Townships, lying between the Counties of Durham and the Lake Simcoe, do constitute and form the East Riding of the County of York.
			Durham, York East & Simcoe. 1800. 40 Geo. III, C.3. An Act for the more equal Representation of the Commons of this Province in Parliament, and for the better defining the Qualification of Electors. . . . That from and after the end of the present Parliament, the representation of the Commons of this Province in the House of Assembly, shall be in manner and form following, that is to say: the County of Durham, the East Riding of the County of York, and the County of Simcoe, be together represented by one Member.
			General Election July 1800.
			On June 11, 1801, the election of Henry Allcock, MPP, Durham, York East & Simcoe, was declared void. A new election was called.
Durham, York East & Simcoe	Angus Macdonell (York)	July 4, 1801*	On June 29, 1801, Angus Macdonell, Clerk of the House, was thanked for his years of service, 1792-1801.
			By-election Date unknown.
			Writ of Election – June 11, 1801. On July 4, 1801, the House was informed of the election

of Angus Macdonell, MPP, Durham, York East & Simcoe in room of Henry Allcock, unseated.

| Essex | Mathew Elliot | May 28, 1801 | Essex. 1798. 38 Geo. III, C.5, Ss.39, 40. An Act for the better Division of this Province. And be it further enacted by the authority aforesaid, That the Townships of Rochester, Mersea, Gosfield, Maidstone, Sandwich, Colchester, Malden, and the tracts of Land occupied by the Huron and other Indians upon the Strait, together with such of the islands as are in the Lakes Erie, Sinclair or the Straits, do constitute and form the County of Essex. . . . And be it further enacted by the authority aforesaid, That the Counties of Essex and Kent, together with so much of this province as is not included within any other District thereof, do constitute and form the Western District. |

Essex. 1800. 40 Geo. III, C.3. An Act for the more equal Representation of the Commons of this Province in Parliament, and for the better defining the Qualification of Electors. . . . That from and after the end of the present Parliament, the representation of the Commons of this Province in the House of Assembly, shall be in manner and form following, that is to say: the County of Essex, shall be represented by two Members.

General Election July 1800.

| Essex | Thomas McKee | June 9, 1801 | Essex. 1798. 38 Geo. III, C.5, Ss.39, 40. An Act for the better Division of this Province. And be it further enacted by the authority aforesaid, that the Townships of Rochester, Mersea, Gosfield, Maidstone, Sandwich, Colchester, Malden, and the tracts of Land occupied by the Huron and other Indians upon the Strait, together with such of the islands as are in the |

Constituency	Member	Sworn In	Comments
Essex — *Continued*			Lakes Erie, Sinclair or the Straits, do constitute and form the County of Essex. . . . And be it further enacted by the authority aforesaid, that the Counties of Essex and Kent, together with so much of this province as is not included within any other District thereof, do constitute and form the Western District.
			Essex. 1800. 40 Geo. III, C.3. An Act for the more equal Representation of the Commons of this Province in Parliament, and for the better defining the Qualification of Electors. . . . That from and after the end of the present Parliament, the representation of the Commons of this Province in the House of Assembly, shall be in manner and form following, that is to say: the County of Essex, shall be represented by two Members.
			General Election July 1800.
Frontenac	John Ferguson	May 28, 1801	Frontenac. 1798. 38 Geo. III, C.5, Ss.14, 18. An Act for the better Division of this Province. And be it further enacted by the authority aforesaid, That the Townships of Pittsburg, Kingston, Loughborough, Portland, Hinchinbroke, Bedford and Wolfe Island, do constitute and form the County of Frontenac. . . . And be it further enacted by the authority aforesaid, That the Counties of Frontenac, the incorporated Counties of Lenox and Addington, Hastings, and Prince Edward, with all that tract of Country which lies between the District of Johnstown and a line drawn north sixteen degrees West from the northwest angle of the Township of Rawdon, till it intersects the northern limits of the province, together with all islands in the Ottawa River, wholly or in greater

part opposite thereto, do constitute and form the Midland District.

Frontenac. 1800. 40 Geo. III, C.3. An Act for the more equal Representation of the Commons of this Province in Parliament, and for the better defining the Qualification of Electors. . . . That from and after the end of the present Parliament, the representation of the Commons of this Province in the House of Assembly, shall be in manner and form following, that is to say: the Counties of Dundas, Grenville, Leeds, Frontenac, and Prince Edward, be each represented by one Member.

General Election July 1800.

| Glengary & Prescott | Alexander McDonell | May 28, 1801 | Sheriff of the Home District. |

Glengary & Prescott. 1798. 38 Geo. III, C.5, Ss.1, 4, 6. An Act for the better division of this Province. . . . and by the authority of the same, that the Townships of Lancaster, [a] Charlottenburg, and Kenyon, together with the tract of land claimed by the St. Regis Indians, and such of the islands in the river Saint Lawrence as are wholly or in greater part opposite thereto, shall constitute and form the County of Glengary. . . . And be it further enacted by the authority aforesaid, That the Townships of Hawkesbury, Longueil, with the tract of land in its rear, Alfred, and Plantagenet, with such of the islands in the Ottawa river as are wholly or in greater part opposite thereto, shall constitute and form the County of Prescott. . . . And be it further enacted by the authority aforesaid, That the Counties of Glengary, Stormont, Dundas, Prescott, and Russell, do constitute and form the Eastern District.

Glengary & Prescott. 1800. 40 Geo. III, C.3. An Act for the more equal Representation of the

Constituency	Member	Sworn In	Comments
Glengary & Prescott — *Continued*			Commons of this Province in Parliament, and for the better defining the Qualification of Electors. . . . That from and after the end of the present Parliament, the representation of the Commons of this Province in the House of Assembly, shall be in manner and form following, that is to say: the Counties of Glengary and Prescott, shall together be represented by two Members.
			General Election July 1800.
Glengary & Prescott	Angus Macdonell (Glengary)	May 28, 1801	Glengary & Prescott. 1798. 38 Geo. III, C.5, Ss.1, 4, 6. An Act for the better division of this Province. . . . and by the authority of the same, That the Townships of Lancaster, [a] Charlottenburg, and Kenyon, together with the tract of land claimed by the St. Regis Indians, and such of the islands in the river Saint Lawrence as are wholly or in greater part opposite thereto, shall constitute and form the County of Glengary. . . . And be it further enacted by the authority aforesaid, That the Townships of Hawkesbury, Longueil, with the tract of land in its rear, Alfred, and Plantagenet, with such of the islands in the Ottawa river as are wholly or in greater part opposite thereto, shall constitute and form the County of Prescott. . . . And be it further enacted by the authority aforesaid, That the Counties of Glengary, Stormont, Dundas, Prescott, and Russell, do constitute and form the Eastern District.
			Glengary & Prescott. 1800. 40 Geo. III, C.3. An Act for the more equal Representation of the Commons of this Province in Parliament, and for the better defining the Qualification of

			Electors. . . . That from and after the end of the present Parliament, the representation of the Commons of this Province in the House of Assembly, shall be in manner and form following, that is to say: the Counties of Glengary and Prescott, shall together be represented by two Members. General Election July 1800.
Grenville	Samuel Sherwood	May 28, 1801	Grenville. 1798. 38 Geo. III, C.5, Ss.6, 10. An Act for the better Division of this Province. And be it further enacted by the authority aforesaid, That the Townships of Edwardsburg, Augusta, Wolford, Oxford on the Rideau, Marlborough, Montague and Gower, called North and South Gower, together with such of the Islands in the River Saint Lawrence as are wholly or in greater part opposite thereto, shall constitute and form the County of Grenville. . . . And be it further enacted by the authority aforesaid, That the Counties of Grenville, Leeds, and Carleton, do constitute and form the District of Johnstown. Grenville. 1800. 40 Geo. III, C.3. An Act for the more equal Representation of the Commons of this Province in Parliament, and for the better defining the Qualification of Electors. . . . That from and after the end of the present Parliament, the representation of the Commons of this Province in the House of Assembly, shall be in manner and form following, that is to say: the Counties of Dundas, Grenville, Leeds, Frontenac, and Prince Edward, be each represented by one Member. General Election July 1800.
Hastings & Northumberland	David McGregor Rogers	May 28, 1801	Hastings & Northumberland. 1798. 38 Geo. III, C.5, Ss.16, 18, 19, 24, 25. An Act for the better Division of this Province. And be it further enacted by the authority aforesaid, that the Townships of Sydney, Thurlow, the tract of

Constituency	Member	Sworn In	Comments
Hastings & Northumberland — *Continued*			Land occupied by the Mohawks, Hungerford, Huntington and Rawdon, do constitute and form the County of Hastings. . . . And be it further enacted by the authority aforesaid, That the Townships of Murray, Cramahe, Haldimand, Hamilton, Elnwick, Percy, and Seymour, with the peninsula of Newcastle, do constitute and form the County of Northumberland. . . . Provided always, and it is hereby further enacted, That when and so soon as the said Counties of Northumberland and Durham shall make it satisfactorily appear to the governor, lieutenant governor, or person administering the government of this province, that there are one thousand souls within the said Counties, and that six of the Townships therein do hold town meetings according to law, [1802. 42 Geo. III, C.2], then the said Counties, with all the land in their rear, confined between their extreme boundaries, produced north sixteen degrees, West, until they intersect the northern limits of the province, shall, and are hereby declared to be, a separate District to be called the District of Newcastle.
			Hastings & Northumberland. 1800. 40 Geo. III, C.3. An Act for the more equal Representation of the Commons of this Province in Parliament, and for the better defining the Qualification of Electors. . . . That from and after the end of the present Parliament, the representation of the Commons of this Province in the House of Assembly, shall be in manner and form following, that is to say: the Counties of Hastings and Northumberland, be together represented by one Member.
			General Election July 1800.

Kent	Thomas McCrae	May 28, 1801	Kent. 1798. 38 Geo. III, C.5, Ss.38, 40. An Act for the better Division of this Province. And be it further enacted by the authority aforesaid, that the Townships of Dover, Chatham, Camden, distinguished by being called Camden West, the Moravian tract of Land, called Orford, distinguished by Orford north and south, Howard, Harwich, Raleigh, Romney, Tilbury, divided into the east and west, with the Township on the river Sainclair, occupied by the Shawney Indians, together with the islands in the Lakes Erie and Sinclair wholly or in greater part opposite thereto, do constitute and form the County of Kent. . . . And be it further enacted by the authority aforesaid, That the Counties of Essex and Kent, together with so much of this province as is not included within any other District thereof, do constitute and form the Western District.
			General Election July 1800.
Leeds	William Buell, Sr.	May 28, 1801	Leeds. 1798. 38 Geo. III, C.5, Ss.7, 10. An Act for the better Division of this Province. And be it further enacted by the authority aforesaid, that the Townships of Elizabeth-Town, Yonge, (including what was formerly called Escot) Lansdown, Leeds, Crosby, Bastard, Burgess, Elmsley, and Kitley, together with such of the Islands in the River Saint Lawrence as are wholly, or in greater part opposite thereto, do constitute and form the County of Leeds. . . . And be it further enacted by the authority aforesaid, That the Counties of Grenville, Leeds, and Carleton, do constitute and form the District of Johnstown.
			Leeds. 1800. 40 Geo. III, C.3. An Act for the more equal Representation of the Commons of this Province in Parliament, and for the better defining the Qualification of Electors. . . . That from and after the end of the present

Constituency	Member	Sworn In	Comments
Leeds — *Continued*			Parliament, the representation of the Commons of this Province in the House of Assembly, shall be in manner and form following, that is to say: the Counties of Dundas, Grenville, Leeds, Frontenac, and Prince Edward, be each represented by one Member.
			General Election July 1800.
Lenox & Addington	Timothy Thompson	May 28, 1801	Lenox & Addington. 1798. 38 Geo. III, C.5, Ss.15, 18. An Act for the better Division of this Province. And be it further enacted by the authority aforesaid, That the Townships of Ernest-Town, Fredericksburg, Adolphustown, Richmond, Camden, (distinguished by being called Camden East,) Amherst Island, and Sheffield, do constitute and form the incorporated Counties of Lenox & Addington. . . . And be it further enacted by the authority aforesaid, That the Counties of Frontenac, the incorporated Counties of Lenox and Addington, Hastings, and Prince Edward, with all that tract of Country which lies between the District of Johnstown and a line drawn north sixteen degrees West from the northwest angle of the Township of Rawdon, till it intersects the northern limits of the province, together with all islands in the Ottawa River, wholly or in greater part opposite thereto, do constitute and form the Midland District.
			Lenox & Addington. 1800. 40 Geo. III, C.3. An Act for the more equal Representation of the Commons of this Province in Parliament, and for the better defining the Qualification of Electors. . . . That from and after the end of the present Parliament, the representation of the Commons of this Province in the House of

Lincoln, 1st R. – See York West, Lincoln, 1st R. & Haldimand

Lincoln, 2nd, 3rd & 4th R.   Ralph Clench   May 28, 1801

Assembly, shall be in manner and form following, that is to say: the incorporated Counties of Lenox and Addington, be together represented by one Member.

General Election July 1800.

Also listed as Ralfe or Ralf.

Lincoln, 2nd, 3rd & 4th R. 1798. 38 Geo. III, C.5, Ss.27, 29, 31. An Act for the better Division of this Province. And be it further enacted by the authority aforesaid, That the Townships of Newark, Grantham and Louth, do constitute and form the second Riding of the County of Lincoln; Provided always, that the Town and Township of Newark, now generally called West Niagara, be henceforth declared and called the Town and Township of Niagara respectively. . . . And be it further enacted by the authority aforesaid, That the Townships of Stamford, Thorold and Pelham, do constitute and form the third Riding of the County of Lincoln. . . . And be it further enacted by the authority aforesaid, That the Townships of Bertie, Willoughby, Crowland, Humberstone, and Wainfleet, do constitute and form the fourth Riding of the County of Lincoln.

Lincoln, 2nd, 3rd & 4th R. 1800. 40 Geo. III, C.3. An Act for the more equal Representation of the Commons of this Province in Parliament, and for the better defining the Qualification of Electors. . . . That from and after the end of the present Parliament, the representation of the Commons of this Province in the House of Assembly, shall be in manner and form following, that is to say: the second, third and fourth Ridings of the County of Lincoln, be together represented by two Members.

General Election July 1800.

Constituency	Member	Sworn In	Comments
Lincoln, 2nd, 3rd, & 4th R.	Isaac Swayze	May 28, 1801	Lincoln, 2nd, 3rd & 4th R. 1798. 38 Geo. III, C.5, Ss.27, 29, 30. An Act for the better Division of this Province. And be it further enacted by the authority aforesaid, That the Townships of Newark, Grantham and Louth, do constitute and form the second Riding of the County of Lincoln; Provided always, that the Town and Township of Newark, now generally called West Niagara, be henceforth declared and called the Town and Township of Niagara respectively. . . . And be it further enacted by the authority aforesaid, That the Townships of Stamford, Thorold and Pelham, do constitute and form the third Riding of the County of Lincoln. . . . And be it further enacted by the authority aforesaid, That the Townships of Bertie, Willoughby, Crowland, Humberstone, and Wainfleet, do constitute and form the fourth Riding of the County of Lincoln.
			1800. 40 Geo. III, C.3. An Act for the more equal Representation of the Commons of this Province in Parliament, and for the better defining the Qualification of Electors. . . . That from and after the end of the present Parliament, the representation of the Commons of this Province in the House of Assembly, shall be in manner and form following, that is to say: the second, third and fourth Ridings of the County of Lincoln, be together represented by two Members.
			General Election July 1800.
Oxford, Middlesex & Norfolk	Hon. David William Smith	May 28, 1801	Oxford, Middlesex & Norfolk. 1798. 38 Geo. III, C.5, Ss.35, 36, 33. An Act for the better Division of this Province. And be it further enacted by the authority aforesaid, That the

Townships of Rainham, Walpole, Woodhouse, Charlotteville, Walsingham, Houghton, Middleton, Windham, and Townsend, together with Turkey Point, and Promontory of Long Point, do constitute and form the County of Norfolk. . . . And be it further enacted by the authority aforesaid, That the Townships of Burford, Norwich, Dereham, Oxford upon the Thames, Blanford, and Blenheim, do constitute and form the County of Oxford. . . . And be it further enacted by the authority aforesaid, That the Townships of London, Westminster, Dorchester, Yarmouth, Southwold, Dunwich, Alborough, and Delaware, do constitute and form the County of Middlesex.

Oxford, Middlesex & Norfolk. 1800. 40 Geo. III, C.3. An Act for the more equal Representation of the Commons of this Province in Parliament, and for the better defining the Qualification of Electors. . . . That from and after the end of the present Parliament, the representation of the Commons of this Province in the House of Assembly, shall be in manner and form following, that is to say: The Counties of Oxford, Middlesex, and Norfolk, shall together be represented by one Member.

General Election July 1800.

On May 28, 1801, David McGregor Rogers, MPP, Northumberland & Hastings, proposed David William Smith, MPP, Oxford, Middlesex & Norfolk, as Speaker. Seconded and resolved. May 28, 1801 – Date took chair.

On Jan. 27, 1803, the House was informed of the absence from the Country of the Speaker, the Hon. David William Smith, MPP, Oxford, Middlesex & Norfolk. A new Speaker was to be chosen.

Prince Edward   Ebenezer Washburn   May 28, 1801

Prince Edward. 1798. 38 Geo. III, C.5, Ss.17, 18. An Act for the better Division of this

Constituency	Member	Sworn In	Comments
Prince Edward — *Continued*			Province. And be it further enacted by the authority aforesaid, That the Townships of Ameliasburg, Hallowell, Sophiasburg, and Marysburg, with such of the Islands in the Bay of Quinty and Lake Ontario, as are wholly, or in greater part opposite thereto, and such as were not formerly included in the County of Ontario, do constitute and form the County of Prince Edward. . . . And be it further enacted by the authority aforesaid, That the Counties of Frontenac, the incorporated Counties of Lenox and Addington, Hastings, and Prince Edward, with all that tract of Country which lies between the District of Johnstown and a line drawn north sixteen degrees West from the northwest angle of the Township of Rawdon, till it intersects the northern limits of the province, together with all islands in the Ottawa River, wholly or in greater part opposite thereto, do constitute and form the Midland District.
			Prince Edward. 1800. 40 Geo. III, C.3. An Act for the more equal Representation of the Commons of this Province in Parliament, and for the better defining the Qualification of Electors. . . . That from and after the end of the present Parliament, the representation of the Commons of this Province in the House of Assembly, shall be in manner and form following, that is to say: the Counties of Dundas, Grenville, Leeds, Frontenac, and Prince Edward, be each represented by one Member.
			General Election July 1800.
Stormont & Russell	Robert Isaac Dey Gray	May 28, 1801	Mr. Solicitor General.

Stormont & Russell. 1798. 38 Geo. III, C.5, Ss.2, 6. An Act for the better Division of this Province. And be it further enacted by the authority aforesaid, That the Townships of Cornwall, Osnaburg, Finch, and Roxburg, together with such of the islands in the river Saint Lawrence as are wholly or in greater part opposite thereto, shall constitute and form the County of Stormont. . . . And be it further enacted by the authority aforesaid, That the Townships of Clarence, Cumberland, Gloucester, Osgoode, Russell, and Cambridge, with such of the islands in the river Ottawa as are wholly or in greater part opposite thereto, shall constitute and form the County of Russell. . . . And be it further enacted by the authority aforesaid, That the Counties of Glengary, Stormont, Dundas, Prescott, and Russell, do constitute and form the Eastern District.

Stormont & Russell. 1800. 40 Geo. III, C.3. An Act for the more equal Representation of the Commons of this Province in Parliament, and for the better defining the Qualification of Electors. . . . That from and after the end of the present Parliament, the representation of the Commons of this Province in the House of Assembly, shall be in manner and form following, that is to say: The Counties of Stormont and Russell, shall together be represented by one Member.

General Election July 1800.

York West, Lincoln, 1st R., & Haldimand	Hon. Richard Beasley	May 28, 1801	York West, Lincoln, 1st R., & Haldimand. 1798. 38 Geo. III, C.5, Ss.22, 26, 27, 31. An Act for the better Division of this Province. And be it further enacted by the authority aforesaid, That the Townships of·Beverly and Flamborough, the latter divided into Flamborough East and West, so much of the tract of land upon the Grand River in the occupation of the Six Nation Indians, as lies to the northward of Dundas

Constituency	Member	Sworn In	Comments
York West, Lincoln, 1st R., & Haldimand — *Continued*			Street, and all the land between the said tract and the East Riding of the County of York, with the reserved lands in the rear of the Townships of Blenheim and Blanford, do constitute and form the west Riding of the County of York. . . . And be it further enacted by the authority aforesaid, That the Counties of Northumberland, Durham, York, and Simcoe, do constitute and form the Home District. . . . And be it further enacted by the authority aforesaid, That the Townships of Clinton, Grimsby, Saltfleet, Barton, Ancaster, Glanford, Binbrook, Gainsborough, and Caistor, do constitute and form the First Riding of the County of Lincoln. . . . And be it further enacted by the authority aforesaid, That so much of the Townships of Glandford as is now comprehended between the southern boundary of the Township of Binbrook, and the boundary of the Six Nation Indians' land, be added to the said Township of Binbrook, and become part thereof. . . . And be it further enacted by the authority aforesaid, That the tract of land on each side of the Grand River, now in the occupation of the Six Nation Indians, and laying to the southward and southeast of Dundas Street, do constitute and form the County of Haldimand.
			York West, Lincoln, 1st R. & Haldimand. 1800. 40 Geo. III, C.3. An Act for the more equal Representation of the Commons of this Province in Parliament, and for the better defining the Qualification of Electors. . . . That from and after the end of the present Parliament, the representation of the Commons of this Province in the House of Assembly,

shall be in manner and form following, that is to say: The West Riding of the County of York, the first Riding of the County of Lincoln, and the County of Haldimand, be together represented by two Members.

General Election July 1800.

On Jan. 27, 1803, John Ferguson, MPP, Frontenac, proposed Richard Beasley, MPP, York West, Lincoln, 1st R. & Haldimand, as Speaker, in room of the Hon. David William Smith, MPP, Oxford, Middlesex & Norfolk, in absentia. Seconded and resolved. Jan. 27, 1803 – Date took chair.

York West, Lincoln, 1st R. & Haldimand	Robert Nelles	May 28, 1801

Also listed as Nellis.

York West, Lincoln, 1st R. & Haldimand. 1798. 38 Geo. III, C.5, Ss.22, 26, 27, 31. An Act for the better Division of this Province. And be it further enacted by the authority aforesaid, That the Townships of Beverly and Flamborough, the latter divided into Flamborough East and West, so much of the tract of land upon the Grand River in the occupation of the Six Nation Indians, as lies to the northward of Dundas Street, and all the land between the said tract and the East Riding of the County of York, with the reserved lands in the rear of the Townships of Blenheim and Blanford, do constitute and form the west Riding of the County of York. . . . And be it further enacted by the authority aforesaid, That the Counties of Northumberland, Durham, York, and Simcoe, do constitute and form the Home District. . . . And be it further enacted by the authority aforesaid, That the Townships of Clinton, Grimsby, Saltfleet, Barton, Ancaster, Glanford, Binbrook, Gainsborough, and Caistor, do constitute and form the First Riding of the County of Lincoln. . . . And be it further

Constituency	Member	Sworn In	Comments
York West, Lincoln, 1st R. & Haldimand — *Continued*			enacted by the authority aforesaid, That so much of the Townships of Glandford as is now comprehended between the southern boundary of the Township of Binbrook, and the boundary of the Six Nation Indians' land, be added to the said Township of Binbrook, and become part thereof. And be it further enacted by the authority aforesaid, That the tract of land on each side of the Grand River, now in the occupation of the Six Nation Indians, and laying to the southward and southeast of Dundas Street, do constitute and form the County of Haldimand. . . . And be it further enacted by the authority aforesaid, That so much of the Townships of Glandford as is now comprehended between the southern boundary of the Township of Binbrook, and the boundary of the Six Nation Indians' land, be added to the said Township of Binbrook, and become part thereof. . . . And be it further enacted by the authority aforesaid, That the tract of land on each side of the Grand River, now in the occupation of the Six Nation Indians, and laying to the southward and southeast of Dundas Street, do constitute and form the County of Haldimand.
			York West, Lincoln, 1st R. & Haldimand. 1800. 40 Geo. III, C.3. An Act for the more equal Representation of the Commons of this Province in Parliament, and for the better defining the Qualification of Electors. . . . That from and after the end of the present Parliament, the representation of the Commons of this Province in the House of Assembly, shall be in manner and form following, that is to say: The West Riding of the County of York,

the first Riding of the County of Lincoln, and the County of Haldimand, be together represented by two Members.

General Election July 1800.

LEGISLATURES OF UPPER CANADA
4th Legislature

General Election   May 1804

Sessions of the Fourth Legislature of Upper Canada: Feb. 1, 1805 – Mar. 16, 1808

First:	Feb. 1, 1805 – Mar. 2, 1805.
Second:	Feb. 4, 1806 – Mar. 3, 1806.
Third:	Feb. 2, 1807 – Mar. 10, 1807.
Fourth:	Jan. 20, 1808 – Mar. 16, 1808.

Alphabetical List of Members

Member	Constituency	Sworn In	Comments
D'Arcy Boulton	Stormont & Russell	Feb. 5, 1806*	Mr. Solicitor General. On Feb. 5, 1806, the House was informed of the election of D'Arcy Boulton, MPP, Stormont & Russell, in room of Robert Isaac Dey Gray, deceased.
Ralph Clench	Lincoln, 2nd, 3rd & 4th R.	Feb. 1, 1805	
David Cowan	Essex	Feb. 1, 1805	
John Crysler	Dundas	Feb. 1, 1805	
Thomas Dorland	Lenox & Addington	Feb. 1, 1805	
Mathew Elliott	Essex	Feb. 1, 1805	
Robert Isaac Dey Gray	Stormont & Russell	Did not take seat	Mr. Solicitor General. Drowned, Oct. 1804, in the shipwreck of *The Speedy*, off Presqu'ile. A new election was called.
Solomon Hill	York West, Lincoln, 1st R. & Haldimand	Feb. 1, 1805	Died, Aug. 30, 1807. A new election was called.
Peter Howard	Leeds	Feb. 1, 1805	

Angus Macdonell	Durham, York East & Simcoe	Did not take seat	Drowned, Oct. 1804, in the shipwreck of *The Speedy*, off Presqu'ile. A new election was called.
Benajah Mallory	Oxford, Middlesex & Norfolk	Feb. 1, 1805	
Hon. Alexander McDonell	Glengary & Prescott	Feb. 1, 1805	On Feb. 1, 1805, Ralph Clench, MPP, Lincoln, 2nd, 3rd & 4th R., proposed Alexander McDonell, MPP, Glengary & Prescott, as Speaker. Seconded and resolved. Feb. 1, 1805 – Date took chair.
John McGregor	Kent	Feb. 1, 1805	
Allan McLean	Frontenac	Feb. 1, 1805	
Robert Nelles	York West, Lincoln, 1st R. & Haldimand	Feb. 1, 1805	
David McGregor Rogers	Hastings & Northumberland	Feb. 1, 1805	
Samuel Sherwood	Grenville	Feb. 1, 1805	
Isaac Swayze	Lincoln, 2nd, 3rd & 4th R.	Feb. 1, 1805	
Robert Thorpe	Durham, York East & Simcoe	Feb. 3, 1807*	Mr. Justice. On Feb. 2, 1807, the House was informed of the election of Robert Thorpe, MPP, Durham, York East & Simcoe, in room of William Weekes, deceased.
Ebenezer Washburn	Prince Edward	Feb. 1, 1805	
William Weekes	Durham, York East & Simcoe	Feb. 27, 1805*	On Feb. 27, 1805, the House was informed of the election of William Weekes, MPP, Durham, York East & Simcoe, in room of Angus Macdonell, deceased. Killed in a duel with William Dickson, Oct. 10, 1806 at Fort Niagara. A new election was called.

*   By-election

Member	Constituency	Sworn In	Comments
Walter Butler Wilkinson	Glengary & Prescott	Feb. 1, 1805	
Joseph Willcocks	York West, Lincoln, 1st. R. & Haldimand	Jan. 26, 1808*	On Jan. 26, 1808, the House was informed of the election of Joseph Willcocks, MPP, York West, Lincoln, 1st R. & Haldimand, in room of Solomon Hill, deceased.
			On Feb. 20, 1808, Joseph Willcocks, MPP, York West, Lincoln, 1st R. & Haldimand, was placed in the Common Gaol of the Home District, having been convicted of contempt of the House of Assembly. On Mar. 16, 1808, Willcocks was ordered discharged from the Gaol.

*   By-election

Alphabetical List of Constituencies
4th Legislature: Feb. 1, 1805 – Mar. 16, 1808.

27

Constituency	Member	Sworn In	Comments
Dundas	John Crysler	Feb. 1, 1805	General Election May 1804.
			Dundas. 1808. 48 Geo. III, C.11, S.2. An Act for the better Representation of the Commons of this Province in Parliament, and to repeat part of an act passed in the fortieth year of his Majesty's reign, entitled, an act for the more equal representation of the Commons of this Province, and for the better defining the Qualification of Electors. And be it further enacted by the authority aforesaid, That from and after the end of the present Parliament, the representation of the Commons of this Province in the House of Assembly, shall be in manner and form following, that is to say: That the Counties of Dundas, Grenville, Leeds, Frontenac and Prince Edward, except the Township of Ameliasburgh, be each represented by one member.
Durham, York East & Simcoe	Angus Macdonell	Did not take seat	General Election May 1804.
			Drowned, Oct. 1804, in the shipwreck of *The Speedy*, off Presqu'ile. A new election was called.
Durham, York East & Simcoe	William Weekes	Feb. 27, 1805*	By-election Date unknown.
			On Feb. 27, 1805, the House was informed of the election of William Weekes, MPP, Durham, York East & Simcoe, in room of Angus Macdonell, deceased.
			Killed in a duel with William Dickson, Oct. 10, 1806 at Fort Niagara. A new election was called.
Durham, York East & Simcoe	Robert Thorpe	Feb. 3, 1807*	Mr. Justice.

By-election Date unknown.

On Feb. 2, 1807, the House was informed of the election of Robert Thorpe, MPP, Durham, York East & Simcoe, in room of William Weekes, deceased.

Essex	David Cowan	Feb. 1, 1805	General Election May 1804.

Essex. 1808. 48 Geo. III, C.11, S.2. An Act for the better Representation of the Commons of this Province in Parliament, and to repeat part of an act passed in the fortieth year of his Majesty's reign, entitled, an act for the more equal representation of the Commons of this Province, and for the better defining the Qualification of Electors. And be it further enacted by the authority aforesaid, That from and after the end of the present Parliament, the representation of the Commons of this Province in the House of Assembly, shall be in manner and form following, that is to say: That the County of Essex, shall be represented by two members.

Essex	Mathew Elliott	Feb. 1, 1805	General Election May 1804.

Essex. 1808. 48 Geo. III, C.11, S.2. An Act for the better Representation of the Commons of this Province in Parliament, and to repeat part of an act passed in the fortieth year of his Majesty's reign, entitled, an act for the more equal representation of the Commons of this Province, and for the better defining the Qualification of Electors. And be it further enacted by the authority aforesaid, That from and after the end of the present Parliament, the representation of the Commons of this Province in the House of Assembly, shall be in manner and form following, that is to say: That

*   By-election

Constituency	Member	Sworn In	Comments
Essex — *Continued*			the County of Essex, shall be represented by two members.
Frontenac	Allan McLean	Feb. 1, 1805	General Election May 1804.
			Frontenac. 1808. 48 Geo. III, C.11, S.2. An Act for the better Representation of the Commons of this Province in Parliament, and to repeat part of an act passed in the fortieth year of his Majesty's reign, entitled, an act for the more equal representation of the Commons of this Province, and for the better defining the Qualification of Electors. And be it further enacted by the authority aforesaid, That from and after the end of the present Parliament, the representation of the Commons of this Province in the House of Assembly, shall be in manner and form following, that is to say: That the Counties of Dundas, Grenville, Leeds, Frontenac and Prince Edward, except the Township of Ameliasburgh, be each represented by one member.
Glengary & Prescott	Hon. Alexander McDonell	Feb. 1, 1805	General Election May 1804.
			On Feb. 1, 1805, Ralph Clench, MPP, Lincoln, 2nd, 3rd & 4th R., proposed Alexander McDonell, MPP, Glengary & Prescott, as Speaker. Seconded and resolved. Feb. 1, 1805 – Date took chair.
Glengary & Prescott	Walter Butler Wilkinson	Feb. 1, 1805	General Election May 1804.
Grenville	Samuel Sherwood	Feb. 1, 1805	General Election May 1804.
			Grenville. 1808. 48 Geo. III, C.11, S.2. An Act for the better Representation of the Commons of this Province in Parliament, and to repeat part of an act passed in the fortieth year of his Majesty's reign, entitled, an act for the more

equal representation of the Commons of this Province, and for the better defining the Qualification of Electors. And be it further enacted by the authority aforesaid, That from and after the end of the present Parliament, the representation of the Commons of this Province in the House of Assembly, shall be in manner and form following, that is to say: That the Counties of Dundas, Grenville, Leeds, Frontenac and Prince Edward, except the Township of Ameliasburgh, be each represented by one member.

Hastings & Northumberland	David McGregor Rogers	Feb. 1, 1805	General Election May 1804.
Kent	John McGregor	Feb. 1, 1805	General Election May 1804.

Kent. 1808. 48 Geo. III, C.11, S.2. An Act for the better Representation of the Commons of this Province in Parliament, and to repeat part of an act passed in the fortieth year of his Majesty's reign, entitled, an act for the more equal representation of the Commons of this Province, and for the better defining the Qualification of Electors. And be it further enacted by the authority aforesaid, That from and after the end of the present Parliament, the representation of the Commons of this Province in the House of Assembly, shall be in manner and form following, that is to say: That the County of Kent shall be represented by one member.

Leeds	Peter Howard	Feb. 1, 1805	General Election May 1804.

Leeds. 1808. 48 Geo. III, C.11, S.2. An Act for the better Representation of the Commons of this Province in Parliament, and to repeat part of an act passed in the fortieth year of his Majesty's reign, entitled, an act for the more equal representation of the Commons of this Province, and for the better defining the Qualification of Electors. And be it further enacted by the authority aforesaid, That from

Constituency	Member	Sworn In	Comments
Leeds — *Continued*			and after the end of the present Parliament, the representation of the Commons of this Province in the House of Assembly, shall be in manner and form following, that is to say: That the Counties of Dundas, Grenville, Leeds, Frontenac and Prince Edward, except the Township of Ameliasburgh, be each represented by one member.
Lenox & Addington	Thomas Dorland	Feb. 1, 1805	General Election May 1804.
			Lenox & Addington. 1808. 48 Geo. III, C.11, S.2. An Act for the better Representation of the Commons of this Province in Parliament, and to repeat part of an act passed in the fortieth year of his Majesty's reign, entitled, an act for the more equal representation of the Commons of this Province, and for the better defining the Qualification of Electors. And be it further enacted by the authority aforesaid, That from and after the end of the present Parliament, the representation of the Commons of this Province in the House of Assembly, shall be in manner and form following, that is to say: That the incorporated Counties of Lenox and Addington, be together represented by two members.
Lincoln, 1st R. – See York West, Lincoln, 1st R. & Haldimand			
Lincoln, 2nd, 3rd & 4th R.	Ralph Clench	Feb. 1, 1805	General Election May 1804.
Lincoln, 2nd, 3rd & 4th R.	Isaac Swayze	Feb. 1, 1805	General Election May 1804.
Oxford, Middlesex & Norfolk	Benajah Mallory	Feb. 1, 1805	General Election May 1804.
Prince Edward	Ebenezer Washburn	Feb. 1, 1805	General Election May 1804.
			Prince Edward. 1808. 48 Geo. III, C.11, S.2. An Act for the better Representation of the

Commons of this Province in Parliament, and to repeat part of an act passed in the fortieth year of his Majesty's reign, entitled, an act for the more equal representation of the Commons of this Province, and for the better defining the Qualification of Electors. And be it further enacted by the authority aforesaid, That from and after the end of the present Parliament, the representation of the Commons of this Province in the House of Assembly, shall be in manner and form following, that is to say: That the Counties of Dundas, Grenville, Leeds, Frontenac and Prince Edward, except the Township of Ameliasburgh, be each represented by one member.

Stormont & Russell	Robert Isaac Dey Gray	Did not take seat	Mr. Solicitor General.

General Election May 1804.

Drowned, Oct. 1804, in the shipwreck of *The Speedy*, off Presqu'ile. A new election was called.

Stormont & Russell	D'Arcy Boulton	Feb. 5, 1806*	Mr. Solicitor General.

By-election Date unknown.

On Feb. 5, 1806, the House was informed of the election of D'Arcy Boulton, MPP, Stormont & Russell, in room of Robert Isaac Dey Gray, deceased.

Stormont & Russell. 1808. 48 Geo. III, C.11, S.2. An Act for the better Representation of the Commons of this Province in Parliament, and to repeat part of an act passed in the fortieth year of his Majesty's reign, entitled, an act for the more equal representation of the Commons of this Province, and for the better defining the Qualification of Electors. And be it further enacted by the authority aforesaid, That from

* By-election

Constituency	Member	Sworn In	Comments
Stormont & Russell — *Continued*			and after the end of the present Parliament, the representation of the Commons of this Province in the House of Assembly, shall be in manner and form following, that is to say: That the Counties of Stormont and Russell shall be represented by one member.
York West, Lincoln, 1st R. & Haldimand	Solomon Hill	Feb. 1, 1805	General Election May 1804. Died, Aug. 30, 1807. A new election was called.
York West, Lincoln, 1st. R. & Haldimand	Joseph Willcocks	Jan. 26, 1808*	By-election Date unknown. On Jan. 26, 1808, the House was informed of the election of Joseph Willcocks, MPP, York West, Lincoln, 1st R. & Haldimand, in room of Solomon Hill, deceased. On Feb. 20, 1808, Joseph Willcocks, MPP, York West, Lincoln, 1st R. & Haldimand, was placed in the Common Gaol of the Home District, having been convicted of contempt of the House of Assembly. On Mar. 16, 1808, Willcocks was ordered discharged from the Gaol.
York West, Lincoln, 1st R. & Haldimand	Robert Nelles	Feb. 1, 1805	General Election May 1804.

*   By-election

LEGISLATURES OF UPPER CANADA
5th Legislature

General Election   May 1808

Sessions of the Fifth Legislature of Upper Canada: Feb. 2, 1809 – Mar. 6, 1812

First:	Feb. 2, 1809 – Mar. 9, 1809.
Second:	Feb. 1, 1810 – Mar. 12, 1810.
Third:	Feb. 1, 1811 – Mar. 13, 1811.
Fourth:	Feb. 3, 1812 – Mar. 6, 1812.

Alphabetical List of Members

Member	Constituency	Sworn In†	Comments
Jean Baptiste Baby	Essex	Feb. 2, 1809	
Richard Beasley	York West	Feb. 2, 1809	In 1809, the election of Richard Beasley, MPP, York West, was declared void. A new election was called.
John Brownell	Stormont & Russell	Did not take seat	Died, Dec. 27, 1808. A new election was called.
Stephen Burritt	Grenville	Feb. 2, 1809	
Willet Casey	Lenox & Addington	Feb. 1, 1811*	On Feb. 1, 1811, the House was informed of the election of Willet Casey, MPP, Lenox & Addington, in room of John Roblin, whose election was declared void.
Thomas Dorland	Lenox & Addington	Feb. 2, 1809	
Mathew Elliott	Essex	Feb. 2, 1809	
Thomas Fraser	Glengary	Feb. 2, 1809	
Thomas Barnes Gough	York East & Simcoe	Feb. 2, 1809	
Peter Howard	Leeds	Feb. 2, 1809	
Levi Lewis	Lincoln, 1st R. & Haldimand	Feb. 2, 1809	

Benajah Mallory	Oxford & Middlesex	Feb. 1, 1810	Absent first Session.
Henry Markle	Dundas	Feb. 1, 1810	Also listed as Marcle or Merkley. Absent first Session.
Abraham Marsh	Stormont & Russell	Feb. 1, 1811*	Writ of Election – Feb. 2, 1810. On Feb. 1, 1811, the House was informed of the election of Abraham Marsh, MPP, Stormont & Russell, in room of John Brownell, deceased.
Alexander McDonell	Glengary	Feb. 2, 1809	
John McGregor	Kent	Feb. 2, 1809	
Allan McLean	Frontenac	Feb. 2, 1809	
James McNabb	Hastings & Ameliasburgh (Twp.)	Feb. 2, 1809	
Thomas Mears	Prescott	Feb. 2, 1809	
John Roblin	Lenox & Addington	Feb. 2, 1809	On Mar. 7, 1810, the election of John Roblin, MPP, Lenox & Addington, was declared void. A new election was called.
David McGregor Rogers	Northumberland & Durham	Feb. 2, 1809	
David Secord	Lincoln, 2nd R.	Feb. 2, 1809	
Philip Sovereign	Norfolk	Feb. 2, 1809	
John Stinson	Prince Edward (except Ameliasburgh, Twp.)	Feb. 1, 1811*	On Feb. 1, 1811, the House was informed of the election of John Stinson, MPP, Prince Edward (except Ameliasburgh, Twp.), in room of James Willson, whose election was declared void.
Hon. Samuel Street	Lincoln, 3rd R.	Feb. 2, 1809	The Journals for the year 1809 are not known to be in existence. As the practice has been to swear in the new Speaker on the first day of the first Session, the date Feb. 2, 1809 has

† The Journals for the year 1809 are not known to be in existence. As the practice has been to swear in new Members on the first day of the first Session, the date Feb. 2, 1809 has been given as the date the Members took their seats in the 5th Parliament.

* By-election

Member	Constituency	Sworn In	Comments
Hon. Samuel Street — *Continued*			been given as the date the Hon. Samuel Street, MPP, Lincoln, 3rd R., took the chair.
			On Feb. 2, 1809, Samuel Street, MPP, Lincoln, 3rd R., was proposed as Speaker. Seconded and resolved. Feb. 2, 1809 – Date took chair.
Joseph Willcocks	Lincoln, 1st R., & Haldimand	Feb. 2, 1809	
James Willson	Prince Edward (except Ameliasburgh, Twp.)	Feb. 2, 1809	Also listed as Wilson.
			On Mar. 3, 1810, the election of James Willson, MPP, Prince Edward (except Ameliasburgh, Twp.) was declared void. A new election was called.
John Willson	York West	Feb. 1, 1810*	Also listed as Wilson.
			On Feb. 1, 1810, the House was informed of the election of John Willson, MPP, York West, in room of Richard Beasley, whose election was declared void.
Crowel Wilson	Lincoln, 4th R.	Feb. 2, 1809	Also listed as Willson.

* By-election

Constituency	Member	Sworn In†	Comments
Dundas	Henry Markle	Feb. 1, 1810	Also listed as Marcle or Merkley. General Election May 1808. Absent first Session.
Essex	Jean Baptiste Baby	Feb. 2, 1809	General Election May 1808.
Essex	Mathew Elliott	Feb. 2, 1809	General Election May 1808.
Frontenac	Allan McLean	Feb. 2, 1809	General Election May 1808.
Glengary	Alexander McDonell	Feb. 2, 1809	Glengary. 1808. 48 Geo. III, C.11, S.2. An Act for the better Representation of the Commons of this Province in Parliament, and to repeat part of an act passed in the fortieth year of his Majesty's reign, entitled, an act for the more equal representation of the Commons of this Province, and for the better defining the Qualification of Electors. And be it further enacted by the authority aforesaid, That from and after the end of the present Parliament, the representation of the Commons of this Province in the House of Assembly, shall be in manner and form following, that is to say: That the County of Glengary shall be represented by two members. General Election May 1808.
Glengary	Thomas Fraser	Feb. 2, 1809	Glengary. 1808. 48 Geo. III, C.11, S.2. An Act for the better Representation of the Commons of this Province in Parliament, and to repeat part of an act passed in the fortieth year of his Majesty's reign, entitled, an act for the more equal representation of the Commons of this Province, and for the better defining the Qualification of Electors. And be it further enacted by the authority aforesaid, That from and after the end of the present Parliament,

the representation of the Commons of this Province in the House of Assembly, shall be in manner and form following, that is to say: That the County of Glengary shall be represented by two members.

General Election May 1808.

Grenville	Stephen Burritt	Feb. 2, 1809	General Election May 1808.
Hastings & Ameliasburgh (Twp.)	James McNabb	Feb. 2, 1809	Hastings & Ameliasburgh (Twp.). 1808. 48 Geo. III, C.11, S.2. An Act for the better Representation of the Commons of this Province in Parliament, and to repeat part of an act passed in the fortieth year of his Majesty's reign, entitled, an act for the more equal representation of the Commons of this Province, and for the better defining the Qualification of Electors. And be it further enacted by the authority aforesaid, That from and after the end of the present Parliament, the representation of the Commons of this Province in the House of Assembly, shall be in manner and form following, that is to say: That the County of Hastings, and the Township of Ameliasburgh, in the County of Prince Edward, be represented by one member. General Election May 1808.
Kent	John McGregor	Feb. 2, 1809	General Election May 1808.
Leeds	Peter Howard	Feb. 2, 1809	General Election May 1808.
Lenox & Addington	Thomas Dorland	Feb. 2, 1809	General Election May 1808.
Lenox & Addington	John Roblin	Feb. 2, 1809	General Election May 1808. On Mar. 7, 1810, the election of John Roblin, MPP, Lenox & Addington, was declared void. A new election was called.
Lenox & Addington	Willet Casey	Feb. 1, 1811*	By-election Date unknown.

* By-election

† The Journals for the year 1809 are not known to be in existence. As the practice has been to swear in new Members on the first day of the first Session, the date Feb. 2, 1809 has been given as the date the Members took their seats in the 5th Parliament.

Constituency	Member	Sworn In	Comments
Lenox & Addington — *Continued*			On Feb. 1, 1811, the House was informed of the election of Willet Casey, MPP, Lenox & Addington, in room of John Roblin, whose election was declared void.
Lincoln, 1st R. & Haldimand	Levi Lewis	Feb. 2, 1809	Lincoln, 1st R. & Haldimand. 1808. 48 Geo. III, C.11, S.2. An Act for the better Representation of the Commons of this Province in Parliament, and to repeat part of an act passed in the fortieth year of his Majesty's reign, entitled, an act for the more equal representation of the Commons of this Province, and for the better defining the Qualification of Electors. And be it further enacted by the authority aforesaid, That from and after the end of the present Parliament, the representation of the Commons of this Province in the House of Assembly, shall be in manner and form following, that is to say: that the first riding of the County of Lincoln and the County of Haldimand shall be represented by two members, in manner following, viz. the Townships of Saltfleet, Ancaster, Barton, Glanford and Binbrook, with so much of the County of Haldimand as lies between Dundas Street and the Onondaga Village, (commonly call Bearsfoot) on the River Ouse, by one member, and the Townships of Grimsby, Clinton, Gainsborough and Caistor, with so much of the County of Haldimand as lies between the Onondaga Village aforesaid and the mouth of the River Ouse, by one member. General Election May 1808.
Lincoln, 1st R., & Haldimand	Joseph Willcocks	Feb. 2, 1809	General Election May 1808.

Lincoln, 1st R. & Haldimand. 1808. 48 Geo. III, C.11, S.2. An Act for the better Representation of the Commons of this Province in Parliament, and to repeat part of an act passed in the fortieth year of his Majesty's reign, entitled, an act for the more equal representation of the Commons of this Province, and for the better defining the Qualification of Electors. And be it further enacted by the authority aforesaid, That from and after the end of the present Parliament, the representation of the Commons of this Province in the House of Assembly, shall be in manner and form following, that is to say: that the first riding of the County of Lincoln and the County of Haldimand shall be represented by two members, in manner following, viz. the Townships of Saltfleet, Ancaster, Barton, Glanford and Binbrook, with so much of the County of Haldimand as lies between Dundas Street and the Onondaga Village, (commonly call Bearsfoot) on the River Ouse, by one member, and the Townships of Grimsby, Clinton, Gainsborough and Caistor, with so much of the County of Haldimand as lies between the Onondaga Village aforesaid and the mouth of the River Ouse, by one member.

Lincoln, 2nd R.   David Secord   Feb. 2, 1809   Lincoln, 2nd R. 1808. 48 Geo. III, C.11, S.2. An Act for the better Representation of the Commons of this Province in Parliament, and to repeat part of an act passed in the fortieth year of his Majesty's reign, entitled, an act for the more equal representation of the Commons of this Province, and for the better defining the Qualification of Electors. And be it further enacted by the authority aforesaid, That from and after the end of the present Parliament, the representation of the Commons of this

Constituency	Member	Sworn In	Comments
Lincoln, 2nd R. — *Continued*			Province in the House of Assembly, shall be in manner and form following, that is to say: That the second riding of the County of Lincoln shall be represented by one member.
			General Election May 1808.
Lincoln, 3rd R.	Hon. Samuel Street	Feb. 2, 1809	Lincoln, 3rd R. 1808. 48 Geo. III, C.11, S.2. An Act for the better Representation of the Commons of this Province in Parliament, and to repeat part of an act passed in the fortieth year of his Majesty's reign, entitled, an act for the more equal representation of the Commons of this Province, and for the better defining the Qualification of Electors. And be it further enacted by the authority aforesaid, That from and after the end of the present Parliament, the representation of the Commons of this Province in the House of Assembly, shall be in manner and form following, that is to say: That the third riding of the County of Lincoln shall be represented by one member.
			General Election May 1808.
			The Journals for the year 1809 are not known to be in existence. As the practice has been to swear in the new Speaker on the first day of the first Session, the date Feb. 2, 1809 has been given as the date the Hon. Samuel Street, MPP, Lincoln, 3rd R., took the chair.
			On Feb. 2, 1809, Samuel Street, MPP, Lincoln, 3rd R., was proposed as Speaker. Seconded and resolved. Feb. 2, 1809 – Date took chair.
Lincoln, 4th R.	Crowel Wilson	Feb. 2, 1809	Also listed as Willson.
			Lincoln, 4th R. 1808. 48 Geo. III, C.11, S.2. An Act for the better Representation of the Commons of this Province in Parliament, and

to repeat part of an act passed in the fortieth year of his Majesty's reign, entitled, an act for the more equal representation of the Commons of this Province, and for the better defining the Qualification of Electors. And be it further enacted by the authority aforesaid, That from and after the end of the present Parliament, the representation of the Commons of this Province in the House of Assembly, shall be in manner and form following, that is to say: That the fourth riding of the County of Lincoln shall be represented by one member.

General Election May 1808.

| Norfolk | Philip Sovereign | Feb. 2, 1809 | Norfolk. 1808. 48 Geo. III, C.11, S.2. An Act for the better Representation of the Commons of this Province in Parliament, and to repeat part of an act passed in the fortieth year of his Majesty's reign, entitled, an act for the more equal representation of the Commons of this Province, and for the better defining the Qualification of Electors. And be it further enacted by the authority aforesaid, That from and after the end of the present Parliament, the representation of the Commons of this Province in the House of Assembly, shall be in manner and form following, that is to say: That the County of Norfolk shall be represented by one member. |

General Election May 1808.

| Northumberland & Durham | David McGregor Rogers | Feb. 2, 1809 | Northumberland & Durham. 1808. 48 Geo. III, C.11, S.2. An Act for the better Representation of the Commons of this Province in Parliament, and to repeat part of an act passed in the fortieth year of his Majesty's reign, entitled, an act for the more equal representation of the Commons of this Province, and for the better defining the Qualification of Electors. And be it further enacted by the authority aforesaid, That from and after the end of the present |

Constituency	Member	Sworn In	Comments
Northumberland & Durham — *Continued*			Parliament, the representation of the Commons of this Province in the House of Assembly, shall be in manner and form following, that is to say: That the Counties of Northumberland and Durham shall together be represented by one member.
			General Election May 1808.
Oxford & Middlesex	Benajah Mallory	Feb. 1, 1810	Oxford & Middlesex. 1808. 48 Geo. III, C.11, S.2. An Act for the better Representation of the Commons of this Province in Parliament, and to repeat part of an act passed in the fortieth year of his Majesty's reign, entitled, an act for the more equal representation of the Commons of this Province, and for the better defining the Qualification of Electors. And be it further enacted by the authority aforesaid, That from and after the end of the present Parliament, the representation of the Commons of this Province in the House of Assembly, shall be in manner and form following, that is to say: That the Counties of Oxford and Middlesex be together represented by one member.
			General Election May 1808.
			Absent first Session.
Prescott	Thomas Mears	Feb. 2, 1809	Prescott. 1808. 48 Geo. III, C.11, S.2. An Act for the better Representation of the Commons of this Province in Parliament, and to repeat part of an act passed in the fortieth year of his Majesty's reign, entitled, an act for the more equal representation of the Commons of this Province, and for the better defining the Qualification of Electors. And be it further enacted by the authority aforesaid, That from and after the end of the present Parliament,

the representation of the Commons of this Province in the House of Assembly, shall be in manner and form following, that is to say: That the County of Prescott shall be represented by one member.

General Election May 1808.

Prince Edward (except Ameliasburgh, Twp.)	James Willson	Feb. 2, 1809	Also listed as Wilson. General Election May 1808. On Mar. 3, 1810, the election of James Willson, MPP, Prince Edward (except Ameliasburgh, Twp.) was declared void. A new election was called.
Prince Edward (except Ameliasburgh, Twp.)	John Stinson	Feb. 1, 1811*	By-election Date unknown. On Feb. 1, 1811, the House was informed of the election of John Stinson, MPP, Prince Edward (except Ameliasburgh, Twp.), in room of James Willson, whose election was declared void.
Stormont & Russell	John Brownell	Did not take seat	General Election May 1808. Died, Dec. 27, 1808. A new election was called.
Stormont & Russell	Abraham Marsh	Feb. 1, 1811*	By-election Date unknown. Writ of Election – Feb. 2, 1810. On Feb. 1, 1811, the House was informed of the election of Abraham Marsh, MPP, Stormont & Russell, in room of John Brownell, deceased.
York East & Simcoe	Thomas Barnes Gough	Feb. 2, 1809	York East & Simcoe. 1808. 48 Geo. III, C.11, S.2. An Act for the better Representation of the Commons of this Province in Parliament, and to repeat part of an act passed in the fortieth year of his Majesty's reign, entitled, an act for the more equal representation of the Commons of this Province, and for the better defining the

*   By-election

Constituency	Member	Sworn In	Comments
York East & Simcoe — *Continued*			Qualification of Electors. And be it further enacted by the authority aforesaid, That from and after the end of the present Parliament, the representation of the Commons of this Province in the House of Assembly, shall be in manner and form following, that is to say: That the east riding of the County of York and the County of Simcoe shall be represented by one member.
			General Election May 1808.
York West	Richard Beasley	Feb. 2, 1809	York West. 1808. 48 Geo. III, C.11, S.2. An Act for the better Representation of the Commons of this Province in Parliament, and to repeat part of an act passed in the fortieth year of his Majesty's reign, entitled, an act for the more equal representation of the Commons of this Province, and for the better defining the Qualification of Electors. And be it further enacted by the authority aforesaid, That from and after the end of the present Parliament, the representation of the Commons of this Province in the House of Assembly, shall be in manner and form following, that is to say: That the west riding of the County of York shall be represented by one member.
			General Election May 1808.
			In 1809, the election of Richard Beasley, MPP, York West, was declared void. A new election was called.
York West	John Willson	Feb. 1, 1810*	Also listed as Wilson.
			By-election Date unknown.
			On Feb. 1, 1810, the House was informed of the election of John Willson, MPP, York West, in room of Richard Beasley, whose election was declared void.

* By-election

LEGISLATURES OF UPPER CANADA
6th Legislature

General Election   June 1812

Sessions of the Sixth Legislature of Upper Canada: July 27, 1812 – Apr. 1, 1816†

First:	July 27, 1812 – Aug. 5, 1812.
Second:	Feb. 25, 1813 – Mar. 13, 1813.
Third:	Feb. 15, 1814 – Mar. 14, 1814.
Fourth:	Feb. 1, 1815 – Mar. 14, 1815.
Fifth:	Feb. 6, 1816 – Apr. 1, 1816.

Alphabetical List of Members

Member	Constituency	Sworn In	Comments
Gideon Adams	Grenville	Date unknown. First appeared in Journals on Feb. 15, 1814.	
John Beikie	Stormont & Russell	Date unknown. First appeared in Journals on Feb. 15, 1814.	
Mahlon Burwell	Oxford & Middlesex	Date unknown. First appeared in Journals on Feb. 19, 1814.	
Ralph Clench	Lincoln, 2nd R.	Date unknown. First appeared in Journals on Feb. 19, 1814.	On Feb. 19, 1814, the House was informed that Ralph Clench, MPP, Dundas, had been taken prisoner by the enemy.
John Crysler	Dundas	Date unknown. First appeared in	

		Journals on Feb. 15, 1814.	
Thomas Dickson	Lincoln, 3rd R.	Date unknown. First appeared in Journals on Feb. 19, 1814.	
James Durand	York West, Saltfleet, Ancaster, & C.	Date unknown. First appeared in Journals on Feb. 7, 1816.*	James Durand, MPP, York West, Saltfleet, Ancaster & C., was duly elected, in room of Abraham Markle, expelled.
Benjamin Fairfield	Lenox & Addington	Date unknown. First appeared in Journals on Feb. 19, 1814.	
John Fanning	Lincoln, 4th R.	Date unknown.	Vacated seat, between the years 1812-1814. A new election was called.
John Macdonell	Glengary	Date unknown.	Died, Oct. 14, 1812, at Queenston Heights. A new election was called.
Abraham Markle	York West, Saltfleet, Ancaster & C.	Date unknown.	Expelled, Feb. 19, 1814, having deserted to the enemy. A new election was called.
William McCormick	Essex	Date unknown. First appeared in Journals on Feb. 18, 1816.	
Alexander McDonell	Glengary	Date unknown. First appeared in Journals on Feb. 19, 1814.*	Also listed as Macdonell. Alexander McDonell, MPP, Glengary, was elected, in room of John Macdonell, deceased. On Feb. 19, 1814, the House was informed that Alexander McDonell, MPP, Glengary, had been taken prisoner by the enemy.

† The Journals for the years 1812, 1813, 1815, and 1816 are not known to be in existence.

* By-election

Member	Constituency	Sworn In	Comments
John McGregor	Kent	Date unknown. First appeared in Journals on Feb. 19, 1814.	On Feb. 19, 1814, the House was informed that John McGregor, MPP, Kent, had been taken prisoner by the enemy
Hon. Allan McLean	Frontenac	Date unknown. First appeared in Journals on Feb. 15, 1814	Hon. Allan McLean, MPP, Frontenac, was proposed as Speaker. Seconded and resolved. Date took chair unknown. First appeared in Journals as Speaker on Feb. 15, 1814.
Alexander McMartin	Glengary	Date unknown. First appeared in Journals on Feb. 19, 1814.	
Thomas Mears	Prescott	Date unknown. First appeared in Journals on Feb. 16, 1814.	
Robert Nelles	Lincoln, 1st R.	Date unknown. First appeared in Journals on Feb. 6, 1816.*	Writ of Election – Feb. 19, 1814. Robert Nelles, MPP, Lincoln, 1st R., was duly elected, in room of Joseph Willcocks, expelled.
Robert Nichol	Norfolk	Date unknown. First appeared in Journals on Feb. 15, 1814.	
Richard Pattinson	Essex	Date unknown. First appeared in Journals on Feb. 19, 1814.	
Thomas Ridout	York East & Simcoe	Date unknown. First appeared in Journals on Feb. 15, 1814.	

David McGregor Rogers	Northumberland & Durham	Date unknown. First appeared in Journals on Feb. 16, 1814.	
Levius P. Sherwood	Leeds	Date unknown. First appeared in Journals on Feb. 15, 1814.	
John Stinson	Prince Edward (except Ameliasburgh, Twp.)	Date unknown. First appeared in Journals on Feb. 15, 1814.	
Isaac Swayze	Lincoln, 4th R.	Date unknown. First appeared in Journals on Feb. 19, 1814.*	Isaac Swayze, MPP, Lincoln, 4th R., was duly elected, in room of John Fanning.
Timothy Thompson	Lenox & Addington	Date unknown. First appeared in Journals on Feb. 19, 1814.	
Joseph Willcocks	Lincoln, 1st R.	Date unknown. First appeared in Journals on Feb. 19, 1814.	Expelled, Feb. 19, 1814, having deserted to the enemy. A new election was called.
John Willson	York West	Date unknown. First appeared in Journals on Feb. 19, 1814.	
James Young	Hastings & Ameliasburgh (Twp.)	Date unknown. First appeared in Journals on Feb. 19, 1814.	

* By-election

Constituency	Member	Sworn In†	Comments
Dundas	John Crysler	Date unknown. First appeared in Journals on Feb. 15, 1814.	General Election June 1812.
Essex	William McCormick	Date unknown. First appeared in Journals on Feb. 18, 1816.	General Election June 1812.
Essex	Richard Pattinson	Date unknown. First appeared in Journals on Feb. 19, 1814.	General Election June 1812.
Frontenac	Hon. Allan McLean	Date unknown. First appeared in Journals on Feb. 15, 1814.	General Election June 1812. Hon. Allan McLean, MPP, Frontenac, was proposed as Speaker. Seconded and resolved. Date took chair unknown. First appeared in Journals as Speaker on Feb. 15, 1814.
Glengary	John Macdonell	Date unknown.	General Election June 1812. Died, Oct. 14, 1812, at Queenston Heights. A new election was called.
Glengary	Alexander McDonell	Date unknown. First appeared in Journals on Feb. 19, 1814.*	Also listed as Macdonell. By-election Date unknown. Alexander McDonell, MPP, Glengary, was duly elected, in room of John Macdonell, deceased. On Feb. 19, 1814, the House was informed that Alexander McDonell, MPP, Glengary, had been taken prisoner by the enemy.

Glengary	Alexander McMartin	Date unknown. First appeared in Journals on Feb. 19, 1814.	General Election June 1812.
Grenville	Gideon Adams	Date unknown. First appeared in Journals on Feb. 15, 1814.	General Election June 1812.
Hastings & Ameliasburgh (Twp.)	James Young	Date unknown. First appeared in Journals on Feb. 19, 1814.	General Election June 1812.
Kent	John McGregor	Date unknown. First appeared in Journals on Feb. 19, 1814.	General Election June 1812. On Feb. 19, 1814, the House was informed that John McGregor, MPP, Kent, had been taken prisoner by the enemy.
Leeds	Levius P. Sherwood	Date unknown. First appeared in Journals on Feb. 15, 1814.	General Election June 1812.
Lenox & Addington	Benjamin Fairfield	Date unknown. First appeared in Journals on Feb. 19, 1814.	General Election June 1812.
Lenox & Addington	Timothy Thompson	Date unknown. First appeared in Journals on Feb. 19, 1814.	General Election June 1812.
Lincoln, 1st R.	Joseph Willcocks	Date unknown. First appeared in Journals on Feb. 19, 1814.	General Election June 1812. Expelled, Feb. 19, 1814, having deserted to the enemy. A new election was called.

† The Journals for the years 1812, 1813, 1815, and 1816 are not known to be in existence.

* By-election

Constituency	Member	Sworn In	Comments
Lincoln, 1st R.	Robert Nelles	Date unknown. First appeared in Journals on Feb. 6, 1816.*	By-election Date unknown. Writ of Election – Feb. 19, 1814. Robert Nelles, MPP, Lincoln, 1st R., was duly elected, in room of Joseph Willcocks, expelled.
Lincoln, 2nd R.	Ralph Clench	Date unknown. First appeared in Journals on Feb. 19, 1814.	General Election June 1812. On Feb. 19, 1814, the House was informed that Ralph Clench, MPP, Dundas, had been taken prisoner by the enemy.
Lincoln, 3rd R.	Thomas Dickson	Date unknown. First appeared in Journals on Feb. 19, 1814.	General Election June 1812.
Lincoln, 4th R.	John Fanning	Date unknown.	General Election June 1812. Vacated seat, between the years 1812-1814. A new election was called.
Lincoln, 4th R.	Isaac Swayze	Date unknown. First appeared in Journals on Feb. 19, 1814.*	By-election Date unknown. Isaac Swayze, MPP, Lincoln, 4th R., was duly elected, in room of John Fanning.
Norfolk	Robert Nichol	Date unknown. First appeared in Journals on Feb. 15, 1814.	General Election June 1812.
Northumberland & Durham	David McGregor Rogers	Date unknown. First appeared in Journals on Feb. 16, 1814.	General Election June 1812.
Oxford & Middlesex	Mahlon Burwell	Date unknown. First appeared in Journals on Feb. 19, 1814.	General Election June 1812.

Prescott	Thomas Mears	Date unknown. First appeared in Journals on Feb. 16, 1814.	General Election June 1812. Prescott. 1816. 56 Geo. III, C.2, Ss.1, 2. An act to repeal part of an act of the parliament of this province, passed in the thirty-eighth year of his Majesty's reign, entitled, An act for the better division of this province, and more effectually to provide for the administration of Justice by constituting the Counties of Prescott and Russell, under certain modifications, a separate District. Whereas from the great extent of the Eastern District of this province, the inhabitants, of the Counties of Prescott and Russell, in the said District, experience much inconvenience in attending his Majesty's courts of justice at present established. . . . And be it further enacted by the authority aforesaid, That from and after the passing of this act, there shall be formed, constituted and established, a new District, to consist of the said Counties of Prescott and Russell, to be called the District of Ottawa.
Prince Edward (except Ameliasburg, Twp.)	John Stinson	Date unknown. First appeared in Journals on Feb. 15, 1814.	General Election June 1812.
Stormont & Russell	John Beikie	Date unknown. First appeared in Journals on Feb. 15, 1814.	General Election June 1812. Stormont & Russell. 1816. 56 Geo. III, C.2, Ss.1, 2. An act to repeal part of an act of the parliament of this province, passed in the thirty-eighth year of his Majesty's reign, entitled, An act for the better division of this province, and more effectually to provide for the administration of Justice by constituting the Counties of Prescott and Russell, under certain modifications, a separate District. Whereas from the great extent of the Eastern District of

*   By-election

Constituency	Member	Sworn In	Comments
Stormont & Russell — *Continued*			this province, the inhabitants, of the Counties of Prescott and Russell, in the said District, experience much inconvenience in attending his Majesty's courts of justice at present established. . . . And be it further enacted by the authority aforesaid, That from and after the passing of this act, there shall be formed, constituted and established, a new District, to consist of the said Counties of Prescott and Russell, to be called the District of Ottawa.
York East & Simcoe	Thomas Ridout	Date unknown. First appeared in Journals on Feb. 15, 1814.	General Election June 1812.
York West, Saltfleet, Ancaster & C.	Abraham Markle	Date unknown.	General Election June 1812. Expelled, Feb. 19, 1814, having deserted to the enemy. A new election was called.
York West, Saltfleet, Ancaster, & C.	James Durand	Date unknown. First appeared in Journals on Feb. 7, 1816.*	By-election Date unknown. James Durand, MPP, York West, Saltfleet, Ancaster & C., was duly elected, in room of Abraham Markle, expelled.
York West	John Willson	Date unknown. First appeared in Journals on Feb. 19, 1814.	General Election June 1812.

*   By-election

LEGISLATURES OF UPPER CANADA
7th Legislature

General Election   Apr. 1816

Sessions of the Seventh Legislature of Upper Canada: Feb. 4, 1817 – Mar. 7, 1820

First:	Feb. 4, 1817 – Apr. 7, 1817.
Second:	Feb. 5, 1818 – Apr. 1, 1818.
Third:	Oct. 12, 1818 – Nov. 27, 1818.
Fourth:	June 7, 1819 – July 12, 1819.
Fifth:	Feb. 21, 1820 – Mar. 7, 1820.

Alphabetical List of Members

Member	Constituency	Sworn In	Comments
Zaccheus Burnham	Northumberland & Durham	Feb. 4, 1817	
Mahlon Burwell	Oxford & Middlesex	Feb. 4, 1817	
John Cameron	Glengary	Feb. 4, 1817	
Willet Casey	Lenox & Addington	Feb. 4, 1817	
Ralph Clench	Lincoln, 2nd R.	Date unknown. First appeared in Journals on Feb. 27, 1817.	
Joshua Cornwall	Kent	Feb. 8, 1817	
James Cotter	Prince Edward (except Ameliasburg, Twp.)	Feb. 4, 1817	
John Crysler	Dundas	Mar. 10, 1817	
James Durand	Wentworth	Feb. 25, 1817	Committed to the Common Goal of the Home District, Mar. 4, 1817, having authored a libel against the Lieutenant Governor, the former House of Assembly and the present Members.

			Expelled, Mar. 7, 1817, having been found guilty of a high contempt of the House's authority, by withdrawing himself without leave from the judgment of the House. A new election was called.
		Feb. 6, 1818*	Writ of Election – Mar. 24, 1817. On Feb. 6, 1818, the House was informed of the election of James Durand, MPP, Wentworth, who was returned as duly elected.
Isaac Fraser	Lenox & Addington	Feb. 4, 1817	
Moses Gamble	Halton	Feb. 25, 1817	On Mar. 3, 1817, the election of Moses Gamble, MPP, Halton was declared void. Gamble had come into this Province from the United States of America which made him ineligible to serve in the Provincial Parliament of the Province and ought not to have been returned for the County of Halton. A new election was called.
George B. Hall	Essex	Feb. 4, 1817	
Richard Hatt	Halton	Feb. 6, 1818*	Writ of Election – Mar. 24, 1817. On Feb. 6, 1818, the House was informed of the election of Richard Hatt, MPP, Halton, in room of Moses Gamble, whose election was declared void.
			Died, Sept. 26, 1819. A new writ was issued on Feb. 21, 1820. [There was no evidence in the Journals that the By-election took place. House was prorogued on Mar. 7, 1820.]
Peter Howard	Leeds	Feb. 4, 1817	
Jonas Jones	Grenville	Feb. 4, 1817	
William McCormick	Essex	Feb. 4, 1817	
John McDonell	Prescott	Feb. 4, 1817	Mr. Attorney General.

*   By-election

Member	Constituency	Sworn In	Comments
Hon. Allan McLean	Frontenac	Feb. 4, 1817	On Feb. 4, 1817, Robert Nichol, MPP, Norfolk, proposed Allan McLean, MPP, Frontenac, as Speaker. Seconded and resolved. Feb. 4, 1817 – Date took chair.
Alexander McMartin	Glengary	Feb. 4, 1817	
James McNabb	Hastings & Ameliasburg (Twp.)	Feb. 4, 1817	
Robert Nelles	Lincoln, 1st R.	Feb. 4, 1817	
Robert Nichol	Norfolk	Feb. 4, 1817	
Peter Robinson	York East	Feb. 4, 1817	
David Secord	Lincoln, 3rd R.	Feb. 4, 1817	
Isaac Swayze	Lincoln, 4th R.	Feb. 4, 1817	Died, Feb. 11, 1828.
Philip VanKoughnet	Stormont & Russell	Feb. 4, 1817	

Constituency	Member	Sworn In	Comments
Dundas	John Crysler	Mar. 10, 1817	General Election Apr. 1816.
Essex	George B. Hall	Feb. 4, 1817	General Election Apr. 1816.
Essex	William McCormick	Feb. 4, 1817	General Election Apr. 1816.
Frontenac	Hon. Allan McLean	Feb. 4, 1817	General Election Apr. 1816.
			On Feb. 4, 1817, Robert Nichol, MPP, Norfolk, proposed Allan McLean, MPP, Frontenac, as Speaker. Seconded and resolved. Feb. 4, 1817 – Date took chair.
Glengary	John Cameron	Feb. 4, 1817	General Election Apr. 1816.
			Glengary. 1818. 59 Geo. III, C.3, Ss.1, 2. An Act for the better Division of the County of Glengary into Townships. Whereas from the great extent of the Township of Lancaster, in the County of Glengary, in the Eastern District of this Province, and the great population therein, the Inhabitants of the said Township experience many inconveniences, in particular in attending Town Meetings; and whereas it has become expedient to divide the said Township, and to constitute the Township of Lancaster. . . . And be it further enacted by the authority aforesaid, That the North or rear nine Concessions of the aforesaid Township of Lancaster, shall form and constitute the Township of Lochiel.
Glengary	Alexander McMartin	Feb. 4, 1817	General Election Apr. 1816.
			Glengary. 1818. 59 Geo. III, C.3, Ss.1, 2. An Act for the better Division of the County of Glengary into Townships. Whereas from the great extent of the Township of Lancaster, in the County of Glengary, in the Eastern District

of this Province, and the great population therein, the Inhabitants of the said Township experience many inconveniences, in particular in attending Town Meetings; and whereas it has become expedient to divide the said Township, and to constitute the Township of Lancaster. . . . And be it further enacted by the authority aforesaid, That the North or rear nine Concessions of the aforesaid Township of Lancaster, shall form and constitute the Township of Lochiel.

| Grenville | Jonas Jones | Feb. 4, 1817 | General Election Apr. 1816. |
| Halton | Moses Gamble | Feb. 25, 1817 | General Election Apr. 1816. |

Halton. 1816. 56 Geo. III, C.19, S.12. An act to erect and form a new District out of certain parts of the Home and Niagara Districts, to be called the DISTRICT OF GORE. And be it further enacted by the authority aforesaid, that the Townships of Trafalgar, Nelson, Flamborough, the latter divided into Flamborough East and West, Beverly, and Blocks Number, one, two, three and four, on the Grand River with the reserved Lands in the rear of the Townships of Blenheim and Blandord, do constitute and form the County of Halton, and the residue of the County of York.

Halton. 1817. 57 Geo. III, C.1, S.1. An Act to Provide for the Representation of the Commons of the Counties of Wentworth and Halton, in Parliament. . . . That from and after the Passing of this Act, the said Counties of Wentworth and Halton, be each represented by one Member.

On Mar. 3, 1817, the election of Moses Gamble, MPP,.Halton was declared void. Gamble had come into this Province from the United States of America which made him ineligible to serve in the Provincial Parliament of the Province and ought not to have been

Constituency	Member	Sworn In	Comments
Halton — *Continued*			returned for the County of Halton. A new election was called.
Halton	Richard Hatt	Feb. 6, 1818*	By-election Date unknown.
			Writ of Election – Mar. 24, 1817. On Feb. 6, 1818, the House was informed of the election of Richard Hatt, MPP, Halton, in room of Moses Gamble, whose election was declared void.
			Died, Sept. 26, 1819. A new writ was issued on Feb. 21, 1820. [There was no evidence in the Journals that the By-election took place. House was prorogued on Mar. 7, 1820.]
Hastings & Ameliasburg (Twp.)	James McNabb	Feb. 4, 1817	General Election Apr. 1816.
Kent	Joshua Cornwall	Feb. 8, 1817	General Election Apr. 1816.
Leeds	Peter Howard	Feb. 4, 1817	General Election Apr. 1816.
Lenox & Addington	Willet Casey	Feb. 4, 1817	General Election Apr. 1816.
Lenox & Addington	Isaac Fraser	Feb. 4, 1817	General Election Apr. 1816.
Lincoln, 1st R.	Robert Nelles	Feb. 4, 1817	General Election Apr. 1816.
Lincoln, 2nd R.	Ralph Clench	Date unknown. First appeared in Journals on Feb. 27, 1817.	General Election Apr. 1816.
Lincoln, 3rd R.	David Secord	Feb. 4, 1817	General Election Apr. 1816.
Lincoln, 4th R.	Isaac Swayze	Feb. 4, 1817	General Election Apr. 1816. Died, Feb. 11, 1828.
Norfolk	Robert Nichol	Feb. 4, 1817	General Election Apr. 1816.
Northumberland & Durham	Zaccheus Burnham	Feb. 4, 1817	General Election Apr. 1816.
Oxford & Middlesex	Mahlon Burwell	Feb. 4, 1817	General Election Apr. 1816.

Prescott	John McDonell	Feb. 4, 1817	Mr. Attorney General. General Election Apr. 1816.
Prince Edward (except Ameliasburg, Twp.)	James Cotter	Feb. 4, 1817	General Election Apr. 1816.
Stormont & Russell	Philip VanKoughnet	Feb. 4, 1817	General Election Apr. 1816.
Wentworth	James Durand	Feb. 25, 1817	General Election Apr. 1816.

Wentworth. 1816. 56 Geo. III, C.19, S.11. An act to erect and form a new District out of certain parts of the Home and Niagara Districts, to be called the DISTRICT OF GORE. And be it further enacted by the authority aforesaid, that the Townships of Saltfleet, Barton, Benbrook, Glanford, Ancaster, and the Beach between Burlington Bay, and Lake Ontario, and the Promontary near Coot's Paradise, and so much of the County of Haldimand as lies between Dundas Street and the Onondaga Village, commonly called Bear's-Foot, including said village, shall form and be called the County of Wentworth, and the residue of the County of Lincoln, and the residue of the County of Haldimand shall from henceforth be and remain the Counties of Lincoln and Haldimand respectively.

Wentworth. 1817. 57 Geo. III, C.1, S.1. An Act to Provide for the Representation of the Commons of the Counties of Wentworth and Halton, in Parliament. . . . That from and after the Passing of this Act, the said Counties of Wentworth and Halton, be each represented by one member.

Committed to the Common Goal of the Home District, Mar. 4, 1817, having authored a libel against the Lieutenant Governor, the former House of Assembly and the present Members.

* By-election

Constituency	Member	Sworn In	Comments
Wentworth — *Continued*			Expelled, Mar. 7, 1817, having been found guilty of a high contempt of the House's authority, by withdrawing himself without leave from the judgment of the House. A new election was called.
		Feb. 6, 1818*	By-election Date unknown.
			Writ of Election – Mar. 24, 1817. On Feb. 6, 1818, the House was informed of the election of James Durand, MPP, Wentworth, who was returned as duly elected.
York East	Peter Robinson	Feb. 4, 1817	General Election Apr. 1816.

LEGISLATURES OF UPPER CANADA
8th Legislature

General Election July 1820

Sessions of the Eighth Legislature of Upper Canada: Jan. 31, 1821 – Jan. 19, 1824

First:	Jan. 31, 1821 – Apr. 14, 1821.
Second:	Nov. 21, 1821 – Jan. 17, 1822.
Third:	Jan. 15, 1823 – Mar. 19, 1823.
Fourth:	Nov. 11, 1823 – Jan. 19, 1824.

Alphabetical List of Members

Member	Constituency	Sworn In	Comments
Francis Baby	Essex	Jan. 31, 1821	
William Warren Baldwin	York & Simcoe	Jan. 31, 1821	
Barnabas Bidwell	Lennox & Addington	Date unknown. First appeared in Journals on Nov. 29, 1821*	Writ of Election – Oct. 2, 1821. On Nov. 24, 1821, the House was informed of the election of Barnabas Bidwell, MPP, Lennox & Addington, in room of Daniel Hagerman, deceased.
			On Jan. 4, 1822, the election of Barnabas Bidwell, MPP, Lennox & Addington, was declared void. A new election was called.
John Bostwick	Middlesex	Mar. 17, 1821	Sheriff of London District.
Mahlon Burwell	Middlesex	Jan. 31, 1821	
Samuel Casey	Lennox & Addington	Jan. 31, 1821	
William Chisholm	Halton	Jan. 31, 1821	
John Clark	Lincoln, 1st R.	Jan. 31, 1821	
Matthew Clark	Lennox & Addington	Jan. 22, 1823*	Writ of Election – Jan. 7, 1822. On Jan. 22, 1823, the House was informed of the election of Matthew Clark, MPP, Lennox & Addington,

			in room of Barnabas Bidwell, whose election was declared void.
			On Feb. 14, 1823, the election of Matthew Clark, MPP, Lennox & Addington, was declared void. A new election was called.
James Crooks	Halton	Jan. 31, 1821	
Walter F. Gates	Grenville	Jan. 31, 1821	
James Gordon	Kent	Jan. 31, 1821	
Christopher Alexander Hagerman	Kingston (Town)	Jan. 31, 1821	
Daniel Hagerman	Lennox & Addington	Did not take seat	Died before the commencement of the first Session of the 8th Legislature. A new election was called.
George Ham	Lennox & Addington	Nov. 11, 1823*	Writ of Election – Feb. 14, 1823. On Nov. 11, 1823, the House was informed of the election of George Ham, MPP, Lennox & Addington, in room of Matthew Clark, whose election was declared void.
			On Dec. 8, 1823, the election of George Ham, MPP, Lennox & Addington, was declared void. A new writ was issued that day. [There was no evidence in the Journals that the By-election took place. House was prorogued on Jan. 19, 1824.]
George Hamilton	Wentworth	Jan. 31, 1821	
Robert Hamilton	Lincoln, 3rd R.	Jan. 31, 1821	
William Hamilton	Prescott & Russell	Jan. 31, 1821	On Mar. 24, 1821, the election of William Hamilton, MPP, Prescott & Russell, was declared void. David Pattie was declared duly elected at the July 10-15, 1820 General Election.
Thomas Hornor	Oxford	Jan. 31, 1821	Also listed as Horner.

* By-election

Member	Constituency	Sworn In	Comments
Charles Jones	Leeds	Jan. 31, 1821	
Jonas Jones	Grenville	Jan. 31, 1821	
William J. Kerr	Lincoln, 2nd R.	Jan. 31, 1821	
William McCormick	Essex	Feb. 12, 1821	
Alexander McDonell	Glengary	Jan. 31, 1821	
Allan McLean	Frontenac	Jan. 31, 1821	Also listed as MacLean.
Archibald McLean	Stormont	Jan. 31, 1821	Also listed as MacLean.
Alexander McMartin	Glengary	Jan. 31, 1821	
William Morris	Carleton	Jan. 31, 1821	
Robert Nichol	Norfolk	Jan. 31, 1821	
David Pattie	Prescott & Russell	Mar. 24, 1821	On Mar. 24, 1821, the House was informed that David Pattie was duly elected as the Member for Prescott & Russell, at the July 10 – 15, 1820 General Election, in room of William Hamilton, whose election was declared void.
Paul Peterson	Prince Edward	Jan. 31, 1821	
Robert Randal	Lincoln, 4th R.	Jan. 31, 1821	Also listed as Randall.
John Beverley Robinson	York (Town)	Jan. 31, 1821	Mr. Attorney General.
Peter Robinson	York & Simcoe	Jan. 31, 1821	
David McGregor Rogers	Northumberland	Jan. 31, 1821	
Henry Ruttan	Northumberland	Jan. 31, 1821	
Peter Shaver	Dundas	Jan. 31, 1821	
Hon. Levius P. Sherwood	Leeds	Jan. 31, 1821	On Jan. 31, 1821, Robert Nichol, MPP, Norfolk, proposed Levius P. Sherwood, MPP, Leeds, as Speaker. Seconded and resolved. Jan. 31, 1821 – Date took chair.

Philip VanKoughnet	Stormont	Jan. 31, 1821
Francis Leigh Walsh	Norfolk	Jan. 31, 1821
Reuben White	Hastings	Jan. 31, 1821
James Willson	Prince Edward	Jan. 31, 1821
John Willson	Wentworth	Jan. 31, 1821
Samuel Street Wilmot	Durham	Jan. 31, 1821

Constituency	Member	Sworn In	Comments
Carleton	William Morris	Jan. 31, 1821	Carleton. 1798. 38 Geo. III, C.5, Ss.9, 10. An act for the better division of this province. And be it further enacted by the authority aforesaid, that the Township of Nepean, with the tract of land to be hereafter laid out into Townships, between Nepean, and a line drawn north sixteen degrees west, from the north west angle of the Township of Crosby, until it intersects the Ottawa River, with such of the Islands in the said River as are wholly, or in greater part opposite thereto, shall constitute and form the County of Carleton. . . . And be it further enacted by the authority aforesaid, That the Counties of Grenville, Leeds and Carleton, do constitute and form the District of Johnstown.
			General Election July 1820.
			Carleton. 1821. 2 Geo. IV, C.3, S.3. An act to repeal part of an act passed in the thirty-eighth year of his late Majesty's reign, entitled, An act for the better division of this province, and to make further provision for the division of the same into Counties and Districts. And be it further enacted by the authority aforesaid, that the Townships of Gouldburn, Beckwith, Drummond, Bathurst, March, Huntly, Ramsay, Lanark, Dalhousie, and Sherbrooke North and South, together with such other Townships as may hereafter be surveyed by direction of the Governor, Lieutenant Governor or Person administering the Government of this Province, lying within the present limits of the County of Carlton, shall continue and remain the County of Carlton.

| | | | Carleton. 1824. 4 Geo. IV, C.5, S.3. An act to divide the County of Carleton, in the Bathurst District.

And be it further enacted by the authority aforesaid, That the Townships of Nepean, Goulbourne, Huntley, March, Pakenham, Fitzroy, and Torbolton, together with such of the Islands in the Ottawa river as are wholly or in greater part opposite thereto, do constitute and form the County of Carleton. . . . that the said Counties of Lanark and Carleton, formed by this act, shall be each represented by one member. |
|---|---|---|---|
| Dundas | Peter Shaver | Jan. 31, 1821 | General Election July 1820. |
| Durham | Samuel Street Wilmot | Jan. 31, 1821 | General Election July 1820. |
| | | | Durham. 1821. 2 Geo. IV, C.3, S.6. An act to repeal part of an act passed in the thirty-eighth year of his late Majesty's reign, entitled, An act for the better division of this province, and to make further provision for the division of the same into Counties and Districts. . . . and the Townships of Cavan, Manvers, Cartwright, Emily, Ops, and Mariposa, to the County of Durham. |
| Essex | Francis Baby | Jan. 31, 1821 | General Election July 1820. |
| Essex | William McCormick | Feb. 12, 1821 | General Election July 1820. |
| Frontenac | Allan McLean | Jan. 31, 1821 | Also listed as MacLean.

General Election July 1820.

Frontenac. 1821. 2 Geo. IV, C.3, S.5. An act to repeal part of an act passed in the thirty-eighth year of his late Majesty's reign, entitled, An act for the better division of this province, and to make further provision for the division of the same into Counties and Districts. And be it further enacted by the authority aforesaid, that the following Townships in the Midland District shall be attached to, and be incorporated with |

Constituency	Member	Sworn In	Comments
Frontenac — *Continued*			the Counties hereinafter mentioned, in the manner following that is to say, the Townships of Oso, Olden, and Kennebec, to the County of Frontenac.
Glengary	Alexander McDonell	Jan. 31, 1821	General Election July 1820.
Glengary	Alexander McMartin	Jan. 31, 1821	General Election July 1820.
Grenville	Walter F. Gates	Jan. 31, 1821	General Election July 1820.
Grenville	Jonas Jones	Jan. 31, 1821	General Election July 1820.
Halton	William Chisholm	Jan. 31, 1821	General Election July 1820.
			Halton. 1821. 2 Geo. IV, C.3, S.9. An act to repeal part of an act passed in the thirty-eighth year of his late Majesty's reign, entitled, An act for the better division of this province, and to make further provision for the division of the same into Counties and Districts. And be it further enacted by the authority aforesaid, that the following Townships, to wit, Esquesing, Erin, Nasagaweya, Eramosa, Garafraxa, and the church land, be annexed to the County of Halton.
Halton	James Crooks	Jan. 31, 1821	General Election July 1820.
			Halton. 1821. 2 Geo. IV, C.3, S.9. An act to repeal part of an act passed in the thirty-eighth year of his late Majesty's reign, entitled, An act for the better division of this province, and to make further provision for the division of the same into Counties and Districts. And be it further enacted by the authority aforesaid, that the following Townships, to wit, Esquesing, Erin, Nasagaweya, Eramosa, Garafraxa, and the church land, be annexed to the County of Halton.

Hastings	Reuben White	Jan. 31, 1821	General Election July 1820.
			Hastings. 1821. 2 Geo. IV, C.3, S.5. An act to repeal part of an act passed in the thirty-eighth year of his late Majesty's reign, entitled, An act for the better division of this province, and to make further provision for the division of the same into Counties and Districts. . . . and the Townships of Elzever, Madoc, and Marmora, to the County of Hastings.
Kent	James Gordon	Jan. 31, 1821	General Election July 1820.
			Kent. 1821. 2 Geo. IV, C.3, S.12. An act to repeal part of an act passed in the thirty-eighth year of his late Majesty's reign, entitled, An act for the better division of this province, and to make further provision for the division of the same into Counties and Districts. And be it further enacted by the authority aforesaid, that the following new Townships in the Western District be attached to the County of Kent, namely, the Townships of Zone, Dawn, Sombra, and Saint Clair.
Kingston (Town)	Christopher Alexander Hagerman	Jan. 31, 1821	General Election July 1820.
Leeds	Charles Jones	Jan. 31, 1821	General Election July 1820.
Leeds	Hon. Levius P. Sherwood	Jan. 31, 1821	General Election July 1820.
			On Jan. 31, 1821, Robert Nichol, MPP, Norfolk, proposed Levius P. Sherwood, MPP, Leeds, as Speaker. Seconded and resolved. Jan. 31, 1821 – Date took chair.
Lennox & Addington	Samuel Casey	Jan. 31, 1821	General Election July 1820.
			Lennox & Addington. 1821. 2 Geo. IV, C.3, S.5. An act to repeal part of an act passed in the thirty-eighth year of his late Majesty's reign, entitled, An act for the better division of this province, and to make further provision for the division of the same into Counties and

Constituency	Member	Sworn In	Comments
Lennox & Addington — *Continued*			Districts. . . . the Township of Kaledar, to the Counties of Lennox and Addington.
Lennox & Addington	Daniel Hagerman	Did not take seat	General Election July 1820.
			Died before the commencement of the first Session of the 8th Legislature. A new election was called.
Lennox & Addington	Barnabas Bidwell	Date unknown. First appeared in Journals on Nov. 29, 1821*	Lennox & Addington. 1821. 2 Geo. IV, C.3, S.5. An act to repeal part of an act passed in the thirty-eighth year of his late Majesty's reign, entitled, An act for the better division of this province, and to make further provision for the division of the same into Counties and Districts. . . . the Township of Kaledar, to the Counties of Lennox and Addington.
			By-election Nov. 5, 1821.
			Writ of Election – Oct. 2, 1821. On Nov. 24, 1821, the House was informed of the election of Barnabas Bidwell, MPP, Lennox & Addington, in room of Daniel Hagerman, deceased.
			On Jan. 4, 1822, the election of Barnabas Bidwell, MPP, Lennox & Addington, was declared void. A new election was called.
Lennox & Addington	Matthew Clark	Jan. 22, 1823*	By-election Feb. 11, 1822.
			Writ of Election – Jan. 7, 1822. On Jan. 22, 1823, the House was informed of the election of Matthew Clark, MPP, Lennox & Addington, in room of Barnabas Bidwell, whose election was declared void.
			On Feb. 14, 1823, the election of Matthew Clark, MPP, Lennox & Addington, was declared void. A new election was called.

Lennox & Addington	George Ham	Nov. 11, 1823*	By-election Mar. 24, 1823.
			Writ of Election – Feb. 14, 1823. On Nov. 11, 1823, the House was informed of the election of George Ham, MPP, Lennox & Addington, in room of Matthew Clark, whose election was declared void.
			On Dec. 8, 1823, the election of George Ham, MPP, Lennox & Addington, was declared void. A new writ was issued that day. [There was no evidence in the Journals that the By-election took place. House was prorogued on Jan. 19, 1824.]
Lincoln, 1st R.	John Clark	Jan. 31, 1821	General Election July 1820.
Lincoln, 2nd R.	William J. Kerr	Jan. 31, 1821	General Election July 1820.
Lincoln, 3rd R.	Robert Hamilton	Jan. 31, 1821	General Election July 1820.
Lincoln, 4th R.	Robert Randal	Jan. 31, 1821	Also listed as Randall.
			General Election July 1820.
Middlesex	John Bostwick	Mar. 17, 1821	Sheriff of London District.
			General Election July 1820.
			Middlesex. 1821. 2 Geo. IV, C.3, S.11. An act to repeal part of an act passed in the thirty-eighth year of his late Majesty's reign, entitled, An act for the better division of this province, and to make further provision for the division of the same into Counties and Districts. . . . and that hereafter the Townships of Moza, Ecfrid, Carradoc, and Lobo, be added to the County of Middlesex, also that a gore of land on the east side of the Township of Norwich, be attached to the Township, and a gore of land on the east of the Township of Dorchester, be attached to the said Township.
Middlesex	Mahlon Burwell	Jan. 31, 1821	General Election July 1820.

*   By-election

Constituency	Member	Sworn In	Comments
Middlesex — *Continued*			Middlesex. 1821. 2 Geo. IV, C.3, S.11. An act to repeal part of an act passed in the thirty-eighth year of his late Majesty's reign, entitled, An act for the better division of this province, and to make further provision for the division of the same into Counties and Districts. . . . and that hereafter the Townships of Moza, Ecfrid, Carradoc, and Lobo, be added to the County of Middlesex, also that a gore of land on the east side of the Township of Norwich, be attached to the Township, and a gore of land on the east of the Township of Dorchester, be attached to the said Township.
Norfolk	Robert Nichol	Jan. 31, 1821	General Election July 1820.
Norfolk	Francis Leigh Walsh	Jan. 31, 1821	General Election July 1820.
Northumberland	David McGregor Rogers	Jan. 31, 1821	General Election July 1820.
			Northumberland. 1821. 2 Geo. IV, C.3, S.6. An act to repeal part of an act passed in the thirty-eighth year of his late Majesty's reign, entitled, An act for the better division of this province, and to make further provision for the division of the same into Counties and Districts. And be it further enacted by the authority aforesaid, that the unattached Townships in the Newcastle District shall be incorporated in manner aforesaid, with the Counties in the said District, as follows, that is to say, the Townships of Asphodel, Otanabee, Monaghan, and Smith, to be attached to the County of Northumberland.
Northumberland	Henry Ruttan	Jan. 31, 1821	General Election July 1820.
			Northumberland. 1821. 2 Geo. IV, C.3, S.6. An act to repeal part of an act passed in the thirty-eighth year of his late Majesty's reign, entitled,

			An act for the better division of this province, and to make further provision for the division of the same into Counties and Districts. And be it further enacted by the authority aforesaid, that the unattached Townships in the Newcastle District shall be incorporated in manner aforesaid, with the Counties in the said District, as follows, that is to say, the Townships of Asphodel, Otanabee, Monaghan, and Smith, to be attached to the County of Northumberland.
Oxford	Thomas Hornor	Jan. 31, 1821	Also listed as Horner.
			General Election July 1820.
			Oxford. 1821. 2 Geo. IV, C.3, S.11. An act to repeal part of an act passed in the thirty-eighth year of his late Majesty's reign, entitled, An act for the better division of this province, and to make further provision for the division of the same into Counties and Districts. And be it further enacted by the authority aforesaid, that the gore of land attached to the Township of Burford, be formed into a separate Township, by the name of the Township of Oakland, and that the said Township of Oakland and the Townships of Nissouri and Zora, be added to the County of Oxford.
Prescott & Russell	William Hamilton	Jan. 31, 1821	General Election July 1820.
			On Mar. 24, 1821, the election of William Hamilton, MPP, Prescott & Russell, was declared void. David Pattie was declared duly elected at the July 10-15, 1820 General Election.
Prescott & Russell	David Pattie	Mar. 24, 1821	On Mar. 24, 1821, the House was informed that David Pattie was duly elected as the Member for Prescott & Russell, at the July 10 – 15, 1820 General Election, in room of William Hamilton, whose election was declared void.
Prince Edward	Paul Peterson	Jan. 31, 1821	General Election July 1820.

Constituency	Member	Sworn In	Comments
Prince Edward	James Willson	Jan. 31, 1821	General Election July 1820.
Stormont	Archibald McLean	Jan. 31, 1821	Also listed as MacLean. General Election July 1820.
Stormont	Philip VanKoughnet	Jan. 31, 1821	General Election July 1820.
Wentworth	George Hamilton	Jan. 31, 1821	General Election July 1820.
Wentworth	John Willson	Jan. 31, 1821	General Election July 1820.
York & Simcoe	William Warren Baldwin	Jan. 31, 1821	General Election July 1820. York & Simcoe. 1821. 2 Geo. IV, C.3, S.7. An act to repeal part of an act passed in the thirty-eighth year of his late Majesty's reign, entitled, An act for the better division of this province, and to make further provision for the division of the same into Counties and Districts. And be it further enacted by the authority aforesaid, That the unattached Townships in the Home District shall be incorporated in manner aforesaid with the Counties in the said Home District as follows, that is to say; the Townships of Reach, Brock, Scott, and Georgiana, shall be attached to the east riding of the County of York; and that hereafter the following Townships, to wit, Chinguacousy, Caledon, Albion, and the gore of Toronto, be added to the west riding of York. . . . and that the following Townships shall constitute and form the County of Simcoe, namely; West Gwillimbury, Tecumseth, Adjala, Mono, Amaranth, Luther, Proton, Melancthon, Mulmar, Tosorontio, Essa, Innisfil, Oro, Vespra, Sunnidale, Flos, Medonta, Aurelia, Merlin, Osprey, Artemisia, Alba, Java, Tina, Tay, Euphrasy, Zero, Matchedash, Thora, Mara, and Ramah.

York & Simcoe	Peter Robinson	Jan. 31, 1821	General Election July 1820.

York & Simcoe. 1821. 2 Geo. IV, C.3, S.7. An act to repeal part of an act passed in the thirty-eighth year of his late Majesty's reign, entitled, An act for the better division of this province, and to make further provision for the division of the same into Counties and Districts. And be it further enacted by the authority aforesaid, that the unattached Townships in the Home District shall be incorporated in manner aforesaid with the Counties in the said Home District as follows, that is to say; the Townships of Reach, Brock, Scott, and Georgiana, shall be attached to the east riding of the County of York; and that hereafter the following Townships, to wit, Chinguacousy, Caledon, Albion, and the gore of Toronto, be added to the west riding of York. . . . and that the following Townships shall constitute and form the County of Simcoe, namely; West Gwillimbury, Tecumseth, Adjala, Mono, Amaranth, Luther, Proton, Melancthon, Mulmar, Tosorontio, Essa, Innisfil, Oro, Vespra, Sunnidale, Flos, Medonta, Aurelia, Merlin, Osprey, Artemisia, Alba, Java, Tina, Tay, Euphrasy, Zero, Matchedash, Thora, Mara, and Ramah.

York (Town)	John Beverley Robinson	Jan. 31, 1821	Mr. Attorney General. General Election July 1820.

LEGISLATURES OF UPPER CANADA
9th Legislature

General Election   July 1824

Sessions of the Ninth Legislature of Upper Canada: Jan. 11, 1825 – Mar. 25, 1828

First:	Jan. 11, 1825 – Apr. 13, 1825.
Second:	Nov. 7, 1825 – Jan. 30, 1826.
Third:	Dec. 5, 1826 – Feb. 17, 1827.
Fourth:	Jan. 15, 1828 – Mar. 25, 1828.

Alphabetical List of Members

Member	Constituency	Sworn In	Comments
James Atkinson	Frontenac	Jan. 11, 1825	
Francis Baby	Essex	Date unknown. First appeared in Journals on Nov. 16, 1825.	On Mar. 24, 1825, the Petition of Francis Baby complaining of the conduct of the Returning Officer at the last Essex General Election was found just. A new election was called.
			Writ of Election – Mar. 25, 1825. Francis Baby was found duly elected for the County of Essex.
Bartholemew C. Beardsley	Lincoln, 2nd & 3rd R.	Jan. 11, 1825	
Richard Beasley	Halton	Jan. 11, 1825	
Marshall Spring Bidwell	Lennox & Addington	Jan. 11, 1825	
George Strange Boulton	Durham	Jan. 11, 1825	On Mar. 1, 1825, the election of George Strange Boulton, MPP, Durham, was declared void. A new election was called.
George T. Burke	Carelton	Date unknown. First appeared in Journals on Nov. 7, 1825.	
Zaccheus Burnham	Northumberland	Jan. 11, 1825	

Duncan Cameron	Glengary	Jan. 11, 1825	Secretary and Registrar. On Mar. 12, 1825, the election of Duncan Cameron, MPP, Glengary, was declared void. A new election was called. [There was no evidence in the Journals of a new Member having been returned for this District.]
John Clark	Lincoln, 1st R.	Jan. 11, 1825	
Thomas Coleman	Hastings	Jan. 11, 1825	
John Crysler	Dundas	Jan. 11, 1825	
John Cumming	Kingston (Town)	Jan. 15, 1825	
Benjamin Ewing	Northumberland	Feb. 24, 1825	On Feb. 23, 1825, the House was informed that Benjamin Ewing was duly elected at the July 13, 1824 Northumberland General Election, in room of James Lyons, whose election was declared void. On Mar. 28, 1825, the election of Benjamin Ewing, MPP, Northumberland, was declared void. James Lyons was duly elected at the July 13, 1824 General Election.
Charles Fothergill	Durham	Mar. 31, 1825*	Government Printer. Writ of Election – Mar. 1, 1825. On Mar. 31, 1825, the House was informed of the election of Charles Fothergill, MPP, Durham, in room of George Strange Boulton, whose election was declared void.
James Gordon	Kent	Jan. 11, 1825	
George Hamilton	Wentworth	Jan. 11, 1825	
Thomas Hornor	Oxford	Jan. 11, 1825	
Charles Ingersol	Oxford	Jan. 11, 1825	
Charles Jones	Leeds	Jan. 11, 1825	

*   By-election

Member	Constituency	Sworn In	Comments
David Jones	Leeds	Jan. 11, 1825	
Jonas Jones	Grenville	Jan. 11, 1825	Counsel for the Crown.
John Johnson Lefferty	Lincoln, 2nd & 3rd. R.	Jan. 11, 1825	
James Lyons	Northumberland	Jan. 11, 1825	On Feb. 23, 1825, the election of James Lyons, MPP, Northumberland, was declared void. Benjamin Ewing was declared duly elected at the July 13, 1824 General Election.
		Mar. 28, 1825	On Mar. 28, 1825, James Lyons was declared duly elected at the July 13, 1824 Northumberland General Election, in room of Benjamin Ewing, whose election was declared void.
John Mathews	Middlesex	Jan. 11, 1825	Also listed as Matthews.
Edward McBride	Niagara (Town)	Jan. 11, 1825	
Duncan McCall	Norfolk	Jan. 11, 1825	
Alexander McDonell	Glengary	Jan. 11, 1825	
Donald McDonell	Prescott & Russell	Jan. 11, 1825	
Archibald McLean	Stormont	Jan. 11, 1825	
William Morris	Lanark	Jan. 11, 1825	
Peter Perry	Lennox & Addington	Jan. 11, 1825	
Paul Peterson	Prince Edward	Jan. 11, 1825	
Eli Playter	York & Simcoe	Jan. 11, 1825	Also listed as Ely. On Feb. 17, 1827, the House was informed that Eli Playter, MPP, York & Simcoe, was indicted for a felony in the Home District and had withdrawn from the Province. A House Committee determined that the finding of an indictment alone did not warrant a Member to vacate his seat.

Robert Randal	Lincoln, 4th R.	Jan. 11, 1825	
John Beverley Robinson	York (Town)	Jan. 11, 1825	Mr. Attorney General.
John Rolph	Middlesex	Jan. 11, 1825	
William Scollick	Halton	Jan. 11, 1825	
William Thompson	York & Simcoe	Jan. 11, 1825	
Hugh Christopher Thomson	Frontenac	Jan. 11, 1825	Also listed as Thompson.
Philip VanKoughnet	Stormont	Jan. 11, 1825	
Hamilton Walker	Grenville	Jan. 11, 1825	
Francis Leigh Walsh	Norfolk	Jan. 11, 1825	
Reuben White	Hastings	Jan. 11, 1825	
John Alexander Wilkinson	Essex	Jan. 11, 1825	
James Willson	Prince Edward	Jan. 15, 1825	
Hon. John Willson	Wentworth	Jan. 11, 1825	On Jan. 11, 1825, George Hamilton, MPP, Wentworth, proposed John Willson, MPP, Wentworth, as Speaker. Seconded and resolved. Jan. 11, 1825 – Date took chair.

Constituency	Member	Sworn In	Comments
Carleton	George T. Burke	Date unknown. First appeared in Journals on Nov. 7, 1825.	General Election July 1824.
Dundas	John Crysler	Jan. 11, 1825	General Election July 1824.
Durham	George Strange Boulton	Jan. 11, 1825	General Election July 1824.
			On Mar. 1, 1825, the election of George Strange Boulton, MPP, Durham, was declared void. A new election was called.
Durham	Charles Fothergill	Mar. 31, 1825*	Government Printer.
			By-election Date unknown.
			Writ of Election – Mar. 1, 1825. On Mar. 31, 1825, the House was informed of the election of Charles Fothergill, MPP, Durham, in room of George Strange Boulton, whose election was declared void.
Essex	Francis Baby	Date unknown. First appeared in Journals on Nov. 16, 1825.	General Election July 1824.
			On Mar. 24, 1825, the Petition of Francis Baby complaining of the conduct of the Returning Officer at the last Essex General Election was found just. A new election was called.
			By-election Date unknown.
			Writ of Election – Mar. 25, 1825. Francis Baby was found duly elected for the County of Essex.
Essex	John Alexander Wilkinson	Jan. 11, 1825	General Election July 1824.
Frontenac	James Atkinson	Jan. 11, 1825	General Election July 1824.
Frontenac	Hugh Christopher Thomson	Jan. 11, 1825	Also listed as Thompson.
			General Election July 1824.

Glengary	Duncan Cameron	Jan. 11, 1825	Secretary and Registrar.
			General Election July 1824.
			On Mar. 12, 1825, the election of Duncan Cameron, MPP, Glengary, was declared void. A new election was called. [There was no evidence in the Journals of a Member having been returned for this District.]
Glengary	Alexander McDonell	Jan. 11, 1825	General Election July 1824.
Grenville	Jonas Jones	Jan. 11, 1825	Counsel for the Crown.
			General Election July 1824.
Grenville	Hamilton Walker	Jan. 11, 1825	General Election July 1824.
Halton	Richard Beasley	Jan. 11, 1825	General Election July 1824.
Halton	William Scollick	Jan. 11, 1825	General Election July 1824.
Hastings	Thomas Coleman	Jan. 11, 1825	General Election July 1824.
Hastings	Reuben White	Jan. 11, 1825	General Election July 1824.
Kent	James Gordon	Jan. 11, 1825	General Election July 1824.
Kingston (Town)	John Cumming	Jan. 15, 1825	General Election July 1824.
Lanark	William Morris	Jan. 11, 1825	Lanark. 1824. 4 Geo. IV, C.5, Ss.2, 3. An Act to divide the County of Carleton, in the Bathurst District. And be it further enacted by the authority aforesaid, that the Townships of Bathurst, Drummond, Beckwith, Dalhousie, Lanark, Ramsay, Darling, Levant, North Sherbroke, South Sherbroke, together with all the unsurveyed lands within the limits of the District of Bathurst, with such of the islands in the Ottawa river as are wholly or in greater part opposite to the said Townships, and unsurveyed land, shall constitute and form the County of Lanark . . . that the said Counties of

* By-election

Constituency	Member	Sworn In	Comments
Lanark — *Continued*			Lanark and Carleton, formed by this act, shall be each represented by one member.
			General Election July 1824.
Leeds	Charles Jones	Jan. 11, 1825	General Election July 1824.
Leeds	David Jones	Jan. 11, 1825	General Election July 1824.
Lennox & Addington	Marshall Spring Bidwell	Jan. 11, 1825	General Election July 1824.
Lennox & Addington	Peter Perry	Jan. 11, 1825	General Election July 1824.
Lincoln, 1st R.	John Clark	Jan. 11, 1825	General Election July 1824.
Lincoln, 2nd & 3rd R.	Bartholemew C. Beardsley	Jan. 11, 1825	General Election July 1824.
Lincoln, 2nd & 3rd. R.	John Johnson Lefferty	Jan. 11, 1825	General Election July 1824.
Lincoln, 4th R.	Robert Randal	Jan. 11, 1825	General Election July 1824.
Middlesex	John Mathews	Jan. 11, 1825	Also listed as Matthews.
			General Election July 1824.
Middlesex	John Rolph	Jan. 11, 1825	General Election July 1824.
Niagara (Town)	Edward McBride	Jan. 11, 1825	General Election July 1824.
Norfolk	Duncan McCall	Jan. 11, 1825	General Election July 1824.
			Norfolk. 1826. 7 Geo. IV, C.13, S.3. An Act to establish the District town of the District of London in a more central position than at present, and to annex the Townships of Walpole and Rainham to the County of Haldimand, in the District of Niagara . . . be it therefore enacted by the authority aforesaid, that so much of a certain act of the parliament of this province passed in the thirty-eighth year of his late Majesty's reign, entitled, An Act for the better division of this province, as enacts that the said Townships of Rainham and

			Walpole shall constitute and form a part of the County of Norfolk, shall be repealed; and that the said Townships of Rainham and Walpole shall be annexed to and shall form part of the County of Haldimand, in the District of Niagara.
Norfolk	Francis Leigh Walsh	Jan. 11, 1825	General Election July 1824.
			Norfolk. 1826. 7 Geo. IV, C.13, S.3. An Act to establish the District town of the District of London in a more central position than at present, and to annex the Townships of Walpole and Rainham to the County of Haldimand, in the District of Niagara . . . be it therefore enacted by the authority aforesaid, that so much of a certain act of the parliament of this province passed in the thirty-eighth year of his late Majesty's reign, entitled, An Act for the better division of this province, as enacts that the said Townships of Rainham and Walpole shall constitute and form a part of the County of Norfolk, shall be repealed; and that the said Townships of Rainham and Walpole shall be annexed to and shall form part of the County of Haldimand, in the District of Niagara.
Northumberland	Zaccheus Burnham	Jan. 11, 1825	General Election July 1824.
Northumberland	James Lyons	Jan. 11, 1825	General Election July 1824.
			On Feb. 23, 1825, the election of James Lyons, MPP, Northumberland, was declared void. Benjamin Ewing was declared duly elected at the July 13, 1824 General Election.
Northumberland	Benjamin Ewing	Feb. 24, 1825	On Feb. 23, 1825, the House was informed that Benjamin Ewing was duly elected at the July 13, 1824 Northumberland General Election, in room of James Lyons, whose election was declared void.
			On Mar. 28, 1825, the election of Benjamin Ewing, MPP, Northumberland, was declared void. James Lyons was duly elected at the July 13, 1824 General Election.

Constituency	Member	Sworn In	Comments
Northumberland	James Lyons	Mar. 28, 1825	On Mar. 28, 1825, James Lyons was declared duly elected at the July 13, 1824 Northumberland General Election, in room of Benjamin Ewing, whose election was declared void.
Oxford	Thomas Hornor	Jan. 11, 1825	General Election July 1824.
Oxford	Charles Ingersol	Jan. 11, 1825	General Election July 1824.
Prescott & Russell	Donald McDonell	Jan. 11, 1825	General Election July 1824.
Prince Edward	Paul Peterson	Jan. 11, 1825	General Election July 1824.
Prince Edward	James Willson	Jan. 15, 1825	General Election July 1824.
Stormont	Archibald McLean	Jan. 11, 1825	General Election July 1824.
Stormont	Philip VanKoughnet	Jan. 11, 1825	General Election July 1824.
Wentworth	George Hamilton	Jan. 11, 1825	General Election July 1824.
Wentworth	Hon. John Willson	Jan. 11, 1825	General Election July 1824. On Jan. 11, 1825, George Hamilton, MPP, Wentworth, proposed John Willson, MPP, Wentworth, as Speaker. Seconded and resolved. Jan. 11, 1825 – Date took chair.
York & Simcoe	Eli Playter	Jan. 11, 1825	Also listed as Ely. General Election July 1824. On Feb. 17, 1827, the House was informed that Eli Playter, MPP, York & Simcoe, was indicted for a felony in the Home District and had withdrawn from the Province. A House Committee determined that the finding of an indictment alone did not warrant a Member to vacate his seat.
York & Simcoe	William Thompson	Jan. 11, 1825	General Election July 1824.
York (Town)	John Beverley Robinson	Jan. 11, 1825	Mr. Attorney General. General Election July 1824.

LEGISLATURES OF UPPER CANADA
10th Legislature

General Election   July 1828

Sessions of the Tenth Legislature of Upper Canada: Jan. 8, 1829 – Mar. 6, 1830

First:	Jan. 8, 1829 – Mar. 20, 1829.
Second:	Jan. 8, 1830 – Mar. 6, 1830.

Alphabetical List of Members

Member	Constituency	Sworn In	Comments
Francis Baby	Essex	Jan. 8, 1829	
Robert Baldwin	York (Town)	Jan. 30, 1830*	Writ of Election – Jan. 19, 1830. On Jan. 30, 1830, the House was informed of the election of Robert Baldwin, MPP, York (Town), in room of John Beverley Robinson, resigned.
William Warren Baldwin	Norfolk	Jan. 8, 1829	
William Berczy	Kent	Date unknown. First appeared in Journals on Jan. 22, 1830.	
Donald Bethune	Kingston (Town)	Jan. 8, 1829	
Hon. Marshall Spring Bidwell	Lennox & Addington	Jan. 8, 1829	On Jan. 8, 1829, John Mathews, MPP, Middlesex, proposed Marshall Spring Bidwell, MPP, Lennox & Addington, as Speaker. Seconded and resolved. Jan. 8, 1829 – Date took chair.
Ambrose Blacklock	Stormont	Jan. 8, 1829	
George Brouse	Dundas	Jan. 8, 1829	
William Buell, Jr.	Leeds	Jan. 8, 1829	

John Cawthra	Simcoe	Jan. 8, 1829	
Thomas Dalton	Frontenac	Jan. 8, 1829	
Robert Dickson	Niagara (Town)	Jan. 8, 1829	
Benjamin Ewing	Northumberland	Jan. 8, 1829	
Charles Fothergill	Durham	Date unknown. First appeared in Journals on Jan. 19, 1829.	
Alexander Fraser	Glengary	Jan. 8, 1829	
George Hamilton	Wentworth	Jan. 8, 1829	
Rufus E. Henderson	Grenville	Jan. 8, 1829	
Caleb Hopkins	Halton	Jan. 8, 1829	
Thomas Hornor	Oxford	Jan. 8, 1829	
Jesse Ketchum	York	Jan. 8, 1829	
John Kilborn	Leeds	Jan. 8, 1829	
John Johnson Lefferty	Lincoln, 3rd R.	Jan. 8, 1829	
Joseph N. Lockwood	Hastings	Jan. 8, 1829	
George Longley	Grenville	Jan. 8, 1829	
James Lyons	Northumberland	Jan. 8, 1829	
William Lyon Mackenzie	York	Jan. 8, 1829	Also listed as McKenzie, MacKenzie.
Finlay Malcolm	Oxford	Jan. 8, 1829	
John Mathews	Middlesex	Jan. 8, 1829	
Duncan McCall	Norfolk	Jan. 8, 1829	
Donald McDonald	Prescott & Russell	Jan. 8, 1829	Sheriff of the Eastern District.
Archibald McLean	Stormont	Jan. 8, 1829	
William Morris	Lanark	Jan. 8, 1829	

* By-election

Member	Constituency	Sworn In	Comments
Peter Perry	Lennox & Addington	Jan. 8, 1829	
Paul Peterson	Prince Edward	Jan. 8, 1829	
Thomas Radenhurst	Carleton	Jan. 8, 1829	
Robert Randal	Lincoln, 4th R.	Jan. 8, 1829	
John Beverley Robinson	York (Town)	Jan. 8, 1829	Mr. Attorney General. On Jan. 14, 1830, the House was informed of the resignation of John Beverley Robinson, MPP, York (Town), who had accepted the appointment of Speaker of the Legislative Council. A new election was called.
George Rolph	Halton	Jan. 8, 1829	
John Rolph	Middlesex	Jan. 8, 1829	
James Hunter Samson	Hastings	Jan. 8, 1829	
Peter Shaver	Dundas	Jan. 8, 1829	
John David Smith	Durham	Jan. 8, 1829	
William Terry	Lincoln, 1st & 2nd R.	Jan. 8, 1829	
Hugh Christopher Thomson	Frontenac	Jan. 8, 1829	
John Alexander Wilkinson	Essex	Jan. 8, 1829	
James Willson	Prince Edward	Jan. 8, 1829	
John Willson	Wentworth	Jan. 8, 1829	
William Woodruff	Lincoln, 1st & 2nd R.	Jan. 8, 1829	

Constituency	Member	Sworn In	Comments
Carleton	Thomas Radenhurst	Jan. 8, 1829	General Election July 1828.
Dundas	George Brouse	Jan. 8, 1829	General Election July 1828.
Dundas	Peter Shaver	Jan. 8, 1829	General Election July 1828.
Durham	Charles Fothergill	Date unknown. First appeared in Journals on Jan. 19, 1829.	General Election July 1828.
Durham	John David Smith	Jan. 8, 1829	General Election July 1828.
Essex	Francis Baby	Jan. 8, 1829	General Election July 1828.
Essex	John Alexander Wilkinson	Jan. 8, 1829	General Election July 1828.
Frontenac	Thomas Dalton	Jan. 8, 1829	General Election July 1828.
Frontenac	Hugh Christopher Thomson	Jan. 8, 1829	General Election July 1828.
Glengary	Alexander Fraser	Jan. 8, 1829	General Election July 1828.
Grenville	Rufus E. Henderson	Jan. 8, 1829	General Election July 1828.
Grenville	George Longley	Jan. 8, 1829	General Election July 1828.
Halton	Caleb Hopkins	Jan. 8, 1829	General Election July 1828.
Halton	George Rolph	Jan. 8, 1829	General Election July 1828.
Hastings	Joseph N. Lockwood	Jan. 8, 1829	General Election July 1828.
Hastings	James Hunter Samson	Jan. 8, 1829	General Election July 1828.
Kent	William Berczy	Date unknown. First appeared in Journals on Jan. 22, 1830.	General Election July 1828.
Kingston (Town)	Donald Bethune	Jan. 8, 1829	General Election July 1828.
Lanark	William Morris	Jan. 8, 1829	General Election July 1828.

Leeds	William Buell, Jr.	Jan. 8, 1829	General Election July 1828.
Leeds	John Kilborn	Jan. 8, 1829	General Election July 1828.
Lennox & Addington	Hon. Marshall Spring Bidwell	Jan. 8, 1829	General Election July 1828. On Jan. 8, 1829, John Mathews, MPP, Middlesex, proposed Marshall Spring Bidwell, MPP, Lennox & Addington, as Speaker. Seconded and resolved. Jan. 8, 1829 – Date took chair.
Lennox & Addington	Peter Perry	Jan. 8, 1829	General Election July 1828.
Lincoln, 1st & 2nd R.	William Terry	Jan. 8, 1829	General Election July 1828.
Lincoln, 1st & 2nd R.	William Woodruff	Jan. 8, 1829	General Election July 1828.
Lincoln, 3rd R.	John Johnson Lefferty	Jan. 8, 1829	General Election July 1828.
Lincoln, 4th R.	Robert Randal	Jan. 8, 1829	General Election July 1828.
Middlesex	John Mathews	Jan. 8, 1829	General Election July 1828.
Middlesex	John Rolph	Jan. 8, 1829	General Election July 1828.
Niagara (Town)	Robert Dickson	Jan. 8, 1829	General Election July 1828.
Norfolk	William Warren Baldwin	Jan. 8, 1829	General Election July 1828.
Norfolk	Duncan McCall	Jan. 8, 1829	General Election July 1828.
Northumberland	Benjamin Ewing	Jan. 8, 1829	General Election July 1828.
Northumberland	James Lyons	Jan. 8, 1829	General Election July 1828.
Oxford	Thomas Hornor	Jan. 8, 1829	General Election July 1828.
Oxford	Finlay Malcolm	Jan. 8, 1829	General Election July 1828.
Prescott & Russell	Donald McDonald	Jan. 8, 1829	Sheriff of the Eastern District. General Election July 1828.
Prince Edward	Paul Peterson	Jan. 8, 1829	General Election July 1828.
Prince Edward	James Willson	Jan. 8, 1829	General Election July 1828.
Simcoe	John Cawthra	Jan. 8, 1829	General Election July 1828.
Stormont	Ambrose Blacklock	Jan. 8, 1829	General Election July 1828.
Stormont	Archibald McLean	Jan. 8, 1829	General Election July 1828.

Constituency	Member	Sworn In	Comments
Wentworth	George Hamilton	Jan. 8, 1829	General Election July 1828.
Wentworth	John Willson	Jan. 8, 1829	General Election July 1828.
York	Jesse Ketchum	Jan. 8, 1829	General Election July 1828.
York	William Lyon Mackenzie	Jan. 8, 1829	Also listed as McKenzie, MacKenzie. General Election July 1828.
York (Town)	John Beverley Robinson	Jan. 8, 1829	Mr. Attorney General. General Election July 1828. On Jan. 14, 1830, the House was informed of the resignation of John Beverley Robinson, MPP, York (Town), who had accepted the appointment of Speaker of the Legislative Council. A new election was called.
York (Town)	Robert Baldwin	Jan. 30, 1830*	By-election Date unknown. Writ of Election – Jan. 19, 1830. On Jan. 30, 1830, the House was informed of the election of Robert Baldwin, MPP, York (Town), in room of John Beverley Robinson, resigned.

LEGISLATURES OF UPPER CANADA
11th Legislature

General Election Oct. 1830

Sessions of the Eleventh Legislature of Upper Canada: Jan. 7, 1831 – Mar. 6, 1834

First:	Jan. 7, 1831 – Mar. 16, 1831.
Second:	Nov. 17, 1831 – Jan. 28, 1832.
Third:	Oct. 31, 1832 – Feb. 13, 1833.
Fourth:	Nov. 19, 1833 – Mar. 6, 1834.

Alphabetical List of Members

Member	Constituency	Sworn In	Comments
Bartholomew C. Beardsley	Lincoln, 2nd & 3rd R.	Jan. 7, 1831	
William Berczy	Kent	Date unknown. First appeared in Journals on Jan. 11, 1831.	
Marshall Spring Bidwell	Lenox & Addington	Jan. 7, 1831	
George Strange Boulton	Durham	Jan. 7, 1831	Mr. Attorney General.
Henry John Boulton	Niagara (Town)	Jan. 7, 1831	
John Brant	Haldimand	Jan. 7, 1831	On Feb. 1, 1831, the election of John Brant, MPP, Haldimand, was declared void. John Warren was duly elected at the Haldimand General Election.
John Brown	Durham	Jan. 7, 1831	
William Buell, Jr.	Leeds	Jan. 7, 1831	
Mahlon Burwell	Middlesex	Jan. 7, 1831	

John Campbell	Frontenac	Date unknown. First appeared in Journals on Jan. 19, 1831.	
William Chisholm	Halton	Jan. 7, 1831	
John Clark	Lincoln, 1st R.	Date unknown. First appeared in Journals on Jan. 20, 1831.	
John Cook	Dundas	Date unknown. First appeared in Journals on Jan. 10, 1831.	
James Crooks	Halton	Date unknown. First appeared in Journals on Jan. 10, 1831.	On Mar. 16, 1831, the House was informed of the resignation of James Crooks, MPP, Halton, who had been appointed to the Legislative Council. A new election was called.
William Crooks	Lincoln, 2nd & 3rd R.	Jan. 7, 1831	
Charles Duncombe	Oxford	Date unknown. First appeared in Journals on Jan. 10, 1831.	
William Elliott	Essex	Jan. 7, 1831	
Alexander Fraser	Glengarry	Jan. 7, 1831	
Donald Fraser	Lanark	Nov. 2, 1832	On Nov. 2, 1832, the House was informed of the election of Donald Fraser, MPP, Lanark.
			On Nov. 30, 1832, the election of Donald Fraser, MPP, Lanark, was declared void. A new election was called.
		Jan. 17, 1832*	Writ of Election – Nov. 30, 1832. On Jan. 15, 1833, the House was informed of the election of Donald Fraser, MPP, Lanark, who was returned as duly elected.

* By-election

Member	Constituency	Sworn In	Comments
Richard Duncan Frazer	Grenville	Jan. 7, 1831	
Christopher Alexander Hagerman	Kingston (Town)	Jan. 7, 1831	Mr. Solicitor General.
Thomas Hornor	Oxford	Nov. 9, 1832*	On Nov. 9, 1832, the House was informed of the election of Thomas Hornor, MPP, Oxford, in room of Charles Ingersol, deceased.
Matthew Munsel Howard	Leeds	Jan. 7, 1831	
Charles Ingersol	Oxford	Jan. 7, 1831	Died during the Inter-session, between the 2nd and 3rd sessions. A new election was called.
William Botsford Jarvis	York (Town)	Jan. 7, 1831	
Edward Jessup	Grenville	Jan. 7, 1831	On Nov. 21, 1831, the House was informed of the death of Edward Jessup, MPP, Grenville. A new election was called.
Henry Jones	Brockville (Town)	Jan. 7, 1831	
Jesse Ketchum	York	Jan. 7, 1831	
John Bower Lewis	Carleton	Jan. 7, 1831	
George Lyon	Carleton	Jan. 17, 1833	On Jan. 16, 1833, the House was informed that George Lyon had been duly elected at the Carleton General Election, in room of Hamnett Pinhey, whose election was declared void.
James Lyons	Northumberland	Date unknown. First appeared in Journals on Jan. 18, 1831.	
William Lyon Mackenzie	York	Jan. 7, 1831	Expelled, Dec. 12, 1831, being guilty of a high breach of the privileges of the House. Mackenzie had been found guilty of authoring scandalous and defamatory articles in his

			newspaper, the Colonial Advocate. A new election was called.
		Jan. 3, 1832*	Writ of Election – Dec. 12, 1831. On Jan. 3, 1832, the House was informed of the election of William Lyon Mackenzie, MPP, York, who was returned as duly elected.
			Expelled, Jan. 7, 1832, for the publication of gross, scandalous and malicious libels in his newspaper, the Colonial Advocate. A new election was called.
		Did not take seat	On Nov. 2, 1832, the House was informed of the election of William Lyon Mackenzie, MPP, York, who was returned as duly elected.
			Expelled, Dec. 2, 1833, having been declared unfit to take a seat as a Member of the same during the present Parliament. A new election was called.
		Did not take seat	Writ of Election – Dec. 2, 1833. On Dec. 17, 1833, the House was informed of the election of William Lyon Mackenzie, MPP, York, who was returned as duly elected.
			Expelled, Dec. 17, 1832, having been declared unfit and unworthy to hold a seat in this House during the continuance of the present Parliament.
			On Feb. 10, 1834, William Lyon Mackenzie was taken into custody at the Bar of the House by the Sergeant-at-arms, for disorderly conduct in the House.
			Admonished by the Speaker and discharged, Feb. 10, 1834, having been guilty of a breach of the privileges of the House, by obtruding himself within the Bar of the House.
Allan Napier MacNab	Wentworth	Jan. 7, 1831	
Jean Baptiste Maçon	Essex	Jan. 7, 1831	

*   By-election

Member	Constituency	Sworn In	Comments
Duncan McCall	Norfolk	Jan. 7, 1831	Died during the Inter-session, between the 2nd and 3rd Sessions. A new election was called.
Archibald McDonald	Northumberland	Jan. 7, 1831	
Donald McDonald	Prescott & Russell	Jan. 7, 1831	
Hon. Archibald McLean	Stormont	Jan. 7, 1831	On Jan. 7, 1831, William Morris, MPP, Lanark, proposed Archibald McLean, MPP, Stormont, as Speaker. Seconded and resolved. Jan. 7, 1831 – Date took chair.
Alexander McMartin	Glengarry	Jan. 7, 1831	
Colin McNeilledge	Norfolk	Jan. 14, 1833*	On Jan. 14, 1833, the House was informed of the election of Colin McNeilledge, MPP, Norfolk, in room of Duncan McCall, deceased.
William Hamilton Merritt	Haldimand	Nov. 7, 1832*	On Nov. 7, 1832, the House was informed of the election of William Hamilton Merritt, MPP, Haldimand, in room of John Warren, deceased.
William Morris	Lanark	Jan. 7, 1831	
Roswell Mount	Middlesex	Jan. 7, 1831	Funeral, Jan. 20, 1834. No By-election was called.
Hiram Norton	Grenville	Dec. 21, 1831*	Writ of Election – Nov. 25, 1831. On Dec. 21, 1831, the House was informed of the election of Hiram Norton, MPP, Grenville, in room of Edward Jessup, deceased.
Peter Perry	Lenox & Addington	Jan. 7, 1831	
Hamnett Pinhey	Carleton	Nov. 2, 1832	On Nov. 2, 1832, the House was informed of the election of Hamnett Pinhey, MPP, Carleton. On Jan. 16, 1833, the election of Hamnett Pinhey, MPP, Carleton, was declared void. George Lyon was declared duly elected at the Carleton General Election.
Robert Randal	Lincoln, 4th R.	Jan. 7, 1831	

William Benjamin Robinson	Simcoe	Jan. 7, 1831	
John Philip Roblin	Prince Edward	Jan. 7, 1831	
James Hunter Samson	Hastings	Jan. 7, 1831	
Absalom Shade	Halton	Nov. 17, 1831*	Writ of Election – Mar. 16, 1831. On Nov. 17, 1831, the House was informed of the election of Absalom Shade, MPP, Halton, in room of James Crooks, resigned.
Peter Shaver	Dundas	Jan. 7, 1831	
Hugh Christopher Thomson	Frontenac	Jan. 7, 1831	
Philip VanKoughnet	Stormont	Date unknown. First appeared in Journals on Jan. 7, 1831.	
John Warren	Haldimand	Feb. 2, 1831	On Feb. 1, 1831, the House was informed that John Warren was duly elected at the Haldimand General Election, in room of John Brant, whose election was declared void.
			Died in the Inter-session, between the 2nd and 3rd Sessions. A new election was called.
Asa Werden	Prince Edward	Jan. 7, 1831	On Jan. 28, 1831, the election of Asa Werden, MPP, Prince Edward, was declared void. A new election was called.
		Nov. 17, 1831*	Writ of Election – Jan. 28, 1831. On Nov. 17, 1831, the House was informed of the election of Asa Werden, MPP, Prince Edward, who was returned as duly elected.
Reuben White	Hastings	Jan. 7, 1831	
John Willson	Wentworth	Jan. 7, 1831	
William Wilson	Norfolk	Jan. 7, 1831	

* By-election

Constituency	Member	Sworn In	Comments
Brockville (Town)	Henry Jones	Jan. 7, 1831	General Election Oct. 1830.
Carleton	John Bower Lewis	Jan. 7, 1831	General Election Oct. 1830.
			1832. 2 Wm. IV, C.18, S.2. An Act to repeal part of an Act passed in the Fourth year of His late Majesty's Reign, entitled, An Act to divide the County of Carleton, in the Bathurst District. And be it further enacted by the authority aforesaid, that after the passing of this Act it shall and may be lawful for the Governor, Lieutenant Governor, or Person Administering the Government of this Province, to issue Writs for the Return of One Member for each of the said Counties [Lanark and Carleton], in addition to the Members now serving, in the same manner as the Governor, Lieutenant Governor or Person Administering the Government issues Writs for the Return of Members in cases of a General Election of Representative to the Provincial Parliament.
Carleton	Hamnett Pinhey	Nov. 2, 1832	General Election Oct. 1830.
			On Nov. 2, 1832, the House was informed of the election of Hamnett Pinhey, MPP, Carleton.
			On Jan. 16, 1833, the election of Hamnett Pinhey, MPP, Carleton, was declared void. George Lyon was declared duly elected at the Carleton General Election.
Carleton	George Lyon	Jan. 17, 1833	On Jan. 16, 1833, the House was informed that George Lyon had been duly elected at the Carleton General Election, in room of Hamnett Pinhey, whose election was declared void.
			Carleton. 1832. 2 Wm. IV, C.18, S.2. An Act to repeal part of an Act passed in the Fourth year

of His late Majesty's Reign, entitled, An Act to divide the County of Carleton, in the Bathurst District. And be it further enacted by the authority aforesaid, that after the passing of this Act it shall and may be lawful for the Governor, Lieutenant Governor, or Person Administering the Government of this Province, to issue Writs for the Return of One Member for each of the said Counties [Lanark and Carleton], in addition to the Members now serving, in the same manner as the Governor, Lieutenant Governor or Person Administering the Government issues Writs for the Return of Members in cases of a General Election of Representative to the Provincial Parliament.

Dundas	John Cook	Date unknown. First appeared in Journals on Jan. 10, 1831.	General Election Oct. 1830.
Dundas	Peter Shaver	Jan. 7, 1831	General Election Oct. 1830.
Durham	George Strange Boulton	Jan. 7, 1831	Mr. Attorney General. General Election Oct. 1830. Durham. 1834. 4 Wm. IV, C.15. An Act to attach certain Townships in the District of Newcastle to the Counties of Northumberland and Durham respectively. Whereas there are several Townships in the District of Newcastle which are not attached to or included within any County of the same, and whereas there are many inhabitants settled in those Townships, and it is therefore desirable to annex the same to some adjoining County . . . and that the Townships of Verulam, Fenelon and Eldon. be annexed to, and form part of the County of Durham.
Durham	John Brown	Jan. 7, 1831	General Election Oct. 1830. Durham. 1834. 4 Wm. IV, C.15. An Act to attach certain Townships in the District of

Constituency	Member	Sworn In	Comments
Durham — *Continued*			Newcastle to the Counties of Northumberland and Durham respectively. Whereas there are several Townships in the District of Newcastle which are not attached to or included within any County of the same, and whereas there are many inhabitants settled in those Townships, and it is therefore desirable to annex the same to some adjoining County . . . and that the Townships of Verulam, Fenelon and Eldon, be annexed to, and form part of the County of Durham.
Essex	William Elliott	Jan. 7, 1831	General Election Oct. 1830.
Essex	Jean Baptiste Maon	Jan. 7, 1831	General Election Oct. 1830.
Frontenac	John Campbell	Date unknown. First appeared in Journals on Jan. 19, 1831.	General Election Oct. 1830.
Frontenac	Hugh Christopher Thomson	Jan. 7, 1831	General Election Oct. 1830.
Glengarry	Alexander Fraser	Jan. 7, 1831	General Election Oct. 1830.
Glengarry	Alexander McMartin	Jan. 7, 1831	General Election Oct. 1830.
Grenville	Richard Duncan Frazer	Jan. 7, 1831	General Election Oct. 1830.
Grenville	Edward Jessup	Jan. 7, 1831	General Election Oct. 1830.
			On Nov. 21, 1831, the House was informed of the death of Edward Jessup, MPP, Grenville. A new election was called.
Grenville	Hiram Norton	Dec. 21, 1831*	By-election Dec. 12, 1831.
			Writ of Election – Nov. 21, 1831. On Dec. 21, 1831, the House was informed of the election of Hiram Norton, MPP, Grenville, in room of Edward Jessup, deceased.

Haldimand	John Brant	Jan. 7, 1831	Haldimand. 1826. 7 Geo. IV, C.13, S.3. An act to establish the district town of the district of London in a more central position that at present, and to annex the townships of Walpole and Rainham to the county of Haldimand, in the district of Niagara. . . . be it therefore enacted by the authority aforesaid, That so much of a certain act of the parliament of this province passed in the thirty-eighth year of his late Majesty's reign, entitled, An act for the better division of this province, as enacts that the said townships of Rainham and Walpole shall constitute and form a part of the county of Norfolk, shall be repealed; and that the said Townships of Rainham and Walpole shall be annexed to and shall form part of the county of Haldimand, in the district of Niagara.
			General Election Oct. 1830.
			On Feb. 1, 1831, the election of John Brant, MPP, Haldimand, was declared void. John Warren was duly elected at the Haldimand General Election.
Haldimand	John Warren	Feb. 2, 1831	On Feb. 1, 1831, the House was informed that John Warren was duly elected at the Haldimand General Election, in room of John Brant, whose election was declared void.
			Died in the Inter-session, between the 2nd and 3rd Sessions. A new election was called.
Haldimand	William Hamilton Merritt	Nov. 7, 1832*	By-election Date unknown.
			On Nov. 7, 1832, the House was informed of the election of William Hamilton Merritt, MPP, Haldimand, in room of John Warren, deceased.
Halton	William Chisholm	Jan. 7, 1831	General Election Oct. 1830.

* By-election

Constituency	Member	Sworn In	Comments
Halton	James Crooks	Date unknown. First appeared in Journals on Jan. 10, 1831.	General Election Oct. 1830. On Mar. 16, 1831, the House was informed of the resignation of James Crooks, MPP, Halton, who had been appointed to the Legislative Council. A new election was called.
Halton	Absalom Shade	Nov. 17, 1831*	By-election Date unknown. Writ of Election – Mar. 16, 1831. On Nov. 17, 1831, the House was informed of the election of Absalom Shade, MPP, Halton, in room of James Crooks, resigned.
Hastings	James Hunter Samson	Jan. 7, 1831	General Election Oct. 1830.
Hastings	Reuben White	Jan. 7, 1831	General Election Oct. 1830.
Kent	William Berczy	Date unknown. First appeared in Journals on Jan. 11, 1831.	General Election Oct. 1830.
Kingston (Town)	Christopher Alexander Hagerman	Jan. 7, 1831	Mr. Solicitor General. General Election Oct. 1830.
Lanark	Donald Fraser	Nov. 2, 1832	General Election Oct. 1830. Lanark. 1832. 2 Wm. IV, C.18, S.2. An Act to repeal part of an Act passed in the Fourth year of His late Majesty's Reign, entitled, An Act to divide the County of Carleton, in the Bathurst District. And be it further enacted by the authority aforesaid, that after the passing of this Act it shall and may be lawful for the Governor, Lieutenant Governor, or Person Administering the Government of this Province, to issue Writs for the Return of One MPP, each of the said Counties [Lanark and Carleton], in addition to the Members now serving, in the

same manner as the Governor, Lieutenant Governor or Person Administering the Government issues Writs for the Return of Members in cases of a General Election of Representatives to the Provincial Parliament.

On Nov. 2, 1832, the House was informed of the election of Donald Fraser, MPP, Lanark.

On Nov. 30, 1832, the election of Donald Fraser, MPP, Lanark, was declared void. A new election was called.

		Jan. 17, 1832*	By-election Date unknown.

Writ of Election – Nov. 30, 1832. On Jan. 15, 1833, the House was informed of the election of Donald Fraser, MPP, Lanark, who was returned as duly elected.

Lanark	William Morris	Jan. 7, 1831	General Election Oct. 1830.

Lanark. 1832. 2 Wm. IV, C.18, S.2. An Act to repeal part of an Act passed in the Fourth year of His late Majesty's Reign, entitled, An Act to divide the County of Carleton, in the Bathurst District. And be it further enacted by the authority aforesaid, that after the passing of this Act it shall and may be lawful for the Governor, Lieutenant Governor, or Person Administering the Government of this Province, to issue Writs for the Return of One MPP, each of the said Counties [Lanark and Carleton], in addition to the Members now serving, in the same manner as the Governor, Lieutenant Governor or Person Administering the Government issues Writs for the Return of Members in cases of a General Election of Representatives to the Provincial Parliament.

Leeds	William Buell, Jr.	Jan. 7, 1831	General Election Oct. 1830.

* By-election

Constituency	Member	Sworn In	Comments
Leeds	Matthew Munsel Howard	Jan. 7, 1831	General Election Oct. 1830.
Lenox & Addington	Marshall Spring Bidwell	Jan. 7, 1831	General Election Oct. 1830.
Lenox & Addington	Peter Perry	Jan. 7, 1831	General Election Oct. 1830.
Lincoln, 1st R.	John Clark	Date unknown. First appeared in Journals on Jan. 20, 1831.	General Election Oct. 1830.
Lincoln, 2nd & 3rd R.	Bartholomew C. Beardsley	Jan. 7, 1831	General Election Oct. 1830.
Lincoln, 2nd & 3rd R.	William Crooks	Jan. 7, 1831	General Election Oct. 1830.
Lincoln, 4th R.	Robert Randal	Jan. 7, 1831	General Election Oct. 1830.
Middlesex	Mahlon Burwell	Jan. 7, 1831	General Election Oct. 1830.
Middlesex	Roswell Mount	Jan. 7, 1831	General Election Oct. 1830. Funeral, Jan. 20, 1834. No By-election was called.
Niagara (Town)	Henry John Boulton	Jan. 7, 1831	General Election Oct. 1830.
Norfolk	Duncan McCall	Jan. 7, 1831	General Election Oct. 1830. Died during the Inter-session, between the 2nd and 3rd Sessions. A new election was called.
Norfolk	Colin McNeilledge	Jan. 14, 1833*	By-election Date unknown. On Jan. 14, 1833, the House was informed of the election of Colin McNeilledge, MPP, Norfolk, in room of Duncan McCall, deceased.
Norfolk	William Wilson	Jan. 7, 1831	General Election Oct. 1830.
Northumberland	James Lyons	Date unknown. First appeared in Journals on Jan. 18, 1831.	General Election Oct. 1830. Northumberland. 1834. 4 Wm. IV, C.15. An Act to attach certain Townships in the District of Newcastle to the Counties of Northumberland

and Durham, respectively. Whereas there are several Townships in the District of Newcastle which are not attached to or included within any County of the same, and whereas there are many inhabitants settled in those Townships, and it is therefore desirable to annex the same to some adjoining County . . . That the Townships of Ennismore, Harvey, Douro, Dummer, Belmont, Burleigh and Methuen, be annexed to, and form part of the County of Northumberland . . .

Northumberland	Archibald McDonald	Jan. 7, 1831	General Election Oct. 1830.

Northumberland. 1834. 4 Wm. IV, C.15. An Act to attach certain Townships in the District of Newcastle to the Counties of Northumberland and Durham, respectively. Whereas there are several Townships in the District of Newcastle which are not attached to or included within any County of the same, and whereas there are many inhabitants settled in those Townships, and it is therefore desirable to annex the same to some adjoining County . . . That the Townships of Ennismore, Harvey, Douro, Dummer, Belmont, Burleigh and Methuen, be annexed to, and form part of the County of Northumberland . . .

Oxford	Charles Duncombe	Date unknown. First appeared in Journals on Jan. 10, 1831.	General Election Oct. 1830.
Oxford	Charles Ingersol	Jan. 7, 1831	General Election Oct. 1830.

Died during the Inter-session, between the 2nd and 3rd sessions. A new election was called.

*   By-election

Constituency	Member	Sworn In	Comments
Oxford	Thomas Hornor	Nov. 9, 1832*	By-election Date unknown.
			On Nov. 9, 1832, the House was informed of the election of Thomas Hornor, MPP, Oxford, in room of Charles Ingersol, deceased.
Prescott & Russell	Donald McDonald	Jan. 7, 1831	General Election Oct. 1830.
Prince Edward	John Philip Roblin	Jan. 7, 1831	General Election Oct. 1830.
			Prince Edward. 1831. 1 Wm. IV, C.7. An act to erect the county of Prince Edward into a separate district. Whereas from the peculiar situation of the county of Prince Edward, in the Midland district of this province, and from various other causes, it has become expedient to erect the said county into a separate district. . . .
Prince Edward	Asa Werden	Jan. 7, 1831	General Election Oct. 1830.
			Prince Edward. 1831. 1 Wm. IV, C.7. An act to erect the county of Prince Edward into a separate district. Whereas from the peculiar situation of the county of Prince Edward, in the Midland district of this province, and from various other causes, it has become expedient to erect the said county into a separate district. . . .
			On Jan. 28, 1831, the election of Asa Werden, MPP, Prince Edward, was declared void. A new election was called.
		Nov. 17, 1831*	Writ of Election – Jan. 28, 1831. On Nov. 17, 1831, the House was informed of the election of Asa Werden, MPP, Prince Edward, who was returned as duly elected.
Simcoe	William Benjamin Robinson	Jan. 7, 1831	General Election Oct. 1830.

Stormont	Hon. Archibald McLean	Jan. 7, 1831	General Election Oct. 1830.
			On Jan. 7, 1831, William Morris, MPP, Lanark, proposed Archibald McLean, MPP, Stormont, as Speaker. Seconded and resolved. Jan. 7, 1831 – Date took chair.
Stormont	Philip VanKoughnet	Date unknown. First appeared in Journals on Jan. 7, 1831.	General Election Oct. 1830.
Wentworth	Allan Napier MacNab	Jan. 7, 1831	General Election Oct. 1830.
Wentworth	John Willson	Jan. 7, 1831	General Election Oct. 1830.
York	Jesse Ketchum	Jan. 7, 1831	General Election Oct. 1830.
			York. 1833. 3 Wm. IV, C.16, Ss. 1, 3. An Act to alter the manner of holding the Elections for Members to represent the Counties of York and Lincoln, in the House of Assembly; more equally to divide the County of York into Ridings, and to increase the Representation of the said County of York. . . . and that from and after the passing of this Act, the County of York shall be divided into Four Ridings, to be called the First, Second, Third and Fourth Ridings, respectively.
York	William Lyon Mackenzie	Jan. 7, 1831	General Election Oct. 1830.
			Expelled, Dec. 12, 1831, being guilty of a high breach of the privileges of the House. Mackenzie had been found guilty of authoring scandalous and defamatory articles in his newspaper, the Colonial Advocate. A new election was called.
		Jan. 3, 1832*	By-election Date unknown.
			Writ of Election – Dec. 12, 1831. On Jan. 3, 1832, the House was informed of the election

*   By-election

Constituency	Member	Sworn In	Comments
York — *Continued*			of William Lyon Mackenzie, MPP, York, who was returned as duly elected.
			Expelled, Jan. 7, 1832, for the publication of gross, scandalous and malicious libels in his newspaper, the Colonial Advocate. A new election was called.
		Did not take seat	On Nov. 2, 1832, the House was informed of the election of William Lyon Mackenzie, MPP, York, who was returned as duly elected.
			Expelled, Dec. 2, 1833, having been declared unfit to take a seat as a Member of the same during the present Parliament. A new election was called.
		Did not take seat	By-election Dec. 16, 1833.
			Writ of Election – Dec. 2, 1833. On Dec. 17, 1833, the House was informed of the election of William Lyon Mackenzie, MPP, York, who was returned as duly elected.
			Expelled, Dec. 17, 1833, having been declared unfit and unworthy to hold a seat in this House during the continuance of the present Parliament.
			York. 1833. 3 Wm. IV, C.16, Ss. 1, 3. An Act to alter the manner of holding the Elections for Members to represent the Counties of York and Lincoln, in the House of Assembly; more equally to divide the County of York into Ridings, and to increase the Representation of the said County of York. . . . and that from and after the passing of this Act, the County of York shall be divided into Four Ridings, to be called the First, Second, Third and Fourth Ridings, respectively.
			On Feb. 10, 1834, William Lyon Mackenzie

was taken into custody at the Bar of the House by the Sergeant-at-arms, for disorderly conduct in the House.

Admonished by the Speaker and discharged, Feb. 10, 1834, having been guilty of a breach of the privileges of the House, by obtruding himself within the Bar of the House.

York (Town)	William Botsford Jarvis	Jan. 7, 1831	General Election Oct. 1830.

LEGISLATURES OF UPPER CANADA
12th Legislature

General Election   Oct. 1834

Sessions of the Twelfth Legislature of Upper Canada: Jan. 15, 1835 – Apr. 20, 1836

First:	Jan. 15, 1835 – Apr. 16, 1835.
Second:	Jan. 14, 1836 – Apr. 20, 1836.

Alphabetical List of Members

Member	Constituency	Sworn In	Comments
Robert Alway	Oxford	Jan. 15, 1835	
Hon. Marshall Spring Bidwell	Lennox & Addington	Jan. 15, 1835	On Jan. 15, 1835, Peter Perry, MPP, Lennox & Addington, proposed Marshall Spring Bidwell, MPP, Lennox & Addington, as Speaker. Seconded and resolved. Jan. 15, 1835 – Date took chair.
George Strange Boulton	Durham	Jan. 15, 1835	
John Brown	Durham	Jan. 15, 1835	
William Bruce	Stormont	Jan. 15, 1835	
William Buell, Jr.	Leeds	Apr. 12, 1836*	Writ of Election – Mar. 8, 1836. On Apr. 12, 1836, the House was informed of the elections of William Buell, Jr. and Matthew Munsel Howard, Members for Leeds, in room of Ogle Robert Gowan and Robert S. Jameson, whose elections were declared void.
Francis Caldwell	Essex	Jan. 15, 1835	
John Chesser	Prescott	Jan. 14, 1831*	Writ of Election – Feb. 27, 1835. On Apr. 2, 1835, the House was informed of the election of John Chesser, MPP, Prescott, in room of Alexander McDonell, deceased.

Alexander Chisholm	Glengarry	Jan. 15, 1835	
John Cook	Dundas	Jan. 15, 1835	
Nathan Cornwall	Kent	Jan. 15, 1835	
Charles Duncombe	Oxford	Jan. 15, 1835	
David Duncombe	Norfolk	Jan. 15, 1835	
Robert Graham Dunlop	Huron	Jan. 14, 1836*	On Jan. 14, 1836, the House was informed of the election of Robert Graham Dunlop, MPP, Huron.
James Durand	Halton	Jan. 15, 1835	
David Gibson	York, 1st R.	Jan. 15, 1835	
John Gilchrist	Northumberland	Jan. 15, 1835	
Ogle Robert Gowan	Leeds	Jan. 15, 1835	On Feb. 14, 1835, the election of Ogle Robert Gowan, MPP, Leeds, was declared void. A new election was called.
		Mar. 21, 1835*	Writ of Election – Feb. 14, 1835. On Mar. 21, 1835, the House was informed of the election of Ogle Robert Gowan, MPP, Leeds, who was returned as duly elected.

On Apr. 10, 1835, the election of Ogle Robert Gowan, MPP, Leeds, was declared void. The Committee appointed to investigate this By-election recommended to the House "that no writ for a new election be ordered until steps are taken to secure the freedom of elections, and enable peaceable and quiet electors of the said county to exercise their elective franchise in peace and safety."

On Mar. 3, 1836, with the passing of the Bill, "An Act to ensure the freedom of Elections in the County of Leeds," a new election was called.

*   By-election

Member	Constituency	Sworn In	Comments
Christopher Alexander Hagerman	Kingston (Town)	Jan. 15, 1835	Solicitor General.
Caleb Hopkins	Halton	Jan. 15, 1835	
Matthew Munsel Howard	Leeds	Apr. 15, 1836*	Writ of Election – Mar. 8, 1836. On Apr. 12, 1836, the House was informed of the elections of Matthew Munsel Howard and William Buell, Jr., Members for Leeds, in room of Ogle Robert Gowan and Robert S. Jameson, whose elections were declared void.
Robert S. Jameson	Leeds	Jan. 15, 1835	Attorney General.
			On Feb. 14, 1835, the election of Robert S. Jameson, MPP, Leeds, was declared void. A new election was called.
		Mar. 21, 1835*	Writ of Election – Feb. 14, 1835. On Mar. 21, 1835, the House was informed of the election of Robert S. Jameson, MPP, Leeds, who was returned as duly elected.
			On Apr. 10, 1835, the election of Robert S. Jameson, MPP, Leeds, was declared void. The Committee appointed to investigate this By-election recommended to the House "that no writ for a new election be ordered until steps are taken to secure the freedom of elections, and enable peaceable and quiet electors of the said county to exercise their elective franchise in peace and safety."
			On Mar. 3, 1836, with the passing of the Bill, "An Act to ensure the freedom of Elections in the County of Leeds," a new election was called.
David Jones	Brockville (Town)	Jan. 15, 1835	
John Johnson Lefferty	Lincoln, 3rd R.	Did not take seat	On Feb. 2, 1835, the election of John Johnson

Lefferty, MPP, Lincoln, 3rd R., was declared void. David Thorburn was duly elected at the Lincoln, 3rd R. General Election.

John Bower Lewis	Carleton	Date unknown. First appeared in Journals on Jan. 22, 1835.	
Samuel Lount	Simcoe	Jan. 15, 1835	
Donald Macdonell	Glengarry	Jan. 15, 1835	Also listed as McDonell.
Donald Aeneas MacDonell	Stormont	Jan. 15, 1835	Also listed as McDonell.
William Lyon Mackenzie	York, 2nd R.	Jan. 15, 1835	
Allan Napier MacNab	Hamilton (City)	Jan. 15, 1835	
Edward Malloch	Carleton	Jan. 15, 1835	
William McCrae	Kent	Jan. 15, 1835	
Alexander McDonell (Northumberland)	Northumberland	Jan. 15, 1835	
Alexander McDonell (Prescott)	Prescott	Jan. 15, 1835	On Feb. 27, 1835, the House was informed of the death of Alexander McDonell, MPP, Prescott. A new election was called.
John McIntosh	York, 4th R.	Jan. 15, 1835	
Thomas McKay	Russell	Jan. 15, 1835	
Archibald McLean	Cornwall (Town)	Jan. 15, 1835	
Gilbert McMicking	Lincoln, 4th R.	Jan. 15, 1835	
William Hamilton Merritt	Haldimand	Jan. 15, 1835	
Elias Moore	Middlesex	Jan. 15, 1835	
William Morris	Lanark	Jan. 15, 1835	On Jan. 27, 1836, the House was informed of the resignation of the Hon. William Morris, MPP, Lanark, who had been appointed to the Legislative Council. A new election was called.

* By-election

Member	Constituency	Sworn In	Comments
Thomas David Morrison	York, 3rd R.	Jan. 15, 1835	
Hiram Norton	Grenville	Jan. 15, 1835	
Thomas Parke	Middlesex	Jan. 15, 1835	
Peter Perry	Lennox & Addington	Jan. 15, 1835	
Charles Richardson	Niagara (Town)	Jan. 15, 1835	
William Benjamin Robinson	Simcoe	Jan. 15, 1835	
John Philip Roblin	Prince Edward	Jan. 15, 1835	
George Rykert	Lincoln, 2nd R.	Jan. 15, 1835	
Jacob Rymal	Wentworth	Jan. 15, 1835	
James Hunter Samson	Hastings	Jan. 15, 1835	On Mar. 30, 1836, the House was informed of the death of James Hunter Samson, MPP, Hastings. A new Writ was issued that day, with the By-election being called for Apr. 25, 1836. [As the House prorogued Apr. 20, 1836, the By-election was not held.]
Peter Shaver	Dundas	Jan. 15, 1835	
Jacob Shibley	Frontenac	Jan. 15, 1835	
James Edward Small	Toronto (City)	Jan. 15, 1835	
Harmannus Smith	Wentworth	Jan. 15, 1835	
John Strange	Frontenac	Jan. 15, 1835	
Josias Tayler	Lanark	Jan. 15, 1835	
Alexander Thom	Lanark	Mar. 2, 1836*	Writ of Election – Jan. 27, 1836. On Mar. 2, 1836, the House was informed of the election of Alexander Thom, MPP, Lanark, in room of the Hon. William Morris, resigned.
David Thorburn	Lincoln, 3rd R.	Date unknown. First appeared in	On Feb. 2, 1835, the House was informed that David Thorburn was duly elected at the

		Journals on Feb. 5, 1835.	Lincoln, 3rd R. General Election, in room of John Johnson Lefferty, whose election was declared void.
Francis Leigh Walsh	Norfolk	Jan. 15, 1835	
Charles Waters	Prescott	Jan. 15, 1835	
William B. Wells	Grenville	Jan. 15, 1835	
John Alexander Wilkinson	Essex	Jan. 15, 1835	
James Willson	Prince Edward	Jan. 15, 1835	
Dennis Woolverton	Lincoln, 1st R.	Jan. 15, 1835	
Henry W. Yager	Hastings	Jan. 15, 1835	

*   By-election

Alphabetical List of Constituencies
12th Legislature: Jan. 15, 1835 – Apr. 20, 1836.

76

Constituency	Member	Sworn In	Comments
Brockville (Town)	David Jones	Jan. 15, 1835	General Election Oct. 1834.
Carleton	John Bower Lewis	Date unknown. First appeared in Journals on Jan. 22, 1835.	General Election Oct. 1834.
Carleton	Edward Malloch	Jan. 15, 1835	General Election Oct. 1834.
Cornwall (Town)	Archibald McLean	Jan. 15, 1835	General Election Oct. 1834.
Dundas	John Cook	Jan. 15, 1835	General Election Oct. 1834.
Dundas	Peter Shaver	Jan. 15, 1835	General Election Oct. 1834.
Durham	George Strange Boulton	Jan. 15, 1835	General Election Oct. 1834.
Durham	John Brown	Jan. 15, 1835	General Election Oct. 1834.
Essex	Francis Caldwell	Jan. 15, 1835	General Election Oct. 1834.
Essex	John Alexander Wilkinson	Jan. 15, 1835	General Election Oct. 1834.
Frontenac	Jacob Shibley	Jan. 15, 1835	General Election Oct. 1834.
Frontenac	John Strange	Jan. 15, 1835	General Election Oct. 1834.
Glengarry	Alexander Chisholm	Jan. 15, 1835	General Election Oct. 1834.
Glengarry	Donald Macdonell	Jan. 15, 1835	Also listed as McDonell. General Election Oct. 1834.
Grenville	Hiram Norton	Jan. 15, 1835	General Election Oct. 1834.
Grenville	William B. Wells	Jan. 15, 1835	General Election Oct. 1834.
Haldimand	William Hamilton Merritt	Jan. 15, 1835	General Election Oct. 1834.
Halton	James Durand	Jan. 15, 1835	General Election Oct. 1834.
Halton	Caleb Hopkins	Jan. 15, 1835	General Election Oct. 1834.
Hamilton (City)	Allan Napier MacNab	Jan. 15, 1835	General Election Oct. 1834.

Hastings	James Hunter Samson	Jan. 15, 1835	General Election Oct. 1834.
			On Mar. 30, 1836, the House was informed of the death of James Hunter Samson, MPP, Hastings. A new Writ was issued that day, with the By-election being called for Apr. 25, 1836. [As the House prorogued Apr. 20, 1836, the By-election was not held.]
Hastings	Henry W. Yager	Jan. 15, 1835	General Election Oct. 1834.
Huron	Robert Graham Dunlop	Jan. 14, 1836*	Huron. 1835. 5 Wm. IV, C.45, S.1. An Act to form certain Townships in the London District into a County, and to attach certain Townships to the Counties of Middlesex and Kent in the London and Western Districts. . . . That the Townships of Williams, McGillivray, Stephen, Hay, Stanley, Goderich, Colborne, Hullet, McKillop, Tuckersmith, Hibbert, Logan, Fullarton, Usborne, Biddulph, Blanchard, Downie, Ellice, North Easthope, and South Easthope, do constitute and form the County of Huron in the London District.
			By-election July 8, 1835.
			On Jan. 14, 1836, the House was informed of the election of Robert Graham Dunlop, MPP, Huron.
Kent	Nathan Cornwall	Jan. 15, 1835	General Election Oct. 1834.
			Kent. 1835. 5 Wm. IV, C.45, S.3. An Act to form certain Townships in the London District into a County, and to attach certain Townships to the Counties of Middlesex and Kent, in the London and Western Districts. And be it further enacted by the authority aforesaid, that the Townships of Moore and Sarnia, (formerly Saint Clair), Plympton, Enniskillen, Warwick, Brooke, and Bosanquet, be attached to and

*   By-election

Constituency	Member	Sworn In	Comments
Kent — *Continued*			form part of the County of Kent, in the Western District.
Kent	William McCrae	Jan. 15, 1835	General Election Oct. 1834.
			Kent. 1835. 5 Wm. IV, C.45, S.3. An Act to form certain Townships in the London District into a County, and to attach certain Townships to the Counties of Middlesex and Kent, in the London and Western Districts. And be it further enacted by the authority aforesaid, that the Townships of Moore and Sarnia, (formerly Saint Clair), Plympton, Enniskillen, Warwick, Brooke, and Bosanquet, be attached to and form part of the County of Kent, in the Western District.
Kingston (Town)	Christopher Alexander Hagerman	Jan. 15, 1835	Solicitor General.
			General Election Oct. 1834.
Lanark	William Morris	Jan. 15, 1835	General Election Oct. 1834.
			On Jan. 27, 1836, the House was informed of the resignation of the Hon. William Morris, MPP, Lanark, who had been appointed to the Legislative Council. A new election was called.
Lanark	Alexander Thom	Mar. 2, 1836*	By-election Feb. 22, 1836.
			Writ of Election – Jan. 27, 1836. On Mar. 2, 1836, the House was informed of the election of Alexander Thom, MPP, Lanark, in room of the Hon. William Morris, resigned.
Lanark	Josias Tayler	Jan. 15, 1835	General Election Oct. 1834.
Leeds	Ogle Robert Gowan	Jan. 15, 1835	General Election Oct. 1834.
			On Feb. 14, 1835, the election of Ogle Robert Gowan, MPP, Leeds, was declared void. A new election was called.

		Mar. 21, 1835*	By-election Mar. 2, 1835.
			Writ of Election – Feb. 14, 1835. On Mar. 21, 1835, the House was informed of the election of Ogle Robert Gowan, MPP, Leeds, who was returned as duly elected.
			On Apr. 10, 1835, the election of Ogle Robert Gowan, MPP, Leeds, was declared void. The Committee appointed to investigate this By-election recommended to the House "that no writ for a new election be ordered until steps are taken to secure the freedom of elections, and enable peaceable and quiet electors of the said county to exercise their elective franchise in peace and safety."
			On Mar. 3, 1836, with the passing of the Bill, "An Act to ensure the freedom of Elections in the County of Leeds," a new election was called.
Leeds	Robert S. Jameson	Jan. 15, 1835	Attorney General.
			General Election Oct. 1834.
			On Feb. 14, 1835, the election of Robert S. Jameson, MPP, Leeds, was declared void. A new election was called.
		Mar. 21, 1835*	By-election Mar. 2, 1835.
			Writ of Election – Feb. 14, 1835. On Mar. 21, 1835, the House was informed of the election of Robert S. Jameson, MPP, Leeds, who was returned as duly elected.
			On Apr. 10, 1835, the election of Robert S. Jameson, MPP, Leeds, was declared void. The Committee appointed to investigate this By-election recommended to the House "that no writ for a new election be ordered until steps are taken to secure the freedom of elections, and enable peaceable and quiet electors of the

*　By-election

Constituency	Member	Sworn In	Comments
Leeds — *Continued*			said county to exercise their elective franchise in peace and safety."
			On Mar. 3, 1836, with the passing of the Bill, "An Act to ensure the freedom of Elections in the County of Leeds," a new election was called.
Leeds	William Buell, Jr.	Apr. 12, 1836*	By-election Mar. 28, 1836.
			Writ of Election – Mar. 8, 1836. On Apr. 12, 1836, the House was informed of the elections of William Buell, Jr. and Matthew Munsel Howard, Members for Leeds, in room of Ogle Robert Gowan and Robert S. Jameson, whose elections were declared void.
Leeds	Matthew Munsel Howard	Apr. 15, 1836*	By-election Mar. 28, 1836.
			Writ of Election – Mar. 8, 1836.
			On Apr. 12, 1836, the House was informed of the elections of Matthew Munsel Howard and William Buell, Jr., Members for Leeds, in room of Ogle Robert Gowan and Robert S. Jameson, whose elections were declared void.
Lennox & Addington	Hon. Marshall Spring Bidwell	Jan. 15, 1835	General Election Oct. 1834.
			On Jan. 15, 1835, Peter Perry, MPP, Lennox & Addington, proposed Marshall Spring Bidwell, MPP, Lennox & Addington, as Speaker. Seconded and resolved. Jan. 15, 1835 – Date took chair.
Lennox & Addington	Peter Perry	Jan. 15, 1835	General Election Oct. 1834.
Lincoln, 1st R.	Dennis Woolverton	Jan. 15, 1835	General Election Oct. 1834.
Lincoln, 2nd R.	George Rykert	Jan. 15, 1835	General Election Oct. 1834.
Lincoln, 3rd R.	John Johnson Lefferty	Did not take seat	General Election Oct. 1834.

			On Feb. 2, 1835, the election of John Johnson Lefferty, MPP, Lincoln, 3rd R., was declared void. David Thorburn was duly elected at the Lincoln, 3rd R. General Election.
Lincoln, 3rd R.	David Thorburn	Date unknown. First appeared in Journals on Feb. 5, 1835.	On Feb. 2, 1835, the House was informed that David Thorburn was duly elected at the Lincoln, 3rd R. General Election, in room of John Johnson Lefferty, whose election was declared void.
Lincoln, 4th R.	Gilbert McMicking	Jan. 15, 1835	General Election Oct. 1834.
Middlesex	Elias Moore	Jan. 15, 1835	General Election Oct. 1834.
Middlesex	Thomas Parke	Jan. 15, 1835	General Election Oct. 1834.
			Middlesex. 1835. 5 Wm. IV, C.45, S.2. An Act to form certain Townships in the London District into a County, and to attach certain Townships to the Counties of Middlesex and Kent, in the London and Western Districts. And be it further enacted by the authority aforesaid, that the Township of Adelaide be attached to and form part of the County of Middlesex, in the London District.
Niagara (Town)	Charles Richardson	Jan. 15, 1835	General Election Oct. 1834.
Norfolk	David Duncombe	Jan. 15, 1835	General Election Oct. 1834.
Norfolk	Francis Leigh Walsh	Jan. 15, 1835	General Election Oct. 1834.
Northumberland	John Gilchrist	Jan. 15, 1835	General Election Oct. 1834.
Northumberland	Alexander McDonell (Northumberland)	Jan. 15, 1835	General Election Oct. 1834.
Oxford	Robert Alway	Jan. 15, 1835	General Election Oct. 1834.
Oxford	Charles Duncombe	Jan. 15, 1835	General Election Oct. 1834.

* By-election

Constituency	Member	Sworn In	Comments
Prescott	Alexander McDonell (Prescott)	Jan. 15, 1835	General Election Oct. 1834. On Feb. 27, 1835, the House was informed of the death of Alexander McDonell, MPP, Prescott. A new election was called.
Prescott	John Chesser	Jan. 14, 1831*	By-election Mar. 17, 1835. Writ of Election – Feb. 27, 1835. On Apr. 2, 1835, the House was informed of the election of John Chesser, MPP, Prescott, in room of Alexander McDonell, deceased.
Prescott	Charles Waters	Jan. 15, 1835	General Election Oct. 1834.
Prince Edward	John Philip Roblin	Jan. 15, 1835	General Election Oct. 1834.
Prince Edward	James Willson	Jan. 15, 1835	General Election Oct. 1834.
Russell	Thomas McKay	Jan. 15, 1835	General Election Oct. 1834.
Simcoe	Samuel Lount	Jan. 15, 1835	General Election Oct. 1834.
Simcoe	William Benjamin Robinson	Jan. 15, 1835	General Election Oct. 1834.
Stormont	William Bruce	Jan. 15, 1835	General Election Oct. 1834.
Stormont	Donald Aeneas MacDonell	Jan. 15, 1835	Also listed as McDonell. General Election Oct. 1834.
Toronto (City)	James Edward Small	Jan. 15, 1835	General Election Oct. 1834.
Wentworth	Jacob Rymal	Jan. 15, 1835	General Election Oct. 1834.
Wentworth	Harmannus Smith	Jan. 15, 1835	General Election Oct. 1834.
York, 1st R.	David Gibson	Jan. 15, 1835	York, 1st R. 1833. 3 Wm. IV, C.16, Ss. 1, 3. An Act to alter the manner of holding the Elections for Members to represent the Counties of York and Lincoln, in the House of Assembly; more equally to divide the County of York into Ridings, and to increase the

Representation of the said County of York. . . . and that the Townships of York, including its Peninsula, Etobicoke, Vaughan and King, do form the First Riding: . . . that each of the said Ridings in the County of York shall be Represented in the House of Assembly by one Member.

General Election Oct. 1834.

| York, 2nd R. | William Lyon Mackenzie | Jan. 15, 1835 | York, 2nd R. 1833. 3 Wm. IV, C.16, Ss. 1, 3. An Act to alter the manner of holding the Elections for Members to represent the Counties of York and Lincoln, in the House of Assembly; more equally to divide the County of York into Ridings, and to increase the Representation of the said County of York. . . . the Townships of Caledon, Chinguacousy, Toronto, Gore of Toronto and Albion, the Second Riding: . . . that each of the said Ridings in the County of York shall be Represented in the House of Assembly by one Member. |

General Election Oct. 1834.

| York, 3rd R. | Thomas David Morrison | Jan. 15, 1835 | York, 3rd. R. 1833. 3 Wm. IV, C.16, Ss. 1, 3. An Act to alter the manner of holding the Elections for Members to represent the Counties of York and Lincoln, in the House of Assembly; more equally to divide the County of York into Ridings, and to increase the Representation of the said County of York. . . . the Townships of Scarborough, Markham, Pickering and Whitby, the Third Riding: . . . that each of the said Ridings in the County of York shall be Represented in the House of Assembly by one Member. |

General Election Oct. 1834.

* By-election

Constituency	Member	Sworn In	Comments
York, 4th R.	John McIntosh	Jan. 15, 1835	York, 4th R. 1833. 3 Wm. IV, C.16, Ss. 1, 3. An Act to alter the manner of holding the Elections for Members to represent the Counties of York and Lincoln, in the House of Assembly; more equally to divide the County of York into Ridings, and to increase the Representation of the said County of York. . . . and the Townships of East Gwillimbury, North Gwillimbury, Scott, Georgina, Brock, Reach, Whitchurch and Uxbridge, the Fourth Riding of the said County. . . . that each of the said Ridings in the County of York shall be Represented in the House of Assembly by one Member.
			General Election Oct. 1834.

LEGISLATURES OF UPPER CANADA
13th Legislature

General Election   July 1836

Sessions of the Thirteenth Legislature of Upper Canada: Nov. 8, 1836 – Feb. 10, 1840

First:	Nov. 8, 1836 – Mar. 4, 1837.
Second:	June 19, 1837 – July 11, 1837.
Third:	Dec. 28, 1837 – Mar. 6, 1838.
Fourth:	Feb. 27, 1839 – May 11, 1839.
Fifth:	Dec. 3, 1839 – Feb. 10, 1840.

Alphabetical List of Members

Member	Constituency	Sworn In	Comments
Michael Aikman	Wentworth	Nov. 8, 1836	
Robert Alway	Oxford	Nov. 8, 1836	
James Rogers Armstrong	Prince Edward	Nov. 8, 1836	
Charles Bockus	Prince Edward	Nov. 8, 1836	
George Strange Boulton	Durham	Nov. 8, 1836	
Henry Burritt	Grenville	Feb. 27, 1839*	Writ of Election – Feb. 27, 1838. On Feb. 27, 1839, the House was informed of the election of Henry Burritt, MPP, Grenville, in room of William B. Wells, expelled.
Mahlon Burwell	London (Town)	Nov. 8, 1836	
Francis Caldwell	Essex	Nov. 8, 1836	
Malcolm Cameron	Lanark	Nov. 8, 1836	
John Solomon Cartwright	Lennox & Addington	Nov. 8, 1836	
Alexander Chisholm	Glengarry	Date unknown. First appeared in Journals on Dec. 6, 1836.	

William Chisholm	Halton	Nov. 8, 1836	
John Cook	Dundas	Nov. 8, 1836	
Nathan Cornwall	Kent	Nov. 8, 1836	
George Hill Detlor	Lennox & Addington	Nov. 8, 1836	
William Henry Draper	Toronto (City)	Nov. 8, 1836	On July 7, 1837, the House was informed that William Henry Draper, MPP, Toronto (City), had accepted the office of Solicitor General. A new election was not called.
Charles Duncombe	Oxford	Date unknown. First appeared in Journals on Dec. 1, 1836.	Expelled, having been seen in arms with rebels against Her Majesty in Dec. 1837 and having fled from justice. A new election was called.
David Duncombe	Norfolk	Nov. 8, 1836	
Robert Graham Dunlop	Huron	Nov. 8, 1836	
George Elliott	Durham	Nov. 8, 1836	
Colin Campbell Ferrie	Hamilton (City)	Nov. 8. 1836	
John William Gamble	York, 1st R.	Feb. 5, 1838*	Writ of Election – Jan. 15, 1838. On Feb. 5, 1838, the House was informed of the election of John William Gamble, MPP, York, 1st R., in room of David Gibson, expelled.
David Gibson	York, 1st R.	Nov. 8, 1836	Expelled, Jan. 15, 1838, having been seen in arms at Montgomery's Tavern with the rebels there assembled, from Dec. 5-7, 1837. A new election was called.
Ogle Robert Gowan	Leeds	Nov. 8, 1836	
Christopher Alexander Hagerman	Kingston (Town)	Nov. 8, 1836	Mr. Attorney General.
Richard Phillips Hotham	Prescott	Nov. 8, 1836	

*   By-election

Member	Constituency	Sworn In	Comments
Roger Rollo Hunter	Oxford	Feb. 27, 1839*	Writ of Election – Jan. 20, 1838. On Feb. 27, 1839, the House was informed of the election of Roger Rollo Hunter, MPP, Oxford, in room of Charles Duncombe, expelled.
George S. Jarvis	Cornwall (Town)	Nov. 8, 1836	
Jonas Jones	Leeds	Nov. 8, 1836	On June 19, 1837, the House was informed of the resignation of Jonas Jones, MPP, Leeds, who had been appointed the Registrar for the County of Dundas. A new election was called.
John Kearns	Prescott	Nov. 8, 1836	
John Bower Lewis	Carleton	Nov. 8, 1836	
Donald Macdonell	Glengarry	Nov. 8, 1836	
Donald Aeneas MacDonell	Stormont	Nov. 8, 1836	
Hon. Allan Napier MacNab	Wentworth	Nov. 8, 1836	On June 19, 1837, Charles Richardson, MPP, Niagara (Town), proposed Allan Napier NacNab, MPP, Wentworth, as Speaker, in room of Archibald McLean, MPP, Stormont, resigned. Seconded and resolved. June 19, 1837 – Date took chair.
			On Dec. 28, 1837, the House was informed of the absence of the Speaker of the House, the Hon. Allan Napier MacNab, MPP, Wentworth, due to public duty in defence of the Province. A new Speaker was to be chosen in his absence.
			On Jan. 24, 1838, the House was informed of the return of the Speaker, the Hon. Allan Napier MacNab, MPP, Wentworth. Henry Ruttan, MPP, Northumberland, was discharged from his duty as Speaker, and the Hon. MacNab resumed the chair.

Edward Malloch	Carleton	Nov. 8, 1836	
Anthony Manahan	Hastings	Nov. 8, 1836	
John Marks	Frontenac	Nov. 8, 1836	
James Mathewson	Frontenac	Nov. 8, 1836	
Milo McCargar	Grenville	Apr. 25, 1839*	Writ of Election – Feb. 27, 1839. On Apr. 25, 1839, the House was informed of the election of Milo McCargar, MPP, Grenville, in room of Hiram Norton, resigned.
William McCrae	Kent	Nov. 8, 1836	
Alexander McDonell	Northumberland	Nov. 8, 1836	
John McIntosh	York, 4th R.	Nov. 8, 1836	
Thomas McKay	Russell	Nov. 8, 1836	
Alexander McLean	Stormont	Dec. 30, 1837*	Writ of Election – June 19, 1837. On Dec. 30, 1837, the House was informed of the election of Alexander McLean, MPP, Stormont, in room of Archibald McLean, resigned.
Hon. Archibald McLean	Stormont	Nov. 8, 1836	On Nov. 8, 1836, William Benjamin Robinson, MPP, Simcoe, proposed Archibald McLean, MPP, Simcoe, as Speaker. Seconded and resolved. Nov. 8, 1836 – Date took chair. On June 19, 1837, the House was informed of the resignation of Archibald McLean, MPP, Stormont, who had been appointed a Judge of His Majesty's Court of King's Bench, in this Province. A new Speaker was to be chosen and a new election was called.
Gilbert McMicking	Lincoln, 4th R.	Nov. 8, 1836	
William Hamilton Merritt	Haldimand	Nov. 8, 1836	
Elias Moore	Middlesex	Nov. 8, 1836	
James Morris	Leeds	Dec. 30, 1837*	Writ of Election – June 19, 1837. On Dec. 30,

* By-election

Member	Constituency	Sworn In	Comments
James Morris — *Continued*			1837, the House was informed of the election of James Morris, MPP, Leeds, in room of Jonas Jones, resigned.
Thomas David Morrison	York, 3rd R.	Nov. 8, 1836	On Mar. 22, 1839, the House was informed of the resignation of Thomas David Morrison, MPP, York, 3rd R., who had left the Province. A new election was called.
Edmund Murney	Hastings	Nov. 8, 1836	
Hiram Norton	Grenville	Nov. 8, 1836	On Feb. 27, 1839, the House was informed of the resignation of Hiram Norton, MPP, Grenville, who had removed to the United States, to permanently reside there. A new election was called.
Thomas Parke	Middlesex	Nov. 8, 1836	
John A.H. Powell	Lanark	Nov. 8, 1836	
John Prince	Essex	Nov. 8, 1836	
Charles Richardson	Niagara (Town)	Nov. 8, 1836	
William Benjamin Robinson	Simcoe	Nov. 8, 1836	
John Rolph	Norfolk	Date unknown. First appeared in Journals on Nov. 15, 1836.	Expelled, having combined, conspired and confederated with the rebels who took up arms in the Province against Her Majesty in the month of Dec. 1837 and having fled from justice to the United States of America. A new election was called.
Hon. Henry Ruttan	Northumberland	Nov. 8, 1836	On Dec. 28, 1837, Ogle Robert Gowan, MPP, Leeds, proposed Henry Ruttan, MPP, Northumberland, as Speaker, in room of the Hon. Allan Napier MacNab, MPP, Wentworth, in absentia. Seconded and resolved. Dec. 28, 1837 – Date took chair.

			Discharged as Speaker, Jan. 24, 1838, with the return of the Hon. Allan Napier MacNab, MPP, Wentworth, who had been absent on public duty, in defence of the Province.
George Rykert	Lincoln, 2nd R.	Nov. 8, 1836	
William Salmon	Norfolk	Feb. 27, 1837*	Writ of Election – Jan. 20, 1838. On Feb. 27, 1838, the House was informed of the election of William Salmon, MPP, Norfolk, in room of John Rolph, expelled.
Absalom Shade	Halton	Nov. 8, 1836	
Peter Shaver	Dundas	Nov. 8, 1836	
Henry Sherwood	Brockville (Town)	Nov. 8, 1836	
James Edward Small	York, 3rd R.	Apr. 29, 1839*	Writ of Election – Mar. 22, 1839. On Apr. 29, 1839, the House was informed of the election of James Edward Small, MPP, York, 3rd R., in room of Thomas David Morrison, resigned.
Edward William Thomson	York, 2nd R.	Nov. 8, 1836	
David Thorburn	Lincoln, 3rd R.	Nov. 8, 1836	
William B. Wells	Grenville	Date unknown. First appeared in Journals on June 24, 1837.	Expelled, having assisted the people (styling themselves patriots) who had assembled at various points in the State of New York, for the purpose of invading Upper Canada and for having fled from justice. A new election was called.
Charles Wickens	Simcoe	Nov. 8, 1836	
Richard Woodruff	Lincoln, 1st R.	Nov. 8, 1836	

* By-election

Constituency	Member	Sworn In	Comments
Brockville (Town)	Henry Sherwood	Nov. 8, 1836	General Election July 1836.
Carleton	John Bower Lewis	Nov. 8, 1836	General Election July 1836.
Carleton	Edward Malloch	Nov. 8, 1836	General Election July 1836.
Cornwall (Town)	George S. Jarvis	Nov. 8, 1836	General Election July 1836.
Dundas	John Cook	Nov. 8, 1836	General Election July 1836.
Dundas	Peter Shaver	Nov. 8, 1836	General Election July 1836.
Durham	George Strange Boulton	Nov. 8, 1836	General Election July 1836.
Durham	George Elliott	Nov. 8, 1836	General Election July 1836.
Essex	Francis Caldwell	Nov. 8, 1836	General Election July 1836.
Essex	John Prince	Nov. 8, 1836	General Election July 1836.
Frontenac	John Marks	Nov. 8, 1836	General Election July 1836.
Frontenac	James Mathewson	Nov. 8, 1836	General Election July 1836.
Glengarry	Alexander Chisholm	Date unknown. First appeared in Journals on Dec. 6, 1836.	General Election July 1836.
Glengarry	Donald Macdonell	Nov. 8, 1836	General Election July 1836.
Grenville	Hiram Norton	Nov. 8, 1836	General Election July 1836. On Feb. 27, 1839, the House was informed of the resignation of Hiram Norton, MPP, Grenville, who had removed to the United States, to permanently reside there. A new election was called.
Grenville	Milo McCargar	Apr. 25, 1839*	By-election Date unknown. Writ of Election – Feb. 27, 1839. On Apr. 25, 1839, the House was informed of the election

			of Milo McCargar, MPP, Grenville, in room of Hiram Norton, resigned.
Grenville	William B. Wells	Date unknown. First appeared in Journals on June 24, 1837.	General Election July 1836. Expelled, having assisted the people (styling themselves patriots) who had assembled at various points in the State of New York, for the purpose of invading Upper Canada and for having fled from justice. A new election was called.
Grenville	Henry Burritt	Feb. 27, 1839*	By-election Date unknown. Writ of Election – Feb. 27, 1838. On Feb. 27, 1839, the House was informed of the election of Henry Burritt, MPP, Grenville, in room of William B. Wells, expelled.
Haldimand	William Hamilton Merritt	Nov. 8, 1836	General Election July 1836.
Halton	William Chisholm	Nov. 8, 1836	General Election July 1836. Halton. 1837. 7 Wm. IV, C.116, Ss. 1, 28. An Act erecting certain parts of the Counties of Halton and Simcoe into a new District, by the name of the District of Wellington. [Royal Assent promulgated by Proclamation, Apr. 20, 1838.] Whereas from the increase of the population of the County of Halton, in the Gore District, and the great distance from the District Town, it is expedient to provide under certain conditions for erecting part of the said County of Halton, in the Gore District, and part of the County of Simcoe, in the Home District, into a separate District, with the Town of Guelph for the District Town: And whereas the Townships of Proton, Luther, Melancthon and Amaranth, from the County of Simcoe, and Garafraxa, Erin, Eramosa, Guelph, Nichol, Waterloo, Wilmot, Woolwich, and reserved lands west of Woolwich and Nichol, the triangular piece of

*   By-election

Constituency	Member	Sworn In	Comments
Halton — *Continued*			land adjoining the said tract in the proposed District of Huron, part of the late purchase from the Indians from Gore, and part of Indian lands do form the said new District, to be named the District of Wellington . . . and the residue of the said County of Halton shall from thenceforth, be and remain the County of Halton, in the District of Gore; and the residue of the said County of Simcoe shall, from thenceforth, be and remain the County of Simcoe.
Halton	Absalom Shade	Nov. 8, 1836	General Election July 1836.
			Halton. 1837. 7 Wm. IV, C.116, Ss. 1, 28. An Act erecting certain parts of the Counties of Halton and Simcoe into a new District, by the name of the District of Wellington. [Royal Assent promulgated by Proclamation, Apr. 20, 1838.] Whereas from the increase of the population of the County of Halton, in the Gore District, and the great distance from the District Town, it is expedient to provide under certain conditions for erecting part of the said County of Halton, in the Gore District, and part of the County of Simcoe, in the Home District, into a separate District, with the Town of Guelph for the District Town: And whereas the Townships of Proton, Luther, Melancthon and Amaranth, from the County of Simcoe, and Garafraxa, Erin, Eramosa, Guelph, Nichol, Waterloo, Wilmot, Woolwich, and reserved lands west of Woolwich and Nichol, the triangular piece of land adjoining the said tract in the proposed District of Huron, part of the late purchase from the Indians from Gore, and part of Indian lands do form the said new District, to be named the District of Wellington . . . and the residue of the

said County of Halton shall from thenceforth, be and remain the County of Halton, in the District of Gore; and the residue of the said County of Simcoe shall, from thenceforth, be and remain the County of Simcoe.

Hamilton (City)	Colin Campbell Ferrie	Nov. 8, 1836	General Election July 1836.
Hastings	Anthony Manahan	Nov. 8, 1836	General Election July 1836.
Hastings	Edmund Murney	Nov. 8, 1836	General Election July 1836.
Huron	Robert Graham Dunlop	Nov. 8, 1836	General Election July 1836.

Huron. 1837-8. 1 Vic., C.26, Ss.1, 23. An Act to authorize the erection of the County of Huron, and certain other Territory adjacent thereto, into a separate District. Whereas the tract of Country lately sold by His Majesty's Government to the Canada Company, and commonly known by the name of the County of Huron, is how attached to the District of London: and whereas, from the great extent of the said tract of land, and its great distance from the District Town of the London District, it is highly expedient and necessary that the said County of Huron should be set off into a distinct and separate District. . . . And be it further enacted by the authority aforesaid, That on any future survey of the territory lying to the northward of said County of Huron, one range of Townships lying immediately contiguous to the northerly boundary of the said County, shall be attached to and become part of the said intended new District; and that at any convenient time subsequent to the survey of the said range of Townships as aforesaid, . . . it shall and may be lawful to and for the Governor, Lieutenant Governor, or Person Administering the Government of this Province, by and with the advice and consent of Her Majesty's Executive Council for the affairs thereof, to divide the said new District into two

Constituency	Member	Sworn In	Comments
Huron — *Continued*			Counties, under such names and with such limits as may be expedient.
			Huron. 1840. 3 Vic., C.38. An Act to attach certain Townships to the County of Halton. . . . That the Township of Ashfield, and such other Townships as may hereafter be surveyed, being the first range of Townships lying immediately contiguous to the Northerly Boundary of the said County, be attached to and form part of the County of Huron, in the said intended New District.
Kent	Nathan Cornwall	Nov. 8, 1836	General Election July 1836.
Kent	William McCrae	Nov. 8, 1836	General Election July 1836.
Kingston (Town)	Christopher Alexander Hagerman	Nov. 8, 1836	Mr. Attorney General. General Election July 1836.
Lanark	Malcolm Cameron	Nov. 8, 1836	General Election July 1836.
Lanark	John A.H. Powell	Nov. 8, 1836	General Election July 1836.
Leeds	Ogle Robert Gowan	Nov. 8, 1836	General Election July 1836.
Leeds	Jonas Jones	Nov. 8, 1836	General Election July 1836.
			On June 19, 1837, the House was informed of the resignation of Jonas Jones, MPP, Leeds, who had been appointed the Registrar for the County of Dundas. A new election was called.
Leeds	James Morris	Dec. 30, 1837*	By-election Date unknown.
			Writ of Election – June 19, 1837. On Dec. 30, 1837, the House was informed of the election of James Morris, MPP, Leeds, in room of Jonas Jones, resigned.
Lennox & Addington	John Solomon Cartwright	Nov. 8, 1836	General Election July 1836.
Lennox & Addington	George Hill Detlor	Nov. 8, 1836	General Election July 1836.

Lincoln, 1st R.	Richard Woodruff	Nov. 8, 1836	General Election July 1836.
Lincoln, 2nd R.	George Rykert	Nov. 8, 1836	General Election July 1836.
Lincoln, 3rd R.	David Thorburn	Nov. 8, 1836	General Election July 1836.
Lincoln, 4th R.	Gilbert McMicking	Nov. 8, 1836	General Election July 1836.
London (Town)	Mahlon Burwell	Nov. 8, 1836	General Election July 1836.
Middlesex	Elias Moore	Nov. 8, 1836	General Election July 1836.
Middlesex	Thomas Parke	Nov. 8, 1836	General Election July 1836.
Niagara (Town)	Charles Richardson	Nov. 8, 1836	General Election July 1836.
Norfolk	David Duncombe	Nov. 8, 1836	General Election July 1836.
Norfolk	John Rolph	Date unknown. First appeared in Journals on Nov. 15, 1836.	General Election July 1836. Expelled, having combined, conspired and confederated with the rebels who took up arms in the Province against Her Majesty in the month of Dec. 1837 and having fled from justice to the United States of America. A new election was called.
Norfolk	William Salmon	Feb. 27, 1837*	By-election Date unknown. Writ of Election – Jan. 20, 1838. On Feb. 27, 1838, the House was informed of the election of William Salmon, MPP, Norfolk, in room of John Rolph, expelled.
Northumberland	Alexander McDonell	Nov. 8, 1836	General Election July 1836.
Northumberland	Hon. Henry Ruttan	Nov. 8, 1836	General Election July 1836. On Dec. 28, 1837, Ogle Robert Gowan, MPP, Leeds, proposed Henry Ruttan, MPP, Northumberland, as Speaker, in room of the Hon. Allan Napier MacNab, MPP, Wentworth, in absentia. Seconded and resolved. Dec. 28, 1837 – Date took chair.

* By-election

Constituency	Member	Sworn In	Comments
Northumberland — *Continued*			Discharged as Speaker, Jan. 24, 1838, with the return of the Hon. Allan Napier MacNab, MPP, Wentworth, who had been absent on public duty, in defence of the Province.
Oxford	Robert Alway	Nov. 8, 1836	General Election July 1836.
			Oxford. 1837. 7 Wm. IV, C.30. Ss. 1, 27. An Act to authorize the erection of the County of Oxford into a separate district, by the name of, the District of Brock. . . . That the Townships of Zorra, Nissouri, Blandford, Blenheim, Oxford (three divisions), Burford, Oakland, Norwich and Dereham, shall form a new and separate District, under the name of the District of Brock, and that the Town of Woodstock shall be the District Town thereof. And be it further enacted by the authority aforesaid, that so soon as the said part of the County of Oxford shall have been formed a separate District, by Proclamation as hereinbefore provided, all the Townships comprised within the limits of the said intended District, shall form and be called the County of Oxford, in the District of Brock.
Oxford	Charles Duncombe	Date unknown. First appeared in Journals on Dec. 1, 1836.	General Election July 1836.
			Oxford. 1837. 7 Wm. IV, C.30. Ss. 1, 27. An Act to authorize the erection of the County of Oxford into a separate district, by the name of, the District of Brock. . . . That the Townships of Zorra, Nissouri, Blandford, Blenheim, Oxford (three divisions), Burford, Oakland, Norwich and Dereham, shall form a new and separate District, under the name of the District of Brock, and that the Town of Woodstock shall be the District Town thereof. And be it further enacted by the authority aforesaid, that so soon as the said part of the County of Oxford

shall have been formed a separate District, by Proclamation as hereinbefore provided, all the Townships comprised within the limits of the said intended District, shall form and be called the County of Oxford, in the District of Brock.

Expelled, having been seen in arms with rebels against Her Majesty in Dec. 1837 and having fled from justice. A new election was called.

Oxford	Roger Rollo Hunter	Feb. 27, 1839*	By-election Date unknown. Writ of Election – Jan. 20, 1838. On Feb. 27, 1839, the House was informed of the election of Roger Rollo Hunter, MPP, Oxford, in room of Charles Duncombe, expelled.
Prescott	Richard Phillips Hotham	Nov. 8, 1836	General Election July 1836.
Prescott	John Kearns	Nov. 8, 1836	General Election July 1836.
Prince Edward	James Rogers Armstrong	Nov. 8, 1836	General Election July 1836.
Prince Edward	Charles Bockus	Nov. 8, 1836	General Election July 1836.
Russell	Thomas McKay	Nov. 8, 1836	General Election July 1836.
Simcoe	William Benjamin Robinson	Nov. 8, 1836	General Election July 1836. Simcoe. 1837. 7 Wm. IV, C.116, Ss. 1, 28. An Act erecting certain parts of the Counties of Halton and Simcoe into a new District, by the name of the District of Wellington. [Royal Assent promulgated by Proclamation, Apr. 20, 1838.] Whereas from the increase of the population of the County of Halton, in the Gore District, and the great distance from the District Town, it is expedient to provide under certain conditions for erecting part of the said County of Halton, in the Gore District, and part of the County of Simcoe, in the Home District, into a separate District, with the Town of Guelph for

* By-election

Constituency	Member	Sworn In	Comments
Simcoe — *Continued*			the District Town: And whereas the Townships of Proton, Luther, Melancthon and Amaranth, from the County of Simcoe, and Garafraxa, Erin, Eramosa, Guelph, Nichol, Waterloo, Wilmot, Woolwich, and reserved lands west of Woolwich and Nichol, the triangular piece of land adjoining the said tract in the proposed District of Huron, part of the late purchase from the Indians from Gore, and part of Indian lands do form the said new District, to be named the District of Wellington . . . and the residue of the said County of Halton shall from thenceforth, be and remain the County of Halton, in the District of Gore; and the residue of the said County of Simcoe shall, from thenceforth, be and remain the County of Simcoe.
Simcoe	Charles Wickens	Nov. 8, 1836	General Election July 1836. Simcoe. 1837. 7 Wm. IV, C.116, Ss. 1, 28. An Act erecting certain parts of the Counties of Halton and Simcoe into a new District, by the name of the District of Wellington. [Royal Assent promulgated by Proclamation, Apr. 20, 1838.] Whereas from the increase of the population of the County of Halton, in the Gore District, and the great distance from the District Town, it is expedient to provide under certain conditions for erecting part of the said County of Halton, in the Gore District, and part of the County of Simcoe, in the Home District, into a separate District, with the Town of Guelph for the District Town: And whereas the Townships of Proton, Luther, Melancthon and Amaranth, from the County of Simcoe, and Garafraxa, Erin, Eramosa, Guelph, Nichol, Waterloo, Wilmot, Woolwich, and reserved lands west of Woolwich and Nichol, the triangular piece of

land adjoining the said tract in the proposed District of Huron, part of the late purchase from the Indians from Gore, and part of Indian lands do form the said new District, to be named the District of Wellington . . . and the residue of the said County of Halton shall from thenceforth, be and remain the County of Halton, in the District of Gore; and the residue of the said County of Simcoe shall, from thenceforth, be and remain the County of Simcoe.

Stormont	Donald Aeneas MacDonell	Nov. 8, 1836	General Election July 1836.
Stormont	Hon. Archibald McLean	Nov. 8, 1836	General Election July 1836.
			On Nov. 8, 1836, William Benjamin Robinson, MPP, Simcoe, proposed Archibald McLean, MPP, Simcoe, as Speaker. Seconded and resolved. Nov. 8, 1836 – Date took chair.
			On June 19, 1837, the House was informed of the resignation of Archibald McLean, MPP, Stormont, who had been appointed a Judge of His Majesty's Court of King's Bench, in this Province. A new Speaker was to be chosen and a new election was called.
Stormont	Alexander McLean	Dec. 30, 1837*	By-election Date unknown.
			Writ of Election – June 19, 1837. On Dec. 30, 1837, the House was informed of the election of Alexander McLean, MPP, Stormont, in room of Archibald McLean, resigned.
Toronto (City)	William Henry Draper	Nov. 8, 1836	General Election July 1836.
			On July 7, 1837, the House was informed that William Henry Draper, MPP, Toronto (City), had accepted the office of Solicitor General. A new election was not called.
Wentworth	Michael Aikman	Nov. 8, 1836	General Election July 1836.

* By-election

Constituency	Member	Sworn In	Comments
Wentworth	Hon. Allan Napier MacNab	Nov. 8, 1836	General Election July 1836.
			On June 19, 1837, Charles Richardson, MPP, Niagara (Town) proposed Allan Napier NacNab, MPP, Wentworth, as Speaker, in room of Archibald McLean, MPP, Stormont, resigned. Seconded and resolved. June 19, 1837 – Date took chair.
			On Dec. 28, 1837, the House was informed of the absence of the Speaker of the House, the Hon. Allan Napier MacNab, MPP, Wentworth, due to public duty in defence of the Province. A new Speaker was to be chosen in his absence.
			On Jan. 24, 1838, the House was informed of the return of the Speaker, the Hon. Allan Napier MacNab, MPP, Wentworth. Henry Ruttan, MPP, Northumberland, was discharged from his duty as Speaker, and the Hon. MacNab resumed the chair.
York, 1st R.	David Gibson	Nov. 8, 1836	General Election July 1836.
			Expelled, Jan. 15, 1838, having been seen in arms at Montgomery's Tavern with the rebels there assembled from Dec. 5-7, 1837. A new election was called.
York, 1st R.	John William Gamble	Feb. 5, 1838*	By-election Date unknown.
			Writ of Election – Jan. 15, 1838. On Feb. 5, 1838, the House was informed of the election of John William Gamble, MPP, York, 1st R., in room of David Gibson, expelled.
York, 2nd R.	Edward William Thomson	Nov. 8, 1836	General Election July 1836.
York, 3rd R.	Thomas David Morrison	Nov. 8, 1836	General Election July 1836.
			On Mar. 22, 1839, the House was informed of the resignation of Thomas David Morrison,

			MPP, York, 3rd R., who had left the Province. A new election was called.
York, 3rd R.	James Edward Small	Apr. 29, 1839*	By-election Apr. 22, 1839.
			Writ of Election – Mar. 22, 1839. On Apr. 29, 1839, the House was informed of the election of James Edward Small, MPP, York, 3rd R., in room of Thomas David Morrison, resigned.
York, 4th R.	John McIntosh	Nov. 8, 1836	General Election July 1836.

LEGISLATURES OF THE PROVINCE OF CANADA
(Canada West)
1st Legislature

General Election Mar. 1841

Sessions of the First Legislature of the Province of Canada: June 14, 1841 – Dec. 9, 1843

First:	June 14, 1841 – Sept. 18, 1841.
Second:	Sept. 8, 1842 – Oct. 12, 1842.
Third:	Sept. 28, 1843 – Dec. 9, 1843.

Alphabetical List of Members

Member	Constituency	Sworn In	Comments
Hon. Austin Cuvillier	Huntingdon (Canada East)	June 14, 1841	On June 14, 1841, Augustin Norbert Morin, MPP, Nicolet (Canada East), proposed Austin Cuvillier, MPP, Huntingdon (Canada East), as Speaker. Seconded and resolved. June 14, 1841 – Date took chair.
Hon. Robert Baldwin	Hastings	June 14, 1841	Solicitor General.
			On Aug. 25, 1841, Robert Baldwin, Member for both the County of Hastings and the County of York, 4th R., chose to serve for the County of Hastings. A new election was called for the County of York, 4th R.
			On Sept. 16, 1842, the House was informed of the resignation of Robert Baldwin, MPP, Hastings, who had been appointed Attorney General of Canada West. A new election was called.
			Writ of Election – Sept. 17, 1842. Special Return of Writ – Oct. 17, 1842. The election was declared void, as a collision took place between the two parties causing conditions to be unsafe to poll all the votes of the County

			within the time prescribed by law. On Oct. 3, 1843, a new election was called.
Hon. Robert Baldwin	York, 4th R.	June 14, 1841	Solicitor General.
			On Aug. 25, 1841, Robert Baldwin, Member for both the County of York, 4th R., and the County of Hastings chose to serve for the County of Hastings. A new election was called for the County of York, 4th R.
George Morss Boswell	Northumberland South	June 14, 1841	
Henry John Boulton	Niagara (Town)	Sept. 28, 1842	On Sept. 26, 1842, the House was informed that Henry John Boulton was duly elected at the Town of Niagara General Election, in room of Edward Clarke Campbell, whose election was declared void.
Isaac Buchanan	Toronto (City)	June 14, 1841	Resigned during the Inter-session, between the 2nd and 3rd Sessions. A new election was called.
Malcolm Cameron	Lanark	June 14, 1841	
Edward Clarke Campbell	Niagara (Town)	June 14, 1841	On Sept. 26, 1842, the election of Edward Clarke Campbell, MPP, Niagara (Town), was declared void. Henry John Boulton was duly elected at the Town of Niagara General Election.
John Solomon Cartwright	Lennox & Addington	June 14, 1841	
Solomon Youmans Chesley	Cornwall (Town)	June 14, 1841	
John Cook	Dundas	June 14, 1841	
Samuel Crane	Grenville	June 14, 1841	
Stewart Derbishire	Bytown (Town)	June 14, 1841	
Hon. William Henry Draper	Russell	June 14, 1841	Attorney General.
			Resigned during the Inter-session, between the 2nd and 3rd Sessions, having been appointed to the Legislative Council. A new election was called.

Member	Constituency	Sworn In	Comments
George Duggan, Jr.	York, 2nd R.	June 14, 1841	On Sept. 26, 1842, the election of George Duggan, Jr., MPP, York, 2nd R., was declared void. A new election was called.
			Writ of Election – Oct. 10, 1842. Return of Writ – Nov. 22, 1842. On Sept. 28, 1843, the House was informed of the election of George Duggan, Jr., MPP, York, 2nd R., who was returned as duly elected.
William Dunlop	Huron	Aug. 20, 1841	On Aug. 20, 1841, the House was informed that William Dunlop was duly elected at the County of Huron General Election, in room of James McGill Strachan, whose election was declared void.
Hon. John Henry Dunn	Toronto (City)	June 14, 1841	Receiver General.
James Durand	Halton West	June 14, 1841	
John Gilchrist	Northumberland North	June 14, 1841	
Hon. Samuel Beasley Harrison	Kingston (Town)	July 1, 1841*	Executive Councillor.
			Writ of Election – June 19, 1841. Return of Writ – July 1, 1841. On July 1, 1841, the House was informed of the election of the Hon. Samuel Beasley Harrison, MPP, Kingston (Town), in room of Anthony Manahan, resigned.
Hon. Francis Hincks	Oxford	June 14, 1841	Resigned during the Inter-session, between the 1st and 2nd Sessions, having been appointed Inspector General. A new election was called.
			Writ of Election – June 16, 1842. Return of Writ – July 6, 1842. On Sept. 8, 1842, the House was informed of the election of the Hon. Francis Hincks, MPP, Oxford, who had been returned as duly elected.

Caleb Hopkins	Halton East	June 14, 1841	
James Johnston	Carleton	June 14, 1841	
Hon. Hamilton Hartley Killaly	London (Town)	June 14, 1841	On Sept. 9, 1842, the House was informed of the resignation of the Hon. Hamilton Hartley Killaly, MPP, London (Town), who had been appointed President of the Board of Works of this Province. A new election was called.

On Sept. 9, 1842, the House was informed of the resignation of the Hon. Hamilton Hartley Killaly, MPP, London (Town), who had been appointed President of the Board of Works of this Province. A new election was called.

Writ of Election – Sept. 12, 1842. Return of Writ – Sept. 28, 1842. On Oct. 3, 1842, the House was informed of the election of the Hon. Hamilton Hartley Killaly, MPP, London (Town), who was returned as duly elected.

Resigned, Nov. 30, 1843, in consequence of the Provisions of the Act of the 4th and 5th Vic., C. 4. No By-election was called.

Hon. Louis Hypolite Lafontaine   York, 4th R.   Sept. 8, 1842*

Writ of Election – Aug. 31, 1841. Return of Writ – Sept. 21, 1841. On Sept. 8, 1842, the House was informed of the election of Louis Hypolite Lafontaine, MPP, York, 4th R., in room of Robert Baldwin, resigned.

On Sept. 16, 1842, the House was informed of the resignation of Louis Hypolite Lafontaine, MPP, York, 4th R., who had been appointed Attorney General of Canada East. A new election was called.

Writ of Election – Sept. 17, 1842. Return of Writ – Oct. 8, 1842. On Sept. 28, 1843, the House was informed of the election of the Hon. Louis Hypolite Lafontaine, MPP, York, 4th R., who was returned as duly elected.

John Sandfield Macdonald	Glengarry	June 14, 1841	
Sir Allan Napier MacNab	Hamilton (Town)	June 14, 1841	
Anthony Manahan	Kingston (Town)	June 14, 1841	Resigned, June 18, 1841, having been appointed to the office of Collector of Customs

*   By-election

Member	Constituency	Sworn In	Comments
Anthony Manahan — *Continued*			for the Port of Toronto. A new election was called.
Donald McDonald	Prescott	June 14, 1841	
Alexander McLean	Stormont	June 14, 1841	
William Hamilton Merritt	Lincoln North	June 14, 1841	
James Morris	Leeds	June 14, 1841	
Edmund Murney	Hastings	Nov. 7, 1843*	Writ of Election – Oct. 9, 1843. Return of Writ – Nov. 4, 1843. On Nov. 7, 1843, the House was informed of the election of Edmund Murney, MPP, Hastings, in room of Robert Baldwin, resigned.
Thomas Parke	Middlesex	June 14, 1841	Resigned, June 16, 1841, having been appointed Surveyor General. A new election was called.
		July 15, 1841*	Writ of Election – June 18, 1841. Return of Writ – July 10, 1841. On July 13, 1841, the House was informed of the election of Thomas Parke, MPP, Middlesex, who was returned as duly elected.
Israel Wood Powell	Norfolk	June 14, 1841	
James Hervey Price	York, 1st R.	June 14, 1841	
John Prince	Essex	June 14, 1841	
John Philip Roblin	Prince Edward	June 14, 1841	
George Sherwood	Brockville (Town)	June 14, 1841	
Hon. Henry Sherwood	Toronto (City)	Sept. 28, 1843*	Queen's Counsel.
			Writ of Election – Feb. 11, 1843. Return of Writ – Mar. 6, 1843. On Sept. 28, 1843, the House was informed of the election of the Hon. Henry Sherwood, MPP, Toronto (City), in room of Isaac Buchanan, resigned.

Hon. James Edward Small	York, 3rd R.	June 14, 1841	On Sept. 26, 1842, the House was informed of the resignation of James Edward Small, MPP, York, 3rd R., who had been appointed Solicitor General of Canada West. A new election was called.
			Writ of Election — Sept. 27, 1842. Return of Writ — Oct. 15, 1842. On Sept. 28, 1843, the House was informed of the election of the Hon. James Edward Small, MPP, York, 3rd R., who was returned as duly elected.
Harmannus Smith	Wentworth	June 14, 1841	
Henry Smith, Jr.	Frontenac	June 14, 1841	
Elmes Steele	Simcoe	June 14, 1841	
William Stewart	Russell	Oct. 30, 1843*	Writ of Election — Aug. 14, 1843. Return of Writ — Sept. 14, 1843. On Sept. 28, 1843, the House was informed of the election of William Stewart, MPP, Russell, in room of the Hon. William Henry Draper, resigned.
James McGill Strachan	Huron	June 14, 1841	On Aug. 20, 1841, the election of James McGill Strachan, MPP, Huron, was declared void. William Dunlop was duly elected at the Huron General Election.
David Thompson	Haldimand	June 14, 1841	
David Thorburn	Lincoln South	June 14, 1841	
John Tucker Williams	Durham	June 14, 1841	
Joseph Woods	Kent	June 17, 1841	

*   By-election

Constituency	Member	Sworn In	Comments
Brockville (Town)	George Sherwood	June 14, 1841	Brockville (Town). 1840. 3 & 4 Vic., C. 35, S. 17. An Act to Reunite the Provinces of Upper and Lower Canada, and the Government of Canada. And be it enacted, That the City of Toronto shall be represented by Two Members, and the Towns of Kingston, Brockville, Hamilton, Cornwall, Niagara, London and Bytown shall each be represented by One Member in the Legislative Assembly of the Province of Canada. General Election Mar. 1841.
Bytown (Town)	Stewart Derbishire	June 14, 1841	Bytown (Town). 3 & 4 Vic., C. 35, S. 17. An Act to Reunite the Provinces of Upper and Lower Canada, and the Government of Canada. And be it enacted, That the City of Toronto shall be represented by Two Members, and the Towns of Kingston, Brockville, Hamilton, Cornwall, Niagara, London and Bytown shall each be represented by One Member in the Legislative Assembly of the Province of Canada. General Election Mar. 1841.
Carleton	James Johnston	June 14, 1841	Carleton. 1840. 3 & 4 Vic., C. 35, S. 16. An Act to Reunite the Provinces of Upper and Lower Canada, and the Government of Canada. And be it enacted, That every County and Riding, other than those hereinbefore specified, which at the time of the passing of this Act was by Law entitled to be represented in the Assembly of the Province of Upper Canada, shall be represented by One Member in the Legislative Assembly of the Province of Canada. General Election Mar. 1841.

Cornwall (Town)	Solomon Youmans Chesley	June 14, 1841	Cornwall (Town). 1840. 3 & 4 Vic., C. 35, S. 17. An Act to Reunite the Provinces of Upper and Lower Canada, and the Government of Canada. And be it enacted, That the City of Toronto shall be represented by Two Members, and the Towns of Kingston, Brockville, Hamilton, Cornwall, Niagara, London and Bytown shall each be represented by One Member in the Legislative Assembly of the Province of Canada.
			General Election Mar. 1841.
Dundas	John Cook	June 14, 1841	Dundas. 1840. 3 & 4 Vic., C. 35, S. 16. An Act to Reunite the Provinces of Upper and Lower Canada, and the Government of Canada. And be it enacted, That every County and Riding, other than those hereinbefore specified, which at the time of the passing of this Act was by Law entitled to be represented in the Assembly of the Province of Upper Canada, shall be represented by One Member in the Legislative Assembly of the Province of Canada.
			General Election Mar. 1841.
Durham	John Tucker Williams	June 14, 1841	Durham. 1840. 3 & 4 Vic., C. 35, S. 16. An Act to Reunite the Provinces of Upper and Lower Canada, and the Government of Canada. And be it enacted, That every County and Riding, other than those hereinbefore specified, which at the time of the passing of this Act was by Law entitled to be represented in the Assembly of the Province of Upper Canada, shall be represented by One Member in the Legislative Assembly of the Province of Canada.
			Generál Election Mar. 1841.
Essex	John Prince	June 14, 1841	Essex. 1840. 3 & 4 Vic., C. 35, S. 16. An Act to Reunite the Provinces of Upper and Lower Canada, and the Government of Canada. And be it enacted, That every County and Riding, other than those hereinbefore specified, which

Constituency	Member	Sworn In	Comments
Essex — *Continued*			at the time of the passing of this Act was by Law entitled to be represented in the Assembly of the Province of Upper Canada, shall be represented by One Member in the Legislative Assembly of the Province of Canada.
			General Election Mar. 1841.
Frontenac	Henry Smith, Jr.	June 14, 1841	Frontenac. 1840. 3 & 4 Vic., C. 35, S. 16. An Act to Reunite the Provinces of Upper and Lower Canada, and the Government of Canada. And be it enacted, That every County and Riding, other than those hereinbefore specified, which at the time of the passing of this Act was by Law entitled to be represented in the Assembly of the Province of Upper Canada, shall be represented by One Member in the Legislative Assembly of the Province of Canada.
			General Election Mar. 1841.
Glengarry	John Sandfield Macdonald	June 14, 1841	Glengarry. 1840. 3 & 4 Vic., C. 35, S. 16. An Act to Reunite the Provinces of Upper and Lower Canada, and the Government of Canada. And be it enacted, That every County and Riding, other than those hereinbefore specified, which at the time of the passing of this Act was by Law entitled to be represented in the Assembly of the Province of Upper Canada, shall be represented by One Member in the Legislative Assembly of the Province of Canada.
			General Election Mar. 1841.
Grenville	Samuel Crane	June 14, 1841	Grenville. 1840. 3 & 4 Vic., C. 35, S. 16. An Act to Reunite the Provinces of Upper and Lower Canada, and the Government of

Canada. And be it enacted, That every County and Riding, other than those hereinbefore specified, which at the time of the passing of this Act was by Law entitled to be represented in the Assembly of the Province of Upper Canada, shall be represented by One Member in the Legislative Assembly of the Province of Canada.

General Election Mar. 1841.

Haldimand	David Thompson	June 14, 1841	Haldimand. 1840. 3 & 4 Vic., C. 35, S. 16. An Act to Reunite the Provinces of Upper and Lower Canada, and the Government of Canada. And be it enacted, That every County and Riding, other than those hereinbefore specified, which at the time of the passing of this Act was by Law entitled to be represented in the Assembly of the Province of Upper Canada, shall be represented by One Member in the Legislative Assembly of the Province of Canada.

General Election Mar. 1841.

Halton East	Caleb Hopkins	June 14, 1841	Halton East. 1840. 3 & 4 Vic., C. 35, S. 13. An Act to Reunite the Provinces of Upper and Lower Canada, and for the Government of Canada. And be it enacted, That the County of Halton in the Province of Upper Canada shall be divided into Two Ridings, to be called respectively the East Riding and the West Riding; and that the East Riding of the said County shall consist of the following Townships, namely, Trafalgar, Nelson, Esquesing, Nasagawega, East Flamborough, West Flamborough, Ering, Beverley; . . . and that the East Riding and West Riding of the said County shall each be represented by One Member in the Legislative Assembly of the Province of Canada.

General Election Mar. 1841.

Constituency	Member	Sworn In	Comments
Halton West	James Durand	June 14, 1841	Halton West. 1840. 3 & 4 Vic., C. 35, S. 13. An Act to Reunite the Provinces of Upper and Lower Canada, and for the Government of Canada. And be it enacted, That the County of Halton in the Province of Upper Canada shall be divided into Two Ridings, to be called respectively the East Riding and the West Riding; . . . and that the West Riding of the said County shall consist of the following Townships, namely, Garafraxa, Nichol, Woolwich, Guelph, Waterloo, Wilmot, Dumfries, Puslinch, Eramosa; and that the East Riding and the West Riding of the said County shall each be represented by One Member in the Legislative Assembly of the Province of Canada.
			General Election Mar. 1841.
Hamilton (Town)	Sir Allan Napier MacNab	June 14, 1841	Hamilton (Town). 1840. 3 & 4 Vic., C. 35, S. 17. An Act to Reunite the Provinces of Upper and Lower Canada, and the Government of Canada. And be it enacted, That the City of Toronto shall be represented by Two Members, and the Towns of Kingston, Brockville, Hamilton, Cornwall, Niagara, London and Bytown shall each be represented by One Member in the Legislative Assembly of the Province of Canada.
			General Election Mar. 1841.
Hastings	Hon. Robert Baldwin	June 14, 1841	Solicitor General.
			Hastings. 1840. 3 & 4 Vic., C. 35, S. 16. An Act to Reunite the Provinces of Upper and Lower Canada, and the Government of Canada. And be it enacted, That every County and Riding, other than those hereinbefore

specified, which at the time of the passing of this Act was by Law entitled to be represented in the Assembly of the Province of Upper Canada, shall be represented by One Member in the Legislative Assembly of the Province of Canada.

General Election Mar. 1841.

On Aug. 25, 1841, Robert Baldwin, Member for both the County of Hastings and the County of York, 4th R., chose to serve for the County of Hastings. A new election was called of the County of York, 4th R.

On Sept. 16, 1842, the House was informed of the resignation of Robert Baldwin, MPP, Hastings, who had been appointed Attorney General of Canada West. A new election was called.

Writ of Election – Sept. 17, 1842. Special Return of Writ – Oct. 17, 1842. The election was declared void, as a collision took place between the two parties causing conditions to be unsafe to poll all the votes of the County within the time prescribed by law. On Oct. 3, 1843, a new election was called.

Hastings	Edmund Murney	Nov. 7, 1843*	By-election Date unknown.

Writ of Election – Oct. 9, 1843. Return of Writ – Nov. 4, 1843. On Nov. 7, 1843, the House was informed of the election of Edmund Murney, MPP, Hastings, in room of Robert Baldwin, resigned.

Huntingdon (Canada East)	Hon. Austin Cuvillier	June 14, 1841	General Election Mar. 1841.

On June 14, 1841, Augustin Norbert Morin, MPP, Nicolet (Canada East), proposed Austin Cuvillier, MPP, Huntingdon (Canada East), as Speaker. Seconded and resolved. June 14, 1841 – Date took chair.

* By-election

Constituency	Member	Sworn In	Comments
Huron	James McGill Strachan	June 14, 1841	Huron. 1840. 3 & 4 Vic., C. 35, S. 16. An Act to Reunite the Provinces of Upper and Lower Canada, and the Government of Canada. And be it enacted, That every County and Riding, other than those hereinbefore specified, which at the time of the passing of this Act was by Law entitled to be represented in the Assembly of the Province of Upper Canada, shall be represented by One Member in the Legislative Assembly of the Province of Canada.
			General Election Mar. 1841.
			On Aug. 20, 1841, the election of James McGill Strachan, MPP, Huron, was declared void. William Dunlop was duly elected at the Huron General Election.
Huron	William Dunlop	Aug. 20, 1841	On Aug. 20, 1841, the House was informed that William Dunlop was duly elected at the County of Huron General Election, in room of James McGill Strachan, whose election was declared void.
Kent	Joseph Woods	June 17, 1841	Kent. 1840. 3 & 4 Vic., C. 35, S. 16. An Act to Reunite the Provinces of Upper and Lower Canada, and the Government of Canada. And be it enacted, That every County and Riding, other than those hereinbefore specified, which at the time of the passing of this Act was by Law entitled to be represented in the Assembly of the Province of Upper Canada, shall be represented by One Member in the Legislative Assembly of the Province of Canada.
			General Election Mar. 1841.
Kingston (Town)	Anthony Manahan	June 14, 1841	Kingston (Town). 1840. 3 & 4 Vic., C. 35, S. 17. An Act to Reunite the Provinces of Upper

and Lower Canada, and the Government of Canada. And be it enacted, That the City of Toronto shall be represented by Two Members, and the Towns of Kingston, Brockville, Hamilton, Cornwall, Niagara, London and Bytown shall each be represented by One Member in the Legislative Assembly of the Province of Canada.

General Election Mar. 1841.

Resigned, June 18, 1841, having been appointed to the office of Collector of Customs for the Port of Toronto. A new election was called.

Kingston (Town)	Hon. Samuel Beasley Harrison	July 1, 1841*	Executive Councillor.

By-election Date unknown.

Writ of Election – June 19, 1841. Return of Writ – July 1, 1841. On July 1, 1841, the House was informed of the election of the Hon. Samuel Beasley Harrison, MPP, Kingston (Town), in room of Anthony Manahan, resigned.

Lanark	Malcolm Cameron	June 14, 1841	Lanark. 1840. 3 & 4 Vic., C. 35, S. 16. An Act to Reunite the Provinces of Upper and Lower Canada, and the Government of Canada. And be it enacted, That every County and Riding, other than those hereinbefore specified, which at the time of the passing of this Act was by Law entitled to be represented in the Assembly of the Province of Upper Canada, shall be represented by One Member in the Legislative Assembly of the Province of Canada.

General Election Mar. 1841.

Leeds	James Morris	June 14, 1841	Leeds. 1840. 3 & 4 Vic., C. 35, S. 16. An Act to Reunite the Provinces of Upper and Lower Canada, and the Government of Canada. And

* By-election

Constituency	Member	Sworn In	Comments
Leeds — *Continued*			be it enacted, That every County and Riding, other than those hereinbefore specified, which at the time of the passing of this Act was by Law entitled to be represented in the Assembly of the Province of Upper Canada, shall be represented by One Member in the Legislative Assembly of the Province of Canada. General Election Mar. 1841.
Lennox & Addington	John Solomon Cartwright	June 14, 1841	Lennox & Addington. 1840. 3 & 4 Vic., C. 35, S. 16. An Act to Reunite the Provinces of Upper and Lower Canada, and the Government of Canada. And be it enacted, That every County and Riding, other than those hereinbefore specified, which at the time of the passing of this Act was by Law entitled to be represented in the Assembly of the Province of Upper Canada, shall be represented by One Member in the Legislative Assembly of the Province of Canada. General Election Mar. 1841.
Lincoln North	William Hamilton Merritt	June 14, 1841	Lincoln North. 1840. 3 & 4 Vic., C. 35, S. 15. An Act to Reunite the Provinces of Upper and Lower Canada, and the Government of Canada. And be it enacted, That the County of Lincoln in the Province of Upper Canada shall be divided into Two Ridings, to be called respectively the North Riding and the South Riding; and that the North Riding shall be formed by uniting the First Riding and Second Riding of the said County . . . and that the North and South Riding of the last mentioned County shall each be represented by One Member in the Legislative Assembly of the Province of Canada.

			General Election Mar. 1841.
Lincoln South	David Thorburn	June 14, 1841	Lincoln South. 1840. 3 & 4 Vic., C. 35, S. 15. An Act to Reunite the Provinces of Upper and Lower Canada, and the Government of Canada. And be it enacted, That the County of Lincoln in the Province of Upper Canada shall be divided into Two Ridings, to be called respectively the North Riding and the South Riding; . . . and the South Riding [shall be formed] by uniting the Third Riding and Fourth Riding of the said County; and that the North and South Riding of the last mentioned County shall each be represented by One Member in the Legislative Assembly of the Province of Canada.
			General Election Mar. 1841.
London (Town)	Hon. Hamilton Hartley Killaly	June 14, 1841	London (Town). 1840. 3 & 4 Vic., C. 35, S. 16. An Act to Reunite the Provinces of Upper and Lower Canada, and the Government of Canada. And be it enacted, That the City of Toronto shall be represented by Two Members, and the Towns of Kingston, Brockville, Hamilton, Cornwall, Niagara, London and Bytown shall each be represented by One Member in the Legislative Assembly of the Province of Canada.
			General Election Mar. 1841.
			On Sept. 9, 1842, the House was informed of the resignation of the Hon. Hamilton Hartley Killaly, MPP, London (Town), who had been appointed President of the Board of Works of this Province. A new election was called.
			By-election Date unknown.
			Writ of Election – Sept. 12, 1842. Return of Writ – Sept. 28, 1842. On Oct. 3, 1842, the House was informed of the election of the Hon. Hamilton Hartley Killaly, MPP, London (Town), who was returned as duly elected.

Constituency	Member	Sworn In	Comments
London (Town) — *Continued*			Resigned, Nov. 30, 1843, in consequence of the Provisions of the Act of the 4th and 5th Vic., C. 4. No By-election was called.
Middlesex	Thomas Parke	July 15, 1841*	Middlesex. 1840. 3 & 4 Vic., C. 35, S. 16. An Act to Reunite the Provinces of Upper and Lower Canada, and the Government of Canada. And be it enacted, That every County and Riding, other than those hereinbefore specified, which at the time of the passing of this Act was by Law entitled to be represented in the Assembly of the Province of Upper Canada, shall be represented by One Member in the Legislative Assembly of the Province of Canada.
			General Election Mar. 1841.
			Resigned, June 16, 1841, having been appointed Surveyor General. A new election was called.
			By-election Date unknown.
			Writ of Election – June 18, 1841. Return of Writ – July 10, 1841. On July 13, 1841, the House was informed of the election of Thomas Parke, MPP, Middlesex, who was returned as duly elected.
Niagara (Town)	Edward Clarke Campbell	June 14, 1841	Niagara (Town). 1840.
			3 & 4 Vic., C. 35, S. 17. An Act to Reunite the Provinces of Upper and Lower Canada, and the Government of Canada. And be it enacted, that the City of Toronto shall be represented by Two Members, and the Towns of Kingston, Brockville, Hamilton, Cornwall, Niagara, London and Bytown shall each be represented by One Member in the Legislative Assembly of the Province of Canada.

			General Election Mar. 1841.
			On Sept. 26, 1842, the election of Edward Clarke Campbell, MPP, Niagara (Town), was declared void. Henry John Boulton was duly elected at the Town of Niagara General Election.
Niagara (Town)	Henry John Boulton	Sept. 28, 1842	On Sept. 26, 1842, the House was informed that Henry John Boulton was duly elected at the Town of Niagara General Election, in room of Edward Clarke Campbell, whose election was declared void.
Norfolk	Israel Wood Powell	June 14, 1841	Norfolk. 1840. 3 & 4 Vic., C. 35, S. 16. An Act to Reunite the Provinces of Upper and Lower Canada, and the Government of Canada. And be it enacted, That every County and Riding, other than those hereinbefore specified, which at the time of the passing of this Act was by Law entitled to be represented in the Assembly of the Province of Upper Canada, shall be represented by One Member in the Legislative Assembly of the Province of Canada. General Election Mar. 1841.
Northumberland North	John Gilchrist	June 14, 1841	Northumberland North. 1840. 3 & 4 Vic., C. 35, S. 14. An Act to Reunite the Provinces of Upper and Lower Canada, and the Government of Canada. And be it enacted, That the County of Northumberland in the Province of Upper Canada shall be divided into Two Ridings, to be called respectively the North riding and the South Riding; and that the North Riding of the last mentioned County shall consist of the following Townships, namely, Monaghan, Otonabee, Asphodel, Smith, Douro, Dummer, Belmont, Methuen, Burleigh, Harvey, Emily, Gore, Ennismore; . . . and that the North

*   By-election

Constituency	Member	Sworn In	Comments
Northumberland North — *Continued*			Riding and South Riding of the last mentioned County shall each be represented by One Member in the Legislative Assembly of the Province of Canada.
			General Election Mar. 1841.
Northumberland South	George Morss Boswell	June 14, 1841	Northumberland South. 1840. 3 & 4 Vic., C. 35, S. 14. An Act to Reunite the Provinces of Upper and Lower Canada, and the Government of Canada. And be it enacted, That the County of Northumberland in the Province of Upper Canada shall be divided into Two Ridings, to be called respectively the North Riding and the South Riding. . . . and that the South Riding of the last mentioned County shall consist of the following Townships, namely, Hamilton, Haldimand, Cramak, Murray, Seymour, Percy; and that the North Riding and South Riding of the last mentioned County shall each be represented by One Member in the Legislative Assembly of the Province of Canada.
			General Election Mar. 1841.
Oxford	Hon. Francis Hincks	June 14, 1841	Oxford. 1840. 3 & 4 Vic., C. 35, S. 16. An Act to Reunite the Provinces of Upper and Lower Canada, and the Government of Canada. And be it enacted, That every County and Riding, other than those hereinbefore specified, which at the time of the passing of this Act was by Law entitled to be represented in the Assembly of the Province of Upper Canada, shall be represented by One Member in the Legislative Assembly of the Province of Canada.
			General Election Mar. 1841.
			Resigned during the Inter-session, between the

			1st and 2nd Sessions, having been appointed Inspector General. A new election was called.
			By-election Date unknown.
			Writ of Election – June 16, 1842. Return of Writ – July 6, 1842. On Sept. 8, 1842, the House was informed of the election of the Hon. Francis Hincks, MPP, Oxford, who had been returned as duly elected.
Prescott	Donald McDonald	June 14, 1841	Prescott. 1840. 3 & 4 Vic., C. 35, S. 16. An Act to Reunite the Provinces of Upper and Lower Canada, and the Government of Canada. And be it enacted, That every County and Riding, other than those hereinbefore specified, which at the time of the passing of this Act was by Law entitled to be represented in the Assembly of the Province of Upper Canada, shall be represented by One Member in the Legislative Assembly of the Province of Canada.
			General Election Mar. 1841.
Prince Edward	John Philip Roblin	June 14, 1841	Prince Edward. 1840. 3 & 4 Vic., C. 35, S. 16. An Act to Reunite the Provinces of Upper and Lower Canada, and the Government of Canada. And be it enacted, That every County and Riding, other than those hereinbefore specified, which at the time of the passing of this Act was by Law entitled to be represented in the Assembly of the Province of Upper Canada, shall be represented by One Member in the Legislative Assembly of the Province of Canada.
			General Election Mar. 1841.
Russell	Hon. William Henry Draper	June 14, 1841	Attorney General.
			Russell. 1840. 3 & 4 Vic., C. 35, S. 16. An Act to Reunite the Provinces of Upper and Lower Canada, and the Government of Canada. And be it enacted, That every County and Riding, other than those hereinbefore specified, which at the time of the passing of this Act was by

Constituency	Member	Sworn In	Comments
Russell — *Continued*			Law entitled to be represented in the Assembly of the Province of Upper Canada, shall be represented by One Member in the Legislative Assembly of the Province of Canada.
			General Election Mar. 1841.
			Resigned during the Inter-session, between the 2nd and 3rd Sessions, having been appointed to the Legislative Council. A new election was called.
Russell	William Stewart	Oct. 30, 1843*	By-election Date unknown.
			Writ of Election – Aug. 14, 1843. Return of Writ – Sept. 14, 1843. On Sept. 28, 1843, the House was informed of the election of William Stewart, MPP, Russell, in room of the Hon. William Henry Draper, resigned.
Simcoe	Elmes Steele	June 14, 1841	Simcoe. 1840. 3 & 4 Vic., C. 35, S. 16. An Act to Reunite the Provinces of Upper and Lower Canada, and the Government of Canada. And be it enacted, That every County and Riding, other than those hereinbefore specified, which at the time of the passing of this Act was by Law entitled to be represented in the Assembly of the Province of Upper Canada, shall be represented by One Member in the Legislative Assembly of the Province of Canada.
			General Election Mar. 1841.
Stormont	Alexander McLean	June 14, 1841	Stormont. 1840. 3 & 4 Vic., C. 35, S. 16. An Act to Reunite the Provinces of Upper and Lower Canada, and the Government of Canada. And be it enacted, That every County and Riding, other than those hereinbefore specified, which at the time of the passing of this Act was by Law entitled to be represented

in the Assembly of the Province of Upper Canada, shall be represented by One Member in the Legislative Assembly of the Province of Canada.

General Election Mar. 1841.

Toronto (City)	Isaac Buchanan	June 14, 1841	Toronto (City). 1840. 3 & 4 Vic., C. 35, S. 17. An Act to Reunite the Provinces of Upper and Lower Canada, and the Government of Canada. And be it enacted, That the City of Toronto shall be represented by Two Members, and the Towns of Kingston, Brockville, Hamilton, Cornwall, Niagara, London and Bytown shall each be represented by One Member in the Legislative Assembly of the Province of Canada.
			General Election Mar. 1841.
			Resigned during the Inter-session, between the 2nd and 3rd Sessions. A new election was called.
Toronto (City)	Hon. Henry Sherwood	Sept. 28, 1843*	Queen's Counsel.
			By-election Date unknown.
			Writ of Election — Feb. 11, 1843. Return of Writ — Mar. 6, 1843. On Sept. 28, 1843, the House was informed of the election of the Hon. Henry Sherwood, MPP, Toronto (City), in room of Isaac Buchanan, resigned.
Toronto (City)	Hon. John Henry Dunn	June 14, 1841	Receiver General.
			Toronto (City). 1840. 3 & 4 Vic., C. 35, S. 17. An Act to Reunite the Provinces of Upper and Lower Canada, and the Government of Canada. And be it enacted, That the City of Toronto shall be represented by Two Members, and the Towns of Kingston, Brockville, Hamilton, Cornwall, Niagara, London and

* By-election

Constituency	Member	Sworn In	Comments
Toronto (City) — *Continued*			Bytown shall each be represented by One Member in the Legislative Assembly of the Province of Canada.
			General Election Mar. 1841.
Wentworth	Harmannus Smith	June 14, 1841	Wentworth. 1840. 3 & 4 Vic., C. 35, S. 16. An Act to Reunite the Provinces of Upper and Lower Canada, and the Government of Canada. And be it enacted, That every County and Riding, other than those hereinbefore specified, which at the time of the passing of this Act was by Law entitled to be represented in the Assembly of the Province of Upper Canada, shall be represented by One Member in the Legislative Assembly of the Province of Canada.
			General Election Mar. 1841.
York, 1st R.	James Hervey Price	June 14, 1841	York, 1st R. 1840. 3 & 4 Vic., C. 35, S. 16. An Act to Reunite the Provinces of Upper and Lower Canada, and the Government of Canada. And be it enacted, That every County and Riding, other than those hereinbefore specified, which at the time of the passing of this Act was by Law entitled to be represented in the Assembly of the Province of Upper Canada, shall be represented by One Member in the Legislative Assembly of the Province of Canada.
			General Election Mar. 1841.
York, 2nd R.	George Duggan, Jr.	June 14, 1841	York, 2nd R. 1840. 3 & 4 Vic., C. 35, S. 16. An Act to Reunite the Provinces of Upper and Lower Canada, and the Government of Canada. And be it enacted, That every County and Riding, other than those hereinbefore specified, which at the time of the passing of

this Act was by Law entitled to be represented in the Assembly of the Province of Upper Canada, shall be represented by One Member in the Legislative Assembly of the Province of Canada.

General Election Mar. 1841.

On Sept. 26, 1842, the election of George Duggan, Jr., MPP, York, 2nd R., was declared void. A new election was called.

By-election Date unknown.

Writ of Election – Oct. 10, 1842. Return of Writ – Nov. 22, 1842. On Sept. 28, 1843, the House was informed of the election of George Duggan, Jr., MPP, York, 2nd R., who was returned as duly elected.

York, 3rd R.	Hon. James Edward Small	June 14, 1841

York, 3rd R. 1840. 3 & 4 Vic., C. 35, S. 16. An Act to Reunite the Provinces of Upper and Lower Canada, and the Government of Canada. And be it enacted, That every County and Riding, other than those hereinbefore specified, which at the time of the passing of this Act was by Law entitled to be represented in the Assembly of the Province of Upper Canada, shall be represented by One Member in the Legislative Assembly of the Province of Canada.

General Election Mar. 1841.

On Sept. 26, 1842, the House was informed of the resignation of James Edward Small, MPP, York, 3rd R., who had been appointed Solicitor General of Canada West. A new election was called.

By-election Date unknown.

Writ of Election – Sept. 27, 1842. Return of Writ – Oct. 15, 1842. On Sept. 28, 1843, the House was informed of the election of the Hon. James Edward Small, MPP, York, 3rd R., who was returned as duly elected.

Constituency	Member	Sworn In	Comments
York, 4th R.	Hon. Robert Baldwin	June 14, 1841	Solicitor General.
			York, 4th R. 1840. 3 & 4 Vic., C. 35, S. 16. An Act to Reunite the Provinces of Upper and Lower Canada, and the Government of Canada. And be it enacted, That every County and Riding, other than those hereinbefore specified, which at the time of the passing of this Act was by Law entitled to be represented in the Assembly of the Province of Upper Canada, shall be represented by One Member in the Legislative Assembly of the Province of Canada.
			General Election Mar. 1841.
			On Aug. 25, 1841, Robert Baldwin, Member for both the County of York, 4th R., and the County of Hastings, chose to serve for the County of Hastings. A new election was called for the County of York, 4th R.
York, 4th R.	Hon. Louis Hypolite Lafontaine	Sept. 8, 1842*	By-election Date unknown.
			Writ of Election – Aug. 31, 1841. Return of Writ – Sept. 21, 1841. On Sept. 8, 1842, the House was informed of the election of Louis Hypolite Lafontaine, MPP, York, 4th R., in room of Robert Baldwin, resigned.
			On Sept. 16, 1842, the House was informed of the resignation of Louis Hypolite Lafontaine, MPP, York, 4th R., who had been appointed Attorney General of Canada East. A new election was called.
			By-election Date unknown.
			Writ of Election – Sept. 17, 1842. Return of Writ – Oct. 8, 1842. On Sept. 28, 1843, the House was informed of the election of the Hon.

Louis Hypolite Lafontaine, MPP, York, 4th R.,
who was returned as duly elected.

LEGISLATURES OF THE PROVINCE OF CANADA
(Canada West)
2nd Legislature

General Election   Oct. 1844

Sessions of the Second Legislature of the Province of Canada: Nov. 28, 1844 – July 28, 1847

First:	Nov. 28, 1844 – Mar. 29, 1845.
Second:	Mar. 20, 1846 – June 9, 1846.
Third:	June 2, 1847 – July 28, 1847.

Alphabetical List of Members

Member	Constituency	Sworn In	Comments
Hon. Robert Baldwin	York, 4th R.	Nov. 28, 1844	
William Henry Boulton	Toronto (City)	Nov. 28, 1844	
John Hillyard Cameron	Cornwall (Town)	June 2, 1847*	Writ of Election – July 13, 1846. Return of Writ – Aug. 17, 1846. On June 2, 1847, the House was informed of the election of John Hillyard Cameron, MPP, Cornwall (Town), in room of Rolland Macdonald, resigned.
Malcolm Cameron	Lanark	Dec. 2, 1844	On Jan. 21, 1845, the election of Malcom Cameron, MPP, Lanark, was declared void. A new election was called. [There was no evidence in the Journals of a By-election ever having taken place.]
Hon. William Cayley	Huron	Mar. 20, 1846*	Inspector General.
			Writ of Election – Jan. 26, 1846. Return of Writ – Feb. 28, 1846. On Mar. 20, 1846, the House was informed of the election of the Hon. William Cayley, MPP, Huron, in room of William Dunlop, resigned.
George Chalmers	Halton East	Nov. 28, 1844	

Roger Bates Conger	Prince Edward	June 2, 1847*	Writ of Election – June 1, 1846. Return of Writ – July 1, 1846. On June 2, 1847, the House was informed of the election of Roger Bates Conger, MPP, Prince Edward, in room of John Philip Roblin, resigned.
James Cummings	Lincoln South	Nov. 28, 1844	
Walter Hamilton Dickson	Niagara (Town)	Nov. 28, 1844	
Hon. William Henry Draper	London (Town)	Feb. 25, 1845*	Attorney General. Writ of Election – Jan. 25, 1845. Return of Writ – Feb. 13, 1845. On Feb. 25, 1845, the House was informed of the election of the Hon. William Henry Draper, MPP, London (Town), in room of Lawrence Lawrason, resigned. Resigned, June 2, 1847, in consequence of the provisions of the Act of the 7 Vic., C. 65. A new election was called.
George Duggan, Jr.	York, 2nd R.	Nov. 28, 1844	
William Dunlop	Huron	Nov. 28, 1844	On Mar. 20, 1846, the House was informed of the resignation of William Dunlop, MPP, Huron, during the Inter-session. A new election had been called.
Edward Ermatinger	Middlesex	Nov. 28, 1844	
Ogle Robert Gowan	Leeds	Nov. 28, 1844	
George Barker Hall	Northumberland South	Nov. 28, 1844	
Hon. Samuel Beasley Harrison	Kent	Nov. 28, 1844	On Jan. 9, 1845, the House was informed of the resignation of the Hon. Samuel Beasley Harrison, MPP, Kent, who had been appointed Judge of the Home District Surrogate Court. A new election was called.
Hamilton Dibble Jessup	Grenville	Nov. 28, 1844	

*   By-election

Member	Constituency	Sworn In	Comments
James Johnston	Carleton	Nov. 28, 1844	Resigned, May 14, 1846, in consequence of the provisions of the Act of the 7 Vic., C. 65. A new election was called.
Lawrence Lawrason	London (Town)	Nov. 28, 1844	Resigned, Jan. 24, 1845, in consequence of the provisions of the Act of the 7 Vic., C. 65. A new election was called.
George Lyon	Carleton	June 2, 1847*	Writ of Election – May 22, 1846. Return of Writ – June 23, 1846. On June 2, 1847, the House was informed of the election of George Lyon, MPP, Carleton, in room of James Johnston, resigned.
John Alexander Macdonald	Kingston (City)	Nov. 28, 1844	On June 2, 1847, the House was informed of the resignation of John Alexander Macdonald, MPP, Kingston (City). A new election was called.
		June 4, 1847*	Writ of Election – May 21, 1847. Return of Writ – June 1, 1847. On June 4, 1847, the House was informed of the election of the Hon. John Alexander Macdonald, MPP, Kingston (City), who was returned as duly elected.
John Sandfield Macdonald	Glengary	Nov. 28, 1844	
Rolland Macdonald	Cornwall (Town)	Nov. 28, 1844	On June 2, 1847, the House was informed of the resignation of Rolland Macdonald, MPP, Cornwall (Town). A new election was called.
Donald Aeneas MacDonell	Stormont	Nov. 28, 1844	
George Macdonell	Dundas	Nov. 28, 1844	
Hon. Sir Allan Napier MacNab	Hamilton (City)	Nov. 28, 1844	On Nov. 28, 1844, Hon. James Smith, MPP, Missiquoi (Canada East), proposed Sir Allan Napier MacNab, MPP, Hamilton (City), as Speaker. Seconded and resolved. Nov. 28, 1844 – Date took chair.

William Hamilton Merritt	Lincoln North	Jan. 7, 1845	
George Monro	York, 3rd R.	Mar. 26, 1846	On Mar. 14, 1845, the House was informed that George Monro was duly elected at the York, 3rd R. General Election, in room of James Edward Small, whose election was declared void.
Edmund Murney	Hastings	Nov. 28, 1844	
Adam Henry Myers	Northumberland North	Nov. 28, 1844	
Archibald Petrie	Russell	Nov. 28, 1844	
Israel Wood Powell	Norfolk	Nov. 28, 1844	
James Hervey Price	York, 1st R.	Nov. 28, 1844	
John Prince	Essex	Nov. 28, 1844	
Robert Riddell	Oxford	Nov. 28, 1844	
Hon. William Benjamin Robinson	Simcoe	Dec. 2, 1844	On Dec. 20, 1844, the House was informed of the resignation of William Benjamin Robinson, MPP, Simcoe, who had been appointed Inspector General of Accounts. A new election was called.
		Jan. 21, 1845*	Writ of Election – Dec. 20, 1844. Return of Writ – Jan. 13, 1845. On Jan. 21, 1845, the House was informed of the election of the Hon. William Benjamin Robinson, MPP, Simcoe, who was returned as duly elected.
			Resigned, June 26, 1846, having been appointed Chief Commissioner of Public Works. A new election was called.
		June 2, 1847*	Writ of Election – July 7, 1846. Return of Writ – July 27, 1846. On June 2, 1847, the House was informed of the election of the Hon. William Benjamin Robinson, MPP, Simcoe, who was returned as duly elected.
John Philip Roblin	Prince Edward	Nov. 28, 1844	On May 22, 1846, the House was informed of the resignation of John Philip Roblin, MPP,

* By-election

Member	Constituency	Sworn In	Comments
John Philip Roblin — *Continued*			Prince Edward, who had been appointed Collector of Customs for the Port of Picton. A new election was called.
Benjamin Seymour	Lennox & Addington	Nov. 28, 1844	
George Sherwood	Brockville (Town)	Nov. 28, 1844	
Hon. Henry Sherwood	Toronto (City)	Nov. 28, 1844	Solicitor General.
			On June 2, 1847, the House was informed of the resignation of the Hon. Henry Sherwood, MPP, Toronto (City), who had been appointed Attorney General of Canada West. A new election was called.
		June 14, 1847*	Writ of Election – May 29, 1847. Return of Writ – June 10, 1847. On June 14, 1847, the House was informed of the election of the Hon. Henry Sherwood, MPP, Toronto (City), who was returned as duly elected.
Hon. James Edward Small	York, 3rd R.	Nov. 28, 1844	On Mar. 14, 1845, the election of James Edward Small, MPP, York, 3rd R., was declared void. George Monro was duly elected at the York, 3rd R. General Election.
Harmannus Smith	Wentworth	Nov. 28, 1844	
Henry Smith, Jr.	Frontenac	Nov. 28, 1844	
Neil Stewart	Prescott	Nov. 28, 1844	
William Stewart	Bytown (Town)	Nov. 28, 1844	
David Thompson	Haldimand	Nov. 28, 1844	
James Webster	Halton West	Nov. 28, 1844	
John Tucker Williams	Durham	Nov. 28, 1844	
John Wilson	London (Town)	July 7, 1847*	Writ of Election – June 9, 1847. Return of Writ – July 3, 1847. On July 7, 1847, the House

was informed of the election of John Wilson, MPP, London (Town), in room of the Hon. William Henry Draper, resigned.

Joseph Woods	Kent	Feb. 25, 1845*	Writ of Election – Jan. 11, 1845. Return of Writ – Feb. 7, 1845. On Feb. 17, 1845, the House was informed of the election of Joseph Woods, MPP, Kent, in room of the Hon. Samuel Beasley Harrison, resigned.

* By-election

Constituency	Member	Sworn In	Comments
Brockville (Town)	George Sherwood	Nov. 28, 1844	General Election Oct. 1844.
Bytown (Town)	William Stewart	Nov. 28, 1844	General Election Oct. 1844.
Carleton	James Johnston	Nov. 28, 1844	General Election Oct. 1844.
			Carleton. 1845. 8 Vic., C. 8. Schedule B. An Act for better defining the limits of the Counties and Districts in Upper Canada, for erecting certain new Townships, from some counties and attaching them to others, and for other purposes relative to the division of Upper Canada into Townships, Counties and Districts. Which shall include and consist of the Townships of Fitzroy, Goulbourn, North Gower, Gloucester, Huntley, March, Marlborough, Nepean, Osgoode and Torbolton, and, except for the purposes of representation in the Legislative Assembly, the Town of Bytown.
			Carleton. 1846. 9 Vic., C. 46. Schedule. An Act to amend the Act for defining the Limits of Counties and Districts in Upper Canada. Which shall include and consist of the Townships of Fitzroy, Goulbourn, that part of North Gower on the north side of the Rideau River, Gloucester, Huntley, March, Marlborough, Nepean, Osgoode and Torbolton, and, except for the purposes of representation in the Legislative Assembly, the Town of Bytown.
			Resigned, May 14, 1846, in consequence of the provisions of the Act of the 7 Vic., C. 65. A new election was called.
Carleton	George Lyon	June 2, 1847*	By-election Date unknown.
			Writ of Election – May 22, 1846. Return of Writ

– June 23, 1846. On June 2, 1847, the House was informed of the election of George Lyon, MPP, Carleton, in room of James Johnston, resigned.

Cornwall (Town)	Rolland Macdonald	Nov. 28, 1844	General Election Oct. 1844.
			On June 2, 1847, the House was informed of the resignation of Rolland Macdonald, MPP, Cornwall (Town). A new election was called.
Cornwall (Town)	John Hillyard Cameron	June 2, 1847*	By-election Date unknown.
			Writ of Election – July 13, 1846. Return of Writ – Aug. 17, 1846. On June 2, 1847, the House was informed of the election of John Hillyard Cameron, MPP, Cornwall (Town), in room of Rolland Macdonald, resigned.
Dundas	George Macdonell	Nov. 28, 1844	General Election Oct. 1844.
			Dundas. 1845. 8 Vic., C. 8. Schedule B. An Act for better defining the limits of the Counties and Districts in Upper Canada, for erecting certain new Townships, from some counties and attaching them to others, and for other purposes relative to the division of Upper Canada into Townships, Counties and Districts. Which shall include and consist of the Townships of Mountain, Matilda, Winchester, and Williamsburgh.
Durham	John Tucker Williams	Nov. 28, 1844	General Election Oct. 1844.
			Durham. 1845. 8 Vic., C. 8. Schedule B. An Act for better defining the limits of the Counties and Districts in Upper Canada, for erecting certain new Townships, from some Counties and attaching them to others, and for other purposes relative to the division of Upper Canada into Townships, Counties and Districts. Which shall include and consist of the

* By-election

Constituency	Member	Sworn In	Comments
Durham — *Continued*			Townships of Clarke, Cavan, Cartwright, Darlington, Hope, and Manvers.
Essex	John Prince	Nov. 28, 1844	General Election Oct. 1844.
			Essex. 1845. 8 Vic., C. 8. Schedule B. An Act for better defining the limits of the Counties and Districts in Upper Canada, for erecting certain new Townships, from some Counties and attaching them to others, and for other purposes relative to the division of Upper Canada into Townships, Counties and Districts. Which shall include and consist of the Townships of Anderdon, Colchester, Gosfield, Maidstone, Mersea, Malden, Rochester, and Sandwich.
Frontenac	Henry Smith, Jr.	Nov. 28, 1844	General Election Oct. 1844.
			Frontenac. 1845. 8 Vic., C. 8. Schedule B. An Act for better defining the limits of the Counties and Districts in Upper Canada, for erecting certain new Townships, from some counties and attaching them to others, and for other purposes relative to the division of Upper Canada into Townships, Counties and Districts. Which shall include and consist of the Townships of Bedford, Barrie, Clarendon, Hinchinbrooke, Kingston, Kennebec, Loughborough, Olden, Oso, Portland, Pittsburgh, which shall include Howe Island, Palmerston, Storrington, and Wolfe Island, and, except for the purposes of representation in the Legislative Assembly, the Town of Kingston.
Glengary	John Sandfield Macdonald	Nov. 28, 1844	General Election Oct. 1844.
			Glengarry. 1845. 8 Vic., C. 8. Schedule B. An Act for better defining the limits of the Counties and Districts in Upper Canada, for erecting

certain new Townships, from some counties and attaching them to others, and for other purposes relative to the division of Upper Canada into Townships, Counties and Districts. Which shall include and consist of the Townships of Charlottenburgh, Kenyon, Lochiel, and Lancaster, and the Indian Reservation adjoining the said Townships of Charlottenburgh and Kenyon.

Grenville	Hamilton Dibble Jessup	Nov. 28, 1844	General Election Oct. 1844.

Grenville. 1845. 8 Vic., C. 8. Schedule B. An Act for better defining the limits of the Counties and Districts in Upper Canada, for erecting certain new Townships, from some counties and attaching them to others, and for other purposes relative to the division of Upper Canada into Townships, Counties and Districts. Which shall include and consist of the Townships of Augusta, Edwardsburgh, South Gower, Oxford and Wolford.

Grenville. 1846. 9 Vic., C. 46. Schedule. An Act to amend the Act for defining the limits of Counties and Districts in Upper Canada. Which shall include and consist of the Townships of Augusta, Edwardsburgh, South Gower, Oxford, Wolford, and that part of North Gower lying on the south side of the River Rideau, which shall be attached to and form part of the Township of South Gower.

Haldimand	David Thompson	Nov. 28, 1844	General Election Oct. 1844.

Haldimand. 1845. 8 Vic., C. 8. Schedule B. An Act for better defining the limits of the Counties and Districts in Upper Canada, for erecting certain new Townships, from some counties and attaching them to others, and for other purposes relative to the division of Upper Canada into Townships, Counties and Districts. Which shall for all purposes include the Townships of Canborough, Cayuga, Dunn,

Constituency	Member	Sworn In	Comments
Haldimand — *Continued*			Moulton, Sherbrooke, – and for the purposes of representation in the Legislative Assembly and of registration of titles only, the Townships of Seneca, Oneida, Rainham and Walpole.
Halton East	George Chalmers	Nov. 28, 1844	General Election Oct. 1844.
			Halton East. 1845. 8 Vic., C. 8, S. 5. An Act for better defining the limits of the Counties and Districts in Upper Canada, for erecting certain new Townships, from some counties and attaching them to others, and for other purposes relative to the division of Upper Canada into Townships, Counties and Districts. And be it enacted, That the North Riding of the County of Northumberland shall hereafter be known and designated by the name of The County of Peterborough, the South Riding of the said County, by the name of The County of Northumberland, the West Riding of The County of Halton, by the name of The County of Waterloo, the East Riding of the same County, by the name of The County of Halton, and the South Riding of The County of Lincoln, by the name of the County of Welland, and the North Riding, by the name of The County of Lincoln.
Halton West	James Webster	Nov. 28, 1844	General Election Oct. 1844.
			Halton West. 1845. 8 Vic., C. 8, S. 5. An Act for better defining the limits of the Counties and Districts in Upper Canada, for erecting certain new Townships, from some counties and attaching them to others, and for other purposes relative to the division of Upper Canada into Townships, Counties and Districts. And be it enacted that the North Riding of the

County of Northumberland shall hereafter be known and designated by the name of The County of Peterborough, the South Riding of the said County, by the name of The County of Northumberland, the West Riding of The County of Halton, by the name of The County of Waterloo, the East Riding of the same County, by the name of The County of Halton, and the South Riding of The County of Lincoln, by the name of The County of Welland, and the North Riding, by the name of The County of Lincoln.

Hamilton (City)	Hon. Sir Allan Napier MacNab	Nov. 28, 1844	General Election Oct. 1844. On Nov. 28, 1844, Hon. James Smith, MPP, Missiquoi (Canada East), proposed Sir Allan Napier MacNab, MPP, Hamilton (City), as Speaker. Seconded and resolved. Nov. 28, 1844 – Date took chair.
Hastings	Edmund Murney	Nov. 28, 1844	General Election Oct. 1844. Hastings. 1845. 8 Vic., C. 8. Schedule B. An Act for better defining the limits of the Counties and Districts in Upper Canada, for erecting certain new Townships, from some counties and attaching them to others, and for other purposes relative to the division of Upper Canada into Townships, Counties and Districts. Which shall include and consist of the Townships of Elzevir, Grimsthorpe, Hungerford, Huntingdon, Lake, Marmora, Madoc, Rawdon, Sydney, Tudor, Thurlow and Tyendinaga.
Huron	William Dunlop	Nov. 28, 1844	General Election Oct. 1844. Huron. 1845. 8 Vic., C. 8. Schedule B. An Act for better defining the limits of the Counties and Districts in Upper Canada, for erecting certain new Townships, from some counties and attaching them to others, and for other purposes relative to the division of Upper Canada into Townships, Counties and Districts.

Constituency	Member	Sworn In	Comments
Huron — *Continued*			Which shall include and consist of the Townships of Ashfield, Biddulph, Blanchard, Colborne, Downie, Ellice, South Easthope, North Easthope, Fullerton, Goderich, Hibbert, Hay, Hullet, Logan, McKillop, McGillivray, Stephen, Stanley, Tuckersmith, Usborne, and Wawanosh.
			On Mar. 20, 1846, the House was informed of the resignation of William Dunlop, MPP, Huron, during the Inter-session. A new election had been called.
Huron	Hon. William Cayley	Mar. 20, 1846*	Inspector General.
			By-election Date unknown.
			Writ of Election – Jan. 26, 1846. Return of Writ – Feb. 28, 1846. On Mar. 20, 1846, the House was informed of the election of the Hon. William Cayley, MPP, Huron, in room of William Dunlop, resigned.
Kent	Hon. Samuel Beasley Harrison	Nov. 28, 1844	General Election Oct. 1844.
			On Jan. 9, 1845, the House was informed of the resignation of the Hon. Samuel Beasley Harrison, MPP, Kent, who had been appointed Judge of the Home District Surrogate Court. A new election was called.
Kent	Joseph Woods	Feb. 25, 1845*	By-election Date unknown.
			Writ of Election – Jan. 11, 1845. Return of Writ – Feb. 7, 1845. On Feb. 17, 1845, the House was informed of the election of Joseph Woods, MPP, Kent, in room of the Hon. Samuel Beasley Harrison, resigned.
			Kent. 1845. 8 Vic., C. 8. Schedule B. An Act for better defining the limits of the Counties

and Districts in Upper Canada, for erecting certain new Townships, from some counties and attaching them to others, and for other purposes relative to the division of Upper Canada into Townships, Counties and Districts. Which shall include and consist of the Townships of Bosanquet, Brooke, Camden, Chatham, Dawn, East Dover, West Dover, Enniskillen, Howard, Harwich, Moore, Orford, Plympton, Raleigh, Romney, Sarnia, Sombra, East Tilbury, West Tilbury, Warwick and Zone.

Kingston (City)	John Alexander Macdonald	Nov. 28, 1844	General Election Oct. 1844.
			On June 2, 1847, the House was informed of the resignation of John Alexander Macdonald, MPP, Kingston (City). A new election was called.
		June 4, 1847*	By-election Date unknown.
			Writ of Election – May 21, 1847. Return of Writ – June 1, 1847. On June 4, 1847, the House was informed of the election of the Hon. John Alexander Macdonald, MPP, Kingston (City), who was returned as duly elected.
Lanark	Malcolm Cameron	Dec. 2, 1844	General Election Oct. 1844.
			On Jan. 21, 1845, the election of Malcom Cameron, MPP, Lanark, was declared void. A new election was called. [There was no evidence in the Journals of a By-election ever having taken place.]
			Lanark. 1845. 8 Vic., C. 8. Schedule B. An Act for better defining the limits of the Counties and Districts in Upper Canada, for erecting certain new Townships, from some counties and attaching them to others, and for other purposes relative to the division of Upper Canada into Townships, Counties and Districts.

*   By-election

Constituency	Member	Sworn In	Comments
Lanark — *Continued*			(Which for the purpose of representation in the Legislative Assembly, shall be united as it now is, with the County of Renfrew), shall include and consist of the Townships of Bathurst, Beckwith, Drummond, Dalhousie, Darling, North Elmsley, North Burgess, Levant, Lanark, Montague, Ramsay, North Sherbrooke, South Sherbrooke.
Leeds	Ogle Robert Gowan	Nov. 28, 1844	General Election Oct. 1844.
			Leeds. 1845. 8 Vic., C. 8. Schedule B. An Act for better defining the limits of the Counties and Districts in Upper Canada, for erecting certain new Townships, from some counties and attaching them to others, and for other purposes relative to the division of Upper Canada into Townships, Counties and Districts. Which shall include and consist of the Townships of Bastard, Burgess, North Crosby, South Crosby, Elmsley, Elizabethtown, Kitley, Lansdown, Leeds, Yonge, and Escott, and except for the purposes of representation in the Legislative Assembly the Town of Brockville.
Lennox & Addington	Benjamin Seymour	Nov. 28, 1844	General Election Oct. 1844.
			Lennox & Addington (Lennox). 1845. 8 Vic., C. 8. Schedule B. An Act for better defining the limits of the Counties and Districts in Upper Canada, for erecting certain new Townships, from some counties and attaching them to others, and for other purposes relative to the division of Upper Canada into Townships, Counties and Districts. (Which shall for the purpose of representation in the Legislative Assembly, be united as it now is, to the County of Addington), shall include and consist of the Townships of Adolphustown, Fredericsburgh,

Fredericsburgh additional and Richmond. (Addington). (Which for the purpose of representation in the Legislative Assembly shall be united as it now is with the County of Lennox), shall include and consist of the Townships of Amherst Island, Camden, Ernestown, Kaladar, Sheffield and Anglesea.

Lincoln North	William Hamilton Merritt	Jan. 7, 1845	General Election Oct. 1844.

Lincoln North. 1845. 8 Vic., C. 8, S. 5. An Act for better defining the limits of the Counties and Districts in Upper Canada, for erecting certain new Townships, from some counties and attaching them to others, and for other purposes relative to the division of Upper Canada into Townships, Counties and Districts. And be it enacted that the North Riding of the County of Northumberland shall hereafter be known and designated by the name of The County of Peterborough, the South Riding of the said County, by the name of The County of Northumberland, the West Riding of The County of Halton, by the name of The County of Waterloo, the East Riding of the same County, by the name of The County of Halton, and the South Riding of The County of Lincoln, by the name of The County of Welland, and the North Riding, by the name of The County of Lincoln.

Lincoln South	James Cummings	Nov. 28, 1844	General Election Oct. 1844.

Lincoln South. 1845. 8 Vic., C. 8, S. 5. An Act for better defining the limits of the Counties and Districts in Upper Canada, for erecting certain new Townships, from some counties and attaching them to others, and for other purposes relative to the division of Upper Canada into Townships, Counties and Districts. And be it enacted that the North Riding of the County of Northumberland shall hereafter be known and designated by the name of The

Constituency	Member	Sworn In	Comments
Lincoln South — *Continued*			County of Peterborough, the South Riding of the said County, by the name of The County of Northumberland, the West Riding of The County of Halton, by the name of The County of Waterloo, the East Riding of the same County, by the name of The County of Halton, and the South Riding of The County of Lincoln, by the name of The County of Welland, and the North Riding, by the name of The County of Lincoln.
London (Town)	Lawrence Lawrason	Nov. 28, 1844	General Election Oct. 1844. Resigned, Jan. 24, 1845, in consequence of the provisions of the Act of the 7 Vic., C. 65. A new election was called.
London (Town)	Hon. William Henry Draper	Feb. 25, 1845*	Attorney General. By-election Date unknown. Writ of Election – Jan. 25, 1845. Return of Writ – Feb. 13, 1845. On Feb. 25, 1845, the House was informed of the election of the Hon. William Henry Draper, MPP, London (Town), in room of Lawrence Lawrason, resigned. Resigned, June 2, 1847, in consequence of the provisions of the Act of the 7 Vic., C. 65. A new election was called.
London (Town)	John Wilson	July 7, 1847*	By-election Date unknown. Writ of Election – June 9, 1847. Return of Writ – July 3, 1847. On July 7, 1847, the House was informed of the election of John Wilson, MPP, London (Town), in room of the Hon. William Henry Draper, resigned.
Middlesex	Edward Ermatinger	Nov. 28, 1844	General Election Oct. 1844. Middlesex. 1845. 8 Vic., C. 8. Schedule B. An

Act for better defining the limits of the Counties and Districts in Upper Canada, for erecting certain new Townships, from some counties and attaching them to others, and for other purposes relative to the division of Upper Canada into Townships, Counties and Districts. Which shall include and consist of the Townships of Adelaide, Aldborough, Bayham, Carradoc, Delaware, Dorchester, Dunwich, Ekfrid, Lobo, London, Metcalfe, Mosa, Malahide, Southwold, Westminster, Williams, Yarmouth, and (except for the purposes of representation in the Legislative Assembly), the Town of London.

Niagara (Town)	Walter Hamilton Dickson	Nov. 28, 1844	General Election Oct. 1844.
Norfolk	Israel Wood Powell	Nov. 28, 1844	General Election Oct. 1844.

Norfolk. 1845. 8 Vic., C. 8. Schedule B. An Act for better defining the limits of the Counties and Districts in Upper Canada, for erecting certain new Townships, from some counties and attaching them to others, and for other purposes relative to the division of Upper Canada into Townships, Counties and Districts. Which shall include and consist of the Townships of Charlotteville, Houghton, Middleton, Townsend, Woodhouse, Windham, Walsingham, and Long Point, and Ryerson's Island in Lake Erie; – and (for all purposes except that of representation in the Legislative Assembly, and that of registration of titles), the Townships of Rainham, and Walpole.

Northumberland North	Adam Henry Myers	Nov. 28, 1844	General Election Oct. 1844.

Northumberland North. 1845. 8 Vic., C. 8, S. 5. An Act for better defining the limits of the Counties and Districts in Upper Canada, for

Constituency	Member	Sworn In	Comments
Northumberland North — *Continued*			erecting certain new Townships, from some counties and attaching them to others, and for other purposes relative to the division of Upper Canada into Townships, Counties and Districts. And be it enacted that the North Riding of the County of Northumberland shall hereafter be known and designated by the name of The County of Peterborough, the South Riding of the said County, by the name of The County of Northumberland, the West Riding of The County of Halton, by the name of The County of Waterloo, the East Riding of the same County, by the name of The County of Halton, and the South Riding of The County of Lincoln, by the name of The County of Welland, and the North Riding, by the name of The County of Lincoln.
Northumberland South	George Barker Hall	Nov. 28, 1844	General Election Oct. 1844.
			Northumberland South. 1845. 8 Vic., C. 8, S. 5. An Act for better defining the limits of the Counties and Districts in Upper Canada, for erecting certain new Townships, from some counties and attaching them to others, and for other purposes relative to the division of Upper Canada into Townships, Counties and Districts. And be it enacted that the North Riding of the County of Northumberland shall hereafter be known and designated by the name of The County of Peterborough, the South Riding of the said County, by the name of The County of Northumberland, the West Riding of The County of Halton, by the name of The County of Waterloo, the East Riding of the same County, by the name of The County of Halton, and the South Riding of The County of Lincoln, by the name of The County of Welland, and

			the North Riding, by the name of The County of Lincoln.
Oxford	Robert Riddell	Nov. 28, 1844	General Election Oct. 1844.
			Oxford. 1845. 8 Vic., C. 8. Schedule B. An Act for better defining the limits of the Counties and Districts in Upper Canada, for erecting certain new Townships, from some counties and attaching them to others, and for other purposes relative to the division of Upper Canada into Townships, Counties and Districts. Which shall include and consist of the Townships of Blandford, Blenheim, Burford, Dereham, Nissouri, North Oxford, East Oxford, West Oxford, Oakland, Norwich, East Zorra, and West Zorra.
Prescott	Neil Stewart	Nov. 28, 1844	General Election Oct. 1844.
			Prescott. 1845. 8 Vic., C. 8. Schedule B. An Act for better defining the limits of the Counties and Districts in Upper Canada, for erecting certain new Townships, from some counties and attaching them to others, and for other purposes relative to the division of Upper Canada into Townships, Counties and Districts. Which shall include and consist of the Townships of Alfred, Caledonia, East Hawkesbury, West Hawkesbury, Longueuil, and Planatagenet.
Prince Edward	John Philip Roblin	Nov. 28, 1844	General Election Oct. 1844.
			Prince Edward. 1845. 8 Vic., C. 8. Schedule B. An Act for better defining the limits of the Counties and Districts in Upper Canada, for erecting certain new Townships, from some counties and attaching them to others, and for other purposes relative to the division of Upper Canada into Townships, Counties and Districts. Which shall include and consist of the Townships of Athol, Ameliasburgh, Hillier, Hallowell, Marysburgh, and Sophiasburgh.

Constituency	Member	Sworn In	Comments
Prince Edward — *Continued*			On May 22, 1846, the House was informed of the resignation of John Philip Roblin, MPP, Prince Edward, who had been appointed Collector of Customs for the Port of Picton. A new election was called.
Prince Edward	Roger Bates Conger	June 2, 1847*	By-election Date unknown.
			Writ of Election – June 1, 1846. Return of Writ – July 1, 1846. On June 2, 1847, the House was informed of the election of Roger Bates Conger, MPP, Prince Edward, in room of John Philip Roblin, resigned.
Russell	Archibald Petrie	Nov. 28, 1844	General Election Oct. 1844.
			Russell. 1845. 8 Vic., C. 8. Schedule B. An Act for better defining the limits of the Counties and Districts in Upper Canada, for erecting certain new Townships, from some counties and attaching them to others, and for other purposes relative to the division of Upper Canada into Townships, Counties and Districts. Which shall include and consist of the Townships of Clarence, Cumberland, Cambridge, and Russell.
Simcoe	Hon. William Benjamin Robinson	Dec. 2, 1844	General Election Oct. 1844.
			On Dec. 20, 1844, the House was informed of the resignation of William Benjamin Robinson, MPP, Simcoe, who had been appointed Inspector General of Accounts. A new election was called.
		Jan. 21, 1845*	By-election Date unknown.
			Writ of Election – Dec. 20, 1844. Return of Writ – Jan. 13, 1845. On Jan. 21, 1845, the House was informed of the election of the Hon.

William Benjamin Robinson, MPP, Simcoe, who was returned as duly elected.

Simcoe. 1845. 8 Vic., C. 8. Schedule B. An Act for better defining the limits of the Counties and Districts in Upper Canada, for erecting certain new Townships, from some counties and attaching them to others, and for other purposes relative to the division of Upper Canada into Townships, Counties and Districts. Which shall include and consist of the Townships of Adjala, Artemesia, Collingwood, Essa, Flos, West Gwillimbury, Innisfil, Medonte, Matchedash, Mulmur, Mono, Notawasaga, Ospry, Oro, North Orillia, South Orillia, Saint Vincent, Sunnidale, Tay, Tecumseth, Tosorontia, Tiny, Uphrasia, and Vespra.

Resigned, June 26, 1846, having been appointed Chief Commissioner of Public Works. A new election was called.

June 2, 1847*   By-election Date unknown.

Writ of Election – July 7, 1846. Return of Writ – July 27, 1846. On June 2, 1847, the House was informed of the election of the Hon. William Benjamin Robinson, MPP, Simcoe, who was returned as duly elected.

Stormont   Donald Aeneas MacDonell   Nov. 28, 1844   General Election Oct. 1844.

Stormont. 1845. 8 Vic., C. 8. Schedule B. An Act for better defining the limits of the Counties and Districts in Upper Canada, for erecting certain new Townships, from some counties and attaching them to others, and for other purposes relative to the division of Upper Canada into Townships, Counties and Districts. Which shall include and consist of the Townships of Cornwall, Finch, Osnabruck,

*   By-election

Constituency	Member	Sworn In	Comments
Stormont — *Continued*			Roxborough, and (except for the purpose of representation in the Legislative Assembly) the Town of Cornwall.
Toronto (City)	William Henry Boulton	Nov. 28, 1844	General Election Oct. 1844.
Toronto (City)	Hon. Henry Sherwood	Nov. 28, 1844	Solicitor General.
			General Election Oct. 1844.
			On June 2, 1847, the House was informed of the resignation of the Hon. Henry Sherwood, MPP, Toronto (City), who had been appointed Attorney General of Canada West. A new election was called.
		June 14, 1847*	By-election Date unknown.
			Writ of Election – May 29, 1847. Return of Writ – June 10, 1847. On June 14, 1847, the House was informed of the election of the Hon. Henry Sherwood, MPP, Toronto (City), who was returned as duly elected.
Wentworth	Harmannus Smith	Nov. 28, 1844	General Election Oct. 1844.
			Wentworth. 1845. 8 Vic., C. 8. Schedule B. An Act for better defining the limits of the Counties and Districts in Upper Canada, for erecting certain new Townships, from some counties and attaching them to others, and for other purposes relative to the division of Upper Canada into Townships, Counties and Districts. Which shall for all purposes include and consist of the Townships of Ancaster, Brantford, Binbrooke, Barton, Glandford, Onondaga, Saltfleet, and Tuscarora, and (for all purposes except that of representation in the Legislative Assembly, and that of Registration of Titles), the Townships of Seneca and Oneida, and (except for the

			purpose of representation in the Legislative Assembly) the Town of Hamilton.
York, 1st R.	James Hervey Price	Nov. 28, 1844	General Election Oct. 1844.
York, 2nd R.	George Duggan, Jr.	Nov. 28, 1844	General Election Oct. 1844.
York, 3rd R.	Hon. James Edward Small	Nov. 28, 1844	General Election Oct. 1844.
			On Mar. 14, 1845, the election of James Edward Small, MPP, York, 3rd R., was declared void. George Monro was duly elected at the York, 3rd R. General Election.
York, 3rd R.	George Monro	Mar. 26, 1846	On Mar. 14, 1845, the House was informed that George Monro was duly elected at the York, 3rd R. General Election, in room of James Edward Small, whose election was declared void.
York, 4th R.	Hon. Robert Baldwin	Nov. 28, 1844	General Election Oct. 1844.

*   By-election

LEGISLATURES OF THE PROVINCE OF CANADA
(Canada West)
3rd Legislature

General Election Dec. 1847

Sessions of the Third Legislature of the Province of Canada: Feb. 25, 1848 – Aug. 30, 1851

First:	Feb. 25, 1848 – Mar. 23, 1848.
Second:	Jan. 18, 1849 – May 30, 1849.
Third:	May 14, 1850 – Aug. 10, 1850.
Fourth:	May 20, 1851 – Aug. 30, 1851.

Alphabetical List of Members

Member	Constituency	Sworn In	Comments
Hon. Augustin Norbert Morin	Bellechase (Canada East)	Feb. 25, 1848	On Feb. 25, 1848, the Hon. Robert Baldwin, MPP, York North, proposed Augustin Norbert Morin, MPP, Bellechasse (Canada East), as Speaker. Seconded and resolved. Feb. 25, 1848 – Date took chair.
Hon. Robert Baldwin	York North	Feb. 25, 1848	On Mar. 13, 1848, the House was informed of the resignation of the Hon. Robert Baldwin, MPP, York North, who had been appointed Attorney General of Canada West. A new election was called.
		Jan. 18, 1849*	Writ of Election – Mar. 15, 1848. Return of Writ – Apr. 1, 1848. On Jan. 18, 1849, the House was informed of the election of the Hon. Robert Baldwin, MPP, York North, who was returned as duly elected.
Robert Bell	Lanark	Feb. 25, 1848	
Hon. William Hume Blake	York East	Feb. 25, 1848	On Mar. 13, 1848, the House was informed of the resignation of William Hume Blake, MPP, York East, who had been appointed Solicitor General of Canada West. A new election was

			called.
		Jan. 18, 1849*	Writ of Election – June 16, 1848. Return of Writ – July 5, 1848. On Jan. 18, 1849, the House was informed of the election of William Hume Blake, MPP, York East, who was returned as duly elected.
			On May 14, 1850, the House was informed of the resignation of William Hume Blake, MPP, York East, who had been appointed Chancellor of Upper Canada. A new election had been called.
Hon. Henry John Boulton	Norfolk	Feb. 25, 1848	
William Henry Boulton	Toronto (City)	Feb. 25, 1848	
Read Burritt	Grenville	Feb. 25, 1848	
Hon. John Hillyard Cameron	Cornwall (Town)	Feb. 25, 1848	
Hon. Malcolm Cameron	Kent	Mar. 2, 1848	On Mar. 16, 1848, the House was informed of the resignation of the Hon. Malcolm Cameron, MPP, Kent, who had been appointed Assistant Commissioner of Public Works in this Province. A new election was called.
		Jan. 18, 1849*	Writ of Election – Mar. 20, 1848. Return of Writ – Apr. 10, 1848. On Jan. 18, 1849, the House was informed of the election of the Hon. Malcolm Cameron, MPP, Kent, who was returned as duly elected.
Peter Carroll	Oxford	Feb. 25, 1848	On Mar. 1, 1848, the election of Peter Carroll, MPP, Oxford, was declared void. Francis Hincks was duly elected at the Oxford General Election.
			On Petition, Judgment was upheld.
Hon. William Cayley	Huron	Feb. 25, 1848	
John Pliny Crysler	Dundas	Feb. 25, 1848	

*   By-election

Member	Constituency	Sworn In	Comments
Walter Hamilton Dickson	Niagara (Town)	Jan. 29, 1849	Absent first Session.
Adam Johnston Fergusson	Waterloo	Feb. 8, 1849	On Feb. 8, 1849, the House was informed that Adam Johnston Fergusson was duly elected at the Waterloo General Election, in room of James Webster, whose election was declared void. [Webster had since resigned his seat.]
Billa Flint	Hastings	Feb. 25, 1848	
James Hall	Peterborough	Feb. 25, 1848	
Hon. Francis Hincks	Oxford	Mar. 1, 1848	On Mar. 1, 1848, the House was informed that Francis Hincks was duly elected at the Oxford General Election, in room of Peter Carroll, whose election was declared void.
			On Petition, Judgment was upheld.
			On Mar. 20, 1848, the House was informed of the resignation of the Hon. Francis Hincks, who had been appointed Inspector General of Public Accounts of this Province. A new election was called.
		Jan. 18, 1849*	Writ of Election – Mar. 24, 1848. Return of Writ – Apr. 28, 1848. On Jan. 18, 1849, the House was informed of the election of the Hon. Francis Hincks, MPP, Oxford, who was returned as duly elected.
Caleb Hopkins	Halton	May 14, 1850*	Writ of Election – Feb. 11, 1850. Return of Writ – Mar. 18, 1850. On May 14, 1850, the House was informed of the election of Caleb Hopkins, MPP, Halton, in room of John Wetenhall, resigned.
Thomas Hall Johnson	Prescott	Feb. 25, 1848	
George Byron Lyon	Russell	Feb. 25, 1848	
Hon. John Alexander Macdonald	Kingston (City)	Feb. 25, 1848	

Hon. John Sandfield Macdonald	Glengary	Feb. 25, 1848	On May 14, 1850, the House was informed of the resignation of John Sandfield Macdonald, MPP, Glengary, who had been appointed Solicitor General of Canada West. A new election had been called.
		May 29, 1850*	Writ of Election – Dec. 28, 1849. Return of Writ – Jan. 11, 1850. On May 14, 1850, the House was informed of the election of the Hon. John Sandfield Macdonald, MPP, Glengary, who was returned as duly elected.
William Lyon Mackenzie	Haldimand	May 20, 1851*	Writ of Election – Mar. 19, 1851. Return of Writ – Apr. 21, 1851. On May 20, 1851, the House was informed of the election of William Lyon Mackenzie, MPP, Haldimand, in room of David Thompson, deceased.
Sir Allan Napier MacNab	Hamilton (City)	Feb. 25, 1848	
Edward Malloch	Carleton	Feb. 25, 1848	
Duncan McFarland	Welland	Feb. 25, 1848	
Alexander McLean	Stormont	Feb. 25, 1848	
Hon. William Hamilton Merritt	Lincoln	Feb. 25, 1848	On Jan. 18, 1849, the House was informed of the resignation of William Hamilton Merritt, MPP, Lincoln, who had been appointed the President of the Executive Council of the Province of Canada. A new election had been called.
		Jan. 18, 1849*	Writ of Election – Sept. 19, 1848. Return of Writ – Oct. 6, 1848. On Jan. 18, 1849, the House was informed of the election of the Hon. William Hamilton Merritt, MPP, Lincoln, who was returned as duly elected.
			On May 14, 1850, the House was informed of the resignation of the Hon. William Hamilton Merritt, MPP, Lincoln, who had been appointed

*   By-election

Member	Constituency	Sworn In	Comments
Hon. William Hamilton Merritt — *Continued*			Chief Commissioner of Public Works of the Province of Canada. A new election had been called.
		May 14, 1850*	Writ of Election – Apr. 20, 1850. Return of Writ – May 4, 1850. On May 14, 1850, the House was informed of the election of the Hon. Malcolm Cameron, MPP, Kent, who was returned as duly elected.
Joseph Curran Morrison	York West	Feb. 25, 1848	
Adam Henry Myers	Northumberland	Feb. 25, 1848	
William Notman	Middlesex	Feb. 25, 1848	
Peter Perry	York East	July 9, 1850*	Writ of Election – Nov. 19, 1849. Return of Writ – Dec. 4, 1849. On May 14, 1850, the House was informed of the election of Peter Perry, MPP, York East, in room of William Hume Blake, resigned.
			On Aug. 26, 1851, the House was informed of the death of Peter Perry, MPP, York East. A new writ was issued that day.
			House was prorogued on Aug. 30, 1851. No By-election was held.
Hon. James Hervey Price	York South	Feb. 25, 1848	On Mar. 13, 1848, the House was informed of the resignation of James Hervey Price, MPP, York South, who had been appointed Commissioner of Crown Lands of this Province. A new election was called.
		Jan. 18, 1849*	Writ of Election – Mar. 15, 1848. Return of Writ – Mar. 31, 1848. On Jan. 18, 1849, the House was informed of the election of the Hon. James Hervey Price, MPP, York South, who was returned as duly elected.
John Prince	Essex	Feb. 25, 1848	

William Buell Richards	Leeds	Feb. 25, 1848	
William Benjamin Robinson	Simcoe	Feb. 25, 1848	
John Scott	Bytown (Town)	Feb. 25, 1848	
Benjamin Seymour	Lenox & Addington	Feb. 25, 1848	
George Sherwood	Brockville (Town)	Feb. 25, 1848	
Hon. Henry Sherwood	Toronto (City)	Feb. 25, 1848	Attorney General.
Harmannus Smith	Wentworth	Feb. 25, 1848	
Henry Smith, Jr.	Frontenac	Feb. 25, 1848	
James Smith	Durham	Feb. 25, 1848	
David Barker Stevenson	Prince Edward	Feb. 25, 1848	
David Thompson	Haldimand	Feb. 25, 1848	On May 20, 1851, the House was informed of the death of David Thompson, MPP, Haldimand. A new election had been called.
James Webster	Waterloo	Feb. 25, 1848	Resigned, Jan. 8, 1849, empowered by 4 & 5 Vic., C.4.
			On Feb. 8, 1849, the election of James Webster, late MPP, Waterloo, was declared void. Adam Johnston Fergusson was duly elected at the Waterloo General Election.
John Wetenhall	Halton	Feb. 25, 1848	On May 14, 1850, the House was informed of the resignation of John Wetenhall, MPP, Halton, who had been appointed Assistant Commissioner of Public Works of this Province. A new election had been called.
John Wilson	London (Town)	Feb. 29, 1848	On May 14, 1850, the House was informed of the resignation of John Wilson, MPP, London (Town). A new election had been called.
		May 31, 1850*	Writ of Election – Dec. 21, 1849. Return of Writ – Jan. 21, 1850. On May 14, 1850, the House

*   By-election

Member	Constituency	Sworn In	Comments
John Wilson — *Continued*			was informed of the election of John Wilson, MPP, London (Town), who was returned as duly elected.

Constituency	Member	Sworn In	Comments
Bellechase (Canada East)	Hon. Augustin Norbert Morin	Feb. 25, 1848	General Election Dec. 1847.
			On Feb. 25, 1848, the Hon. Robert Baldwin, MPP, York North, proposed Augustin Norbert Morin, MPP, Bellechasse (Canada East), as Speaker. Seconded and resolved. Feb. 25, 1848 – Date took chair.
Brockville (Town)	George Sherwood	Feb. 25, 1848	General Election Dec. 1847.
Bytown (Town)	John Scott	Feb. 25, 1848	General Election Dec. 1847.
Carleton	Edward Malloch	Feb. 25, 1848	General Election Dec. 1847.
			Carleton. 1851. 14 & 15 Vic., C.5, S.5. Schedule A. An Act to make certain alterations in the Territorial Divisions of Upper Canada. The County of Carleton shall consist of the Townships of Fitzroy, Goulburn, Gower North, Gloucester, Huntley, March, Marlborough, Osgood, Tarbolton and Nepean.
Cornwall (Town)	Hon. John Hillyard Cameron	Feb. 25, 1848	General Election Dec. 1847.
Dundas	John Pliny Crysler	Feb. 25, 1848	General Election Dec. 1847.
			Dundas. 1851. 14 & 15 Vic., C.5, S.8. Schedule A. An Act to make certain alterations in the Territorial Divisions of Upper Canada. The County of Dundas shall consist of the Townships of Mountain, Matilda, Winchester and Williamsburgh.
Durham	James Smith	Feb. 25, 1848	General Election Dec. 1847.
			Durham. 1851. 14 & 15 Vic., C.5, S.17. Schedule A. An Act to make certain alterations in the Territorial Divisions of Upper Canada. The County of Durham shall consist of the Townships of Hope, Clarke, Darlington, Cavan,

			Manvers and Cartwright.
Essex	John Prince	Feb. 25, 1848	General Election Dec. 1847.
			Essex. 1851. 14 & 15 Vic., C.5, S.34. Schedule A. An Act to make certain alterations in the Territorial Divisions of Upper Canada. The County of Essex shall consist of the Townships of Mersea, Gosfield, Colchester, Rochester, Maidstone, Malden, Anderdon, Tilbury West and Sandwich.
Frontenac	Henry Smith, Jr.	Feb. 25, 1848	General Election Dec. 1847.
			Frontenac. 1851. 14 & 15 Vic., C.5, S.11. Schedule A. An Act to make certain alterations in the Territorial Divisions of Upper Canada. The County of Frontenac shall consist of the Townships of Wolfe Island, (including Simcoe Island, Garden Island, Horse Shoe Island and Mud Island,) Clarendon, Barrie, Palmerston, Kennebec, Olden, Oso, Hinchinbrooke, Bedford, Portland, Loughborough, Storrington, Pittsburgh, Howe Island and Kingston.
Glengary	Hon. John Sandfield Macdonald	Feb. 25, 1848	General Election Dec. 1847.
			On May 14, 1850, the House was informed of the resignation of John Sandfield Macdonald, MPP, Glengary, who had been appointed Solicitor General of Canada West. A new election had been called.
		May 29, 1850*	By-election Date unknown.
			Writ of Election – Dec. 28, 1849. Return of Writ – Jan. 11, 1850. On May 14, 1850, the House was informed of the election of the Hon. John Sandfield Macdonald, MPP, Glengary, who was returned as duly elected.
			Glengarry. 1851. 14 & 15 Vic., C.5, S.1. Schedule A. An Act to make certain alterations

*   By-election

Constituency	Member	Sworn In	Comments
Glengary — *Continued*			in the Territorial Divisions of Upper Canada. The County of Glengarry shall consist of the Townships of Charlottenburgh, Kenyon, Lochiel, Lancaster and the Indian reservation adjoining the said Townships of Charlottenburgh and Kenyon.
Grenville	Read Burritt	Feb. 25, 1848	General Election Dec. 1847.
			Grenville. 1851. 14 & 15 Vic., C.5, S.9. Schedule A. An Act to make certain alterations in the Territorial Divisions of Upper Canada. The County of Grenville shall consist of the Townships of Edwardsburgh, Wolford, Gower South, Oxford and Augusta.
Haldimand	David Thompson	Feb. 25, 1848	General Election Dec. 1847.
			Haldimand. 1851. 14 & 15 Vic., C.5, S.39. Schedule A. An Act to make certain alterations in the Territorial Divisions of Upper Canada. The County of Haldimand shall consist of the Townships of Walpole, Oneida, Seneca, North Cayuga, South Cayuga, Canborough, Rainham, Dunn, Moulton and Sherbrooke.
			On May 20, 1851, the House was informed of the death of David Thompson, MPP, Haldimand. A new election had been called.
Haldimand	William Lyon Mackenzie	May 20, 1851*	By-election Date unknown.
			Writ of Election – Mar. 19, 1851. Return of Writ – Apr. 21, 1851. On May 20, 1851, the House was informed of the election of William Lyon Mackenzie, MPP, Haldimand, in room of David Thompson, deceased.
Halton	John Wetenhall	Feb. 25, 1848	Halton. 1845. 8 Vic., C.8. Schedule B. An Act for better defining the limits of the Counties

and Districts in Upper Canada, for erecting certain new Townships, from some Counties and attaching them to others, and for other purposes relative to the division of Upper Canada into Townships, Counties and Districts. Which shall include and consist of the Townships of Beverly, Esquesing, East Flamborough, West Flamborough, Nassagaweya, Nelson, and Trafalgar, and for all purposes except that of representation in the Legislative Assembly, the Township of Dumfries, and for the purpose of representation in the Legislative Assembly only, the Township of Erin.

General Election Dec. 1847.

On May 14, 1850, the House was informed of the resignation of John Wetenhall, MPP, Halton, who had been appointed Assistant Commissioner of Public Works of this Province. A new election had been called.

Halton	Caleb Hopkins	May 14, 1850*	By-election Date unknown.

Writ of Election – Feb. 11, 1850. Return of Writ – Mar. 18, 1850. On May 14, 1850, the House was informed of the election of Caleb Hopkins, MPP, Halton, in room of John Wetenhall, resigned.

Halton. 1851. 14 & 15 Vic., C.5, S.24. Schedule A. An Act to make certain alterations in the Territorial Divisions of Upper Canada. The County of Halton shall consist of the Townships of Esquesing, Trafalgar, Nassagaweya and Nelson.

Hamilton (City)	Sir Allan Napier MacNab	Feb. 25, 1848	General Election Dec. 1847.

* By-election

Constituency	Member	Sworn In	Comments
Hastings	Billa Flint	Feb. 25, 1848	General Election Dec. 1847. Hastings. 1851. 14 & 15 Vic., C.5, S.15. Schedule A. An Act to make certain alterations in the Territorial Divisions of Upper Canada. The County of Hastings shall consist of the Townships of Lake, Tudor, Grimsthorpe, Marmora, Madoc, Elzevir, Rawdon, Huntingdon, Hungerford, Sidney, Thurlow and Tyendinaga.
Huron	Hon. William Cayley	Feb. 25, 1848	General Election Dec. 1847. Huron. 1851. 14 & 15 Vic., C.5, Ss.2, 30, 31, 29. Schedules C, A. Counties United for the Purpose of Representation. An Act to make certain alterations in the Territorial Divisions of Upper Canada. Huron, Perth and Bruce, as the County of Huron. . . . The County of Huron shall consist of the Townships of Hay, Stephen, McGillivray, Biddulph, Usborne, Howick, McKillop, Grey, Morris, Turnberry, Ashfield, Wawanosh, Colborne, Hullett, Tuckersmith, Stanley and Goderich. . . . The County of Perth shall consist of the Townships of Blanchard, Hibbert, Fullarton, Downie, including the Gore of Downie, Logan, Ellice, Easthope North and Easthope South, Elma, Wallace and Mornington. . . . The County of Bruce shall consist of the Townships of Huron, Kinloss, Culross, Carrick, Kincardine, Greenock, Brant, Bruce, Saugeen, Elderslie and Arran, together with all that portion of the Peninsular Tract of Land known as the Indian Reserve, and not included in the County of Grey, together with all the Islands in Lake Huron and the Georgian Bay contiguous thereto.

Kent	Hon. Malcolm Cameron	Mar. 2, 1848	General Election Dec. 1847.
			On Mar. 16, 1848, the House was informed of the resignation of the Hon. Malcolm Cameron, MPP, Kent, who had been appointed Assistant Commissioner of Public Works in this Province. A new election was called.
		Jan. 18, 1849*	By-election Date unknown.
			Writ of Election — Mar. 20, 1848. Return of Writ — Apr. 10, 1848. On Jan. 18, 1849, the House was informed of the election of the Hon. Malcolm Cameron, MPP, Kent, who was returned as duly elected.
			Kent. 1851. 14 & 15 Vic., C.5, Ss.1, 33, 32. Schedules C, A. Counties United for the Purpose of Representation. An Act to make certain alterations in the Territorial Divisions of Upper Canada. Kent and Lambton, as the County of Kent. . . . The County of Kent shall consist of the Townships of Orford, Howard, Camden, Chatham, Harwich, Dover East, Dover West, Raleigh, Tilbury East, Romney and Zone. . . . The County of Lambton shall consist of the Townships of Bosanquet, Plympton, Warwick, Sarnia, Moore, Enniskillen, Brooke, Sombra, including Walpoole Islands, St. Ann's Island, and the other Islands at the Mouth of the River St. Clair, Dawn and Euphemia.
Kingston (City)	Hon. John Alexander Macdonald	Feb. 25, 1848	General Election Dec. 1847.
Lanark	Robert Bell	Feb. 25, 1848	General Election Dec. 1847.
			Lanark. 1851. 14 & 15 Vic., C.5, Ss.8, 7. Schedules C, A. Counties United for the Purpose of Representation. An Act to make certain alterations in the Territorial Divisions of

*   By-election

Constituency	Member	Sworn In	Comments
Lanark — *Continued*			Upper Canada. Lanark and Renfrew, as the County of Lanark. . . . The County of Lanark shall consist of the Townships of Montague, Elmsley North, Burgess North, Sherbrooke North, Sherbrooke South, Bathurst, Drummond, Beckwith, Dalhousie, Lanark, Ramsay, Lavant, Darling and Pakenham.
			Renfrew. 1845. 8 Vic., C.8. Schedule B. An Act for better defining the limits of the Counties and Districts in Upper Canada, for erecting certain new Townships from some Counties and attaching them to others, and for other purposes relative to the division of Upper Canada into Townships, Counties and Districts. (Which shall for the purpose of representation in the Legislative Assembly, be united as it now is with the County of Lanark,) shall include and consist of the Townships of Admaston, Blithefield, Bagot, Bromley, Horton, MacNab, Packenham, Pembroke, Ross, Stafford, and Westmeath.
			Renfrew. 1851. 14 & 15 Vic., C.5, S.6. Schedule A. An Act to make certain alterations in the Territorial Divisions of Upper Canada. The County of Renfrew shall consist of the Townships of Admaston, Blithfield, Bagot, Bromley, Horton, McNab, Pembroke, Ross, Stafford, Westmeath, and all that tract of land lying between the Western Boundaries of the Townships of Lavant, Blithfield, Admaston, Bromley, Stafford and Pembroke and the Ottawa River and a line drawn parallel to the general course of the said Boundaries of the said Townships from the western corner of the Township of Clarendon to the Ottawa River.

Leeds	William Buell Richards	Feb. 25, 1848	General Election Dec. 1847.

Leeds. 1851. 14 & 15 Vic., C.5, S.10. Schedule A. An Act to make certain alterations in the Territorial Divisions of Upper Canada. The County of Leeds shall consist of the Townships of North Crosby, South Crosby, Burgess, Bastard, Elmsley, Kitley, front of Leeds and Lansdown, rear of Leeds and Lansdown, Escott, Yonge and Elizabethtown.

Lenox & Addington	Benjamin Seymour	Feb. 25, 1848	General Election Dec. 1847.

Lennox and Addington. 1851. 14 & 15 Vic., C.5, Ss.7, 13. Schedules C, A. Counties United for the Purpose of Representation. An Act to make certain alterations in the Territorial Divisions of Upper Canada. Lennox and Addington, as the County of Lennox and Addington. . . . The County of Lennox shall consist of the Townships of Adolphustown, Fredericksburg, Fredericksburg additional, and Richmond. . . . The County of Addington shall consist of the Townships of Camden, Ernestown, Kalader, Anglesea, Sheffield and Amherst Island.

Lincoln	Hon. William Hamilton Merritt	Feb. 25, 1848	Lincoln. 1845. 8 Vic., C.8. Schedule B. An Act

for better defining the limits of the Counties and Districts in Upper Canada, for erecting certain new Townships from some Counties and attaching them to others, and for other purposes relative to the division of Upper Canada into Townships, Counties and Districts. Which shall include and consist of the Townships of Caistor, Clinton, Gainsborough, Grantham, Grimsby, Louth, Niagara, and (except for the purposes of representation in the Legislative Assembly) the town of Niagara.

General Election Dec. 1847.

On Jan. 18, 1849, the House was informed of the resignation of William Hamilton Merritt, MPP, Lincoln, who had been appointed the

Constituency	Member	Sworn In	Comments
Lincoln — *Continued*			President of the Executive Council of the Province of Canada. A new election had been called.
		Jan. 18, 1849*	By-election Date unknown.
			Writ of Election – Sept. 19, 1848. Return of Writ – Oct. 6, 1848. On Jan. 18, 1849, the House was informed of the election of the Hon. William Hamilton Merritt, MPP, Lincoln, who was returned as duly elected.
			On May 14, 1850, the House was informed of the resignation of the Hon. William Hamilton Merritt, MPP, Lincoln, who had been appointed Chief Commissioner of Public Works of the Province of Canada. A new election had been called.
		May 14, 1850*	By-election Date unknown.
			Writ of Election – Apr. 20, 1850. Return of Writ – May 4, 1850. On May 14, 1850, the House was informed of the election of the Hon. Malcolm Cameron, MPP, Kent, who was returned as duly elected.
			Lincoln. 1851. 14 & 15 Vic., C.5, S.41. Schedule A. An Act to make certain alterations in the Territorial Divisions of Upper Canada. The County of Lincoln shall consist of the Townships of Grimsby, Clinton, Louth, Grantham, Caistor, Gainsborough and Niagara.
London (Town)	John Wilson	Feb. 29, 1848	General Election Dec. 1847.
			On May 14, 1850, the House was informed of the resignation of John Wilson, MPP, London (Town). A new election was called.
		May 31, 1850*	By-election Date unknown.

Writ of Election – Dec. 21, 1849. Return of Writ – Jan. 21, 1850. On May 14, 1850, the House was informed of the election of John Wilson, MPP, London (Town), who was returned as duly elected.

Middlesex	William Notman	Feb. 25, 1848	General Election Dec. 1847.

Middlesex. 1851. 14 & 15 Vic., C.5, Ss.3, 36, 35. Schedules C, A. Counties United for the Purpose of Representation. An Act to make certain alterations in the Territorial Divisions of Upper Canada. Middlesex and Elgin, as the County of Middlesex. . . . The County of Middlesex shall consist of the Townships of Mosa, Ekfrid, Carradoc, Metcalfe, Adelaide, Williams, Lobo, Nissouri West, North Dorchester, Delaware, Westminster and London. . . . The County of Elgin shall consist of the Townships of Aldborough, Dunwich, Southwold, Yarmouth, Malahide, Bayham and South Dorchester.

Niagara (Town)	Walter Hamilton Dickson	Jan. 29, 1849	General Election Dec. 1847.

Absent first Session.

Norfolk	Hon. Henry John Boulton	Feb. 25, 1848	General Election Dec. 1847.

Norfolk. 1851. 14 & 15 Vic., C.5, S.37. Schedule A. An Act to make certain alterations in the Territorial Divisions of Upper Canada. The County of Norfolk shall consist of the Townships of Houghton, Middleton, Charlotteville, Windham, Townsend, Woodhouse, Walsingham, including Long Point.

Northumberland	Adam Henry Myers	Feb. 25, 1848	Northumberland. 1845. 8 Vic., C.8. Schedule

B. An Act for better defining the limits of the Counties and Districts in Upper Canada, for erecting certain new Townships from some

*   By-election

Constituency	Member	Sworn In	Comments
Northumberland — *Continued*			Counties and attaching them to others, and for other purposes relative to the division of Upper Canada into Townships, Counties and Districts. Which shall include and consist of the Townships of Alnwick, Cramahé, Hamilton, Haldimand, South Monaghan, Murray, Percy and Seymour.
			General Election Dec. 1847.
			Northumberland. 1851. 14 & 15 Vic., C.5, S.16. Schedule A. An Act to make certain alterations in the Territorial Divisions of Upper Canada. The County of Northumberland shall consist of the Townships of Murray, Brighton, Cramahe, Haldimand, Hamilton, Seymour, Percy, Alnwich and Monaghan South.
Oxford	Peter Carroll	Feb. 25, 1848	General Election Dec. 1847.
			On Mar. 1, 1848, the election of Peter Carroll, MPP, Oxford, was declared void. Francis Hincks was duly elected at the Oxford General Election.
			On Petition, Judgment was upheld.
Oxford	Hon. Francis Hincks	Mar. 1, 1848	On Mar. 1, 1848, the House was informed that Francis Hincks was duly elected at the Oxford General Election, in room of Peter Carroll, whose election was declared void.
			On Petition, Judgment was upheld.
			On Mar. 20, 1848, the House was informed of the resignation of the Hon. Francis Hincks, who had been appointed Inspector General of Public Accounts of this Province. A new election was called.
		Jan. 18, 1849*	By-election Date unknown.

Writ of Election – Mar. 24, 1848. Return of Writ – Apr. 28, 1848. On Jan. 18, 1849, the House was informed of the election of the Hon. Francis Hincks, MPP, Oxford, who was returned as duly elected.

Oxford. 1851. 14 & 15 Vic., C.5, S.38. Schedule A. An Act to make certain alterations in the Territorial Divisions of Upper Canada. The County of Oxford shall consist of the Townships of Zorra East, Zorra West, Oxford North, Oxford East, Oxford West, Dereham, Norwich, Blenheim, Blandford, Nissouri East and the Village of Woodstock.

Peterborough	James Hall	Feb. 25, 1848	

Peterborough. 1845. 8 Vic., C.8. Schedule B. An Act for better defining the limits of the Counties and Districts in Upper Canada, for erecting certain new Townships from some Counties and attaching them to others, and for other purposes relative to the division of Upper Canada into Townships, Counties and Districts. Which shall include and consist of the Townships of Asphodel, Belmont, Burleigh, Bexley, Dummer, Douro, Ennismore, Emily, Eldon, Fenelon, Harvey, Methuen, Mariposa, Otonabee, Ops, Smith, Somerville, Verulam, and North Monaghan.

General Election Dec. 1847.

Peterborough. 1851. 14 & 15 Vic., C.5, Ss.6, 18, 19. Schedules C, A. Counties United for the Purpose of Representation. An Act to make certain alterations in the Territorial Divisions of Upper Canada. Peterborough and Victoria, as the County of Peterborough. . . . The County of Peterborough shall consist of the Townships of Belmont, Methuen, Burleigh, Dummer, Harvey, Douro, Smith, Monaghan North, Asphodel,

*   By-election

Constituency	Member	Sworn In	Comments
Peterborough — *Continued*			Ennismore and Otonabee. . . . The County of Victoria shall consist of the Townships of Mariposa, Ops, Emily, Eldon, Fenelon, Bexley, Verulam and Somerville.
Prescott	Thomas Hall Johnson	Feb. 25, 1848	General Election Dec. 1847.
			Prescott. 1851. 14 & 15 Vic., C.5, S.3. Schedule A. An Act to make certain alterations in the Territorial Divisions of Upper Canada. The County of Prescott shall consist of the Townships of Alfred, Caledonia, Hawkesbury East, Hawkesbury West, Longueuil, Plantagenet North and Plantagenet South.
Prince Edward	David Barker Stevenson	Feb. 25, 1848	General Election Dec. 1847.
			Prince Edward. 1851. 14 & 15 Vic., C.5, S.14. Schedule A. An Act to make certain alterations in the Territorial Divisions of Upper Canada. The County of Prince Edward shall consist of the Townships of Athol, Ameliasburg, Hillier, Hallowell, Marysburgh and Sophiasburgh.
Russell	George Byron Lyon	Feb. 25, 1848	General Election Dec. 1847.
			Russell. 1851. 14 & 15 Vic., C.5, S.4. Schedule A. An Act to make certain alterations in the Territorial Divisions of Upper Canada. The County of Russell shall consist of the Townships of Clarence, Cumberland, Cambridge and Russell.
Simcoe	William Benjamin Robinson	Feb. 25, 1848	General Election Dec. 1847.
			Simcoe. 1851. 14 & 15 Vic., C.5, S.20. Schedule A. An Act to make certain alterations in the Territorial Divisions of Upper Canada. The County of Simcoe shall consist of the Townships of Orillia, Matchedash, Tay, Medonte, Oro, Vespra, Flos, Tiny, Sunnidale,

Nottawasaga, Gwillimbury West, Essa, Tecumseth, Adjala, Tossorontio, Mulmur, Mono and Innisfil, together with the tract of land bounded on the East by the line between the late Home and Newcastle Districts prolonged to French River, on the West by Lake Huron, on the North by French River, and on the South by the River Severn and the Township of Rama, and the Islands in Lakes Simcoe and Huron, lying wholly, or for the most part, opposite to the said County of Simcoe, or any part thereof and contiguous thereto.

| Stormont | Alexander McLean | Feb. 25, 1848 | General Election Dec. 1847. |

Stormont. 1851. 14 & 15 Vic., C.5, S.2. Schedule A. An Act to make certain alterations in the Territorial Divisions of Upper Canada. The County of Stormont shall consist of the Townships of FInch, Osnabruck, Roxborough and Cornwall.

| Toronto (City) | William Henry Boulton | Feb. 25, 1848 | General Election Dec. 1847. |
| Toronto (City) | Hon. Henry Sherwood | Feb. 25, 1848 | General Election Dec. 1847. |

Attorney General.

| Waterloo | James Webster | Feb. 25, 1848 | Waterloo. 1845. 8 Vic., C.8. Schedule B. An Act for better defining the limits of the Counties and Districts in Upper Canada, for erecting certain new Townships from some Counties and attaching them to others, and for other purposes relative to the division of Upper Canada into Townships, Counties and Districts. Which shall include and consist of the Townships of Arthur, Amaranth, Bentinck, Derby, Eramosa, Egremont, Guelph, Glenelg, Garrafraxa, Holland, Luther, Mornington, Minto, Maryborough, Melancthon, Normanby, Nichol, Peel, Proton, Puslinch, Sydenham, Sullivan, Waterloo, Wilmot, Woolwich, and Wellesley, and for the purpose of representation in the Legislative Assembly only, the Township of |

Constituency	Member	Sworn In	Comments
Waterloo — *Continued*			Dumfries, and for all purposes except that of representation in the Legislative Assembly, the Township of Erin.
			General Election Dec. 1847.
			Resigned, Jan. 8, 1849, empowered by 4 & 5 Vic., C.4.
			On Feb. 8, 1849, the election of James Webster, late MPP, Waterloo, was declared void. Adam Johnston Fergusson was duly elected at the Waterloo General Election.
Waterloo	Adam Johnston Fergusson	Feb. 8, 1849	On Feb. 8, 1849, the House was informed that Adam Johnston Fergusson was duly elected at the Waterloo General Election, in room of James Webster, whose election was declared void. [Webster had since resigned his seat.]
			Waterloo. 1851. 14 & 15 Vic., C.5, Ss.5, 25, 27, 28. Schedules C, A. Counties United for the Purpose of Representation. An Act to make certain alterations in the Territorial Divisions of Upper Canada. Waterloo, Wellington and Grey, as the County of Waterloo. . . . The County of Waterloo shall consist of the Townships of North Dumfries, Waterloo, Wilmot, Woolwich and Wellesley. . . . The County of Wellington shall consist of the Townships of Erin, Puslinch, Guelph, Nichol, Garafraxa, Eramosa, Peel, Maryborough, Minto, Arthur, Luther, Amaranth and Pilkington. . . . The County of Grey shall consist of the Townships of Derby, Sydenham, Saint Vincent, Sullivan, Holland, Euphrasia, Collingwood, Bentinck, Glenelg, Artemesia, Osprey, Normanby, Egremont, Proton and Melancthon, together with that portion of the Peninsular Tract of Land known

as the Indian Reserve, and situated between a line drawn northward from the north-east angle of Arran and the north-west angle of Derby, until it strikes Colpoy's Bay on the east side of the Indian Village, and the waters of the Georgian Bay, together with the Islands contiguous thereto.

Welland	Duncan McFarland	Feb. 25, 1848	Welland. 1845. 8 Vic., C.8. Schedule B. An Act for better defining the limits of the Counties and Districts in Upper Canada, for erecting certain new Townships from some Counties and attaching them to others, and for other purposes relative to the division of Upper Canada into Townships, Counties and Districts. Which shall include and consist of the Townships of Bertie, Crowland, Humberstone, Pelham, Stamford, Thorold, Wainfleet, and Willoughby.
			General Election Dec. 1847.
			Welland. 1851. 14 & 15 Vic., C.5, S.40. Schedule A. An Act to make certain alterations in the Territorial Divisions of Upper Canada. The County of Welland shall consist of the Townships of Pelham, Thorold, Stamford, Crowland, Willoughby, Wainfleet, Humberstone and Bertie.
Wentworth	Harmannus Smith	Feb. 25, 1848	General Election Dec. 1847.
			Wentworth. 1851. 14 & 15 Vic., C.5, Ss.4, 42, 26. Schedules C, A. Counties United for the Purpose of Representation. An Act to make certain alterations in the Territorial Divisions of Upper Canada. Wentworth and Brant, as the County of Wentworth. . . . The County of Wentworth shall consist of the Townships of Beverly, Flamborough East, Flamborough West, Ancaster, Glanford, Binbrook, Saltfleet and Barton. . . . The County of Brant shall consist of the Townships of Brantford,

Constituency	Member	Sworn In	Comments
Wentworth — *Continued*			Onondaga, Tuscarora, Oakland, South Dumfries and Burford, and the Village of Paris.
York East	Hon. William Hume Blake	Feb. 25, 1848	York East. 1845. 8 Vic., C.8. Schedule B. An Act for better defining the limits of the Counties and Districts in Upper Canada, for erecting certain new Townships from some Counties and attaching them to others, and for other purposes relative to the division of Upper Canada into Townships, Counties and Districts. Which shall include and consist of the Townships of Markham, Pickering, Scarborough, and Whitby.
			General Election Dec. 1847.
			On Mar. 13, 1848, the House was informed of the resignation of William Hume Blake, MPP, York East, who had been appointed Solicitor General of Canada West. A new election was called.
		Jan. 18, 1849*	By-election Date unknown.
			Writ of Election – June 16, 1848. Return of Writ – July 5, 1848. On Jan. 18, 1849, the House was informed of the election of William Hume Blake, MPP, York East, who was returned as duly elected.
			On May 14, 1850, the House was informed of the resignation of William Hume Blake, MPP, York East, who had been appointed Chancellor of Upper Canada. A new election had been called.
York East	Peter Perry	July 9, 1850*	By-election Date unknown.
			Writ of Election – Nov. 19, 1849. Return of Writ – Dec. 4, 1849. On May 14, 1850, the House was informed of the election of Peter Perry,

MPP, York East, in room of William Hume Blake, resigned.

York. 1851. 14 & 15 Vic., C.5, S.21. Schedule A. An Act to make certain alterations in the Territorial Divisions of Upper Canada. The County of York shall consist of the Townships of Etobicoke, Vaughan, Markham, Scarborough, York, King, Whitchurch, Gwillimbury East and Gwillimbury North.

On Aug. 26, 1851, the House was informed of the death of Peter Perry, MPP, York East. A new writ was issued that day.

House was prorogued on Aug. 30, 1851. No By-election was held.

York North	Hon. Robert Baldwin	Feb. 25, 1848	York North. 1845. 8 Vic., C.8. Schedule B. An Act for better defining the limits of the Counties and Districts in Upper Canada, for erecting certain new Townships from some Counties and attaching them to others, and for other purposes relative to the division of Upper Canada into Townships, Counties and Districts. Which shall include and consist of the Townships of Brock, North Gwillimbury, East Gwillimbury, Georgina, Mara, Reach, Rama, Scott, Thora, Uxbridge, and Whitchurch.
			General Election Dec. 1847.
			On Mar. 13, 1848, the House was informed of the resignation of the Hon. Robert Baldwin, MPP, York North, who had been appointed Attorney General of Canada West. A new election was called.
		Jan. 18, 1849*	By-election Date unknown.
			Writ of Election – Mar. 15, 1848. Return of Writ – Apr. 1, 1848. On Jan. 18, 1849, the House was informed of the election of the Hon. Robert

*   By-election

Constituency	Member	Sworn In	Comments
York North — *Continued*			Baldwin, MPP, York North, who was returned as duly elected.
			York. 1851. 14 & 15 Vic., C.5, S.21. Schedule A. An Act to make certain alterations in the Territorial Divisions of Upper Canada. The County of York shall consist of the Townships of Etobicoke, Vaughan, Markham, Scarborough, York, King, Whitchurch, Gwillimbury East and Gwillimbury North.
York South	Hon. James Hervey Price	Feb. 25, 1848	York South. 1845. 8 Vic., C.8. Schedule B. An Act for better defining the limits of the Counties and Districts in Upper Canada, for erecting certain new Townships from some Counties and attaching them to others, and for other purposes relative to the division of Upper Canada into Townships, Counties and Districts. Which shall include and consist of the Townships of Etobicoke, King, Vaughan, and York, and for the purposes of Registration of Titles only, the City of Toronto.
			General Election Dec. 1847.
			On Mar. 13, 1848, the House was informed of the resignation of James Hervey Price, MPP, York South, who had been appointed Commissioner of Crown Lands of this Province. A new election was called.
		Jan. 18, 1849*	By-election Date unknown.
			Writ of Election – Mar. 15, 1848. Return of Writ – Mar. 31, 1848. On Jan. 18, 1849, the House was informed of the election of the Hon. James Hervey Price, MPP, York South, who was returned as duly elected.
			York. 1851. 14 & 15 Vic., C.5, S.21. Schedule A. An Act to make certain alterations in the

York West   Joseph Curran Morrison   Feb. 25, 1848

Territorial Divisions of Upper Canada. The County of York shall consist of the Townships of Etobicoke, Vaughan, Markham, Scarborough, York, King, Whitchurch, Gwillimbury East and Gwillimbury North.

York West. 1845. 8 Vic., C.8. Schedule B. An Act for better defining the limits of the Counties and Districts in Upper Canada, for erecting certain new Townships from some Counties and attaching them to others, and for other purposes relative to the division of Upper Canada into Townships, Counties and Districts. Which shall include and consist of the Townships of Albion, Caledon, Chinguacousy, Toronto Gore, and Toronto.

General Election Dec. 1847.

York. 1851. 14 & 15 Vic., C.5, S.21. Schedule A. An Act to make certain alterations in the Territorial Divisions of Upper Canada. The County of York shall consist of the Townships of Etobicoke, Vaughan, Markham, Scarborough, York, King, Whitchurch, Gwillimbury East and Gwillimbury North.

*   By-election

LEGISLATURES OF THE PROVINCE OF CANADA
(Canada West)
4th Legislature

General Election   Nov. – Dec. 1851

Sessions of the Fourth Legislature of the Province of Canada: Aug. 19, 1852 – June 22, 1854

First: Aug. 19, 1852 – June 14, 1853.
Second: June 13, 1854 – June 22, 1854.

Alphabetical List of Members

Member	Constituency	Sworn In	Comments
William Henry Boulton	Toronto (City)	Aug. 19, 1852	On Mar. 29, 1853, the election of William Henry Boulton, MPP, Toronto (City), was declared void. A new election was called.
George Brown	Kent	Aug. 19, 1852	
Asa A. Burnham	Northumberland	Aug. 19, 1852	
Hon. Malcolm Cameron	Huron	Aug. 19, 1852*	Resigned prior to the commencement of the 4th Legislature, having been appointed President of the Executive Council of the said Province of Canada. A new election was called.
			Writ of Election – Apr. 14, 1852. Return of Writ – May 12, 1852. The Hon. Malcolm Cameron, MPP, Huron, was returned as duly elected.
David Christie	Wentworth	Aug. 19, 1852	
George Crawford	Brockville (Town)	Aug. 19, 1852	
Jesse Delong	Leeds	June 13, 1854*	Writ of Election – June 28, 1853. Return of Writ – July 30, 1853. On June 13, 1854, the House was informed of the election of Jesse Delong, MPP, Leeds, in room of the Hon. William Buell Richards, resigned.

Thomas C. Dixon	London (Town)	Aug. 19, 1852	
Adam Johnston Fergusson	Waterloo	Aug. 19, 1852	
John William Gamble	York South	Aug. 19, 1852	
Joseph Hartman	York North	Aug. 19, 1852	
Hon. Francis Hincks	Niagara (Town)	Aug. 19, 1852	On Sept. 7, 1852, having been elected Member for both the County of Oxford and the Town of Niagara, the Hon. Francis Hincks chose to serve for the County of Oxford. A new election was called for the Town of Niagara.
Hon. Francis Hincks	Oxford	Aug. 19, 1852	On Sept. 7, 1852, having been elected Member for both the County of Oxford and the Town of Niagara, the Hon. Francis Hincks chose to serve for the County of Oxford. A new election was called for the Town of Niagara.
Thomas Hall Johnson	Prescott	Aug. 19, 1852	
John Langton	Peterborough	Aug. 19, 1852	
George Byron Lyon	Russell	Aug. 19, 1852	
Hon. John Alexander Macdonald	Kingston (City)	Aug. 19, 1852	
Hon. John Sandfield Macdonald	Glengary	Aug. 19, 1852	On Aug. 19, 1852, the Hon. Francis Hincks, Member for both the County of Oxford and the Town of Niagara, proposed John Sandfield Macdonald, MPP, Glengary, as Speaker. Seconded and resolved. Aug. 19, 1852 – Date took chair.
William Lyon Mackenzie	Haldimand	Aug. 19, 1852	
Sir Allan Napier MacNab	Hamilton (City)	Aug. 19, 1852	
Edward Malloch	Carleton	Aug. 19, 1852	
William D. Mattice	Stormont	Aug. 19, 1852	

*   By-election

Member	Constituency	Sworn In	Comments
Roderick McDonald	Cornwall (Town)	Aug. 19, 1852	
Daniel McLachlin	Bytown (Town)	Aug. 19, 1852	
Hon. William Hamilton Merritt	Lincoln	Aug. 19, 1852	
Joseph Curran Morrison	Niagara (Town)	Sept. 29, 1852*	Writ of Election – Sept. 8, 1852. Return of Writ – Sept. 25, 1852. On Sept. 29, 1852, the House was informed of the election of Joseph Curran Morrison, MPP, Niagara (Town), in room of the Hon. Francis Hincks, resigned.
			On June 13, 1854, the House was informed of the resignation of Joseph Curran Morrison, MPP, Niagara (Town), who had been appointed Solicitor General of Canada West.
		June 13, 1854*	Writ of Election – June 27, 1853. Return of Writ – July 13, 1853. On June 13, 1854, the House was informed of the election of the Hon. Joseph Curran Morrison, MPP, Niagara (Town), who was returned as duly elected.
Edmund Murney	Hastings	Aug. 19, 1852	
William Patrick	Grenville	Aug. 19, 1852	
John Prince	Essex	Aug. 30, 1852	
Hon. William Buell Richards	Leeds	Aug. 19, 1852	Attorney General.
			On June 13, 1854, the House was informed of the resignation of the Hon. William Buell Richards, MPP, Leeds, who had been appointed one of the Judges of the Court of Common Pleas of Canada West. A new election was called.
George Percival Ridout	Toronto (City)	Aug. 19, 1852	
William Benjamin Robinson	Simcoe	Aug. 19, 1852	
Hon. John Rolph	Norfolk	Aug. 19, 1852	

Jesse Wright Rose	Dundas	Aug. 19, 1852
Benjamin Seymor	Lenox & Addington	Aug. 19, 1852
James Shaw	Lanark	Aug. 19, 1852
Hon. Henry Sherwood	Toronto (City)	May 4, 1853*

Writ of Election – Mar. 31, 1853. Return of Writ – Apr. 28, 1853. On May 3, 1853, the House was informed of the election of the Hon. Henry Sherwood, MPP, Toronto (City), in room of William Henry Boulton, whose election was declared void.

Henry Smith, Jr.	Frontenac	Aug. 19, 1852
James Smith	Durham	Aug. 19, 1852
David Barker Stevenson	Prince Edward	Aug. 19, 1852
Thomas Clark Street	Welland	Aug. 19, 1852
John White	Halton	Aug. 19, 1852
Crowel Willson	Middlesex	Aug. 19, 1852
Amos Wright	York East	Aug. 19, 1852
George Wright	York West	Aug. 19, 1852

* By-election

Constituency	Member	Sworn In	Comments
Brockville (Town)	George Crawford	Aug. 19, 1852	General Election Nov. – Dec. 1851.
			Brockville (Town). 1853. 16 Vic., C.152. II. S.24. An Act to enlarge the Representation of the People of this Province in Parliament. The Town of Brockville shall form an Electoral Division, and shall, for the purpose of Representation only, include in addition to its present limits, the whole of the Township of Elizabethtown, which shall for the said purpose be detached from the County of Leeds.
Bytown (Town)	Daniel McLachlin	Aug. 19, 1852	General Election Nov. – Dec. 1851.
			Bytown (Town). 1853. 16 Vic., C.152. II. S.28. An Act to enlarge the Representation of the People of this Province in Parliament. The Town of Bytown shall form an Electoral Division.
Carleton	Edward Malloch	Aug. 19, 1852	General Election Nov. – Dec. 1851.
			Carleton. 1853. 16 Vic., C.152. II. Ss.19, 20. An Act to enlarge the Representation of the People of this Province in Parliament. Each of the other Counties in Upper Canada, that is to say, each of the Counties of Carleton, Dundas, Essex, Frontenac, Glengarry, Grey, Haldimand, Halton, Kent, Lambton, Lincoln, Norfolk, Peterborough, Peel, Perth, Prescott, Prince Edward, Renfrew, Russell, Stormont, Victoria and Welland, shall form an Electoral Division. Provided always, That the Townships of Gloucester and Osgoode shall, for the purpose of Representation only, be detached from the County of Carleton and attached to the County of Russell.
Cornwall (Town)	Roderick McDonald	Aug. 19, 1852	General Election Nov. – Dec. 1851.

			Cornwall (Town). 1853. 16 Vic., C.152. II. S.26. An Act to enlarge the Representation of the People of this Province in Parliament. The Town of Cornwall shall form an Electoral Division, and shall, for the purpose of Representation only, include, in addition to its present limits, the whole of the Township of Cornwall, which shall be detached from the County of Stormont.
Dundas	Jesse Wright Rose	Aug. 19, 1852	General Election Nov. – Dec. 1851.
			Dundas. 1853. 16 Vic., C.152. II. S.19. An Act to enlarge the Representation of the People of this Province in Parliament. Each of the other Counties in Upper Canada, that is to say, each of the Counties of Carleton, Dundas, Essex, Frontenac, Glengarry, Grey, Haldimand, Halton, Kent, Lambton, Lincoln, Norfolk, Peterborough, Peel, Perth, Prescott, Prince Edward, Renfrew, Russell, Stormont, Victoria and Welland, shall form an Electoral Division.
Durham	James Smith	Aug. 19, 1852	General Election Nov. – Dec. 1851.
			Durham. 1853. 16 Vic., C.152. II. S.8. An Act to enlarge the Representation of the People of this Province in Parliament. The County of Durham shall be divided into two Ridings, to be called respectively the East Riding and the West Riding.
Essex	John Prince	Aug. 30, 1852	General Election Nov. – Dec. 1851.
			Essex. 1853. 16 Vic., C.152. II. S.19. An Act to enlarge the Representation of the People of this Province in Parliament. Each of the other Counties in Upper Canada, that is to say, each of the Counties of Carleton, Dundas, Essex, Frontenac, Glengarry, Grey, Haldimand, Halton, Kent, Lambton, Lincoln, Norfolk, Peterborough, Peel, Perth, Prescott, Prince Edward, Renfrew, Russell, Stormont, Victoria and Welland, shall form an Electoral Division.

Constituency	Member	Sworn In	Comments
Frontenac	Henry Smith, Jr.	Aug. 19, 1852	General Election Nov. – Dec. 1851.
			Frontenac. 1853. 16 Vic., C.152. II. S.19. An Act to enlarge the Representation of the People of this Province in Parliament. Each of the other Counties in Upper Canada, that is to say, each of the Counties of Carleton, Dundas, Essex, Frontenac, Glengarry, Grey, Haldimand, Halton, Kent, Lambton, Lincoln, Norfolk, Peterborough, Peel, Perth, Prescott, Prince Edward, Renfrew, Russell, Stormont, Victoria and Welland, shall form an Electoral Division.
Glengary	Hon. John Sandfield Macdonald	Aug. 19, 1852	General Election Nov. – Dec. 1851.
			On Aug. 19, 1852, the Hon. Francis Hincks, Member for both the County of Oxford and the Town of Niagara, proposed John Sandfield Macdonald, MPP, Glengary, as Speaker. Seconded and resolved. Aug. 19, 1852 – Date took chair.
			Glengarry. 1853. 16 Vic., C.152. II. S.19. An Act to enlarge the Representation of the People of this Province in Parliament. Each of the other Counties in Upper Canada, that is to say, each of the Counties of Carleton, Dundas, Essex, Frontenac, Glengarry, Grey, Haldimand, Halton, Kent, Lambton, Lincoln, Norfolk, Peterborough, Peel, Perth, Prescott, Prince Edward, Renfrew, Russell, Stormont, Victoria and Welland, shall form an Electoral Division.
Grenville	William Patrick	Aug. 19, 1852	General Election Nov. – Dec. 1851.
			Grenville. 1853. 16 Vic., C.152. II. S.14. An Act to enlarge the Representation of the People of this Province in Parliament. The Counties of Leeds and Grenville shall be formed into three

Ridings, to be called respectively the North Riding of Leeds and Grenville, the South Riding of Leeds, and the South Riding of Grenville.

Haldimand	William Lyon Mackenzie	Aug. 19, 1852	General Election Nov. – Dec. 1851.
			Haldimand. 1853. 16 Vic., C.152. II. S.19. An Act to enlarge the Representation of the People of this Province in Parliament. Each of the other Counties in Upper Canada, that is to say, each of the Counties of Carleton, Dundas, Essex, Frontenac, Glengarry, Grey, Haldimand, Halton, Kent, Lambton, Lincoln, Norfolk, Peterborough, Peel, Perth, Prescott, Prince Edward, Renfrew, Russell, Stormont, Victoria and Welland, shall form an Electoral Division.
Halton	John White	Aug. 19, 1852	General Election Nov. – Dec. 1851.
			Halton. 1853. 16 Vic., C.152. II. S.19. An Act to enlarge the Representation of the People of this Province in Parliament. Each of the other Counties in Upper Canada, that is to say, each of the Counties of Carleton, Dundas, Essex, Frontenac, Glengarry, Grey, Haldimand, Halton, Kent, Lambton, Lincoln, Norfolk, Peterborough, Peel, Perth, Prescott, Prince Edward, Renfrew, Russell, Stormont, Victoria and Welland, shall form an Electoral Division.
Hamilton (City)	Sir Allan Napier MacNab	Aug. 19, 1852	General Election Nov. – Dec. 1851.
			Hamilton (City). 1853. 16 Vic., C.152. II. S.23. An Act to enlarge the Representation of the People of this Province in Parliament. The City of Hamilton shall form an Electoral Division.
Hastings	Edmund Murney	Aug. 19, 1852	General Election Nov. – Dec. 1851.
			Hastings. 1853. 16 Vic., C.152. II. S.7. An Act to enlarge the Representation of the People of this Province in Parliament. The County of Hastings shall form an Electoral Division, and shall be divided into two Ridings to be called

Constituency	Member	Sworn In	Comments
Hastings — *Continued*			respectively the North Riding and the South Riding.
Huron	Hon. Malcolm Cameron	Aug. 19, 1852*	General Election Nov. – Dec. 1851.
			Resigned prior to the commencement of the 4th Legislature, having been appointed President of the Executive Council of the said Province of Canada. A new election was called.
			By-election Date unknown.
			Writ of Election – Apr. 14, 1852. Return of Writ – May 12, 1852. The Hon. Malcolm Cameron, MPP, Huron, was returned as duly elected.
			Huron. 1853. 16 Vic., C.152. II. S.2. An Act to enlarge the Representation of the People of this Province in Parliament. The Counties of Huron and Bruce, and the Counties of Lennox and Addington, shall respectively be united for the purpose of representation; and each such Union of two Counties shall form an Electoral Division.
Kent	George Brown	Aug. 19, 1852	General Election Nov. – Dec. 1851.
			Kent. 1853. 16 Vic., C.152. II. S.19. An Act to enlarge the Representation of the People of this Province in Parliament. Each of the other Counties in Upper Canada, that is to say, each of the Counties of Carleton, Dundas, Essex, Frontenac, Glengarry, Grey, Haldimand, Halton, Kent, Lambton, Lincoln, Norfolk, Peterborough, Peel, Perth, Prescott, Prince Edward, Renfrew, Russell, Stormont, Victoria and Welland, shall form an Electoral Division.
Kingston (City)	Hon. John Alexander Macdonald	Aug. 19, 1852	General Election Nov. – Dec. 1851.

Kingston (City). 1853. 16 Vic., C.152. II. S.22. An Act to enlarge the Representation of the People of this Province in Parliament. The City of Kingston shall form an Electoral Division.

Lanark	James Shaw	Aug. 19, 1852	General Election Nov. – Dec. 1851.

Lanark. 1853. 16 Vic., C.152. II. S.12. An Act to enlarge the Representation of the People of this Province in Parliament. The County of Lanark shall be divided into two Ridings, to be called respectively the North Riding and the South Riding.

Leeds	Hon. William Buell Richards	Aug. 19, 1852	Attorney General.

General Election Nov. – Dec. 1851.

Leeds. 1853. 16 Vic., C.152. II. Ss.14, 24. An Act to enlarge the Representation of the People of this Province in Parliament. The Counties of Leeds and Grenville shall be formed into three Ridings, to be called respectively the North Riding of Leeds and Grenville, the South Riding of Leeds, and the South Riding of Grenville. The Town of Brockville shall form an Electoral Division, and shall, for the purpose of Representation only, include in addition to its present limits, the whole of the Township of Elizabethtown, which shall for the said purpose be detached from the County of Leeds.

On June 13, 1854, the House was informed of the resignation of the Hon. William Buell Richards, MPP, Leeds, who had been appointed one of the Judges of the Court of Common Pleas of Canada West. A new election was called.

* By-election

Constituency	Member	Sworn In	Comments
Leeds	Jesse Delong	June 13, 1854*	By-election Date unknown.
			Writ of Election – June 28, 1853. Return of Writ – July 30, 1853. On June 13, 1854, the House was informed of the election of Jesse Delong, MPP, Leeds, in room of the Hon. William Buell Richards, resigned.
Lenox & Addington	Benjamin Seymor	Aug. 19, 1852	General Election Nov. – Dec. 1851.
			Lennox & Addington. 1853. 16 Vic., C.152. II. S.2. An Act to enlarge the Representation of the People of this Province in Parliament. The Counties of Huron and Bruce, and the Counties of Lennox and Addington shall respectively be united for the purpose of representation; and each such Union of two Counties shall form an Electoral Division.
Lincoln	Hon. William Hamilton Merritt	Aug. 19, 1852	General Election Nov. – Dec. 1851.
			Lincoln. 1853. 16 Vic., C.152. II. Ss.19, 25. An Act to enlarge the Representation of the People of this Province in Parliament. Each of the other Counties in Upper Canada, that is to say, each of the Counties of Carleton, Dundas, Essex, Frontenac, Glengarry, Grey, Haldimand, Halton, Kent, Lambton, Lincoln, Norfolk, Peterborough, Peel, Perth, Prescott, Prince Edward, Renfrew, Russell, Stormont, Victoria and Welland, shall form an Electoral Division. The Town of Niagara shall form an Electoral Division, and shall, for the purpose of Representation only, include in addition to its present limits, the whole of the Township of Niagara, which shall for the said purpose be detached from the County of Lincoln.
London (Town)	Thomas C. Dixon	Aug. 19, 1852	General Election Nov. – Dec. 1851.

			London (Town). 1853. 16 Vic., C.152. II. S.27. An Act to enlarge the Representation of the People of this Province in Parliament. The Town of London shall form an Electoral Division.
Middlesex	Crowel Willson	Aug. 19, 1852	General Election Nov. – Dec. 1851.
			Middlesex. 1853. 16 Vic., C.152. II. S.5. An Act to enlarge the Representation of the People of this Province in Parliament. The County of Middlesex shall be divided into two Ridings, to be called respectively the East Riding and West Riding.
Niagara (Town)	Hon. Francis Hincks	Aug. 19, 1852	General Election Nov. – Dec. 1851.
			On Sept. 7, 1852, having been elected Member for both the County of Oxford and the Town of Niagara, the Hon. Francis Hincks chose to serve for the County of Oxford. A new election was called for the Town of Niagara.
Niagara (Town)	Joseph Curran Morrison	Sept. 29, 1852*	By-election Date unknown.
			Writ of Election – Sept. 8, 1852. Return of Writ – Sept. 25. 1852. On Sept. 29, 1852, the House was informed of the election of Joseph Curran Morrison, MPP, Niagara (Town), in room of the Hon. Francis Hincks, resigned.
			Niagara (Town). 1853. 16 Vic., C.152. II. S.25. An Act to enlarge the Representation of the People of this Province in Parliament. The Town of Niagara shall form an Electoral Division, and shall, for the purpose of Representation only, include in addition to its present limits, the whole of the Township of Niagara, which shall for the said purpose be detached from the County of Lincoln.
			On June 13, 1854, the House was informed of the resignation of Joseph Curran Morrison,

*   By-election

Constituency	Member	Sworn In	Comments
Niagara (Town) — *Continued*			MPP, Niagara (Town), who had been appointed Solicitor General for Canada West.
		June 13, 1854*	By-election Date unknown.
			Writ of Election – June 27, 1853. Return of Writ – July 13, 1853. On June 13, 1854, the House was informed of the election of the Hon. Joseph Curran Morrison, MPP, Niagara (Town), who was returned as duly elected.
Norfolk	Hon. John Rolph	Aug. 19, 1852	General Election Nov. – Dec. 1851.
			Norfolk. 1853. 16 Vic., C.152. II. S.19. An Act to enlarge the Representation of the People of this Province in Parliament. Each of the other Counties in Upper Canada, that is to say, each of the Counties of Carleton, Dundas, Essex, Frontenac, Glengarry, Grey, Haldimand, Halton, Kent, Lambton, Lincoln, Norfolk, Peterborough, Peel, Perth, Prescott, Prince Edward, Renfrew, Russell, Stormont, Victoria and Welland, shall form an Electoral Division.
Northumberland	Asa A. Burnham	Aug. 19, 1852	General Election Nov. – Dec. 1851.
			Northumberland. 1853. 16 Vic., C.152. II. S.9. An Act to enlarge the Representation of the People of this Province in Parliament. The County of Northumberland shall be divided into two Ridings, to be called respectively the East Riding and the West Riding.
Oxford	Hon. Francis Hincks	Aug. 19, 1852	General Election Nov. – Dec. 1851.
			On Sept. 7, 1852, having been elected Member for both the County of Oxford and the Town of Niagara, the Hon. Francis Hincks chose to serve for the County of Oxford. A new election was called for the Town of Niagara.
			Oxford. 1853. 16 Vic., C.152. II. S.6. An Act to

enlarge the Representation of the People of this Province in Parliament. The County of Oxford shall be divided into two Ridings, to be called respectively the North Riding and the South Riding.

Peterborough	John Langton	Aug. 19, 1852	General Election Nov. – Dec. 1851.

Peterborough. 1853. 16 Vic., C.152. II. S.19. An Act to enlarge the Representation of the People of this Province in Parliament. Each of the other Counties in Upper Canada, that is to say, each of the Counties of Carleton, Dundas, Essex, Frontenac, Glengarry, Grey, Haldimand, Halton, Kent, Lambton, Lincoln, Norfolk, Peterborough, Peel, Perth, Prescott, Prince Edward, Renfrew, Russell, Stormont, Victoria and Welland, shall form an Electoral Division.

Prescott	Thomas Hall Johnson	Aug. 19, 1852	General Election Nov. – Dec. 1851.

Prescott. 1853. 16 Vic., C.152. II. S.19. An Act to enlarge the Representation of the People of this Province in Parliament. Each of the other Counties in Upper Canada, that is to say, each of the Counties of Carleton, Dundas, Essex, Frontenac, Glengarry, Grey, Haldimand, Halton, Kent, Lambton, Lincoln, Norfolk, Peterborough, Peel, Perth, Prescott, Prince Edward, Renfrew, Russell, Stormont, Victoria and Welland, shall form an Electoral Division.

Prince Edward	David Barker Stevenson	Aug. 19, 1852	General Election Nov. – Dec. 1851.

Prince Edward. 1853. 16 Vic., C.152. II. S.19. An Act to enlarge the Representation of the People of this Province in Parliament. Each of the other Counties in Upper Canada, that is to say, each of the Counties of Carleton, Dundas, Essex, Frontenac, Glengarry, Grey, Haldimand, Halton, Kent, Lambton, Lincoln, Norfolk,

*   By-election

Constituency	Member	Sworn In	Comments
Prince Edward — *Continued*			Peterborough, Peel, Perth, Prescott, Prince Edward, Renfrew, Russell, Stormont, Victoria and Welland, shall form an Electoral Division.
Russell	George Byron Lyon	Aug. 19, 1852	General Election Nov. – Dec. 1851.
			Russell. 1853. 16 Vic., C.152. II. Ss.19, 20. An Act to enlarge the Representation of the People of this Province in Parliament. Each of the other Counties in Upper Canada, that is to say, each of the Counties of Carleton, Dundas, Essex, Frontenac, Glengarry, Grey, Haldimand, Halton, Kent, Lambton, Lincoln, Norfolk, Peterborough, Peel, Perth, Prescott, Prince Edward, Renfrew, Russell, Stormont, Victoria and Welland, shall form an Electoral Division. Provided always, That the Townships of Gloucester and Osgoode shall, for the purpose of Representation only, be detached from the County of Carleton and attached to the County of Russell.
Simcoe	William Benjamin Robinson	Aug. 19, 1852	General Election Nov. – Dec. 1851.
			Simcoe. 1853. 16 Vic., C.152. II. S.13. An Act to enlarge the Representation of the People of this Province in Parliament. The County of Simcoe shall be divided into two Ridings, to be called respectively the North Riding and the South Riding.
Stormont	William D. Mattice	Aug. 19, 1852	General Election Nov. – Dec. 1851.
			Stormont. 1853. 16 Vic., C.152. II. Ss.19, 26. An Act to enlarge the Representation of the People of this Province in Parliament. Each of the other Counties in Upper Canada, that is to say, each of the Counties of Carleton, Dundas, Essex, Frontenac, Glengarry, Grey, Haldimand,

Halton, Kent, Lambton, Lincoln, Norfolk, Peterborough, Peel, Perth, Prescott, Prince Edward, Renfrew, Russell, Stormont, Victoria and Welland, shall form an Electoral Division. The Town of Cornwall shall form an Electoral Division, and shall, for the purpose of Representation only, include in addition to its present limits, the whole of the Township of Cornwall, which shall for the said purpose be detached from the County of Stormont.

Toronto (City)	William Henry Boulton	Aug. 19, 1852	General Election Nov. – Dec. 1851.
			On Mar. 29, 1853, the election of William Henry Boulton, MPP, Toronto (City), was declared void. A new election was called.
Toronto (City)	Hon. Henry Sherwood	May 4, 1853*	By-election Date unknown.
			Writ of Election – Mar. 31, 1853. Return of Writ – Apr. 28, 1853. On May 3, 1853, the House was informed of the election of the Hon. Henry Sherwood, MPP, Toronto (City), in room of William Henry Boulton, whose election was declared void.
			Toronto (City). 1853. 16 Vic., C.152. II. S.21. An Act to enlarge the Representation of the People of this Province in Parliament. The City of Toronto shall form an Electoral Division.
Toronto (City)	George Percival Ridout	Aug. 19, 1852	General Election Nov. – Dec. 1851.
			Toronto (City). 1853. 16 Vic., C.152. II. S.21. An Act to enlarge the Representation of the People of this Province in Parliament. The City of Toronto shall form an Electoral Division.
Waterloo	Adam Johnston Fergusson	Aug. 19, 1852	General Election Nov. – Dec. 1851.
			Waterloo. 1853. 16 Vic., C.152. II. S.16. An Act to enlarge the Representation of the People of

* By-election

Constituency	Member	Sworn In	Comments
Waterloo — *Continued*			this Province in Parliament. The County of Waterloo shall be divided into two Ridings, to be called respectively, the North Riding and the South Riding.
Welland	Thomas Clark Street	Aug. 19, 1852	General Election Nov. – Dec. 1851.
			Welland. 1853. 16 Vic., C.152. II. S.19. An Act to enlarge the Representation of the People of this Province in Parliament. Each of the other Counties in Upper Canada, that is to say, each of the Counties of Carleton, Dundas, Essex, Frontenac, Glengarry, Grey, Haldimand, Halton, Kent, Lambton, Lincoln, Norfolk, Peterborough, Peel, Perth, Prescott, Prince Edward, Renfrew, Russell, Stormont, Victoria and Welland, shall form an Electoral Division.
Wentworth	David Christie	Aug. 19, 1852	General Election Nov. – Dec. 1851.
			Wentworth. 1853. 16 Vic., C.152. II. S.11. An Act to enlarge the Representation of the People of this Province in Parliament. The County of Wentworth shall be divided into two Ridings, to be called respectively the North Riding and the South Riding.
York East	Amos Wright	Aug. 19, 1852	General Election Nov. – Dec. 1851.
			York East. 1853. 16 Vic., C.152. II. S.4. An Act to enlarge the Representation of the People of this Province in Parliament. The County of York shall be divided into three Ridings, to be called respectively the North Riding, the East Riding, and the West Riding. The East Riding shall consist of the Townships of Markham, Scarborough, and that portion of the Township of York lying East of Yonge Street and the Village of Yorkville.

York North	Joseph Hartman	Aug. 19, 1852	General Election Nov. – Dec. 1851. York North. 1853. 16 Vic., C.152. II. S.4. An Act to enlarge the Representation of the People of this Province in Parliament. The County of York shall be divided into three Ridings, to be called respectively the North Riding, the East Riding, and the West Riding. The North Riding shall consist of the Townships of King, Whitchurch, Georgina, East Gwillimbury and North Gwillimbury.
York South	John William Gamble	Aug. 19, 1852	General Election Nov. – Dec. 1851. York South. 1853. 16 Vic., C.152. II. S.4. An Act to enlarge the Representation of the People of this Province in Parliament. The County of York shall be divided into three Ridings, to be called respectively the North Riding, the East Riding, and the West Riding.
York West	George Wright	Aug. 19, 1852	General Election Nov. – Dec. 1851. York West. 1853. 16 Vic., C.152. II. S.4. An Act to enlarge the Representation of the People of this Province in Parliament. The County of York shall be divided into three Ridings, to be called respectively the North Riding, the East Riding, and the West Riding. The West Riding shall consist of the Townships of Etobicoke, Vaughan, and that portion of the Township of York lying West of Yonge Street.

LEGISLATURES OF THE PROVINCE OF CANADA
(Canada West)
5th Legislature

General Election   July – Aug. 1854

Sessions of the Fifth Legislature of the Province of Canada: Sept. 5, 1854 – June 10, 1857

First:	Sept. 5, 1854 – Dec. 18, 1854 and
	Feb. 23, 1854 – May 30, 1855.
Second:	Feb. 15, 1856 – July 1, 1856.
Third:	Feb. 26, 1857 – June 10, 1857.

Alphabetical List of Members

Member	Constituency	Sworn In	Comments
Hon. Louis Victor Sicotte	Saint Hyacinthe (Canada East)	Sept. 5, 1854	On Sept. 5, 1854, Antoine Aimé Dorion, MPP, Montreal (City) (Canada East), proposed Louis Victor Sicotte, MPP, Saint Hyacinthe (Canada East), as Speaker. Seconded and resolved. Sept. 5, 1854 – Date took chair.
James C. Aikens	Peel	Sept. 5, 1854	
Robert Bell	Lanark North	Sept. 5, 1854	
George Benjamin	Hastings North	Feb. 26, 1857*	Writ of Election – Oct. 6, 1856. Return of Writ – Oct. 27, 1856. On Feb. 26, 1857, the House was informed of the election of George Benjamin, MPP, Hastings North, in room of Edmund Murney, resigned.
Herbert Biggar	Brant West	Sept. 5, 1854	
John George Bowes	Toronto (City)	Sept. 5, 1854	
George Brown	Lambton	Sept. 5, 1854	
Francis Henry Burton	Durham East	Sept. 5, 1854	
Hon. John Hillyard Cameron	Toronto (City)	Sept. 5, 1854	

Hon. William Cayley	Huron & Bruce	Sept. 5, 1854	On Sept. 13, 1854, the House was informed of the resignation of the Hon. William Cayley, MPP, Huron & Bruce, who had been appointed Inspector General of this Province. A new election was called.
			Writ of Election – Sept. 14, 1854. Return of Writ – Oct. 4, 1854. On Oct. 10, 1854, the House was informed of the election of the Hon. William Cayley, MPP, Huron & Bruce, who was returned as duly elected.
George K. Chisholm	Halton	Sept. 5, 1854	
David Christie	Brant East	Mar. 12, 1855	On Mar. 12, 1855, the House was informed that David Christie was duly elected at the Brant East General Election, in room of Daniel McKerlie, whose election was declared void.
Basil Rorison Church	Leeds North & Grenville North	Sept. 5, 1854	
William Clarke	Wellington North	Sept. 5, 1854	
Wilson Seymour Conger	Peterborough	Feb. 15, 1856*	Writ of Election – Dec. 31, 1855. Return of Writ – Jan. 26, 1856. On Feb. 15, 1856, the House was informed of the election of Wilson Seymour Conger, MPP, Peterborough, in room of John Langton, resigned.
Ephraim Cook	Oxford South	Oct. 25, 1854*	Writ of Election – Sept. 22, 1854. Return of Writ – Oct. 9, 1854. On Oct. 17, 1854, the House was informed of the election of Ephraim Cook, MPP, Oxford South, in room of the Hon. Francis Hincks, resigned.
George Crawford	Brockville (Town)	Sept. 6, 1854	
John Pliny Crysler	Dundas	Sept. 5, 1854	
Thomas Mayne Daly	Perth	Sept. 8, 1854	
Jesse Delong	Leeds South	Sept. 5, 1854	

* By-election

Member	Constituency	Sworn In	Comments
Adam Johnston Fergusson	Wellington South	Sept. 5, 1854	
Robert Ferrie	Waterloo South	Sept. 5, 1854	
Billa Flint	Hastings South	Sept. 25, 1854	
Michael Hamilton Foley	Waterloo North	Sept. 5, 1854	
John Frazer	Welland	Sept. 5, 1854	
Samuel Black Freeman	Wentworth South	Sept. 5, 1854	
John William Gamble	York West	Sept. 5, 1854	
Joseph Gould	Ontario North	Sept. 5, 1854	
Joseph Hartman	York North	Sept. 5, 1854	
Hon. Francis Hincks	Oxford South	Sept. 5, 1854	On Sept. 18, 1854, the Hon. Francis Hincks, Member for both the County of Oxford South and the County of Renfrew, chose to sit for the County of Renfrew. A new election was called for the County of Oxford South.
Hon. Francis Hincks	Renfrew	Sept. 5, 1854	On Sept. 18, 1854, the Hon. Francis Hincks, Member for both the County of Oxford South and the County of Renfrew, chose to sit for the County of Renfrew. A new election was called for the County of Oxford South. Resigned, Nov. 16, 1855. A new election was called.
George Jackson	Grey	Sept. 5, 1854	
John Langton	Peterborough	Sept. 5, 1854	On Feb. 15, 1856, the House was informed of the resignation of John Langton, MPP, Peterborough, who had been appointed Auditor. A new election was called.
Edwin Larwill	Kent	Sept. 5, 1854	

John MacVeigh Lumsden	Ontario South	Sept. 5, 1854	
George Byron Lyon	Russell	Sept. 5, 1854	
George Macbeth	Elgin West	Sept. 5, 1854	
Hon. John Alexander Macdonald	Kingston (City)	Sept. 5, 1854	On Sept. 13, 1854, the House was informed of the resignation of John Alexander Macdonald, MPP, Kingston (City), who had been appointed Attorney General of Canada West. A new election was called. Writ of Election – Sept. 14, 1854. Return of Writ – Sept. 28, 1854. On Oct. 2, 1854, the House was informed of the election of the Hon. John Alexander Macdonald, MPP, Kingston (City), who was returned as duly elected.
Hon. John Sandfield Macdonald	Glengarry	Sept. 5, 1854	
William Lyon Mackenzie	Haldimand	Sept. 5, 1854	
Hon. Sir Allan Napier MacNab	Hamilton (City)	Sept. 5, 1854	On Sept. 13, 1854, the House was informed of the resignation of the Hon. Sir Allan Napier MacNab, MPP, Hamilton (City), who had been appointed President of the Committees of the Executive Council of this Province. A new election was called. Writ of Election – Sept. 14, 1854. Return of Writ – Oct. 2, 1854. On Oct. 10, 1854, the House was informed of the election of the Hon. Sir Allan Napier MacNab, MPP, Hamilton (City), who was returned as duly elected.
Donald Matheson	Oxford North	Sept. 5, 1854	
William D. Mattice	Stormont	Sept. 5, 1854	
Henry Wellesley McCann	Prescott	Sept. 5, 1854	
Roderick McDonald	Cornwall (Town)	Sept. 5, 1854	
Daniel McKerlie	Brant East	Sept. 5, 1854	On Mar. 12, 1855, the election of Daniel McKerlie, MPP, Brant East, was declared void. David Christie was duly elected at the Brant East General Election.

Member	Constituency	Sworn In	Comments
Hon. William Hamilton Merritt	Lincoln	Sept. 5, 1854	
Angus Morrison	Simcoe North	Sept. 5, 1854	
Hon. Joseph Curran Morrison	Niagara (Town)	Sept. 5, 1854	On Apr. 21, 1856, the House was informed that Joseph Curran Morrison, MPP, Niagara (Town), had been appointed to the Executive Council.
			On Apr. 21, 1856, the House resolved that the acceptance of office by the Hon. Joseph Curran Morrison, MPP, Niagara (Town), without any emolument attached thereto, is not such an acceptance of office as vacates his seat in the House.
			On May 26, 1856, the House was informed of the resignation of the Hon. Joseph Curran Morrison, who had been appointed Receiver General of this Province. A new election was called.
			Writ of Election – May 27, 1856. Return of Writ – June 20, 1856. On June 20, 1856, the House was informed of the election of the Hon. Joseph Curran Morrison, MPP, Niagara (Town), who was returned as duly elected.
Henry Munro	Durham West	Sept. 5, 1854	
Edmund Murney	Hastings North	Sept. 5, 1854	Resigned, Sept. 15, 1856, in pursuance of the provisions of 7 Vic., C.65. A new election was called.
William Niles	Middlesex East	Sept. 5, 1854	
William Patrick	Grenville South	Sept. 5, 1854	
William Frederick Powell	Carleton	Sept. 5, 1854	
Arthur Rankin	Essex	Sept. 7, 1854	

William Benjamin Robinson	Simcoe South	Sept. 5, 1854
David Roblin	Lenox & Addington	Sept. 5, 1854
Hon. John Rolph	Norfolk	Sept. 5, 1854
James Ross	Northumberland East	Sept. 5, 1854
John Scatcherd	Middlesex West	Sept. 5, 1854
James Shaw	Lanark South	Sept. 5, 1854
Hon. Henry Smith, Jr.	Frontenac	Sept. 5, 1854

On Sept. 13, 1854, the House was informed of the resignation of Henry Smith, Jr., MPP, Frontenac, who had been appointed Solicitor General of Canada West. A new election was called.

Writ of Election – Sept. 14, 1854. Return of Writ – Sept. 28, 1854. On Oct. 2, 1854, the House was informed of the election of the Hon. Henry Smith, Jr., MPP, Frontenac, who had been returned as duly elected.

James Smith	Victoria	Sept. 5, 1854
Sidney Smith	Northumberland West	Sept. 5, 1854
George Southwick	Elgin East	Sept. 5, 1854
Hon. Robert Spence	Wentworth North	Sept. 5, 1854

On Sept. 13, 1854, the House was informed of the resignation of the Hon. Robert Spence, MPP, Wentworth North, who had been appointed Postmaster General of the Province of Canada. A new election was called.

Writ of Election – Sept. 14, 1854. Return of Writ – Oct. 13, 1854. On Oct. 19, 1854, the House was informed of the election of the Hon. Robert Spence, MPP, Wentworth North, who had béen returned as duly elected.

David Barker Stevenson	Prince Edward	Sept. 5, 1854

Member	Constituency	Sworn In	Comments
John Supple	Renfrew	Apr. 11, 1856*	On Apr. 11, 1856, having presented the Indenture of his Election for the County of Renfrew, John Supple took his seat.
			On Apr. 11, 1856, the House resolved that in admitting John Supple, MPP, Renfrew, to take his seat, on the production of the Duplicate Indenture only, and without the Return of the Indenture to the Clerk of the Crown in Chancercy, and the Certificate of the latter Officer, it still recommends a strict adherence to the requirement of producing the usual Certificate.
			Writ of Election – Feb. 27, 1856. Return of Writ – Mar. 31, 1856. On Apr. 15, 1856, the House was informed of the election of John Supple, MPP, Renfrew, in room of the Hon. Francis Hincks, resigned.
John Wilson	London (Town)	Sept. 5, 1854	
Amos Wright	York East	Sept. 5, 1854	
Agar Yielding	Bytown (Town)	Sept. 5, 1854	

*　By-election

Constituency	Member	Sworn In	Comments
Brant East	Daniel McKerlie	Sept. 5, 1854	Brant East. 1853. 16 Vic., C.152. II. S.17. An Act to enlarge the Representation of the People of this Province in Parliament. The County of Brant shall be divided into two Ridings, to be called respectively the East Riding and the West Riding. The East Riding shall consist of the Townships of South Dumfries, Onondaga, East Brantford, and the Village of Paris; . . . The Township of East Brantford to include and consist of all that portion of the present Township of Brantford which lies on the east side of the Grand River.
			General Election July-Aug. 1854.
			On Mar. 12, 1855, the election of Daniel McKerlie, MPP, Brant East, was declared void. David Christie was duly elected at the Brant East General Election.
Brant East	David Christie	Mar. 12, 1855	On Mar. 12, 1855, the House was informed that David Christie was duly elected at the Brant East General Election, in room of Daniel McKerlie, whose election was declared void.
Brant West	Herbert Biggar	Sept. 5, 1854	Brant West. 1853. 16 Vic., C.152. II. S.17. An Act to enlarge the Representation of the People of this Province in Parliament. The County of Brant shall be divided into two Ridings, to be called respectively the East Riding and the West Riding. The West Riding shall consist of the Townships of Burford, Oakland, Tuscarora, West Brantford, and the Town of Brantford. And the Township of West Brantford to include and consist of all the remainder of the present Township of Brantford.

			General Election July-Aug. 1854.
Brockville (Town)	George Crawford	Sept. 6, 1854	General Election July-Aug. 1854.
Bytown (Town)	Agar Yielding	Sept. 5, 1854	General Election July-Aug. 1854.
Carleton	William Frederick Powell	Sept. 5, 1854	General Election July-Aug. 1854.
Cornwall (Town)	Roderick McDonald	Sept. 5, 1854	General Election July-Aug. 1854.
Dundas	John Pliny Crysler	Sept. 5, 1854	General Election July-Aug. 1854.
Durham East	Francis Henry Burton	Sept. 5, 1854	Durham East. 1853. 16 Vic., C.152. II. S.8. An Act to enlarge the Representation of the People of this Province in Parliament. The East Riding shall consist of the Townships of Cavan, Manvers, Hope and the Town of Port Hope. General Election July-Aug. 1854.
Durham West	Henry Munro	Sept. 5, 1854	Durham West. 1853. 16 Vic., C.152. II. S.8. An Act to enlarge the Representation of the People of this Province in Parliament. The West Riding shall consist of the Townships of Clarke, Darlington and Cartwright. General Election July-Aug. 1854.
Elgin East	George Southwick	Sept. 5, 1854	Elgin East. 1853. 16 Vic., C.152. II. S.18. An Act to enlarge the Representation of the People of this Province in Parliament. The County of Elgin shall be divided into two Ridings, to be called respectively the East Riding and the West Riding. The East Riding shall consist of the Townships of Bayham, Malahide, Yarmouth, South Dorchester and the Village of St. Thomas. General Election July-Aug. 1854.
Elgin West	George Macbeth	Sept. 5, 1854	Elgin West. 1853. 16 Vic., C.152. II. S.18. An Act to enlarge the Representation of the People of this Province in Parliament. The County of Elgin shall be divided into two Ridings, to be called respectively the East Riding and the West Riding. The West Riding

Constituency	Member	Sworn In	Comments
Elgin West — *Continued*			shall consist of the Townships of Southwold, Dunwich and Aldborough.
			General Election July-Aug. 1854.
Essex	Arthur Rankin	Sept. 7, 1854	General Election July-Aug. 1854.
Frontenac	Hon. Henry Smith, Jr.	Sept. 5, 1854	General Election July-Aug. 1854.
			On Sept. 13, 1854, the House was informed of the resignation of Henry Smith, Jr., MPP, Frontenac, who had been appointed Solicitor General of Canada West. A new election was called.
			Writ of Election – Sept. 14, 1854. Return of Writ – Sept. 28, 1854. On Oct. 2, 1854, the House was informed of the election of the Hon. Henry Smith, Jr., MPP, Frontenac, who had been returned as duly elected.
Glengarry	Hon. John Sandfield Macdonald	Sept. 5, 1854	General Election July-Aug. 1854.
Grenville South	William Patrick	Sept. 5, 1854	Grenville South. 1853. 16 Vic., C.152. II. S.14. An Act to enlarge the Representation of the People of this Province in Parliament. The South Riding of Grenville shall consist of the Townships of Edwardsburgh and Augusta, and the Town of Prescott.
			Grenville South. 1853. 16 Vic., C.226. II. S.1. An Act to divide the Townships of Yonge and Escott in the United Counties of Leeds and Grenville. . . . That upon, from and after the first day of January next after the passing of this Act, the sixth, seventh, eighth, ninth, tenth and eleventh Concessions of the Townships of Yonge, and the seventh, eighth, ninth and tenth Concessions of the Township of Escott,

shall, for all Municipal and Election purposes, be united together, and form a Township, to be called the "Rear of Yonge and Escott," and that the remainder of the said Townships of Yonge and Escott, together with the Islands in the River St. Lawrence, at present forming part of these Townships, shall, for the like purposes, be together united and form a Township, to be called the "Front of Yonge and Escott."

General Election July-Aug. 1854.

Grey	George Jackson	Sept. 5, 1854	Grey. 1853. 16 Vic., C.152. II. S.19. An Act to enlarge the Representation of the People of this Province in Parliament. Each of the Counties in Upper Canada, that is to say, each of the Counties of Carleton, Dundas, Essex, Frontenac, Glengarry, Grey, Haldimand, Halton, Kent, Lambton, Lincoln, Norfolk, Peterborough, Peel, Perth, Prescott, Prince Edward, Renfrew, Russell, Stormont, Victoria and Welland, shall form an Electoral Division.

General Election July-Aug. 1854.

Haldimand	William Lyon Mackenzie	Sept. 5, 1854	General Election July-Aug. 1854.
Halton	George K. Chisholm	Sept. 5, 1854	General Election July-Aug. 1854.
Hamilton (City)	Hon. Sir Allan Napier MacNab	Sept. 5, 1854	General Election July-Aug. 1854.

On Sept. 13, 1854, the House was informed of the resignation of the Hon. Sir Allan Napier MacNab, MPP, Hamilton (City), who had been appointed President of the Committees of the Executive Council of this Province. A new election was called.

By-election Date unknown.

Writ of Election – Sept. 14, 1854. Return of Writ – Oct. 2, 1854. On Oct. 10, 1854, the House was informed of the election of the Hon. Sir Allan Napier MacNab, MPP, Hamilton (City), who was returned as duly elected.

Constituency	Member	Sworn In	Comments
Hastings North	Edmund Murney	Sept. 5, 1854	Hastings North. 1853. 16 Vic., C.152. II. S.7. An Act to enlarge the Representation of the People of this Province in Parliament. The North Riding shall consist of the Townships of Lake, Tudor, Grimsthorpe, Marmora, Madoc, Elzevir, Rawdon, Huntingdon and Hungerford.
			General Election July-Aug. 1854.
			Resigned, Sept. 15, 1856, in pursuance of the provisions of 7 Vic., C.65. A new election was called.
Hastings North	George Benjamin	Feb. 26, 1857*	By-election Date unknown.
			Writ of Election – Oct. 6, 1856. Return of Writ – Oct. 27, 1856. On Feb. 26, 1857, the House was informed of the election of George Benjamin, MPP, Hastings North, in room of Edmund Murney, resigned.
Hastings South	Billa Flint	Sept. 25, 1854	Hastings South. 1853. 16 Vic., C.152. II. S.7. An Act to enlarge the Representation of the People of this Province in Parliament. The South Riding shall consist of the Townships of Sidney, Thurlow, Tyendinaga, the Village of Trenton, and the Town of Belleville.
			General Election July-Aug. 1854.
Huron & Bruce	Hon. William Cayley	Sept. 5, 1854	Huron & Bruce. 1853. 16 Vic., C.152. II. S.2. An Act to enlarge the Representation of the People of this Province in Parliament. The Counties of Huron and Bruce, and the Counties of Lennox and Addington, shall respectively be united for the purpose of representation and each such Union of two Counties shall form an Electoral Division.
			General Election July-Aug. 1854.

On Sept. 13, 1854, the House was informed of the resignation of the Hon. William Cayley, MPP, Huron & Bruce, who had been appointed Inspector General of this Province. A new election was called.

By-election Date unknown.

Writ of Election – Sept. 14, 1854. Return of Writ – Oct. 4, 1854. On Oct. 10, 1854, the House was informed of the election of the Hon. William Cayley, MPP, Huron & Bruce, who was returned as duly elected.

Kent	Edwin Larwill	Sept. 5, 1854	General Election July-Aug. 1854.
Kingston (City)	Hon. John Alexander Macdonald	Sept. 5, 1854	General Election July-Aug. 1854.

On Sept. 13, 1854, the House was informed of the resignation of John Alexander Macdonald, MPP, Kingston (City), who had been appointed Attorney General of Canada West. A new election was called.

By-election Date unknown.

Writ of Election – Sept. 14, 1854. Return of Writ – Sept. 28, 1854. On Oct. 2, 1854, the House was informed of the election of the Hon. John Alexander Macdonald, MPP, Kingston (City), who was returned as duly elected.

Lambton	George Brown	Sept. 5, 1854	Lambton. 1853. 16 Vic., C.152. II. S.19. An Act to enlarge the Representation of the People of this Province in Parliament. Each of the Counties in Upper Canada, that is to say, each of the Counties of Carleton, Dundas, Essex, Frontenac, Glengarry, Grey, Haldimand, Halton, Kent, Lambton, Lincoln, Norfolk, Peterborough, Peel, Perth, Prescott, Prince Edward, Renfrew, Russell, Stormont, Victoria and Welland, shall form an Electoral Division.

General Election July-Aug. 1854.

*   By-election

Constituency	Member	Sworn In	Comments
Lanark North	Robert Bell	Sept. 5, 1854	Lanark North. 1853. 16 Vic., C.152. II. S.12. An Act to enlarge the Representation of the People of this Province in Parliament. The North Riding shall consist of the Townships of Sherbrooke North, Dalhousie, Lanark, Ramsay, Lavant, Darling and Pakenham.
			General Election July-Aug. 1854.
Lanark South	James Shaw	Sept. 5, 1854	Lanark South. 1853. 16 Vic., C.152. II. S.12. An Act to enlarge the Representation of the People of this Province in Parliament. The South Riding shall consist of the Townships of Montague, Elmsley North, Burgess North, Sherbrooke South, Beckwith, Drummond, Bathurst and the Town of Perth.
			General Election July-Aug. 1854.
Leeds North & Grenville North	Basil Rorison Church	Sept. 5, 1854	Leeds North & Grenville North. 1853. 16 Vic., C.152. II. S.14. An Act to enlarge the Representation of the People of this Province in Parliament. The North Riding of Leeds and Grenville shall consist of the Townships of Kitley, Elmsley, Wolford, Oxford and South Gower.
			Leeds North & Grenville North. 1853. 16 Vic., C.226. II. S.1. An Act to divide the Townships of Yonge and Escott in the United Counties of Leeds and Grenville. . . . That upon, from and after the first day of January next after the passing of this Act, the sixth, seventh, eighth, ninth, tenth and eleventh Concessions of the Townships of Yonge, and the seventh, eighth, ninth and tenth Concessions of the Township of Escott, shall, for all Municipal and Election purposes, be united together, and form a Township, to be called the "Rear of Yonge and Escott," and that the remainder of the said

			Townships of Yonge and Escott, together with the Islands in the River St. Lawrence, at present forming part of these Townships, shall, for the like purposes, be together united and form a Township, to be called the "Front of Yonge and Escott."
			General Election July-Aug. 1854.
Leeds South	Jesse Delong	Sept. 5, 1854	Leeds South. 1853. 16 Vic., C.152. II. S.14. An Act to enlarge the Representation of the People of this Province in Parliament. The South Riding of Leeds shall consist of the Townships of Yonge, Escott, Front of Leeds and Lansdowne, Rear of Leeds and Landsdowne, South Crosby, North Crosby, Bastard and Burgess.
			Leeds South. 1853. 16 Vic., C.226. II. S.1. An Act to divide the Townships of Yonge and Escott in the United Counties of Leeds and Grenville. . . . That upon, from and after the first day of January next after the passing of this Act, the sixth, seventh, eighth, ninth, tenth and eleventh Concessions of the Townships of Yonge, and the seventh, eighth, ninth and tenth Concessions of the Township of Escott, shall, for all Municipal and Election purposes, be united together, and form a Township, to be called the "Rear of Yonge and Escott," and that the remainder of the said Townships of Yonge and Escott, together with the Islands in the River St. Lawrence, at present forming part of these Townships, shall, for the like purposes, be together united and form a Township, to be called the "Front of Yonge and Escott."
			General Election July-Aug. 1854.
Lenox & Addington	David Roblin	Sept. 5, 1854	General Election July-Aug. 1854.
Lincoln	Hon. William Hamilton Merritt	Sept. 5, 1854	General Election July-Aug. 1854.
London (Town)	John Wilson	Sept. 5, 1854	General Election July-Aug. 1854.

Constituency	Member	Sworn In	Comments
Middlesex East	William Niles	Sept. 5, 1854	Middlesex East. 1853. 16 Vic., C.152. II. S.5. An Act to enlarge the Representation of the People of this Province in Parliament. The East Riding shall consist of the Townships of West Nissouri, North Dorchester, Westminster and London.
			General Election July-Aug. 1854.
Middlesex West	John Scatcherd	Sept. 5, 1854	Middlesex West. 1853. 16 Vic., C.152. II. S.5. An Act to enlarge the Representation of the People of this Province in Parliament. The West Riding shall consist of the Townships of Mosa, Eckfrid, Caradoc, Metcalfe, Adelaide, Williams, Lobo, and Delaware.
			General Election July-Aug. 1854.
Niagara (Town)	Hon. Joseph Curran Morrison	Sept. 5, 1854	General Election July-Aug. 1854.
			On Apr. 21, 1856, the House was informed that Joseph Curran Morrison, MPP, Niagara (Town), had been appointed to the Executive Council.
			On Apr. 21, 1856, the House resolved that the acceptance of office by the Hon. Joseph Curran Morrison, MPP, Niagara (Town), without any emolument attached thereto, is not such an acceptance of office as vacates his seat in the House.
			On May 26, 1856, the House was informed of the resignation of the Hon. Joseph Curran Morrison, who had been appointed Receiver General of this Province. A new election was called.
			By-election Date unknown.
			Writ of Election – May 27, 1856. Return of Writ – June 20, 1856. On June 20, 1856, the House

			was informed of the election of the Hon. Joseph Curran Morrison, MPP, Niagara (Town), who was returned as duly elected.
Norfolk	Hon. John Rolph	Sept. 5, 1854	General Election July-Aug. 1854.
Northumberland East	James Ross	Sept. 5, 1854	Northumberland East. 1853. 16 Vic., C.152. II. S.9. An Act to enlarge the Representation of the People of this Province in Parliament. The East Riding shall consist of the Townships of Cramahe, Brighton, Murray, Seymour and Percy. General Election July-Aug. 1854.
Northumberland West	Sidney Smith	Sept. 5, 1854	Northumberland West. 1853. 16 Vic., C.152. II. S.9. An Act to enlarge the Representation of the People of this Province in Parliament. The West Riding shall consist of the Townships of Hamilton, Haldimand, Alnwick, South Monaghan and the Town of Cobourg. General Election July-Aug. 1854.
Ontario North	Joseph Gould	Sept. 5, 1854	Ontario. 1851. 14 & 15 Vic., C.5. II. S.23. Schedule A. An Act to make certain alterations in the Territorial Divisions of Upper Canada. The County of Ontario shall consist of the Townships of Whitby, Pickering, Uxbridge, Reach, Brock, Georgina, Scott, Thora, Mara, Scugog and Rama. Ontario North. 1853. 16 Vic., C.152. II. S.10. An Act to enlarge the Representation of the People of this Province in Parliament. The County of Ontario shall be divided into two Ridings, to be called respectively the North Riding and the South Riding. The North Riding shall consist of the Townships of Reach, Uxbridge, Brock, Scott, Thorah, Mara, Rama and Scugog. General Election July-Aug. 1854.
Ontario South	John MacVeigh Lumsden	Sept. 5, 1854	Ontario. 1851. 14 & 15 Vic., C.5. II. S.23. Schedule A. An Act to make certain alterations

Constituency	Member	Sworn In	Comments
Ontario South — *Continued*			in the Territorial Divisions of Upper Canada. The County of Ontario shall consist of the Townships of Whitby, Pickering, Uxbridge, Reach, Brock, Georgina, Scott, Thora, Mara, Scugog and Rama.
			Ontario South. 1853. 16 Vic., C.152. II. S.10. An Act to enlarge the Representation of the People of this Province in Parliament. The County of Ontario shall be divided into two Ridings, to be called respectively the North Riding and the South Riding. The South Riding shall consist of the Townships of Whitby, Pickering and the Village of Oshawa.
			General Election July-Aug. 1854.
Oxford North	Donald Matheson	Sept. 5, 1854	Oxford North. 1853. 16 Vic., C.152. S.6. An Act to enlarge the Representation of the People of this Province in Parliament. The North Riding shall consist of the Townships of East Nissouri, East Zorra, West Zorra, Blandford, Blenheim, and the Town of Woodstock.
			General Election July-Aug. 1854.
Oxford South	Hon. Francis Hincks	Sept. 5, 1854	Oxford South. 1853. 16 Vic., C.152. II. S.6. An Act to enlarge the Representation of the People of this Province in Parliament. The South Riding shall consist of the Townships of North Oxford, West Oxford, East Oxford, Norwich and Dereham.
			General Election July-Aug. 1854.
			On Sept. 18, 1854, the Hon. Francis Hincks, Member for both the County of Oxford South and the County of Renfrew, chose to sit for the County of Renfrew. A new election was called for the County of Oxford South.

Oxford South	Ephraim Cook	Oct. 25, 1854*	By-election Date unknown.
			Writ of Election – Sept. 22, 1854. Return of Writ – Oct. 9, 1854. On Oct. 17, 1854, the House was informed of the election of Ephraim Cook, MPP, Oxford South, in room of the Hon. Francis Hincks, resigned.
Peel	James C. Aikens	Sept. 5, 1854	Peel. 1851. 14 & 15 Vic., C.5. S.22. Schedule A. An Act to make certain alterations in the Territorial Divisions of Upper Canada. The County of Peel shall consist of the Townships of Albion, Caledon, Chinguacousy, Toronto and Toronto Gore.
			Peel. 1853. 16 Vic., C.152. II. S.19. An Act to enlarge the Representation of the People of this Province in Parliament. Each of the Counties in Upper Canada, that is to say, each of the Counties of Carleton, Dundas, Essex, Frontenac, Glengarry, Grey, Haldimand, Halton, Kent, Lambton, Lincoln, Norfolk, Peterborough, Peel, Perth, Prescott, Prince Edward, Renfrew, Russell, Stormont, Victoria and Welland, shall form an Electoral Division.
			General Election July-Aug. 1854.
Perth	Thomas Mayne Daly	Sept. 8, 1854	Perth. 1853. 16 Vic., C.152. II. S.19. An Act to enlarge the Representation of the People of this Province in Parliament. Each of the Counties in Upper Canada, that is to say, each of the Counties of Carleton, Dundas, Essex, Frontenac, Glengarry, Grey, Haldimand, Halton, Kent, Lambton, Lincoln, Norfolk, Peterborough, Peel, Perth, Prescott, Prince Edward, Renfrew, Russell, Stormont, Victoria and Welland, shall form an Electoral Division.
			General Election July-Aug. 1854.

*   By-election

Constituency	Member	Sworn In	Comments
Peterborough	John Langton	Sept. 5, 1854	General Election July-Aug. 1854.
			On Feb. 15, 1856, the House was informed of the resignation of John Langton, MPP, Peterborough, who had been appointed Auditor. A new election was called.
Peterborough	Wilson Seymour Conger	Feb. 15, 1856*	By-election Date unknown.
			Writ of Election – Dec. 31, 1855. Return of Writ – Jan. 26, 1856. On Feb. 15, 1856, the House was informed of the election of Wilson Seymour Conger, MPP, Peterborough, in room of John Langton, resigned.
Prescott	Henry Wellesley McCann	Sept. 5, 1854	General Election July-Aug. 1854.
Prince Edward	David Barker Stevenson	Sept. 5, 1854	General Election July-Aug. 1854.
Renfrew	Hon. Francis Hincks	Sept. 5, 1854	Renfrew. 1853. 16 Vic., C.152. II. S.19. An Act to enlarge the Representation of the People of this Province in Parliament. Each of the Counties in Upper Canada, that is to say, each of the Counties of Carleton, Dundas, Essex, Frontenac, Glengarry, Grey, Haldimand, Halton, Kent, Lambton, Lincoln, Norfolk, Peterborough, Peel, Perth, Prescott, Prince Edward, Renfrew, Russell, Stormont, Victoria and Welland, shall form an Electoral Division.
			General Election July-Aug. 1854.
			On Sept. 18, 1854, the Hon. Francis Hincks, Member for both the County of Oxford South and the County of Renfrew, chose to sit for the County of Renfrew. A new election was called for the County of Oxford South.
			Resigned, Nov. 16, 1855. A new election was called.

Renfrew	John Supple	Apr. 11, 1856*	By-election Date unknown.
			On Apr. 11, 1856, having presented the Indenture of his Election for the County of Renfrew, John Supple took his seat.
			On Apr. 11, 1856, the House resolved that in admitting John Supple, MPP, Renfrew, to take his seat, on the production of the Duplicate Indenture only, and without the Return of the Indenture to the Clerk of the Crown in Chancercy, and the Certificate of the latter Officer, it still recommends a strict adherence to the requirement of producing the usual Certificate.
			Writ of Election – Feb. 27, 1856. Return of Writ – Mar. 31, 1856. On Apr. 15, 1856, the House was informed of the election of John Supple, MPP, Renfrew, in room of the Hon. Francis Hincks, resigned.
Russell	George Byron Lyon	Sept. 5, 1854	General Election July-Aug. 1854.
Saint Hyacinthe (Canada East)	Hon. Louis Victor Sicotte	Sept. 5, 1854	General Election July-Aug. 1854.
			On Sept. 5, 1854, Antoine Aimé Dorion, MPP, Montreal (City) (Canada East), proposed Louis Victor Sicotte, MPP, Saint Hyacinthe (Canada East), as Speaker. Seconded and resolved. Sept. 5, 1854 – Date took chair.
Simcoe North	Angus Morrison	Sept. 5, 1854	Simcoe North. 1853. 16 Vic., C.152. II. S.13. An Act to enlarge the Representation of the People of this Province in Parliament. The North Riding shall consist of the Townships of Nottawasaga, Sunnidale, Vespra, Flos, Oro, Medonte, Orillia, Tiny, Tay, Matchedash and the Town of Barrie.
			General Election July-Aug. 1854.

* By-election

Constituency	Member	Sworn In	Comments
Simcoe South	William Benjamin Robinson	Sept. 5, 1854	Simcoe South. 1853. 16 Vic., C.152. II. S.13. An Act to enlarge the Representation of the People of this Province in Parliament. The South Riding shall consist of the Townships of West Gwillimbury, Tecumseth, Innisfil, Essa, Adjala, Tosorontio, Mulmer and Mono. General Election July-Aug. 1854.
Stormont	William D. Mattice	Sept. 5, 1854	General Election July-Aug. 1854.
Toronto (City)	John George Bowes	Sept. 5, 1854	General Election July-Aug. 1854.
Toronto (City)	Hon. John Hillyard Cameron	Sept. 5, 1854	General Election July-Aug. 1854.
Victoria	James Smith	Sept. 5, 1854	Victoria. 1853. 16 Vic., C.152. II. S.19. An Act to enlarge the Representation of the People of this Province in Parliament. Each of the Counties in Upper Canada, that is to say, each of the Counties of Carleton, Dundas, Essex, Frontenac, Glengarry, Grey, Haldimand, Halton, Kent, Lambton, Lincoln, Norfolk, Peterborough, Peel, Perth, Prescott, Prince Edward, Renfrew, Russell, Stormont, Victoria and Welland, shall form an Electoral Division. General Election July-Aug. 1854.
Waterloo North	Michael Hamilton Foley	Sept. 5, 1854	Waterloo North. 1853. 16 Vic., C.152. II. S.16. An Act to enlarge the Representation of the People of this Province in Parliament. The North Riding shall consist of the Townships of North Waterloo (including the Town of Berlin,) Woolwich and Wellesley; the Township of North Waterloo to include and consist of that part of the present Township of Waterloo lying within the following limits, that is to say: commencing at the south-west angle of lot Number forty-six in the said Township, thence

easterly along the southerly limits of the said lot, and of the lots Numbers forty-seven, forty-eight, fifty, fifty-one and fifty-three, and the prolongation thereof, to the middle of the Grand River, thence along the middle of the said River against the stream to the prolongation of the limit between Lots Numbers one hundred and thirteen and one hundred and fourteen, and along the prolongation of the limit between the said Lots Numbers one hundred and thirteen and one hundred and fourteen, and along the limits between the said Lots Numbers one hundred and thirteen and one hundred and fourteen, northerly and easterly, to the westerly limits of Lot one hundred and seven, thence along the westerly limits of the said Lot Number one hundred and seven, northerly, to the northerly limits thereof, thence along the northerly limits of the said Lot Number one hundred and seven and of Lots Number one hundred and six, eighty-four and ninety-six, easterly to the easterly boundary of the said Township, thence along the easterly, northerly and westerly boundaries of the said Township, in a northerly, westerly and southerly direction respectively, to the place of beginning.

General Election July-Aug. 1854.

Waterloo South	Robert Ferrie	Sept. 5, 1854	Waterloo South. 1853. 16 Vic., C.152. II. S.16. An Act to enlarge the Representation of the People of this Province in Parliament. The South Riding shall consist of the villages of Galt and Preston, and the Townships of South Waterloo, North Dumfries and Wilmot; And the Township of South Waterloo to include and consist of all the remaining part of the said present Township of Waterloo.
			General Election July-Aug. 1854.
Welland	John Frazer	Sept. 5, 1854	General Election July-Aug. 1854.

Constituency	Member	Sworn In	Comments
Wellington North	William Clarke	Sept. 5, 1854	Wellington North. 1853. 16 Vic., C.152. II. S.15. An Act to enlarge the Representation of the People of this Province in Parliament. The County of Wellington shall be divided into two Ridings, to be called respectively the South Riding and the North Riding. The North Riding shall consist of the Townships of Nichol, Garafraxa, Pilkington, Peel, Arthur, Maryborough, Amaranth, Luther and Minto. General Election July-Aug. 1854.
Wellington South	Adam Johnston Fergusson	Sept. 5, 1854	Wellington South. 1853. 16 Vic., C.152. II. S.15. An Act to enlarge the Representation of the People of this Province in Parliament. The County of Wellington shall be divided into two Ridings, to be called respectively the South Riding and the North Riding. The South Riding shall consist of the Town and Township of Guelph, and the Townships of Puslinch, Eramosa and Erin. General Election July-Aug. 1854.
Wentworth North	Hon. Robert Spence	Sept. 5, 1854	Wentworth North. 1853. 16 Vic., C.152. II. S.11. An Act to enlarge the Representation of the People of this Province in Parliament. The North Riding shall consist of the Townships of Beverly, Flamborough East, Flamborough West and the Town of Dundas. General Election July-Aug. 1854. On Sept. 13, 1854, the House was informed of the resignation of the Hon. Robert Spence, MPP, Wentworth North, who had been appointed Postmaster General of the Province of Canada. A new election was called. By-election Date unknown.

			Writ of Election – Sept. 14, 1854. Return of Writ – Oct. 13, 1854. On Oct. 19, 1854, the House was informed of the election of the Hon. Robert Spence, MPP, Wentworth North, who had been returned as duly elected.
Wentworth South	Samuel Black Freeman	Sept. 5, 1854	Wentworth South. 1853. 16 Vic., C.152. II. S.11. An Act to enlarge the Representation of the People of this Province in Parliament. The South Riding shall consist of the Townships of Saltfleet, Binbrook, Glanford, Barton and Ancaster.
			General Election July-Aug. 1854.
York East	Amos Wright	Sept. 5, 1854	General Election July-Aug. 1854.
York North	Joseph Hartman	Sept. 5, 1854	General Election July-Aug. 1854.
York West	John William Gamble	Sept. 5, 1854	General Election July-Aug. 1854.

LEGISLATURES OF THE PROVINCE OF CANADA
(Canada West)
6th Legislature

General Election   Dec. 1857 – Jan. 1858

Sessions of the Sixth Legislature of the Province of Canada: Feb. 25, 1858 – May 18, 1861

First:	Feb. 25, 1858 – Aug. 16, 1858.
Second:	Jan. 29, 1859 – May 4, 1859.
Third:	Feb. 28, 1860 – May 19, 1860.
Fourth:	Mar. 16, 1861 – May 18, 1861.

Alphabetical List of Members

Member	Constituency	Sworn In	Comments
James C. Aikins	Peel	Feb. 25, 1858	
Charles Allan	Wellington North	Feb. 25, 1858	On July 14, 1858, the election of Charles Allan, MPP, Wellington North, was declared void. A new election was called.
		Did not take seat	Writ of Election – July 16, 1858. Return of Writ – Aug. 21, 1858. On Jan. 29, 1859, the House was informed of the election of Charles Allan, MPP, Wellington North, who had been returned as duly elected.
			Died, Jan. 13, 1859. A new election was called.
Robert Bell	Lanark North	Feb. 25, 1858	Resigned, Sept. 24, 1860. A new election was called.
		Mar. 18, 1861*	Writ of Election – Oct. 8, 1860. Return of Writ – Oct. 26, 1860. On Mar. 16, 1861, the House was informed of the election of Robert Bell, MPP, Lanark, who was returned as duly elected.

George Benjamin	Hastings North	Feb. 25, 1858	
Herbert Biggar	Brant West	Feb. 25, 1858	
George Brown	Oxford North	Feb. 25, 1858	On Apr. 19, 1858, George Brown, Member for both the County of Oxford North and the City of Toronto, chose to serve for the City of Toronto. A new election was called for the County of Oxford North.
Hon. George Brown	Toronto (City)	Feb. 25, 1858	On Apr. 19, 1858, George Brown, Member for both the City of Toronto and the County of Oxford North, chose to serve for the City of Toronto. A new election was called for the County of Oxford North.
			On Aug. 4, 1858, the House was informed of the resignation of George Brown, MPP, Toronto (City), who had been appointed Inspector General of this Province. A new election was called.
		Jan. 29, 1859*	Writ of Election – Aug. 6, 1858. Return of Writ – Sept. 1, 1858. On Jan. 29, 1859, the House was informed of the election of the Hon. George Brown, MPP, Toronto (City), who was returned as duly elected.
Isaac Buchanan	Hamilton (City)	Feb. 25, 1858	
Francis Henry Burton	Durham East	Feb. 25, 1858	
Leonidas Burwell	Elgin East	Feb. 25, 1858	
John Cameron	Victoria	Feb. 25, 1858	
Hon. Malcolm Cameron	Lambton	Feb. 25, 1858	Resigned, Sept. 21, 1860. A new election was called.
John Carling	London (City)	Feb. 25, 1858	
Hon. William Cayley	Renfrew	Mar. 4, 1858*	Writ of Election – Feb. 8, 1858. Return of Writ – Mar. 3, 1858. On Mar. 4, 1858, the House

* By-election

Member	Constituency	Sworn In	Comments
Hon. William Cayley — *Continued*			was informed of the election of the Hon. William Cayley, MPP, Renfrew, in room of John Lorn McDougall, resigned.
David Christie	Brant East	Feb. 25, 1858	Resigned, Oct. 4, 1858. A new election was called.
Basil Rorison Church	Leeds North & Grenville North	Feb. 25, 1858	On Apr. 7, 1858, the House was informed of the death of Basil Rorison Church, MPP, Leeds North & Grenville North. A new election was called.
John Robert Clarke	Northumberland East	Feb. 25, 1858	
Skeffington Connor	Oxford South	Feb. 25, 1858	On Aug. 4, 1858, the House was informed of the resignation of Skeffington Connor, MPP, Oxford South, who had been appointed Solicitor General of Canada West. A new election was called.
		Jan. 29, 1859*	Writ of Election – Aug. 6, 1858. Return of Writ – Sept. 7, 1858. On Jan. 29, 1859, the House was informed of the election of Skeffington Connor, MPP, Oxford South, who was returned as duly elected.
James William Cook	Dundas	Feb. 25, 1858	
Robert Craik	Middlesex East	Mar. 16, 1861*	Writ of Election – Apr. 27, 1860. Return of Writ – May 31, 1860. On Mar. 16, 1861, the House was informed of the election of Robert Craik, MPP, Middlesex East, in room of Marcus Talbot, deceased.
Thomas Mayne Daly	Perth	Feb. 25, 1858	
Willet Casey Dorland	Prince Edward	Feb. 25, 1858	
George Byron Lyon Fellowes	Russell	Feb. 25, 1858	Changed name to Fellowes. For further reference, see, An Act to change the name of

George Byron Lyon, and of his family, by adding the name of Fellowes, 19 Vic. 1856 C. 33.

Resigned, Nov. 1, 1859. A new election was called.

Thomas Roberts Ferguson	Simcoe South	Feb. 25, 1858	
Hugh Finlayson	Brant East	Jan. 29, 1859*	Writ of Election — Oct. 18, 1858. Return of Writ — Dec. 1, 1858. On Jan. 29, 1859, the House was informed of the election of Hugh Finlayson, MPP, Brant East, in room of David Christie, resigned.
Hon. Michael Hamilton Foley	Waterloo North	Feb. 25, 1858	On Aug. 4, 1858, the House was informed of the resignation of Michael Hamilton Foley, MPP, Waterloo North, who had been appointed Postmaster General of this Province. A new election was called.
		Jan. 29, 1859*	Writ of Election — Aug. 6, 1858. Return of Writ — Aug. 23, 1858. On Jan. 29, 1859, the House was informed of the election of the Hon. Michael Hamilton Foley, MPP, Waterloo North, who was returned as duly elected.
Joseph Gould	Ontario North	Feb. 25, 1858	
Ogle Robert Gowan	Leeds North & Grenville North	May 25, 1858*	Writ of Election — Apr. 19, 1858. Return of Writ — May 21, 1858. On May 25, 1858, the House was informed of the election of Ogle Robert Gowan, MPP, Leeds North & Grenville North, in room of Basil Rorison Church, deceased.
Michael Harcourt	Haldimand	Jan. 29, 1859*	Writ of Election — Aug. 21, 1858. Return of Writ — Oct. 7, 1858. On Jan. 29, 1859, the House was informed of the election of Michael Harcourt, MPP, Haldimand, in room of William Lyon Mackenzie, resigned.

* By-election

Member	Constituency	Sworn In	Comments
Joseph Hartman	York North	Feb. 25, 1858	On Feb. 28, 1860, the House was informed of the death of Joseph Hartman, MPP, York North. A new election was called.
John Sheridan Hogan	Grey	Feb. 25, 1858	On Mar. 16, 1861, the House was informed of the death of John Sheridan Hogan, MPP, Grey. A new election had been called.
John Holmes	Huron & Bruce	Feb. 25, 1858	
William Pearce Howland	York West	Feb. 25, 1858	
John W. Loux	Russell	Feb. 28, 1860*	Writ of Election – Nov. 18, 1859. Return of Writ – Dec. 21, 1859. On Feb. 28, 1860, the House was informed of the election of John W. Loux, MPP, Russell, in room of George Byron Lyon Fellowes, resigned.
George Macbeth	Elgin West	Feb. 25,1858	
Donald Alexander Macdonald	Glengarry	Feb. 25, 1858	
Hon. John Alexander Macdonald	Kingston (City)	Feb. 25, 1858	Attorney General.
Hon. John Sandfield Macdonald	Cornwall (Town)	Feb. 25, 1858	On Aug. 4, 1858, the House was informed of the resignation of the Hon. John Sandfield Macdonald, MPP, Cornwall (Town), who had been appointed Attorney General of Canada West. A new election was called.
		Jan. 29, 1859*	Writ of Election – Aug. 6, 1858. Return of Writ – Sept. 1, 1858. On Jan. 29, 1859, the House was informed of the election of the Hon. John Sandfield Macdonald, MPP, Cornwall (Town), who was returned as duly elected.
Hope Fleming Mackenzie	Lambton	Mar. 18, 1861*	Writ of Election – Oct. 13, 1860. Return of Writ – Nov. 19, 1860. On Mar. 16, 1861, the House was informed of the election of Hope Fleming Mackenzie, MPP, Lambton, in room of the

			Hon. Malcolm Cameron, resigned.
William Lyon Mackenzie	Haldimand	Feb. 25, 1858	Resigned, Aug. 16, 1858. A new election was called.
John MacLeod	Essex	Feb. 25, 1858	
William D. Mattice	Stormont	Feb. 25, 1858	
Henry Wellesley McCann	Prescott	Feb. 25, 1858	
Angus Peter McDonald	Middlesex West	Aug. 9, 1858*	On Aug. 9, 1858, having presented the Indenture of his Election for the County of Middlesex West, Angus Peter McDonald took his seat.
			On Aug. 9, 1858, the House resolved that in admitting Angus Peter McDonald, MPP, Middlesex West, to take his seat, on the Production of the Duplicate Indenture only, and without the Return of the Indenture to the Clerk of the Crown in Chancery, and the Certificate of the latter Officer, it still recommends a strict adherence to the requirement of producing the usual Certificate.
			Writ of Election – June 28, 1858. Return of Writ – Aug. 5, 1858. On Aug. 16, 1858, the House was informed of the election of Angus Peter McDonald, MPP, Middlesex West, in room of John Scatcherd, deceased.
John Lorn McDougall	Renfrew	Did not take seat	Resigned, having been appointed Associate Coroner for the United Counties of Lanark and Renfrew. A new election was called.
William McDougall	Oxford North	May 14, 1858*	On May 14, 1858, having presented the Indenture of his Election for the County of Oxford North, William McDougall took his seat.
			On May 14, 1858, the House resolved that in admitting William McDougall, MPP, Oxford North, to take his seat, on the production of the Duplicate Indenture only, and without the

* By-election

Member	Constituency	Sworn In	Comments
William McDougall — *Continued*			Return of the Indenture to the Clerk of the Crown in Chancery, and the Certificate of the latter Officer, it still recommends a strict adherence to the requirement of producing the usual Certificate.
			Writ of Election – Apr. 20, 1858. Return of Writ – May 14, 1858. On May 27, 1858, the House was informed of the election of William McDougall, MPP, Oxford North, in room of George Brown, resigned.
Archibald McKellar	Kent	Feb. 25, 1858	
Gilbert McMicken	Welland	Feb. 25, 1858	
Hon. William Hamilton Merritt	Lincoln	May 25, 1858	Resigned, Sept. 21, 1860. A new election was called.
Angus Morrison	Simcoe North	Feb. 25, 1858	
Hon. Oliver Mowat	Ontario South	Feb. 25, 1858	On Aug. 4, 1858, the House was informed of the resignation of Oliver Mowat, MPP, Ontario South, who had been appointed Secretary and Registrar of this Province. A new election was called.
		Jan. 29, 1859*	Writ of Election – Aug. 6, 1858. Return of Writ – Sept. 4, 1858. On Jan. 28, 1859, the House was informed of the election of the Hon. Oliver Mowat, MPP, Ontario South, who was returned as duly elected.
Henry Munro	Durham West	Feb. 25, 1858	
William Notman	Wentworth North	Feb. 25, 1858	
William Patrick	Grenville South	Feb. 25, 1858	
Andrew William Playfair	Lanark South	Feb. 25, 1858	
Walker Powell	Norfolk	Feb. 25, 1858	

William Frederick Powell	Carleton	Feb. 25, 1858	
Jesse Thomas Purdy	Grey	Mar. 16, 1861*	Writ of Election – Jan. 25, 1861. Return of Writ – Mar. 4, 1861. On Mar. 16, 1861, the House was informed of the election of Jesse Thomas Purdy, MPP, Grey, in room of John Sheridan Hogan, deceased.
John Beverley Robinson, Jr.	Toronto (City)	Feb. 25, 1858	
David Roblin	Lennox & Addington	Mar. 16, 1858	
James Ross	Wellington North	Feb. 24, 1859*	On Feb. 24, 1859, having presented the Indenture of his Election for the County of Wellington North, James Ross took his seat.
			On Feb. 24, 1859, the House resolved that in admitting James Ross, MPP, Wellington North, to take his seat on the production of the Duplicate Indenture only, and without the Return of the Indenture to the Clerk of the Crown in Chancery, and the Certificate of the latter Officer, it still recommends a strict adherence to the requirement of producing the usual Certificate.
			Writ of Election – Jan. 27, 1859. Return of Writ – Feb. 23, 1859. On Feb. 28, 1859, the House was informed of the election of James Ross, MPP, Wellington North, in room of Charles Allan, deceased.
John Charles Rykert	Lincoln	Mar. 18, 1861*	Writ of Election – Oct. 8, 1860. Return of Writ – Nov. 7, 1860. On Mar. 16, 1861, the House was informed of the election of John Charles Rykert, MPP, Lincoln, in room of the Hon. William Hamilton Merritt, resigned.
Joseph Rymal	Wentworth South	Feb. 25, 1858	
John Scatcherd	Middlesex West	Feb. 25, 1858	Died, June 25, 1858. A new election was called.

* By-election

Member	Constituency	Sworn In	Comments
Richard William Scott	Ottawa (City)	Feb. 25, 1858	
William Scott	Waterloo South	Feb. 25, 1858	
Hon. George Sherwood	Brockville (Town)	Feb. 25, 1858	On Aug. 10, 1858, the House was informed of the resignation of George Sherwood, MPP, Brockville (Town), who had been appointed Receiver General of this Province. A new election was called.
		Jan. 29, 1859*	Writ of Election – Aug. 11, 1858. Return of Writ – Sept. 2, 1858. On Jan. 29, 1859, the House was informed of the election of the Hon. George Sherwood, MPP, Brockville (Town), who was returned as duly elected.
Thomas Short	Peterborough	Feb. 25, 1858	
John Simpson	Niagara (Town)	Feb. 25, 1858	
Hon. Henry Smith, Jr.	Frontenac	Feb. 25, 1858	On Feb. 25, 1858, the Hon. John Alexander Macdonald, MPP, Kingston (City), proposed Henry Smith, Jr., MPP, Frontenac, as Speaker. Seconded and resolved. Feb. 25, 1858 – Date took chair.
Hon. Sidney Smith	Northumberland West	Feb. 25, 1858*	President of the Executive Council.
			Resigned prior to the 1st Session, having been appointed Postmaster General of the Province. A new election was called.
			Writ of Election – Feb. 2, 1858. Return of Writ – Feb. 22, 1858. The Hon. Sidney Smith, MPP, Northumberland West, was returned as duly elected.
David Stirton	Wellington South	Feb. 25, 1858	
Marcus Talbot	Middlesex East	Feb. 25, 1858	On Mar. 26, 1860, the House was informed of the death of Marcus Talbot, MPP, Middlesex East. A new election was called.

Benjamin Tett	Leeds South	Feb. 25, 1858	
Lewis Wallbridge	Hastings South	Feb. 25, 1858	
John White	Halton	Feb. 25, 1858	
Adam Wilson	York North	Feb. 29, 1860*	Writ of Election – Dec. 19, 1859. Return of Writ – Jan. 14, 1860. On Feb. 28, 1860, the House was informed of the election of Adam Wilson, MPP, York North, in room of Joseph Hartman, deceased.
Amos Wright	York East	Feb. 25, 1858	

* By-election

Alphabetical List of Constituencies
6th Legislature: Feb. 25, 1858 – May 18, 1861.

156

Constituency	Member	Sworn In	Comments
Brant East	David Christie	Feb. 25, 1858	General Election Dec. 1857 – Jan. 1858.
			Resigned, Oct. 4, 1858. A new election was called.
Brant East	Hugh Finlayson	Jan. 29, 1859*	By-election Date unknown.
			Writ of Election – Oct. 18, 1858. Return of Writ – Dec. 1, 1858. On Jan. 29, 1859, the House was informed of the election of Hugh Finlayson, MPP, Brant East, in room of David Christie, resigned.
Brant West	Herbert Biggar	Feb. 25, 1858	General Election Dec. 1857 – Jan. 1858.
Brockville (Town)	Hon. George Sherwood	Feb. 25, 1858	General Election Dec. 1857 – Jan. 1858.
			On Aug. 10, 1858, the House was informed of the resignation of George Sherwood, MPP, Brockville (Town), who had been appointed Receiver General of this Province. A new election was called.
		Jan. 29, 1859*	By-election Date unknown.
			Writ of Election – Aug. 11, 1858. Return of Writ – Sept. 2, 1858. On Jan. 29, 1859, the House was informed of the election of the Hon. George Sherwood, MPP, Brockville (Town), who was returned as duly elected.
Carleton	William Frederick Powell	Feb. 25, 1858	General Election Dec. 1857 – Jan. 1858.
Cornwall (Town)	Hon. John Sandfield Macdonald	Feb. 25, 1858	General Election Dec. 1857 – Jan. 1858.
			On Aug. 4, 1858, the House was informed of the resignation of the Hon. John Sandfield Macdonald, MPP, Cornwall (Town), who had been appointed Attorney General of Canada West. A new election was called.
		Jan. 29, 1859*	By-election Date unknown.

			Writ of Election — Aug. 6, 1858. Return of Writ — Sept. 1, 1858. On Jan. 29, 1859, the House was informed of the election of the Hon. John Sandfield Macdonald, MPP, Cornwall (Town), who was returned as duly elected.
Dundas	James William Cook	Feb. 25, 1858	General Election Dec. 1857 — Jan. 1858.
Durham East	Francis Henry Burton	Feb. 25, 1858	General Election Dec. 1857 — Jan. 1858.
Durham West	Henry Munro	Feb. 25, 1858	General Election Dec. 1857 — Jan. 1858.
Elgin East	Leonidas Burwell	Feb. 25, 1858	General Election Dec. 1857 — Jan. 1858.
Elgin West	George Macbeth	Feb. 25,1858	General Election Dec. 1857 — Jan. 1858.
Essex	John MacLeod	Feb. 25, 1858	General Election Dec. 1857 — Jan. 1858.
Frontenac	Hon. Henry Smith, Jr.	Feb. 25, 1858	General Election Dec. 1857 — Jan. 1858.
			On Feb. 25, 1858, the Hon. John Alexander Macdonald, MPP, Kingston (City), proposed Henry Smith, Jr., MPP, Frontenac, as Speaker. Seconded and resolved. Feb. 25, 1858 — Date took chair.
			Frontenac. 1860. 23 Vic., C. 39, S. 2. An Act to amend An Act respecting the Territorial Division of Upper Canada. The Townships of Miller, Canonto, otherwise called North and South Canonto, shall be added to and form part of the County of Frontenac, for all purposes whatever.
Glengarry	Donald Alexander Macdonald	Feb. 25, 1858	General Election Dec. 1857 — Jan. 1858.
Grenville South	William Patrick	Feb. 25, 1858	General Election Dec. 1857 — Jan. 1858.
Grey	John Sheridan Hogan	Feb. 25, 1858	General Election Dec. 1857 — Jan. 1858.
			On Mar. 16, 1861, the House was informed of the death of John Sheridan Hogan, MPP, Grey. A new election had been called.

*   By-election

Constituency	Member	Sworn In	Comments
Grey	Jesse Thomas Purdy	Mar. 16, 1861*	By-election Date unknown.
			Writ of Election – Jan. 25, 1861. Return of Writ – Mar. 4, 1861. On Mar. 16, 1861, the House was informed of the election of Jesse Thomas Purdy, MPP, Grey, in room of John Sheridan Hogan, deceased.
Haldimand	William Lyon Mackenzie	Feb. 25, 1858	General Election Dec. 1857 – Jan. 1858.
			Resigned, Aug. 16, 1858. A new election was called.
Haldimand	Michael Harcourt	Jan. 29, 1859*	By-election Date unknown.
			Writ of Election – Aug. 21, 1858. Return of Writ – Oct. 7, 1858. On Jan. 29, 1859, the House was informed of the election of Michael Harcourt, MPP, Haldimand, in room of William Lyon Mackenzie, resigned.
Halton	John White	Feb. 25, 1858	General Election Dec. 1857 – Jan. 1858.
Hamilton (City)	Isaac Buchanan	Feb. 25, 1858	General Election Dec. 1857 – Jan. 1858.
Hastings North	George Benjamin	Feb. 25, 1858	General Election Dec. 1857 – Jan. 1858.
			Hastings North. 1858. 22 Vic., C. 14, S. 2. An Act to annex certain new Townships to the counties of Victoria and Peterborough and the North Riding of the County of Hastings. . . . And the said Townships of McClure, Herschel, Faraday, Wollaston, Wicklow, Monteagle, Dunganan, Limerick, Bangor, Carlow, Mayo and Cashel, shall be attached to and to form part of the North Riding of the County of Hastings for all purposes whatsoever.
Hastings South	Lewis Wallbridge	Feb. 25, 1858	General Election Dec. 1857 – Jan. 1858.
Huron & Bruce	John Holmes	Feb. 25, 1858	General Election Dec. 1857 – Jan. 1858.
Kent	Archibald McKellar	Feb. 25, 1858	General Election Dec. 1857 – Jan. 1858.

Kent. 1859. 22 Vic., C. 80, S. 1. An Act to annex parts of the Townships of Sombra and Dawn, in the County of Lambton, to the Townships of Chatham and Camden, in the County of Kent. Upon, from and after the first day of Jan., one thousand eight hundred and sixty, all that portion of the Township of Sombra, in the County of Lambton, lying south of the line between the fourth and fifth concessions of that Township, shall be separated from Dawn and annexed to the North Gore of that Township of Chatham, in the County of Kent; and all that part of the Township of Dawn, in the said County of Lambton lying south of the line between lots ten and eleven in all the concessions, in the said Township, shall be annexed to and form part of the Township of Camden, in the County of Kent.

Kingston (City)	Hon. John Alexander Macdonald	Feb. 25, 1858	Attorney General. General Election Dec. 1857 – Jan. 1858.
Lambton	Hon. Malcolm Cameron	Feb. 25, 1858	General Election Dec. 1857 – Jan. 1858. Lambton. 1859. 22 Vic., C. 80, S. 1. An Act to annex parts of the Townships of Sombra and Dawn, in the County of Lambton, to the Townships of Chatham and Camden, in the County of Kent. Upon, from and after the first day of Jan., one thousand eight hundred and sixty, all that portion of the Township of Sombra, in the County of Lambton, lying south of the line between the fourth and fifth concessions of that Township, shall be separated from Dawn and annexed to the North Gore of that Township of Chatham, in the County of Kent; and all that part of the Township of Dawn, in the said County of

*   By-election

Constituency	Member	Sworn In	Comments
Lambton — *Continued*			Lambton lying south of the line between lots ten and eleven in all the concessions, in the said Township, shall be annexed to and form part of the Township of Camden, in the County of Kent.
			Resigned, Sept. 21, 1860. A new election was called.
Lambton	Hope Fleming Mackenzie	Mar. 18, 1861*	By-election Date unknown.
			Writ of Election – Oct. 13, 1860. Return of Writ – Nov. 19, 1860. On Mar. 16, 1861, the House was informed of the election of Hope Fleming Mackenzie, MPP, Lambton, in room of the Hon. Malcolm Cameron, resigned.
Lanark North	Robert Bell	Feb. 25, 1858	General Election Dec. 1857 – Jan. 1858.
			Resigned, Sept. 24, 1860. A new election was called.
		Mar. 18, 1861*	By-election Date unknown.
			Writ of Election – Oct. 8, 1860. Return of Writ – Oct. 26, 1860. On Mar. 16, 1861, the House was informed of the election of Robert Bell, MPP, Lanark, who was returned as duly elected.
Lanark South	Andrew William Playfair	Feb. 25, 1858	General Election Dec. 1857 – Jan. 1858.
Leeds North & Grenville North	Basil Rorison Church	Feb. 25, 1858	General Election Dec. 1857 - Jan. 1858.
			On Apr. 7, 1858, the House was informed of the death of Basil Rorison Church, MPP, Leeds North & Grenville North. A new election was called.
Leeds North & Grenville North	Ogle Robert Gowan	May 25, 1858*	By-election Date unknown.
			Writ of Election – Apr. 19, 1858. Return of Writ

| | | | — May 21, 1858. On May 25, 1858, the House was informed of the election of Ogle Robert Gowan, MPP, Leeds North & Grenville North, in room of Basil Rorison Church, deceased. |

Leeds South	Benjamin Tett	Feb. 25, 1858	General Election Dec. 1857 – Jan. 1858.
Lennox & Addington	David Roblin	Mar. 16, 1858	General Election Dec. 1857 – Jan. 1858.
			Lennox & Addington. 1860. 23 Vic., C. 39, Ss. 1, 3. An Act to amend An Act respecting the Territorial Division of Upper Canada. From and after the passing of this Act, the County of Lennox shall be incorporated with the County of Addington, and they shall together form one County, for all purposes whatever, by the name of "the County of Lennox and Addington," -- which County shall be united with the County of Frontenac, as the Counties of Lennox and Addington now are, and shall form the Junior County of the two United Counties of Frontenac, and Lennox and Addington. . . . The Townships of Effingham, Abinger, Ashby and Denbigh, shall be added to and form part of the County of Addington, for all purposes whatever.
Lincoln	Hon. William Hamilton Merritt	May 25, 1858	General Election Dec. 1857 – Jan. 1858.
			Resigned, Sept. 21, 1860. A new election was called.
Lincoln	John Charles Rykert	Mar. 18, 1861*	By-election Date unknown.
			Writ of Election – Oct. 8, 1860. Return of Writ – Nov. 7, 1860. On Mar. 16, 1861, the House was informed of the election of John Charles Rykert, MPP, Lincoln, in room of the Hon. William Hamilton Merritt, resigned.
London (City)	John Carling	Feb. 25, 1858	General Election Dec. 1857 – Jan. 1858.

*   By-election

Constituency	Member	Sworn In	Comments
Middlesex East	Marcus Talbot	Feb. 25, 1858	General Election Dec. 1857 – Jan. 1858.
			On Mar. 26, 1860, the House was informed of the death of Marcus Talbot, MPP, Middlesex East. A new election was called.
Middlesex East	Robert Craik	Mar. 16, 1861*	By-election Date unknown.
			Writ of Election – Apr. 27, 1860. Return of Writ – May 31, 1860. On Mar. 16, 1861, the House was informed of the election of Robert Craik, MPP, Middlesex East, in room of Marcus Talbot, deceased.
Middlesex West	John Scatcherd	Feb. 25, 1858	General Election Dec. 1857 – Jan. 1858.
			Died, June 25, 1858. A new election was called.
Middlesex West	Angus Peter McDonald	Aug. 9, 1858*	By-election Date unknown.
			On Aug. 9, 1858, having presented the Indenture of his Election for the County of Middlesex West, Angus Peter McDonald took his seat.
			On Aug. 9, 1858, the House resolved that in admitting Angus Peter McDonald, MPP, Middlesex West, to take his seat, on the Production of the Duplicate Indenture only, and without the Return of the Indenture to the Clerk of the Crown in Chancery, and the Certificate of the latter Officer, it still recommends a strict adherence to the requirement of producing the usual Certificate.
			Writ of Election – June 28, 1858. Return of Writ – Aug. 5, 1858. On Aug. 16, 1858, the House was informed of the election of Angus Peter McDonald, MPP, Middlesex West, in room of John Scatcherd, deceased.

Niagara (Town)	John Simpson	Feb. 25, 1858	General Election Dec. 1857 – Jan. 1858.
Norfolk	Walker Powell	Feb. 25, 1858	General Election Dec. 1857 – Jan. 1858.
Northumberland East	John Robert Clarke	Feb. 25, 1858	General Election Dec. 1857 – Jan. 1858.
Northumberland West	Hon. Sidney Smith	Feb. 25, 1858*	President of the Executive Council.
			General Election Dec. 1857 – Jan. 1858.
			Resigned prior to the 1st Session, having been appointed Postmaster General of the Province. A new election was called.
			By-election Date unknown.
			Writ of Election – Feb. 2, 1858. Return of Writ – Feb. 22, 1858. The Hon. Sidney Smith, MPP, Northumberland West, was returned as duly elected.
Ontario North	Joseph Gould	Feb. 25, 1858	General Election Dec. 1857 – Jan. 1858.
Ontario South	Hon. Oliver Mowat	Feb. 25, 1858	General Election Dec. 1857 – Jan. 1858.
			On Aug. 4, 1858, the House was informed of the resignation of Oliver Mowat, MPP, Ontario South, who had been appointed Secretary and Registrar of this Province. A new election was called.
		Jan. 29, 1859*	By-election Date unknown.
			Writ of Election – Aug. 6, 1858. Return of Writ – Sept. 4, 1858. On Jan. 28, 1859, the House was informed of the election of the Hon. Oliver Mowat, MPP, Ontario South, who was returned as duly elected.
Ottawa (City)	Richard William Scott	Feb. 25, 1858	General Election Dec. 1857 – Jan. 1858.
Oxford North	George Brown	Feb. 25, 1858	General Election Dec. 1857 – Jan. 1858.
			On Apr. 19, 1858, George Brown, Member for both the County of Oxford North and the City of Toronto, chose to serve for the City of

* By-election

Constituency	Member	Sworn In	Comments
Oxford North — *Continued*			Toronto. A new election was called for the County of Oxford North.
Oxford North	William McDougall	May 14, 1858*	By-election Date unknown.
			On May 14, 1858, having presented the Indenture of his Election for the County of Oxford North, William McDougall took his seat.
			On May 14, 1858, the House resolved that in admitting William McDougall, MPP, Oxford North, to take his seat, on the production of the Duplicate Indenture only, and without the Return of the Indenture to the Clerk of the Crown in Chancery, and the Certificate of the latter Officer, it still recommends a strict adherence to the requirement of producing the usual Certificate.
			Writ of Election – Apr. 20, 1858. Return of Writ – May 14, 1858. On May 27, 1858, the House was informed of the election of William McDougall, MPP, Oxford North, in room of George Brown, resigned.
Oxford South	Skeffington Connor	Feb. 25, 1858	General Election Dec. 1857 – Jan. 1858.
			On Aug. 4, 1858, the House was informed of the resignation of Skeffington Connor, MPP, Oxford South, who had been appointed Solicitor General of Canada West. A new election was called.
		Jan. 29, 1859*	By-election Date unknown.
			Writ of Election – Aug. 6, 1858. Return of Writ – Sept. 7, 1858. On Jan. 29, 1859, the House was informed of the election of Skeffington Connor, MPP, Oxford South, who was returned as duly elected.

Peel	James C. Aikins	Feb. 25, 1858	General Election Dec. 1857 – Jan. 1858.
Perth	Thomas Mayne Daly	Feb. 25, 1858	General Election Dec. 1857 – Jan. 1858.
Peterborough	Thomas Short	Feb. 25, 1858	General Election Dec. 1857 – Jan. 1858.
			Peterborough. 1858. 22 Vic., C. 14, S. 2. An Act to annex certain new Townships to the Counties of Victoria and Peterborough and the North Riding of the County of Hastings. From and after the passing of this Act the said Townships of Snowdon, Minden, Stanhope, Guilford, Dysart, Glamorgan, Monmouth, Dudley, Harburn, Bruton, Harcourt, Cardiff and Chandos, shall be attached to and form part of the County of Peterborough for all purposes whatsoever.
Prescott	Henry Wellesley McCann	Feb. 25, 1858	General Election Dec. 1857 – Jan. 1858.
Prince Edward	Willet Casey Dorland	Feb. 25, 1858	General Election Dec. 1857 – Jan. 1858.
Renfrew	John Lorn McDougall	Did not take seat	General Election Dec. 1857 – Jan. 1858.
			Resigned, having been appointed Associate Coroner for the United Counties of Lanark and Renfrew. A new election was called.
Renfrew	Hon. William Cayley	Mar. 4, 1858*	By-election Date unknown.
			Writ of Election – Feb. 8, 1858. Return of Writ – Mar. 3, 1858. On Mar. 4, 1858, the House was informed of the election of the Hon. William Cayley, MPP, Renfrew, in room of John Lorn McDougall, resigned.
			Renfrew. 1860. 23 Vic., C. 39, S. 4. An Act to amend An Act respecting the Territorial Division of Upper Canada. The Townships of Raglan, Lyndoch, Radcliffe and Brudenell shall be added to and form part of the County of Renfrew, for all purposes whatever.

*   By-election

Constituency	Member	Sworn In	Comments
Russell	George Byron Lyon Fellowes	Feb. 25, 1858	Changed name to Fellowes. For further reference, see, An Act to change the name of George Byron Lyon, and of his family, by adding the name of Fellowes, 19 Vic. 1856 C. 33.
			General Election Dec. 1857. – Jan. 1858.
			Resigned, Nov. 1, 1859. A new election was called.
Russell	John W. Loux	Feb. 28, 1860*	By-election Date unknown.
			Writ of Election – Nov. 18, 1859. Return of Writ – Dec. 21, 1859. On Feb. 28, 1860, the House was informed of the election of John W. Loux, MPP, Russell, in room of George Byron Lyon Fellowes, resigned.
Simcoe North	Angus Morrison	Feb. 25, 1858	General Election Dec. 1857 – Jan. 1858.
			Simcoe North. 1860. 23 Vic., C. 40, S. 3. An Act to amend the Act respecting the representation of the People in the Legislative Assembly, and the Act respecting the Territorial Division of Upper Canada. And whereas by error the Township of "Morrison," in the North Riding of the County of Simcoe, has, in both the said Acts, been called the Township of "Robinson," therefore the enumeration of the Townships, included in the North Riding of the said County, in the tenth sub-section of the eighth section of the Act first above cited, [C. 2 of the Consolidated Statutes for Upper Canada] and the enumeration of the Townships, included in the said County, in the twentieth subsection of the first section of the Act secondly above cited, shall be respectively amended by striking out of each of them the

			word "Robinson" and inserting in lieu thereof the word "Morrison".
Simcoe South	Thomas Roberts Ferguson	Feb. 25, 1858	General Election Dec. 1857 – Jan. 1858.
Stormont	William D. Mattice	Feb. 25, 1858	General Election Dec. 1857 – Jan. 1858.
Toronto (City)	Hon. George Brown	Feb. 25, 1858	General Election Dec. 1857 – Jan. 1858.
			On Apr. 19, 1858, George Brown, Member for both the City of Toronto and the County of Oxford North, chose to serve for the City of Toronto. A new election was called for the County of Oxford North.
			On Aug. 4, 1858, the House was informed of the resignation of George Brown, MPP, Toronto (City), who had been appointed Inspector General of this Province. A new election was called.
		Jan. 29, 1859*	By-election Date unknown.
			Writ of Election – Aug. 6, 1858. Return of Writ – Sept. 1, 1858. On Jan. 29, 1859, the House was informed of the election of the Hon. George Brown, MPP, Toronto (City), who was returned as duly elected.
Toronto (City)	John Beverley Robinson, Jr.	Feb. 25, 1858	General Election Dec. 1857 – Jan. 1858.
Victoria	John Cameron	Feb. 25, 1858	General Election Dec. 1857 – Jan. 1858.
			Victoria. 1858. 22 Vic., C. 14, S. 1. An Act to annex certain new Townships to the Counties of Victoria and Peterborough and the North Riding of the County of Hastings. From and after the passing of this Act the said Townships of Carden, Dalton, Ryde, Draper, Macaulay, Digby, Longford, Oakley, Lutterworth, Anson, Hindon and Laxton, shall be attached to and

* By-election

Constituency	Member	Sworn In	Comments
Victoria — *Continued*			form part of the said County of Victoria for all purposes whatsoever.
Waterloo North	Hon. Michael Hamilton Foley	Feb. 25, 1858	General Election Dec. 1857 – Jan. 1858.
			On Aug. 4, 1858, the House was informed of the resignation of Michael Hamilton Foley, MPP, Waterloo North, who had been appointed Postmaster General of this Province. A new election was called.
		Jan. 29, 1859*	By-election Date unknown.
			Writ of Election – Aug. 6, 1858. Return of Writ – Aug. 23, 1858. On Jan. 29, 1859, the House was informed of the election of the Hon. Michael Hamilton Foley, MPP, Waterloo North, who was returned as duly elected.
			Waterloo North. 1860. 23 Vic., C. 40, S. 1. An Act to amend the Act respecting the representation of the People in the Legislative Assembly, and the Act respecting the Territorial Division of Upper Canada. The second paragraph of sub-section number thirteenth of the eighth section of Chapter two of the Consolidated Statutes of Canada, is hereby amended so as to read as follows: "The North Riding shall consist of the Townships of North Waterloo, Woolwich and Wellesley, the Town of Berlin and the Village of Waterloo."
Waterloo South	William Scott	Feb. 25, 1858	General Election Dec. 1857 – Jan. 1858.
Welland	Gilbert McMicken	Feb. 25, 1858	General Election Dec. 1857 – Jan. 1858.
Wellington North	Charles Allan	Feb. 25, 1858	General Election Dec. 1857 – Jan. 1858.
			On July 14, 1858, the election of Charles Allan, MPP, Wellington North, was declared void. A new election was called.

		Did not take seat	By-election Date unknown.
			Writ of Election – July 16, 1858. Return of Writ – Aug. 21, 1858. On Jan. 29, 1859, the House was informed of the election of Charles Allan, MPP, Wellington North, who had been returned as duly elected.
			Died, Jan. 13, 1859. A new election was called.
Wellington North	James Ross	Feb. 24, 1859*	By-election Date unknown.
			On Feb. 24, 1859, having presented the Indenture of his Election for the County of Wellington North, James Ross took his seat.
			On Feb. 24, 1859, the House resolved that in admitting James Ross, MPP, Wellington North, to take his seat on the production of the Duplicate Indenture only, and without the Return of the Indenture to the Clerk of the Crown in Chancery, and the Certificate of the latter Officer, it still recommends a strict adherence to the requirement of producing the usual Certificate.
			Writ of Election – Jan. 27, 1859. Return of Writ – Feb. 23, 1859. On Feb. 28, 1859, the House was informed of the election of James Ross, MPP, Wellington North, in room of Charles Allan, deceased.
Wellington South	David Stirton	Feb. 25, 1858	General Election Dec. 1857 – Jan. 1858.
Wentworth North	William Notman	Feb. 25, 1858	General Election Dec. 1857 – Jan. 1858.
Wentworth South	Joseph Rymal	Feb. 25, 1858	General Election Dec. 1857 – Jan. 1858.
York East	Amos Wright	Feb. 25, 1858	General Election Dec. 1857 – Jan. 1858.

*   By-election

Constituency	Member	Sworn In	Comments
York North	Joseph Hartman	Feb. 25, 1858	General Election Dec. 1857 – Jan. 1858. On Feb. 28, 1860, the House was informed of the death of Joseph Hartman, MPP, York North. A new election was called.
York North	Adam Wilson	Feb. 29, 1860*	By-election Date unknown. Writ of Election – Dec. 19, 1859. Return of Writ – Jan. 14, 1860. On Feb. 28, 1860, the House was informed of the election of Adam Wilson, MPP, York North, in room of Joseph Hartman, deceased.
York West	William Pearce Howland	Feb. 25, 1858	General Election Dec. 1857 – Jan. 1858.

*　By-election

LEGISLATURES OF THE PROVINCE OF CANADA
(Canada West)
7th Legislature

General Election June – July, 1861

Sessions of the Seventh Legislature of the Province of Canada: Mar. 20, 1862 – May 12, 1863

First: Mar. 20, 1862 – June 9, 1862.
Second: Feb. 12, 1863 – May 12, 1863.

Alphabetical List of Members

Member	Constituency	Sworn In	Comments
Hon. Joseph Edouard Turcotte	Three Rivers (City) (Canada East)	Mar. 20, 1862	On Mar. 20, 1862, the Hon. George Etienne Cartier, MPP, Montreal East (Canada East), proposed Joseph Edouard Turcotte, MPP, Three Rivers (City) (Canada East) as Speaker. Seconded and resolved. Mar. 20, 1862 – Date took chair.
William Anderson, Jr.	Prince Edward	Mar. 20, 1862	
Samuel Ault	Stormont	Mar. 20, 1862	
Robert Bell	Lanark North	Mar. 20, 1862	
Robert Bell	Russell	Mar. 20, 1862	
George Benjamin	Hastings North	Mar. 20, 1862	
James Lyons Biggar	Northumberland East	Mar. 20, 1862	
John Young Bown	Brant East	Mar. 20, 1862	
Hon. George Brown	Oxford South	Apr. 13, 1863*	Writ of Election – Feb. 9, 1863. Return of Writ – Mar. 9, 1863. On Mar. 16, 1863, the House was informed of the election of the Hon. George Brown, MPP, Oxford South, in room of Skeffington Connor, resigned.
Isaac Buchanan	Hamilton (City)	Apr. 29, 1862	

Leonidas Burwell	Elgin East	Mar. 20, 1862	
Hon. John Hillyard Cameron	Peel	Mar. 20, 1862	
Matthew Crooks Cameron	Ontario North	Mar. 27, 1862	
Hon. John Carling	London (City)	Mar. 20, 1862	On Mar. 27, 1862, the House was informed of the resignation of the Hon. John Carling, MPP, London (City), who had been appointed Receiver General. A new election was called.
		Apr. 24, 1862*	Writ of Election – Mar. 27, 1862. Return of Writ – Apr. 7, 1862. On Apr. 24, 1862, the House was informed of the election of the Hon. John Carling, MPP, London (City), who was returned as duly elected.
William Clarke	Wellington North	Mar. 31, 1862	
James Cockburn	Northumberland West	Mar. 20, 1862	
Skeffington Connor	Oxford South	Mar. 20, 1862	On Feb. 12, 1863, the House was informed of the resignation of Skeffington Connor, MPP, Oxford South, who had been appointed Puisné Judge in the Court of Queen's Bench in Canada West. A new election was called.
James Cowan	Waterloo South	Mar. 20, 1862	
John Crawford	Toronto East	Mar. 24, 1862	
Thomas Mayne Daly	Perth	Feb. 13, 1863*	Writ of Election – June 6, 1862. Return of Writ – July 3, 1862. On Feb. 12, 1862, the House was informed of the election of Thomas Mayne Daly, MPP, Perth, in room of the Hon. Michael Hamilton Foley, resigned.
James Dickson	Huron & Bruce	Mar. 20, 1862	
James Wicks Dunsford	Victoria	Mar. 20, 1862	
Thomas Roberts Ferguson	Simcoe South	Mar. 20, 1862	

*   By-election

Member	Constituency	Sworn In	Comments
Hon. Michael Hamilton Foley	Perth	Mar. 20, 1862	On May 31, 1862, the House was informed of the resignation of the Hon. Michael Hamilton Foley, MPP, Perth, who had been appointed Postmaster General of this Province. A new election was called.
Hon. Michael Hamilton Foley	Waterloo North	Mar. 20, 1862	On May 27, 1862, the House was informed of the resignation of the Hon. Michael Hamilton Foley, MPP, Waterloo North, who had been appointed Postmaster General of this Province. A new election was called.
		Feb. 12, 1863*	Writ of Election – May 27, 1862. Return of Writ – June 9, 1862. On Feb. 12, 1863, the House was informed of the election of the Hon. Michael Hamilton Foley, MPP, Waterloo North, who was returned as duly elected.
Michael Harcourt	Haldimand	Mar. 20, 1862	
Frederick William Haultain	Peterborough	Mar. 27, 1862	
Augustus F. Hooper	Lennox & Addington	Mar. 20, 1862	
Hon. William Pearce Howland	York West	Mar. 20, 1862	On May 26, 1862, the House was informed of the resignation of William Pearce Howland, MPP, York West, who had been appointed Minister of Finance of this Province. A new election was called.
		Feb. 26, 1863*	Writ of Election – May 27, 1862. Return of Writ – June 12, 1862. On Feb. 12, 1863, the House was informed of the election of the Hon. William Pearce Howland, MPP, York West, who was returned as duly elected.
George Jackson	Grey	Mar. 20, 1862	
Francis Jones	Leeds North & Grenville North	Mar. 20, 1862	
George Macbeth	Elgin West	Mar. 20, 1862	On Feb. 23, 1863, the election of George

Macbeth, MPP, Elgin West, was declared void. John Scoble was duly elected at the Elgin West General Election.

Donald Alexander Macdonald	Glengarry	Mar. 20, 1862	
Hon. John Alexander Macdonald	Kingston (City)	Mar. 20, 1862	
Hon. John Sandfield Macdonald	Cornwall (Town)	Mar. 20, 1862	On May 26, 1862, the House was informed of the resignation of the Hon. John Sandfield Macdonald, MPP, Cornwall (Town), who had been appointed Attorney General of Canada West. A new election was called.
		Feb. 12, 1863*	Writ of Election – May 27, 1862. Return of Writ – June 14, 1862. On Feb. 12, 1863, the House was informed of the election of the Hon. John Sandfield Macdonald, MPP, Cornwall (Town), who was returned as duly elected.
Alexander Mackenzie	Lambton	Mar. 20, 1862	Also listed as MacKenzie.
Henry Wellesley McCann	Prescott	Mar. 20, 1862	
Hon. William McDougall	Oxford North	Mar. 20, 1862	On May 26, 1862, the House was informed of the resignation of William McDougall, MPP, Oxford North, who had been appointed Commissioner of Crown Lands of this Province. A new election was called.
		Feb. 12, 1863*	Writ of Election – May 27, 1862. Return of Writ – June 14, 1862. On Feb. 12, 1863, the House was informed of the election of the Hon. William McDougall, MPP, Oxford North, who was returned as duly elected.
Archibald McKellar	Kent	Mar. 20, 1862	
Daniel McLachlin	Renfrew	Mar. 20, 1862	
Alexander Morris	Lanark South	Mar. 20, 1862	
Angus Morrison	Simcoe North	Mar. 20, 1862	
James Morton	Frontenac	Mar. 20, 1862	

* By-election

Member	Constituency	Sworn In	Comments
Hon. Oliver Mowat	Ontario South	Mar. 20, 1862	
Henry Munro	Durham West	Mar. 20, 1862	
William Notman	Wentworth North	Mar. 20, 1862	
John O'Connor, Jr.	Essex	Apr. 15, 1863*	Writ of Election – Mar. 10, 1863. Return of Writ – Apr. 7, 1863. On Apr. 13, 1863, the House was informed of the election of John O'Connor, Jr., MPP, Essex, in room of Arthur Rankin, whose election was declared void.
William Patrick	Grenville South	Mar. 20, 1862	
Hon. Maurice Berkeley Portman	Middlesex East	Mar. 20, 1862	
William Frederick Powell	Carleton	Mar. 20, 1862	
Arthur Rankin	Essex	Mar. 20, 1862	On Mar. 9, 1863, the election of Arthur Rankin, MPP, Essex, was declared void. A new election was called.
Hon. John Beverley Robinson, Jr.	Toronto West	Mar. 20, 1862	On Mar. 27, 1862, the House was informed of the resignation of the Hon. John Beverley Robinson, Jr., MPP, Toronto West, who had been appointed President of the Committees of the Executive Council. A new election was called.
		Apr. 28, 1862*	Writ of Election – Mar. 27, 1862. Return of Writ – Apr. 22, 1862. On Apr. 24, 1862, the House was informed of the election of the Hon. John Beverley Robinson, Jr., MPP, Toronto West, who was returned as duly elected.
John Sylvester Ross	Dundas	Mar. 20, 1862	
William Ryerson	Brant West	Mar. 20, 1862	
John Charles Rykert	Lincoln	Mar. 20, 1862	
Joseph Rymal	Wentworth South	Mar. 20, 1862	

Thomas Scatcherd	Middlesex West	Mar. 20, 1862	
John Scoble	Elgin West	Feb. 23, 1863	On Feb. 23, 1863, the House was informed that John Scoble was duly elected at the Elgin West General Election, in room of George Macbeth, whose election was declared void.
Richard William Scott	Ottawa (City)	Mar. 20, 1862	
Hon. George Sherwood	Brockville (Town)	Mar. 20, 1862	
John Simpson	Niagara (Town)	Mar. 20, 1862	
John Shuter Smith	Durham East	Mar. 20, 1862	On Apr. 30, 1863, the election of John Shuter Smith, MPP, Durham East, was declared void. A new writ was issued on May 5, 1863. [House was prorogued on May 12, 1863. No By-election was held.]
David Stirton	Wellington South	Mar. 20, 1862	
Thomas Clark Street	Welland	Mar. 20, 1862	
Benjamin Tett	Leeds South	Mar. 20, 1862	
Lewis Wallbridge	Hastings South	Mar. 20, 1862	
Aquila Walsh	Norfolk	Mar. 20, 1862	
John White	Halton	Mar. 20, 1862	
Hon. Adam Wilson	York North	Mar. 20, 1862	On May 26, 1862, the House was informed of the resignation of Adam Wilson, MPP, York North, who had been appointed Solicitor General. A new election was called.
		Feb. 12, 1863*	Writ of Election – May 27, 1862. Return of Writ – June 13, 1862. On Feb. 12, 1863, the House was informed of the election of the Hon. Adam Wilson, MPP, York North, who was returned as duly elected.
Amos Wright	York East	Mar. 20, 1862	

* By-election

Alphabetical List of Constituencies
7th Legislature: Mar. 20, 1862 – May 12, 1863.

Constituency	Member	Sworn In	Comments
Brant East	John Young Bown	Mar. 20, 1862	General Election June – July 1861.
Brant West	William Ryerson	Mar. 20, 1862	General Election June – July 1861.
Brockville (Town)	Hon. George Sherwood	Mar. 20, 1862	General Election June – July 1861.
Carleton	William Frederick Powell	Mar. 20, 1862	General Election June – July 1861.
Cornwall (Town)	Hon. John Sandfield Macdonald	Mar. 20, 1862	General Election June – July 1861.
			On May 26, 1862, the House was informed of the resignation of the Hon. John Sandfield Macdonald, MPP, Cornwall (Town), who had been appointed Attorney General of Canada West. A new election was called.
		Feb. 12, 1863*	By-election Date unknown.
			Writ of Election – May 27, 1862. Return of Writ – June 14, 1862. On Feb. 12, 1863, the House was informed of the election of the Hon. John Sandfield Macdonald, MPP, Cornwall (Town), who was returned as duly elected.
Dundas	John Sylvester Ross	Mar. 20, 1862	General Election June – July 1861.
Durham East	John Shuter Smith	Mar. 20, 1862	General Election June – July 1861.
			On Apr. 30, 1863, the election of John Shuter Smith, MPP, Durham East, was declared void. A new writ was issued on May 5, 1863. [House was prorogued on May 12, 1863. No By-election was held.]
Durham West	Henry Munro	Mar. 20, 1862	General Election June – July 1861.
Elgin East	Leonidas Burwell	Mar. 20, 1862	General Election June – July 1861.
Elgin West	George Macbeth	Mar. 20, 1862	General Election June – July 1861.
			On Feb. 23, 1863, the election of George Macbeth, MPP, Elgin West, was declared void.

			John Scoble was duly elected at the Elgin West General Election.
Elgin West	John Scoble	Feb. 23, 1863	General Election June – July 1861.
			On Feb. 23, 1863, the House was informed that John Scoble was duly elected at the Elgin West General Election, in room of George Macbeth, whose election was declared void.
Essex	Arthur Rankin	Mar. 20, 1862	General Election June – July 1861.
			On Mar. 9, 1863, the election of Arthur Rankin, MPP, Essex, was declared void. A new election was called.
Essex	John O'Connor, Jr.	Apr. 15, 1863*	By-election Date unknown.
			Writ of Election – Mar. 10, 1863. Return of Writ – Apr. 7, 1863. On Apr. 13, 1863, the House was informed of the election of John O'Connor, Jr., MPP, Essex, in room of Arthur Rankin, whose election was declared void.
Frontenac	James Morton	Mar. 20, 1862	General Election June – July 1861.
Glengarry	Donald Alexander Macdonald (by acclamation)	Mar. 20, 1862	General Election June – July 1861.
Grenville South	William Patrick	Mar. 20, 1862	General Election June – July 1861.
Grey	George Jackson	Mar. 20, 1862	General Election June – July 1861.
Haldimand	Michael Harcourt	Mar. 20, 1862	General Election June – July 1861.
Halton	John White	Mar. 20, 1862	General Election June – July 1861.
Hamilton (City)	Isaac Buchanan	Apr. 29, 1862	General Election June – July 1861.
Hastings North	George Benjamin	Mar. 20, 1862	General Election June – July 1861.
Hastings South	Lewis Wallbridge	Mar. 20, 1862	General Election June – July 1861.
Huron & Bruce	James Dickson	Mar. 20, 1862	General Election June – July 1861.
Kent	Archibald McKellar	Mar. 20, 1862	General Election June – July 1861.

* By-election

Constituency	Member	Sworn In	Comments
Kingston (City)	Hon. John Alexander Macdonald	Mar. 20, 1862	General Election June – July 1861.
Lambton	Alexander Mackenzie	Mar. 20, 1862	Also listed as MacKenzie. General Election June – July 1861.
Lanark North	Robert Bell (by acclamation)	Mar. 20, 1862	General Election June – July 1861.
Lanark South	Alexander Morris	Mar. 20, 1862	General Election June – July 1861.
Leeds North & Grenville North	Francis Jones	Mar. 20, 1862	General Election June – July 1861.
Leeds South	Benjamin Tett	Mar. 20, 1862	General Election June – July 1861.
Lennox & Addington	Augustus F. Hooper	Mar. 20, 1862	General Election June – July 1861.
Lincoln	John Charles Rykert (by acclamation)	Mar. 20, 1862	General Election June – July 1861.
London (City)	Hon. John Carling (by acclamation)	Mar. 20, 1862	General Election June – July 1861. On Mar. 27, 1862, the House was informed of the resignation of the Hon. John Carling, MPP, London (City), who had been appointed Receiver General. A new election was called.
		Apr. 24, 1862*	By-election Date unknown. Writ of Election – Mar. 27, 1862. Return of Writ – Apr. 7, 1862. On Apr. 24, 1862, the House was informed of the election of the Hon. John Carling, MPP, London (City), who was returned as duly elected.
Middlesex East	Hon. Maurice Berkeley Portman	Mar. 20, 1862	General Election June – July 1861.
Middlesex West	Thomas Scatcherd	Mar. 20, 1862	General Election June – July 1861.
Niagara (Town)	John Simpson	Mar. 20, 1862	General Election June – July 1861.
Norfolk	Aquila Walsh	Mar. 20, 1862	General Election June – July 1861.

Northumberland East	James Lyons Biggar	Mar. 20, 1862	General Election June – July 1861.
Northumberland West	James Cockburn	Mar. 20, 1862	General Election June – July 1861.
Ontario North	Matthew Crooks Cameron	Mar. 27, 1862	General Election June – July 1861.
Ontario South	Hon. Oliver Mowat	Mar. 20, 1862	General Election June – July 1861.
Ottawa (City)	Richard William Scott (by acclamation)	Mar. 20, 1862	General Election June – July 1861.
Oxford North	Hon. William McDougall	Mar. 20, 1862	General Election June – July 1861.
			On May 26, 1862, the House was informed of the resignation of William McDougall, MPP, Oxford North, who had been appointed Commissioner of Crown Lands of this Province. A new election was called.
		Feb. 12, 1863*	By-election Date unknown.
			Writ of Election – May 27, 1862. Return of Writ – June 14, 1862. On Feb. 12, 1863, the House was informed of the election of the Hon. William McDougall, MPP, Oxford North, who was returned as duly elected.
Oxford South	Skeffington Connor	Mar. 20, 1862	General Election June – July 1861.
			On Feb. 12, 1863, the House was informed of the resignation of Skeffington Connor, MPP, Oxford South, who had been appointed Puisné Judge in the Court of Queen's Bench in Canada West. A new election was called.
Oxford South	Hon. George Brown	Apr. 13, 1863*	By-election Date unknown.
			Writ of Election – Feb. 9, 1863. Return of Writ – Mar. 9, 1863. On Mar. 16, 1863, the House was informed of the election of the Hon. George Brown, MPP, Oxford South, in room of Skeffington Connor, resigned.

* By-election

Constituency	Member	Sworn In	Comments
Peel	Hon. John Hillyard Cameron	Mar. 20, 1862	General Election June – July 1861.
Perth	Hon. Michael Hamilton Foley	Mar. 20, 1862	General Election June – July 1861.
			On May 31, 1862, the House was informed of the resignation of the Hon. Michael Hamilton Foley, MPP, Perth, who had been appointed Postmaster General of this Province. A new election was called.
Perth	Thomas Mayne Daly	Feb. 13, 1863*	By-election Date unknown.
			Writ of Election –. June 6, 1862. Return of Writ – July 3, 1862. On Feb. 12, 1862, the House was informed of the election of Thomas Mayne Daly, MPP, Perth, in room of the Hon. Michael Hamilton Foley, resigned.
Peterborough	Frederick William Haultain	Mar. 27, 1862	General Election June – July 1861.
Prescott	Henry Wellesley McCann	Mar. 20, 1862	General Election June – July 1861.
Prince Edward	William Anderson, Jr.	Mar. 20, 1862	General Election June – July 1861.
Renfrew	Daniel McLachlin	Mar. 20, 1862	General Election June – July 1861.
Russell	Robert Bell	Mar. 20, 1862	General Election June – July 1861.
Simcoe North	Angus Morrison	Mar. 20, 1862	General Election June – July 1861.
Simcoe South	Thomas Roberts Ferguson	Mar. 20, 1862	General Election June – July 1861.
Stormont	Samuel Ault	Mar. 20, 1862	General Election June – July 1861.
Three Rivers (City) (Canada East)	Hon. Joseph Edouard Turcotte	Mar. 20, 1862	General Election June – July 1861.
			On Mar. 20, 1862, the Hon. George Etienne Cartier, MPP, Montreal East (Canada East), proposed Joseph Edouard Turcotte, MPP, Three Rivers (City) (Canada East) as Speaker. Seconded and resolved. Mar. 20, 1862 – Date took chair.

| Toronto East | John Crawford | Mar. 24, 1862 | Toronto East. 1860. 23 Vic., C. 1, Ss. 3(2), 4. An Act to amend the Act respecting the Representation of the People in the Legislative Assembly. The City of Toronto shall be divided into two Electoral Divisions, to be called respectively [West Toronto and East Toronto]: East Toronto, which shall consist of all that part of the said City, lying East of the said central line of Yonge Street. Each of the said Electoral Divisions shall be represented in the Legislative Assembly by one Member, and shall be dealt with as a separate City Electoral Division, under chapter six of the Consolidated Statutes of Canada, subject to the provisions of this Act.

General Election June – July 1861. |
| Toronto West | Hon. John Beverley Robinson, Jr. | Mar. 20, 1862 | Toronto West. 1860. 23 Vic., C. 1, Ss. 3(1), 4. An Act to amend the Act respecting the Representation of the People in the Legislative Assembly. The City of Toronto shall be divided into two Electoral Divisions, to be called respectively [West Toronto and East Toronto]: West Toronto shall consist of all that part of the said City, lying West of the Centre line of Yonge Street; . . . Each of the said Electoral Divisions shall be represented in the Legislative Assembly by one Member, and shall be dealt with as a separate City Electoral Division, under chapter six of the Consolidated Statutes of Canada, subject to the provisions of this Act.

General Election June – July 1861.

On Már. 27, 1862, the House was informed of the resignation of the Hon. John Beverley Robinson, Jr., MPP, Toronto West, who had been appointed President of the Committees of the Executive Council. A new election was called. |

*   By-election

Constituency	Member	Sworn In	Comments
Toronto West — *Continued*		Apr. 28, 1862*	By-election Date unknown.
			Writ of Election – Mar. 27, 1862. Return of Writ – Apr. 22, 1862. On Apr. 24, 1862, the House was informed of the election of the Hon. John Beverley Robinson, Jr., MPP, Toronto West, who was returned as duly elected.
Victoria	James Wicks Dunsford	Mar. 20, 1862	General Election June – July 1861.
Waterloo North	Hon. Michael Hamilton Foley	Mar. 20, 1862	General Election June – July 1861.
			On May 27, 1862, the House was informed of the resignation of the Hon. Michael Hamilton Foley, MPP, Waterloo North, who had been appointed Postmaster General of this Province. A new election was called.
		Feb. 12, 1863*	By-election Date unknown.
			Writ of Election – May 27, 1862. Return of Writ – June 9, 1862. On Feb. 12, 1863, the House was informed of the election of the Hon. Michael Hamilton Foley, MPP, Waterloo North, who was returned as duly elected.
Waterloo South	James Cowan	Mar. 20, 1862	General Election June – July 1861.
Welland	Thomas Clark Street	Mar. 20, 1862	General Election June – July 1861.
Wellington North	William Clarke	Mar. 31, 1862	General Election June – July 1861.
Wellington South	David Stirton (by acclamation)	Mar. 20, 1862	General Election June – July 1861.
Wentworth North	William Notman	Mar. 20, 1862	General Election June – July 1861.
Wentworth South	Joseph Rymal	Mar. 20, 1862	General Election June – July 1861.
York East	Amos Wright	Mar. 20, 1862	General Election June – July 1861.
York North	Hon. Adam Wilson	Mar. 20, 1862	General Election June – July 1861.
			On May 26, 1862, the House was informed of

			the resignation of Adam Wilson, MPP, York North, who had been appointed Solicitor General. A new election was called.
		Feb. 12, 1863*	By-election Date unknown.
			Writ of Election – May 27, 1862. Return of Writ – June 13, 1862. On Feb. 12, 1863, the House was informed of the election of the Hon. Adam Wilson, MPP, York North, who was returned as duly elected.
York West	Hon. William Pearce Howland	Mar. 20, 1862	General Election June – July 1861.
			On May 26, 1862, the House was informed of the resignation of William Pearce Howland, MPP, York West, who had been appointed Minister of Finance of this Province. A new election was called.
		Feb. 26, 1863*	By-election Date unknown.
			Writ of Election – May 27, 1862. Return of Writ – June 12, 1862. On Feb. 12, 1863, the House was informed of the election of the Hon. William Pearce Howland, MPP, York West, who was returned as duly elected.

*   By-election

LEGISLATURES OF THE PROVINCE OF CANADA
(Canada West)
8th Legislature

General Election   June-July 1863

Sessions of the Eighth Legislature of the Province of Canada: Aug. 13, 1863 – Aug. 15, 1866

First:	Aug. 13, 1863 – Oct. 15, 1863.
Second:	Feb. 19, 1864 – June 30, 1864.
Third:	Jan. 19, 1865 – Mar. 18, 1865.
Fourth:	Aug. 8, 1865 – Sept. 18, 1865.
Fifth:	June 8, 1866 – Aug. 15, 1866.

Alphabetical List of Members

Member	Constituency	Sworn In	Comments
Samuel Ault	Stormont	Aug. 13, 1863	
Robert Bell	Lanark North	Aug. 13, 1863	Resigned, Oct. 4, 1864. A new election was called.
Robert Bell	Russell	Aug. 13, 1863	
James Lyons Biggar	Northumberland East	Aug. 13, 1863	
Isaac Erb Bowman	Waterloo North	May 4, 1864*	On May 4, 1864, having presented the Indenture of his election for the County of Waterloo North, Isaac Erb Bowman took his seat.
			On May 4, 1864, the House resolved that in admitting Isaac Erb Bowman, MPP, Waterloo North, to take his seat, on the production of the Duplicate Indenture only, and without the Return of the Indenture to the Clerk of the Crown in Chancery, and the Certificate of the latter Officer, it still recommends a strict adherence to the requirement of producing the usual Certificate.

			Writ of Election – Mar. 31, 1864. Return of Writ – Apr. 26, 1864. On May 11, 1864, the House was informed of the election of Isaac Erb Bowman, MPP, Waterloo North, in room of the Hon. Michael Hamilton Foley, resigned.
John Young Bown	Brant East	Aug. 13, 1863	
Hon. George Brown	Oxford South	Aug. 13, 1863	On Jan. 19, 1865, the House was informed of the resignation of the Hon. George Brown, MPP, Oxford South, who was appointed President of the Committees of the Executive Council. A new election had been called.
		Jan. 19, 1865*	Writ of Election – June 30, 1864. Return of Writ – July 11, 1864. On Jan. 19, 1865, the House was informed of the election of the Hon. George Brown, MPP, Oxford South, who was returned as duly elected.
Hon. Isaac Buchanan	Hamilton (City)	Sept. 9, 1863	On Mar. 30, 1864, the House was informed of the resignation of Isaac Buchanan, MPP, Hamilton (City), who had been appointed President of the Executive Council of the Province of Canada. A new election was called.
		May 3, 1864*	Writ of Election – Mar. 31, 1864. Return of Writ – Apr. 29, 1864. On May 3, 1864, the House was informed of the election of the Hon. Isaac Buchanan, MPP, Hamilton (City), who was returned as duly elected.
			Resigned, Jan. 17, 1865. A new election was called.
Leonidas Burwell	Elgin East	Aug. 13, 1863	
Hon. John Hillyard Cameron	Peel	Aug. 13, 1863	
Malcolm Crooks Cameron	Ontario North	Jan. 31, 1865*	Writ of Election.– July 5, 1864. Return of Writ – July 30, 1864. On Jan. 19, 1865, the House

* By-election

Member	Constituency	Sworn In	Comments
Malcolm Crooks Cameron — *Continued*			was informed of the election of Matthew Crooks Cameron, MPP, Ontario North, in room of the Hon. William McDougall, resigned.
Hon. John Carling	London (City)	Aug. 13, 1863	
Richard John Cartwright	Lennox & Addington	Aug. 13, 1863	
Fitzwilliam Henry Chambers	Brockville (Town)	Aug. 13, 1863	
Hon. James Cockburn	Northumberland West	Aug. 19, 1863	On Mar. 30, 1864, the House was informed of the resignation of James Cockburn, MPP, Northumberland West, who had been appointed Solicitor General of Canada West. A new election was called.
		May 3, 1864*	Writ of Election – Mar. 31, 1864. Return of Writ – Apr. 23, 1864. On May 3, 1864, the House was informed of the election of the Hon. James Cockburn, MPP, Northumberland West, who was returned as duly elected.
Wilson Seymour Conger	Peterborough	Aug. 13, 1863	On Jan. 19, 1865, the House was informed of the death of Wilson Seymour Conger, MPP, Peterborough. A new election had been called.
James Cowan	Waterloo South	Aug. 13, 1863	
Joseph M. Currier	Ottawa (City)	Aug. 13, 1863	
James Dickson	Huron & Bruce	Aug. 13, 1863	
James Wicks Dunsford	Victoria	Aug. 13, 1863	
Thomas Robert Ferguson	Simcoe South	Aug. 13, 1863	
William Ferguson	Frontenac	Aug. 13, 1863	
Hon. Michael Hamilton Foley	Waterloo North	Aug. 13, 1863	On Mar. 30, 1864, the House was informed of the resignation of the Hon. Michael Hamilton Foley, MPP, Waterloo North, who had been

			appointed Postmaster General of the Province of Canada. A new election was called.
Thomas Nicholson Gibbs	Ontario South	Jan. 31, 1865*	Writ of Election – Dec. 28, 1864. Return of Writ – Jan. 18, 1865. On Jan. 24, 1865, the House was informed of the election of Thomas Nicholson Gibbs, MPP, Ontario South, in room of the Hon. Oliver Mowat, resigned.
Frederick William Haultain	Peterborough	Jan. 19, 1865*	Writ of Election – Aug. 11, 1864. Return of Writ – Sept. 14, 1864. On Jan. 19, 1865, the House was informed of the election of Frederick William Haultain, MPP, Peterborough, in room of Wilson Seymour Conger, deceased.
Thomas Higginson	Prescott	Aug. 13, 1863	
Hon. William Pearce Howland	York West	Aug. 13, 1863	On Jan. 19, 1865, the House was informed of the resignation of the Hon. William Pearce Howland, MPP, York West, who had been appointed Postmaster General. A new election had been called.
		Jan. 19, 1865*	Writ of Election – Nov. 29, 1864. Return of Writ – Dec. 14, 1864. On Jan. 19, 1865, the House was informed of the election of the Hon. William Pearce Howland, MPP, York West, who was returned as duly elected.
George Jackson	Grey	Aug. 13, 1863	
David Ford Jones	Leeds South	Feb. 22, 1864*	Writ of Election – Jan. 4, 1864. Return of Writ – Jan. 30, 1864. On Feb. 19, 1864, the House was informed of the election of David Ford Jones, MPP, Leeds South, in room of the Hon. Albert Norton Richards, resigned.
Francis Jones	Leeds North & Grenville North	Aug. 13, 1863	

*   By-election

Member	Constituency	Sworn In	Comments
Hon. John Alexander Macdonald	Kingston (City)	Aug. 13, 1863	On Mar. 30, 1864, the House was informed of the resignation of the Hon. John Alexander Macdonald, MPP, Kingston (City), who had been appointed Attorney General of Canada West. A new election was called.
		May 3, 1864*	Writ of Election – Mar. 31, 1864. Return of Writ – Apr. 11, 1864. On May 3, 1864, the House was informed of the election of the Hon. John Alexander Macdonald, MPP, Kingston (City), who was returned as duly elected.
Hon. John Sandfield Macdonald	Cornwall (Town)	Aug. 13, 1863	
Robert Macfarlane	Perth	Aug. 13, 1863	
Alexander Mackenzie	Lambton	Aug. 13, 1863	
Hope Fleming Mackenzie	Oxford North	Aug. 13, 1863	On June 13, 1866, the House was informed of the death of Hope Fleming Mackenzie, MPP, Oxford North. A new election was called.
Charles Magill	Hamilton (City)	Feb. 27, 1865*	Writ of Election – Jan. 27, 1865. Return of Writ – Feb. 21, 1865. On Feb. 23, 1865, the House was informed of the election of Charles Magill, MPP, Hamilton (City), in room of the Hon. Isaac Buchanan, resigned.
Thomas David McConkey	Simcoe North	Aug. 13, 1863	
Donald Alexander McDonald	Glengarry	Aug. 13, 1863	
John McDonald	Toronto West	Aug. 13, 1863	
Hon. William McDougall	Lanark North	Jan. 19, 1865*	Writ of Election – Oct. 11, 1864. Return of Writ – Nov. 4, 1864. On Jan. 19, 1865, the House was informed of the election of the Hon. William McDougall, MPP, Lanark North, in room of Robert Bell, resigned.

Hon. William McDougall	Ontario North	Aug. 13, 1863	On Jan. 19, 1865, the House was informed of the resignation of the Hon. William McDougall, MPP, Ontario North, who had been appointed Provincial Secretary. A new election had been called.
William McGiverin	Lincoln	Aug. 13, 1863	
Robert McIntyre	Renfrew	Aug. 13, 1863	
Archibald McKellar	Kent	Aug. 13, 1863	
James McMonies	Wentworth North	June 8, 1866*	Writ of Election – Sept. 30, 1865. Return of Writ – Nov. 1, 1865. On June 8, 1866, the House was informed of the election of James McMonies, MPP, Wentworth North, in room of William Notman, deceased.
Alexander Morris	Lanark South	Aug. 13, 1863	
Angus Morrison	Niagara (Town)	Jan. 19, 1865*	Writ of Election – Aug. 17, 1864. Return of Writ – Sept. 7, 1864. On Jan. 19, 1865, the House was informed of the election of Angus Morrison, MPP, Niagara (Town), in room of the Hon. John Simpson, resigned.
Hon. Oliver Mowat	Ontario South	Aug. 13, 1863	On Jan. 19, 1865, the House was informed of the resignation of the Hon. Oliver Mowat, MPP, Ontario South, who had been appointed Postmaster General of this Province. A new election had been called.
		Did not take seat	Writ of Election – July 5, 1864. Return of Writ – July 18, 1864. On Jan. 19, 1865, the House was informed of the election of the Hon. Oliver Mowat, MPP, Ontario South, who was returned as duly elected.
			On Jan. 19, 1865, the House was informed of the resignation of the Hon. Oliver Mowat, MPP, Ontario South, who had been appointed Vice-Chancellor in the Court of Chancery of Canada West. A new election had been called.

* By-election

Member	Constituency	Sworn In	Comments
Henry Munro	Durham West	Aug. 13, 1863	
William Notman	Wentworth North	Aug. 13, 1863	On June 8, 1866, the House was informed of the death of William Notman, MPP, Wentworth North. A new election had been called.
Thomas Oliver	Oxford North	July 17, 1866*	On July 17, 1866, having presented the Indenture of his election for the County of Oxford North, Thomas Oliver took his seat.
			On July 17, 1866, the House resolved that in admitting Thomas Oliver, MPP, Oxford North, to take his seat, on the production of the Duplicate Indenture only, and without the Return of the Indenture to the Clerk of the Crown in Chancery, and the Certificate of the latter Officer, it still recommends a strict adherence to the requirement of producing the usual Certificate.
			Writ of Election – June 20, 1866. Return of Writ – July 14, 1866. On July 23, 1866, the House was informed of the election of Thomas Oliver, MPP, Oxford North, in room of Hope Fleming Mackenzie, deceased.
Thomas Sutherland Parker	Wellington North	Aug. 13, 1863	
William Frederick Powell	Carleton	Aug. 13, 1863	
Arthur Rankin	Essex	May 17, 1864	On May 17, 1864, the House was informed that Arthur Rankin was duly elected at the Essex General Election.
Hon. Albert Norton Richards	Leeds South	Aug. 13, 1863	On Feb. 19, 1864, the House was informed of the resignation of the Hon. Albert Norton Richards, MPP, Leeds South, who had been appointed Solicitor General of Canada West. A new election had been called.

John Sylvester Ross	Dundas	Aug. 13, 1863	
Walter Ross	Prince Edward	Aug. 13, 1863	
Joseph Rymal	Wentworth South	Aug. 13, 1863	
Thomas Scatcherd	Middlesex West	Aug. 13, 1863	
John Scoble	Elgin West	Aug. 13, 1863	
Walter Shanly	Grenville South	Aug. 13, 1863	
Hon. John Simpson	Niagara (Town)	Aug. 13, 1863	On Mar. 30, 1864, the House was informed of the resignation of John Simpson, MPP, Niagara (Town), who had been appointed Secretary and Registrar of the Province of Canada. A new election was called.
		May 3, 1864*	Writ of Election – Mar. 31, 1864. Return of Writ – Apr. 11, 1864. On May 3, 1864, the House was informed of the election of the Hon. John Simpson, MPP, Niagara (Town), who was returned as duly elected.
			On Jan. 19, 1865, the House was informed of the resignation of the Hon. John Simpson, MPP, Niagara (Town), who had been appointed Assistant Auditor. A new election had been called.
Alexander Mortimer Smith	Toronto East	Aug. 13, 1863	
John Shuter Smith	Durham East	Aug. 13, 1863	
David Stirton	Wellington South	Aug. 13, 1863	
Thomas Clark Street	Welland	Aug. 13, 1863	
David Thompson	Haldimand	Aug. 13, 1863	
Hon. Lewis Wallbridge	Hastings South	Aug. 13, 1863	On Aug. 13, 1863, the Hon. John Sandfield Macdonald, MPP, Cornwall (Town), proposed the Hon. Lewis Wallbridge, MPP, Hastings South, as Speaker. Seconded and resolved. Aug. 13, 1863 – Date took chair.

* By-election

Member	Constituency	Sworn In	Comments
Thomas Campbell Wallbridge	Hastings North	Aug. 13, 1863	
Aquila Walsh	Norfolk	Aug. 13, 1863	
James Pearson Wells	York North	Aug. 13, 1863	
John White	Halton	Aug. 13, 1863	
Crowel Willson	Middlesex East	Aug. 13, 1863	
Edmund Burke Wood	Brant West	Aug. 13, 1863	
Amos Wright	York East	Aug. 13, 1863	

Constituency	Member	Sworn In	Comments
Brant East	John Young Bown	Aug. 13, 1863	General Election June – July 1863.
Brant West	Edmund Burke Wood	Aug. 13, 1863	General Election June – July 1863.
Brockville (Town)	Fitzwilliam Henry Chambers	Aug. 13, 1863	General Election June – July 1863.
Carleton	William Frederick Powell	Aug. 13, 1863	General Election June – July 1863.
Cornwall (Town)	Hon. John Sandfield Macdonald (by acclamation)	Aug. 13, 1863	General Election June – July 1863.
Dundas	John Sylvester Ross	Aug. 13, 1863	General Election June – July 1863.
Durham East	John Shuter Smith	Aug. 13, 1863	General Election June – July 1863.
Durham West	Henry Munro	Aug. 13, 1863	General Election June – July 1863.
Elgin East	Leonidas Burwell	Aug. 13, 1863	General Election June – July 1863.
Elgin West	John Scoble	Aug. 13, 1863	General Election June – July 1863.
Essex	Arthur Rankin	May 17, 1864	General Election June – July 1863. On May 17, 1864, the House was informed that Arthur Rankin was duly elected at the Essex General Election.
Frontenac	William Ferguson	Aug. 13, 1863	General Election June – July 1863.
Glengarry	Donald Alexander McDonald (by acclamation)	Aug. 13, 1863	General Election June – July 1863.
Grenville South	Walter Shanly	Aug. 13, 1863	General Election June – July 1863.
Grey	George Jackson	Aug. 13, 1863	General Election June – July 1863.
Haldimand	David Thompson	Aug. 13, 1863	General Election June – July 1863.
Halton	John White	Aug. 13, 1863	General Election June – July 1863.

Hamilton (City)	Hon. Isaac Buchanan (by acclamation)	Sept. 9, 1863	General Election June – July 1863.
			On Mar. 30, 1864, the House was informed of the resignation of Isaac Buchanan, MPP, Hamilton (City), who had been appointed President of the Executive Council of the Province of Canada. A new election was called.
		May 3, 1864*	By-election Date unknown.
			Writ of Election – Mar. 31, 1864. Return of Writ – Apr. 29, 1864. On May 3, 1864, the House was informed of the election of the Hon. Isaac Buchanan, MPP, Hamilton (City), who was returned as duly elected.
			Resigned, Jan. 17, 1865. A new election was called.
Hamilton (City)	Charles Magill	Feb. 27, 1865*	By-election Date unknown.
			Writ of Election – Jan. 27, 1865. Return of Writ – Feb. 21, 1865. On Feb. 23, 1865, the House was informed of the election of Charles Magill, MPP, Hamilton (City), in room of the Hon. Isaac Buchanan, resigned.
Hastings North	Thomas Campbell Wallbridge	Aug. 13, 1863	General Election June – July 1863.
Hastings South	Hon. Lewis Wallbridge (by acclamation)	Aug. 13, 1863	General Election June – July 1863.
			On Aug. 13, 1863, the Hon. John Sandfield Macdonald, MPP, Cornwall (Town), proposed the Hon. Lewis Wallbridge, MPP, Hastings South, as Speaker. Seconded and resolved. Aug. 13, 1863 – Date took chair.
Huron & Bruce	James Dickson (by acclamation)	Aug. 13, 1863	General Election June – July 1863.
Kent	Archibald McKellar	Aug. 13, 1863	General Election June – July 1863.

* By-election

Constituency	Member	Sworn In	Comments
Kingston (City)	Hon. John Alexander Macdonald	Aug. 13, 1863	General Election June – July 1863.
			On Mar. 30, 1864, the House was informed of the resignation of the Hon. John Alexander Macdonald, MPP, Kingston (City), who had been appointed Attorney General of Canada West. A new election was called.
		May 3, 1864*	By-election Date unknown.
			Writ of Election – Mar. 31, 1864. Return of Writ – Apr. 11, 1864. On May 3, 1864, the House was informed of the election of the Hon. John Alexander Macdonald, MPP, Kingston (City), who was returned as duly elected.
Lambton	Alexander Mackenzie (by acclamation)	Aug. 13, 1863	General Election June – July 1863.
Lanark North	Robert Bell	Aug. 13, 1863	General Election June – July 1863.
			Resigned, Oct. 4, 1864. A new election was called.
Lanark North	Hon. William McDougall	Jan. 19, 1865*	By-election Date unknown.
			Writ of Election – Oct. 11, 1864. Return of Writ – Nov. 4, 1864. On Jan. 19, 1865, the House was informed of the election of the Hon. William McDougall, MPP, Lanark North, in room of Robert Bell, resigned.
Lanark South	Alexander Morris	Aug. 13, 1863	General Election June – July 1863.
Leeds North & Grenville North	Francis Jones	Aug. 13, 1863	General Election June – July 1863.
Leeds South	Hon. Albert Norton Richards	Aug. 13, 1863	General Election June – July 1863.
			On Feb. 19, 1864, the House was informed of the resignation of the Hon. Albert Norton Richards, MPP, Leeds South, who had been appointed Solicitor General of Canada West. A new election had been called.

Leeds South	David Ford Jones	Feb. 22, 1864*	By-election Date unknown.
			Writ of Election – Jan. 4, 1864. Return of Writ – Jan. 30, 1864. On Feb. 19, 1864, the House was informed of the election of David Ford Jones, MPP, Leeds South, in room of the Hon. Albert Norton Richards, resigned.
Lennox & Addington	Richard John Cartwright	Aug. 13, 1863	General Election June – July 1863.
Lincoln	William McGiverin	Aug. 13, 1863	General Election June – July 1863.
London (City)	Hon. John Carling	Aug. 13, 1863	General Election June – July 1863.
Middlesex East	Crowel Willson	Aug. 13, 1863	General Election June – July 1863.
Middlesex West	Thomas Scatcherd	Aug. 13, 1863	General Election June – July 1863.
Niagara (Town)	Hon. John Simpson	Aug. 13, 1863	General Election June – July 1863.
			On Mar. 30, 1864, the House was informed of the resignation of John Simpson, MPP, Niagara (Town), who had been appointed Secretary and Registrar of the Province of Canada. A new election was called.
		May 3, 1864*	By-election Date unknown.
			Writ of Election – Mar. 31, 1864. Return of Writ – Apr. 11, 1864. On May 3, 1864, the House was informed of the election of the Hon. John Simpson, MPP, Niagara (Town), who was returned as duly elected.
			On Jan. 19, 1865, the House was informed of the resignation of the Hon. John Simpson, MPP, Niagara (Town), who had been appointed Assistant Auditor. A new election had been called.
Niagara (Town)	Angus Morrison	Jan. 19, 1865*	By-election Date unknown.
			Writ of Election – Aug. 17, 1864. Return of Writ – Sept. 7, 1864. On Jan. 19, 1865, the House was informed of the election of Angus

* By-election

Constituency	Member	Sworn In	Comments
Niagara (Town) — *Continued*			Morrison, MPP, Niagara (Town), in room of the Hon. John Simpson, resigned.
Norfolk	Aquila Walsh	Aug. 13, 1863	General Election June – July 1863.
Northumberland East	James Lyons Biggar	Aug. 13, 1863	General Election June – July 1863.
Northumberland West	Hon. James Cockburn (by acclamation)	Aug. 19, 1863	General Election June – July 1863.
			On Mar. 30, 1864, the House was informed of the resignation of James Cockburn, MPP, Northumberland West, who had been appointed Solicitor General of Canada West. A new election was called.
		May 3, 1864*	By-election Date unknown.
			Writ of Election – Mar. 31, 1864. Return of Writ – Apr. 23, 1864. On May 3, 1864, the House was informed of the election of the Hon. James Cockburn, MPP, Northumberland West, who was returned as duly elected.
Ontario North	Hon. William McDougall	Aug. 13, 1863	General Election June – July 1863.
			On Jan. 19, 1865, the House was informed of the resignation of the Hon. William McDougall, MPP, Ontario North, who had been appointed Provincial Secretary. A new election had been called.
Ontario North	Malcolm Crooks Cameron	Jan. 31, 1865*	By-election Date unknown.
			Writ of Election – July 5, 1864. Return of Writ – July 30, 1864. On Jan. 19, 1865, the House was informed of the election of Matthew Crooks Cameron, MPP, Ontario North, in room of the Hon. William McDougall, resigned.
Ontario South	Hon. Oliver Mowat	Aug. 13, 1863	General Election June – July 1863.
			On Jan. 19, 1865, the House was informed of the resignation of the Hon. Oliver Mowat, MPP, Ontario South, who had been appointed

			Postmaster General of this Province. A new election was called.
		Did not take seat	By-election Date unknown.
			Writ of Election – July 5, 1864. Return of Writ – July 18, 1864. On Jan. 19, 1865, the House was informed of the election of the Hon. Oliver Mowat, MPP, Ontario South, who was returned as duly elected.
			On Jan. 19, 1865, the House was informed of the resignation of the Hon. Oliver Mowat, MPP, Ontario South, who had been appointed Vice-Chancellor in the Court of Chancery of Canada West. A new election had been called.
Ontario South	Thomas Nicholson Gibbs	Jan. 31, 1865*	By-election Date unknown.
			Writ of Election – Dec. 28, 1864. Return of Writ – Jan. 18, 1865. On Jan. 24, 1865, the House was informed of the election of Thomas Nicholson Gibbs, MPP, Ontario South, in room of the Hon. Oliver Mowat, resigned.
Ottawa (City)	Joseph M. Currier	Aug. 13, 1863	General Election June – July 1863.
Oxford North	Hope Fleming Mackenzie	Aug. 13, 1863	General Election June – July 1863.
			On June 13, 1866, the House was informed of the death of Hope Fleming Mackenzie, MPP, Oxford North. A new election was called.
Oxford North	Thomas Oliver	July 17, 1866*	By-election Date unknown.
			On July 17, 1866, having presented the Indenture of his election for the County of Oxford North, Thomas Oliver took his seat.
			On July 17, 1866, the House resolved that in admitting Thomas Oliver, MPP, Oxford North, to take his seat, on the production of the Duplicate Indenture only, and without the Return of the Indenture to the Clerk of the Crown in Chancery, and the Certificate of the

* By-election

Constituency	Member	Sworn In	Comments
Oxford North — *Continued*			latter Officer, it still recommends a strict adherence to the requirement of producing the usual Certificate.
			Writ of Election – June 20, 1866. Return of Writ – July 14, 1866. On July 23, 1866, the House was informed of the election of Thomas Oliver, MPP, Oxford North, in room of Hope Fleming Mackenzie, deceased.
Oxford South	Hon. George Brown	Aug. 13, 1863	General Election June – July 1863.
			On Jan. 19, 1865, the House was informed of the resignation of the Hon. George Brown, MPP, Oxford South, who had been appointed President of the Committees of the Executive Council. A new election had been called.
		Jan. 19, 1865*	By-election Date unknown.
			Writ of Election – June 30, 1864. Return of Writ – July 11, 1864. On Jan. 19, 1865, the House was informed of the election of the Hon. George Brown, MPP, Oxford South, who was returned as duly elected.
Peel	Hon. John Hillyard Cameron	Aug. 13, 1863	General Election June – July 1863.
Perth	Robert Macfarlane	Aug. 13, 1863	General Election June – July 1863.
Peterborough	Wilson Seymour Conger (by acclamation)	Aug. 13, 1863	General Election June – July 1863.
			On Jan. 19, 1865, the House was informed of the death of Wilson Seymour Conger, MPP, Peterborough. A new election had been called.
Peterborough	Frederick William Haultain	Jan. 19, 1865*	By-election Date unknown.
			Writ of Election – Aug. 11, 1864. Return of Writ – Sept. 14, 1864. On Jan. 19, 1865, the House was informed of the election of Frederick

			William Haultain, MPP, Peterborough, in room of Wilson Seymour Conger, deceased.
Prescott	Thomas Higginson	Aug. 13, 1863	General Election June – July 1863.
Prince Edward	Walter Ross	Aug. 13, 1863	General Election June – July 1863.
Renfrew	Robert McIntyre	Aug. 13, 1863	General Election June – July 1863.
Russell	Robert Bell	Aug. 13, 1863	General Election June – July 1863.
Simcoe North	Thomas David McConkey	Aug. 13, 1863	General Election June – July 1863.
Simcoe South	Thomas Robert Ferguson (by acclamation)	Aug. 13, 1863	General Election June – July 1863.
Stormont	Samuel Ault	Aug. 13, 1863	General Election June – July 1863.
Toronto East	Alexander Mortimer Smith	Aug. 13, 1863	General Election June – July 1863.
Toronto West	John McDonald	Aug. 13, 1863	General Election June – July 1863.
Victoria	James Wicks Dunsford	Aug. 13, 1863	General Election June – July 1863.
Waterloo North	Hon. Michael Hamilton Foley	Aug. 13, 1863	General Election June – July 1863.
			On Mar. 30, 1864, the House was informed of the resignation of the Hon. Michael Hamilton Foley, MPP, Waterloo North, who had been appointed Postmaster General of the Province of Canada. A new election was called.
Waterloo North	Isaac Erb Bowman	May 4, 1864*	By-election Date unknown.
			On May 4, 1864, having presented the Indenture of his election for the County of Waterloo North, Isaac Erb Bowman took his seat.
			On May 4, 1864, the House resolved that in admitting Isaac Erb Bowman, MPP, Waterloo North, to take his seat, on the production of the Duplicate Indenture only, and without the Return of the Indenture to the Clerk of the

* By-election

Constituency	Member	Sworn In	Comments
Waterloo North — *Continued*			Crown in Chancery, and the Certificate of the latter Officer, it still recommends a strict adherence to the requirement of producing the usual Certificate.
			Writ of Election – Mar. 31, 1864. Return of Writ – Apr. 26, 1864. On May 11, 1864, the House was informed of the election of Isaac Erb Bowman, MPP, Waterloo North, in room of the Hon. Michael Hamilton Foley, resigned.
Waterloo South	James Cowan	Aug. 13, 1863	General Election June – July 1863.
Welland	Thomas Clark Street	Aug. 13, 1863	General Election June – July 1863.
Wellington North	Thomas Sutherland Parker	Aug. 13, 1863	General Election June – July 1863.
Wellington South	David Stirton (by acclamation)	Aug. 13, 1863	General Election June – July 1863.
Wentworth North	William Notman	Aug. 13, 1863	General Election June – July 1863.
			On June 8, 1866, the House was informed of the death of William Notman, MPP, Wentworth North. A new election had been called.
Wentworth North	James McMonies	June 8, 1866*	By-election Date unknown.
			Writ of Election – Sept. 30, 1865. Return of Writ – Nov. 1, 1865. On June 8, 1866, the House was informed of the election of James McMonies, MPP, Wentworth North, in room of William Notman, deceased.
Wentworth South	Joseph Rymal	Aug. 13, 1863	General Election June – July 1863.
York East	Amos Wright	Aug. 13, 1863	General Election June – July 1863.
York North	James Pearson Wells	Aug. 13, 1863	General Election June – July 1863.
York West	Hon. William Pearce Howland	Aug. 13, 1863	General Election June – July 1863.
			On Jan. 19, 1865, the House was informed of

the resignation of the Hon. William Pearce Howland, MPP, York West, who had been appointed Postmaster General. A new election had been called.

Jan. 19, 1865*   By-election Date unknown.

Writ of Election — Nov. 29, 1864. Return of Writ — Dec. 14, 1864. On Jan. 19, 1865, the House was informed of the election of the Hon. William Pearce Howland, MPP, York West, who was returned as duly elected.

*   By-election